D1592096

Christianity

A HISTORICAL ATLAS

Cambridge, Massachusetts
London, England
2020

Printed in the United States of America

CIP data for this book is available from the Library of Congress

978-0-674-24235-7

Christianity

A HISTORICAL ATLAS

Edited by

Alec Ryrie

CONTRIBUTORS
Andrew Avenell
Elizabeth Wyse

THE BELKNAP PRESS *of* HARVARD UNIVERSITY PRESS
Cambridge, Massachusetts, and London, England

2020

Contents

CHRISTIANITY IN THE MIDDLE AGES

THE AGE OF REFORM 1500–1800

CHRISTIANITY IN THE MODERN WORLD 1800–2020

Introduction

The Hereford Mappa Mundi dates from c. 1300 and is on display in Hereford Cathedral, England.

A HISTORICAL ATLAS of Christianity is, on the face of it, a strange project. Religion and geography are not obviously connected. The Christian God is, supposedly, the same at every time and place. Religion is a matter of metaphysics and eternal verities, not local variety. Or it is a matter of inner and individual spiritual experience, which is so varied that the attempt to depict it through blocks of solid color on a map seems hopelessly reductionist.

And yet Christianity is a profoundly geographical religion, and maps have a particular power to tell its story. Christians' understanding of the physical spaces they occupy has always been sacralized, both at the local level of churches, shrines, and sites of pilgrimage, and at the global level. For such a profoundly historical religion, this is perhaps unavoidable: because nothing survives better from the ancient past than the geography we inherit from it. It is hard to proclaim the historical Christ without the thought that those feet, in ancient times, walked upon Judaea's mountains, where we can still, perhaps, go ourselves. The Hebrew Bible's narrative is unshakeably rooted in physical space. Jerusalem, for Christians, is a theological principle, the heavenly city to come; but it is also a real place, layered with relics, endlessly fought over, filled with people for whom it is simply home.

The history of cartography itself tells this story. The earliest attempts to map the world which survive down to the present were less sober attempts at accurate representation than they were theological statements. This 8th-century sketch, one of the very oldest world maps we have, makes that eminently clear. The world is divided simply into its three ancient continents, Africa, Asia and Europe, with each assigned to one of the sons of Noah; east, the direction of Jerusalem, is placed at the top; the world-ocean encloses everything. This is a depiction of God's sovereignty and providence, not a navigational aid.

The same is true of a much more elaborate successor, which is recognizably a variant on the same theme: the famous Mappa Mundi at Hereford Cathedral, the largest surviving medieval world map, dating from around 1300. Far more detailed, elaborate, and beautiful than its Frankish predecessor, it would not be of much more practical use to a traveler. Nor should we imagine that the monks who created it believed that they were producing a photo-realist representation of what a viewer stationed far above the earth's surface would see. Apart from anything else, they knew (like the Frankish doodler) that the world is a globe, and that no point on its surface is a

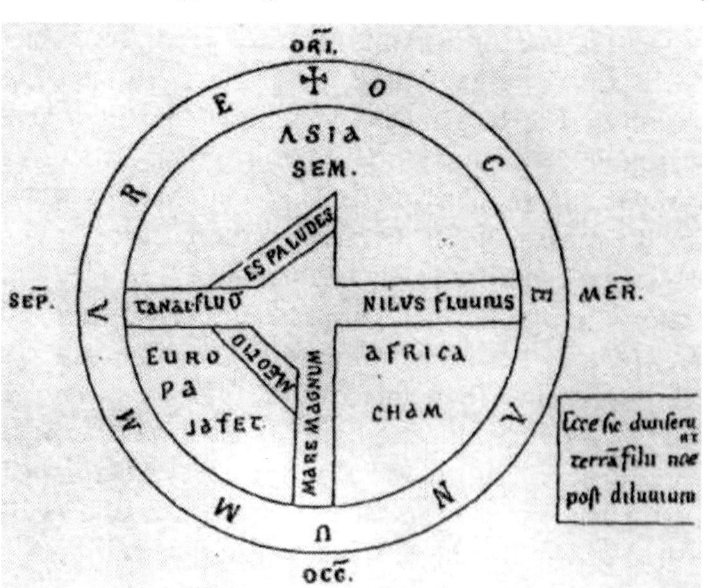

8th-century Frankish world map, showing Jerusalem at the top.

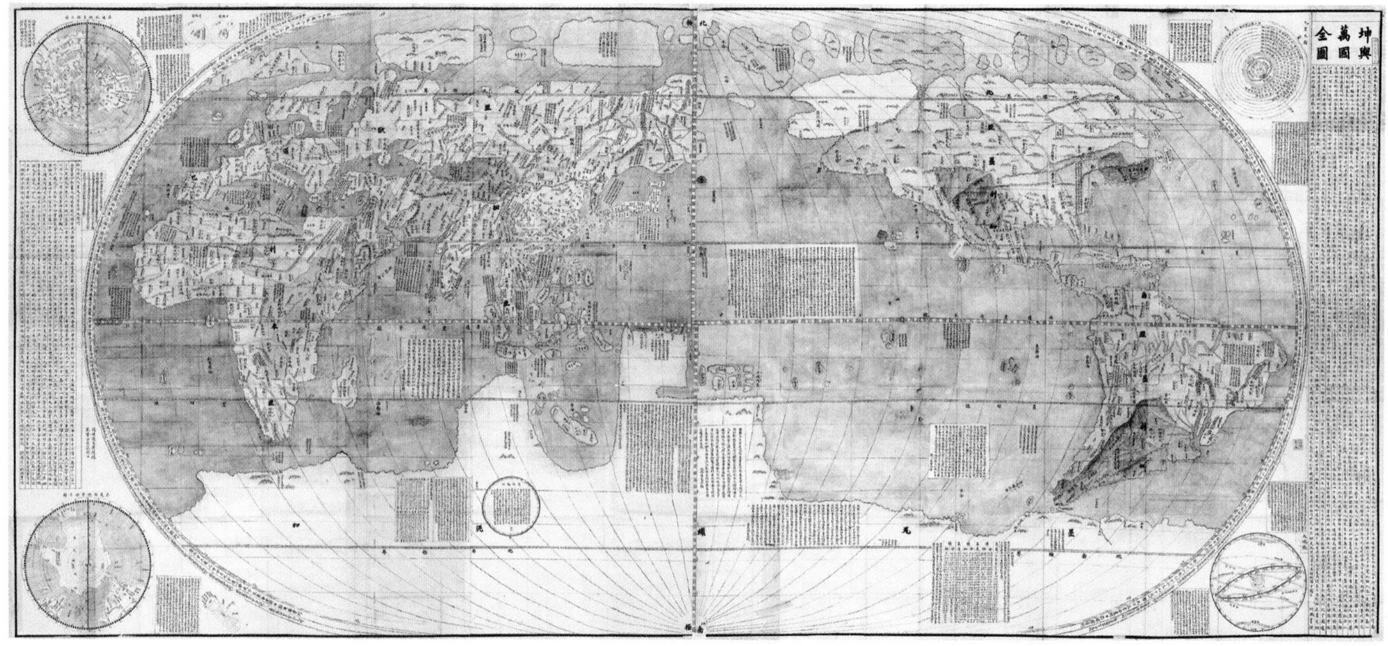

Two-page colored Japanese copy of by Matteo Ricci, c. 1602.

"center," rather than (as shown here) a wheel with Jerusalem as its hub. The fact that Jerusalem sits near the meeting point of the three traditional continents, however, allows for some basic geographical facts to be imbued with sacred meaning. Once again, east is at the top: Britain and Ireland are squeezed in, their shape distorted, at the bottom left-hand corner. Once again, Christ in glory presides over the whole. The map is packed with details garnered from the Bible, from ancient geographers, from more recent travelers' tales and, we must assume, from the mapmakers' own imagination. To ask whether they truly believed that the Red Sea, as shown in the top right, is that color, is to misunderstand their enterprise.

Three short centuries later, and Christian cartography had been transformed. The global maritime opening that western Christians pioneered from the 15th century onward led, in the three decades from 1492–1522, to the first circumnavigation of Africa for two millennia, the first ever crossing of the open Atlantic and the first ever circumnavigation of the globe. Global mapping became an urgently practical business, and the maps produced by geographers such as Gerardus Mercator and Willem Blaeu were pragmatic, secular images. The principle behind Mercator's famous projection, which has become controversial in the modern world for the way it misrepresents the size of equatorial as against polar regions, was not to depict a spheroid planet on a flat surface as accurately as possible, but to allow navigators' routes of constant bearing to be depicted as straight lines. Even the decoration on world maps from this era tended to invoke the ancient pagan symbolism beloved of the Renaissance rather than explicitly Christian symbols. Yet, as the Italian Jesuit missionary Matteo Ricci discovered when he was trying to bring the best Christian scholarship to his hosts at the Chinese imperial court in the 1590s, the new cartography could still be very Christian. There were not many fields of learning in which the western Christian world had outpaced China by the 16th century, but cartography was one, along with its twin, astronomy. Of the various gifts with which Ricci tried to impress his hosts, none had more impact than his world map. Shown here in a Japanese version made in 1604, this is on the face of it a sober and entirely secular object. It is far more accurate than its predecessor, although the "terra inhabitabilis" of the Frankish map still has a successor in Ricci's speculative southern continent. Yet nothing indicates it as a Christian creation. Jerusalem is unmarked. This is, however, a case of secular learning being deployed in the service of Christian mission, with Ricci's Jesuits attempting to use their ability to encompass the whole globe, not merely to show off Christian scholarship but to demonstrate that Christianity is a universal faith that finds its home throughout the world.

As European Christendom's global opening moved from trade and missions to ever more expansive imperial conquests, the way it imagined the world through maps kept pace. Missionaries and imperialists aimed to convert and to conquer both people and land. The people whom they encountered were typically described as heathen or pagan – both words which are linked, etymologically, to notions of rural, wild, and uncultivated land, or "heath." Christi-

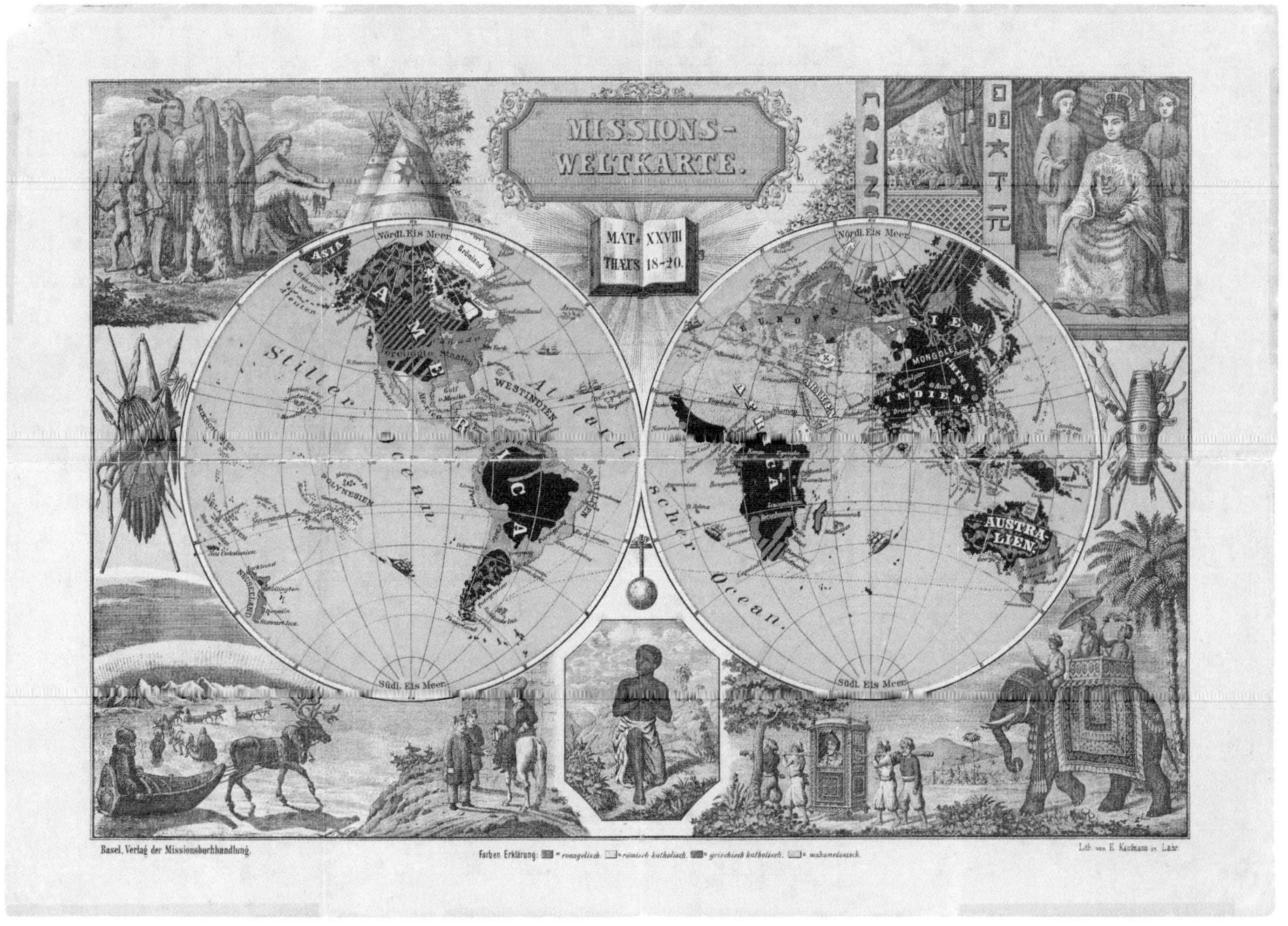

Dutch missionary map dating to 1891.

anity and empire planted civility and cultivation among such wild people, and it could do so either by converting and acculturating them or, if that failed, by displacing them and replacing them with European Christian settlers: which it was often assumed would be the more likely course in the long run, as more backward peoples inevitably died out. This queasy slippage between people and land is represented in the popular genre of missionary maps, widely used by Euro-American missionary agencies in the 19th century and beyond to communicate their ambitions and achievements, to guide their supporters in their prayers for the missionary task, and to mobilize donations. The Dutch map of 1891 on the preceeding page divides the world into five colors: three varieties of Christian – Protestant, Catholic, and Eastern Orthodox; the Muslim world, a perennially awkward category, shown as an undifferentiated block enclosing the ancient Christian societies of Armenia and Abyssinia; and, unlabelled on the key, black for the heathen world, the realm of spiritual darkness where Christianity had yet to penetrate and where its advance was expected to be swift and decisive, a single color uniting diverse "pagan"peoples on five continents. This time, the symbolic framing around the map is of course explicitly Christian, with a key Biblical verse – the risen Christ's command to go and make disciples of all nations – referenced in the center. Although the mapping is cartographically perfectly accurate, the continent of Antarctica is omitted entirely: since it is uninhabited, for these purposes it may as well not exist.

The imperial moment has passed and Christian missionary ambitions have moved on, but the geographical framing of the faith continues. The perennial significance attached to Jerusalem and the "Holy Land" has been powerfully revived in modern times by the creation of the state of Israel, which many Protestants interpret as an apocalyptic event, a step towards the epoch-ending battle expected at Megiddo ("Armageddon") in Israel's north. But there are many other Christian geographies in the modern world. The missionary task is still often framed in this way: in the 1990s evangelicals were enthused by the notion of the "10/40 window," that is, the regions of North Africa and southern and eastern Asia between 10 and 40 degrees north of the equator. This framing was a means of focusing missionary attention on this heavily populated and overwhelmingly non-Christian region. Other sacred geographies have been more assertive. Christians in modern Britain, northern Ireland, South Africa, South Korea, and many others have at times claimed that God's plan for human history marks their land out for a distinct role. Many Chinese Christians treasure the so-called "back to Jerusalem" notion, that the Christian gospel, so long exiled from its ancient Middle Eastern homelands, will soon be swept there on the back of a wave of revival moving west from China. American Christians, too, have wanted to write their once-unknown continents into Christianity's story. One offshoot of American Christianity, Mormonism, has rewritten the entire sacred narrative to put the Americas at center stage.

Students of the history of Christianity generally do not want to embrace these sacred geographies, but geographical framing of the stories that we do tell can nevertheless be illuminating, as this book seeks to show. It is of course true that the spiritual lives of millions cannot be accurately represented by colors on a map, but it is also plainly the case that Christians' religious experiences have usually been communal and have been profoundly affected by the place and time in which they live. Russian Christianity, for example, is not defined or confined by its Russian identity, but nor can we properly understand it apart from that identity.

Telling the stories of Christian history geographically has two particular advantages. One, appropriately enough for an incarnational, historically grounded tradition, it is an antidote to excessive abstraction. Some histories of Christianity have a tendency to reduce themselves to a history of theology, which, while essential, is not intangible: it is a human phenomenon created within specific historical and geographical contexts. Post-Enlightenment Christianity especially has a recurrent tendency to aspire to universal statements and to a God's-eye view of the world, losing sight of the messy historical specificities in which human beings are of necessity mired. Likewise, some histories of Christianity have concentrated to excess on a handful of leading ecclesiastical and political actors, rather than on the whole mass of believers. A geographically-framed story is, however, unavoidably the story of whole populations in specific places. Mapping the earth keeps our feet on the ground.

The other advantage is more important still. The history of Christianity is sometimes still told as a single master narrative, a story that inevitably attends to certain centers and neglects peripheries. Yet the experience of a scattered, disparate religion cannot be reduced to a single story in any age. We have become increasingly aware that there is a cacophany of regional stories to be heard, and that the histories which are usually treated as peripheral – Nestorianism, the kingdom of Kongo, the Jesuit republics of the Paraguayan highlands, the Baptists of Assam – need to be accorded their rightful place. A map is, amongst other things, a device for reminding the viewer that even those parts of the world that are not commanding our immediate attention continue stubbornly to exist, nor does their people's religious experience cease simply because the story as conventionally told neglects it.

This book could not and does not attend equally to every part of the world. Inevitably, it makes narrative choices and privileges some parts of the Christian experience over others. Yet it does try, as befits a global story, to tell it in the round, and to notice its breadth and variety. A principle often underpinning sacred geographies has been the hope to discern a single thread of narrative meaning from the chaotic variety of religious history. To modern eyes, the experience of the historical mapping of Christianity teaches a rather different lesson: that this is a tradition too rich, diverse, quarrelsome, contradictory, and unpredictable for its stories to be told in any other way.

Alec Ryrie

+ ihs xps · Matheus homo

onginneð godspelles

incipit euangelii

genelogia mathei

boc

cynnreccenisse

LIBER

GENERATI

ONIS IHU

XPI FILII DAUID FILII ABRAHAM

cneurisse

hælendes cristes

dauides sunu

abrahames sunu

Christianity

IN THE BEGINNING

Folio 27r from the Lindisfarne Gospels, containing the incipit from the Gospel of Matthew, 8th century CE

Israel: The Crucible of Christianity

Solomon ruled over a united kingdom of Israel, with Judah having its own political authority and special privileges. David, Solomon's father and predecessor, had turned Edom and Moab into Israelite vassal states. After David's death, they became rebellious and difficult to control. The core territories were the twelve provinces of Israel, formed from the twelve tribes of Israel.

ARMAGEDDON IS BELIEVED to refer to the plain near the town of Megiddo, a pass between the Judaean uplands, and the place where the Bronze Age superpowers – Egypt and Sumer, the Hittites, and Mitanni, frequently clashed. From the surrounding hills, Neolithic Judaean farmers would have had a clear view of these spectacles, rendering it the natural site for their religion's apocalyptic battle to end all battles.

The late Bronze Age witnessed the near simultaneous collapse of the empires that had long vied for supremacy in the Near East. The tribes of the Levant were able to exploit the ensuing power vacuum to coalesce into a series of independent polities of varying, size, strength, and durability: Edom, Moab, Ammon… and Israel. According to the biblical account, Joshua established the rudiments of the state of Israel in the aftermath of the exodus from Egypt in around the 13th century BCE with repeated assistance, from a stalled sunset and giant hailstones to the celebrated tumbling walls of Jericho, from the God they called YHWH.

The earliest Israelite state had no centralized political or religious leadership, but in the 11th century BCE Saul claimed an overall kingship, uniting the Israelites in a series of conquests before his defeat by the Philistines and death at Mount Gilboa. Saul's kingdom was salvaged and consolidated by his successor, David, before reaching its apogee under Solomon, the builder of the first temple in Jerusalem.

There followed a long period of decline ending in near annihilation. After Solomon's death the kingdom split into a northern state (Israel) and a southern one (Judah), a division cemented after the brutal battle of Zemaraim in c. 913 BCE. Enfeebled and splintered, the two kingdoms were exposed to resurgent regional empires. The Assyrians conquered the kingdom of Israel in 720 BCE and came close to taking Judah in 701 BCE; eventually Judah fell to the Babylonians in 587 BCE. In both cases there was wholesale deportation of the subjugated populations. However, during the reign of King Josiah of Judah (640–609 BCE), the rediscovery (or creation) of a "book of the law" ascribed to Moses (perhaps the Book of Deuteronomy) powered a revival of the exclusive worship of YHWH, and a wholesale rewriting and expansion of religious and historical texts. This period of renewal gave the Judaean elites the theological and cultural resilience to weather a 70-year exile in Babylon.

The Babylonian captivity proved catalytic in the development of Judaism: while there, the Jews (as we can now call them) were restricted but not isolated, and may have enriched their religious texts with imports from the foundation lore of their captors: the Tower of Babel, Noah's Ark and the Great Flood. The role of prophets such as Jeremiah, Ezekiel and Deutero-Isaiah was critical, convincing their followers of the importance of faithfulness to YHWH, rather than adapting to the culture of their captors. During this period, religious scholars adopted a new alphabet and calendar, and consolidated the foundation texts of their beliefs in the Torah. The subsequent conquest of Babylon by the Persians in 539 BCE permitted their return to Israel before wholesale assimilation could occur. By c. 516 BCE a second temple had been built in Jerusalem.

Old Testament references to sites clustered in the Israelite heartland of the North Judaean hills are redolent of both the trauma of displacement and yearning for a past golden age. Ramah, for instance, was a transit camp for the Israelites en route to Babylon. During the Babylonian period, the Jews also made an important innovation: monotheism, moving beyond the claim that foreign gods should not be worshiped to the belief that YHWH is the only and universal God. One consequence of this universal claim was that it was no longer necessary to have been born a Jew to be admitted to the Jewish faith: it was sufficient to accept Jewish customs and beliefs and (for males) to undergo ritual circumcision. Such flexibility was unusual in the ancient world: it would be by both copying, and radically extending, this relaxation that Christianity would become a religion that spread across the world.

Solomon's Core Territories
970–931 BCE
Traditional tribal boundaries divided into twelve provinces with a Governor for each province
N
35°
36°
33°
32°
31°
ARAM
PHOENICIA
Tyre
Dan
CABUL
GALILEE
Kedesh
Madon
Lake Huleh
Achzib
ASHER
Hazor
VIII
NAPHTALI
GESHUR
Acco
IX
Sea of Chinnereth
(Sea of Galilee)
BEALOTH
ZEBULUN
ISSACHAR
Yarmuk
Shimron
X
Jokneam
Great Sea
Dor
IV
Western Sea
Megiddo
Jezreel
V
Taanach
Ramoth-gilead
Arubboth
Beth-shan
ARGOB
VI
HEPHER
III
Socoh
Abel-meholah
Tirzah
I
Jordan
Shechem
Succoth
Mahmoim
EPHRAIM
Jabbok
Zarethan
Adam
Joppa
VII
GILEAD
Jazer
Jogbehah
II
Bethel
XI
Rabbah
Shaalbim
BENJAMIN
AMMON
Aijalon
Gibeon
Anathoth
Jericho
Abel-keramim
Beth-shemesh
Jerusalem
(Jebus)
Heshbon
Beth-jeshimoth
Gath?
Jarmuth
Medeba
Adullam
Libnah
GAD
Lachish
XII
Gaza
Hebron
JUDAH
Shephelah
Wilderness
Salt Sea
(Dead Sea)
Dibon
PHILISTIA
Arnon
Aroer
MOAB
Beer-sheba
Negev
EDOM
0
20 km
0
20 miles

A Turbulent Province: Roman Judaea

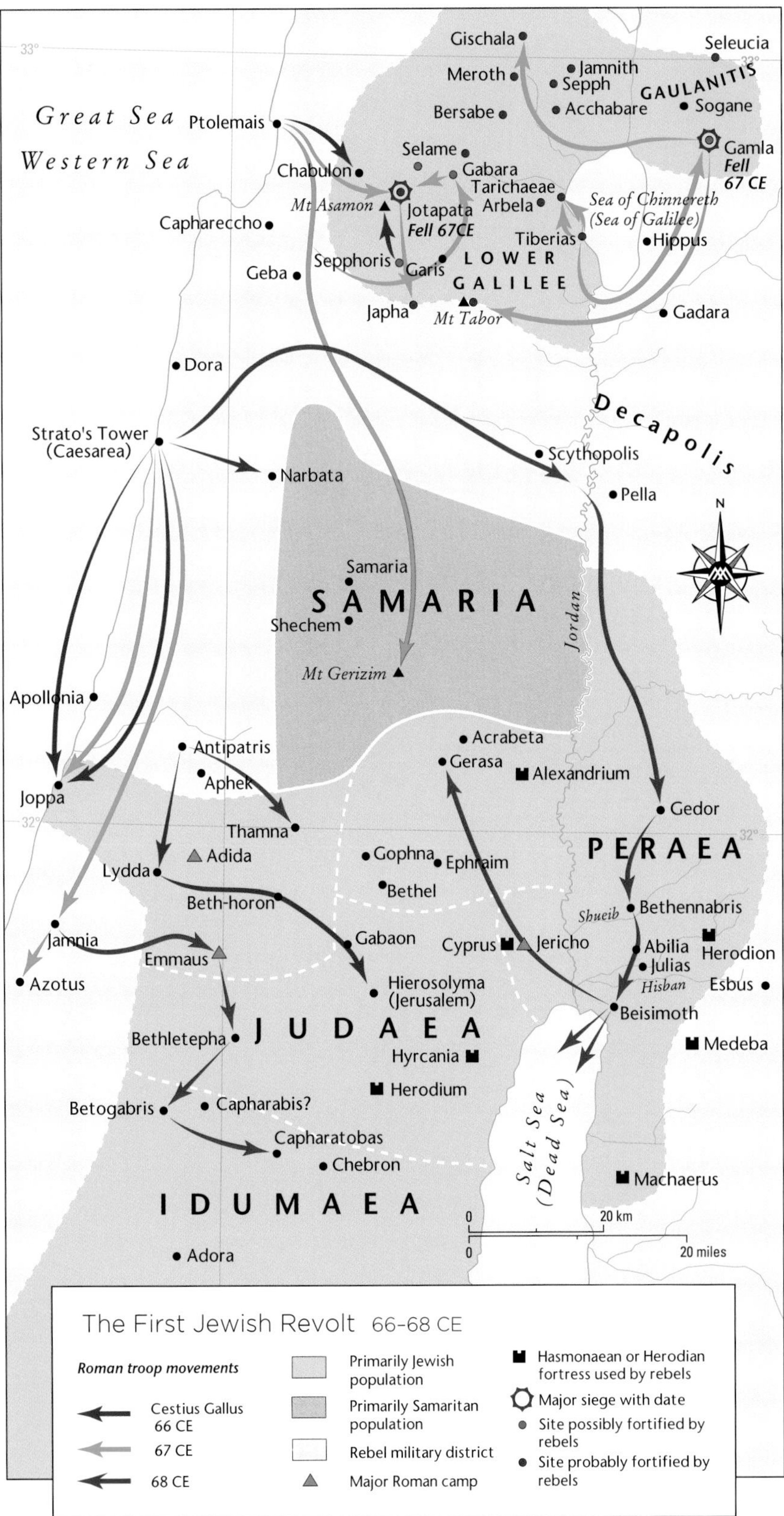

THROUGH EXILE, CAPTIVITY and centuries of imperial rule, the Jews had maintained and reinforced their cultural identity through devotion to their faith. When, in the second century BCE, their Seleucid King Antiochus IV attempted to impose Greek religious rites on his Jewish subjects, the subsequent revolt secured independence and the native rule of the Hasmonean dynasty. With this precedent of successful rebellion, the Jews were never likely to be docile instruments of the Roman imperium.

Herod the Great (74/73–4 BCE) ruled as a Roman client king of Judaea, famous for his colossal building projects, but reviled by many as the tyrant who ordered the Massacre of the Innocents. The decades after the Roman assumption of direct administration of Judaea in 6 CE were littered with unrest, generally with taxes or offenses against the religious sensibilities of the Jews at their core (Caligula repeatedly attempted to have statues of himself erected in synagogues and the Temple of Jerusalem). Overt rebellions were quelled, however, and in 66 CE a new procurator, Gessius Florus, decided to take a more robust approach. In response to a tax boycott, he ordered a raid on the Temple, plundering its treasury to claim reparation. This act of desecration outraged the population and the situation rapidly escalated: when riots broke out in Jerusalem, Florus ordered the crucifixion of a number of local dignitaries. The rebels then besieged, captured, and slaughtered the Roman garrison, while Zealot militias rampaged through the countryside and captured the fortress of Masada.

Belatedly appreciating the scale of the crisis, Rome's regional governor, Cestius Gallus, landed at Caesarea with over 30,000 troops, only to be ambushed in the mountain pass at Beth Horon and routed with massive casualties. While the rebel leadership in Jerusalem squabbled over how to exploit their triumph, the humiliated Gallus was replaced by the highly competent Vespasian. Landing in Ptolemais, Vespasian methodically captured the rebel bases in Galilee in 67–8 CE, effectively securing the province's eastern borders from any potential intervention on behalf of the rebels by Rome's enemy, Parthia. After an amphibious assault down the coast he took Joppa and Lydda, then headed through the Judaean hills toward Jerusalem.

Expelled from their provincial strongholds, militia refugees flooded into Jerusalem, exacerbating the already intense factional infighting, and the rebels' best opportunity to mount a counteroffensive passed. With the death of Nero, the Roman Empire itself descended into political chaos. 69 CE became the "Year of Four Emperors" as rivals fought for the prize. The eventual victor was none other than Vespasian, who departed for Rome to assume the purple, handing command in Judaea to his son Titus. By the spring of 70 CE, Titus was ready to lay siege to Jerusalem itself. Meanwhile, the defenders continued to fight one another: the Zealots even destroyed most of the city's food store, apparently to encourage a fight to the death, which Titus abetted by building a wall round the city, preventing resupply from outside. When the Romans breached the city walls and captured the fortress of Antonia the end was in sight. A desperate last stand in the Temple ended when the walls were set on fire. The blaze destroyed the Temple and much of the city. Surviving rebel leaders (and many others) were executed and much of the remaining population enslaved.

The fortresses at Herodion and Machaerus were taken to eliminate the remnants of Jewish resistance, leaving Masada on the shores of the Dead Sea as the last redoubt of the rebellion. The new Roman legate (the ferocity of the rebellion had led to an upgrading of the post from procurator), Lucius Flavius Silva, left nothing to chance, investing the bleak fastness with a whole legion. A surrounding wall and siege ramp was built in preparation for the final assault. At the end, in 73 CE, when the walls were breached, defenders were found to have committed mass suicide. No mass deportation of Jews followed this revolt; that was to occur after the next revolt in 132–136.

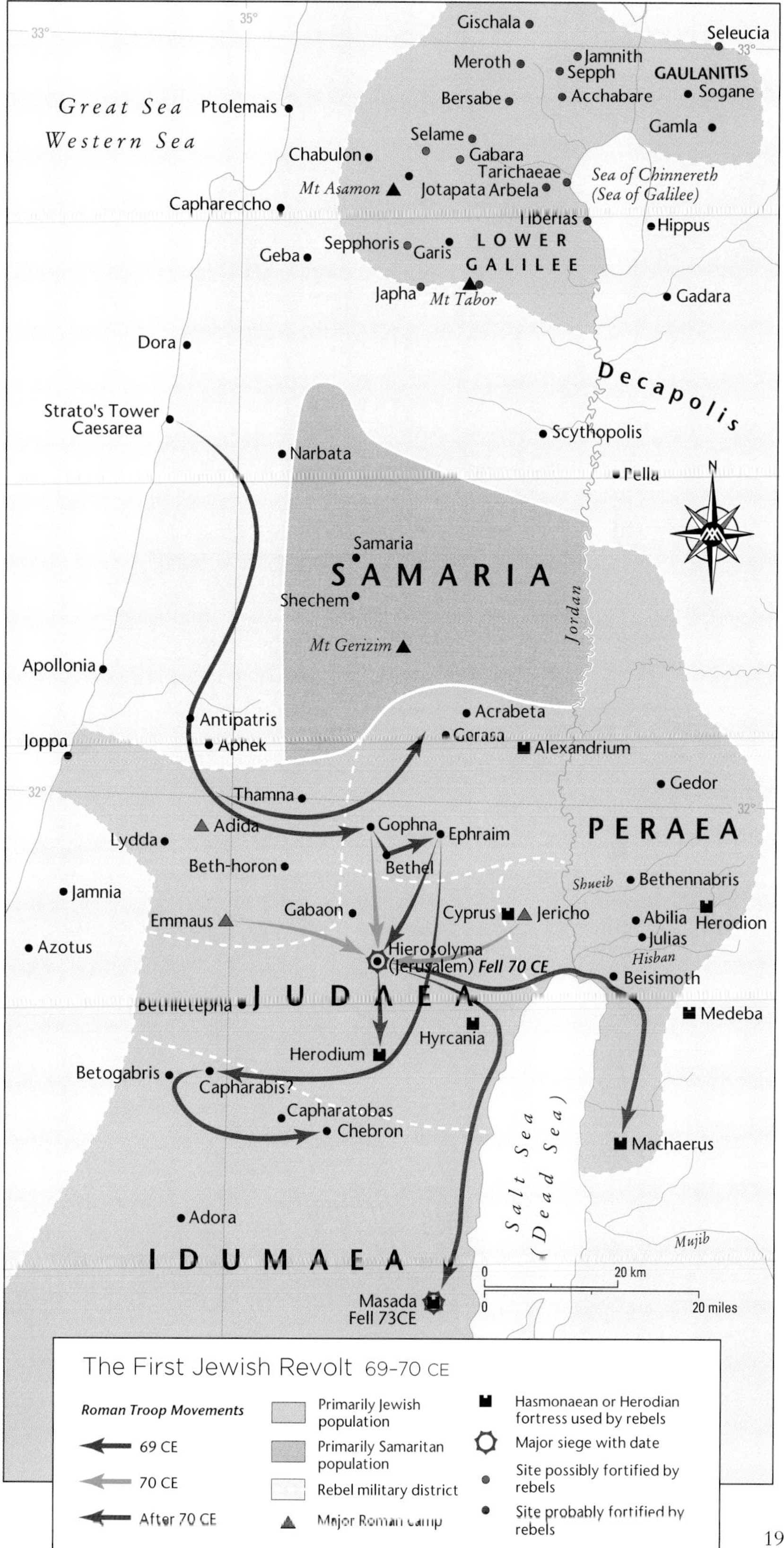

Jerusalem: The Focus of Christianity

Discoveries at Tell-es-Sultan, Jericho, and most recently, Motza, three miles west of Jerusalem, evidence the existence of sophisticated urban cultures in eastern Judaea during the Neolithic, some 9,000 years ago. These ancient settlements had populations of around 3,000, rectilinear street plans, and a range of artifacts indicating transregional trade.

Some 6,000 years later, the Jerusalem captured by David in c. 1010 BCE, after repeated failed attempts, was puny by comparison with its Neolithic predecessors. A village of perhaps 500 inhabitants, the Jebusites (a Canaanite tribe) perched on a spur below Temple Mount; its primary asset was the Gihon spring, which guaranteed a supply of fresh water in a siege. To safeguard this prize, Jebusite defenders had built a set of massive fortifications and taunted David that even if "blind and lame" they could repulse his army. But eventually David made a successful assault, possibly by means of the Warren's Shaft tunnel system adjoining the spring, and, in appreciation of its defensive qualities, made Jerusalem his base. The archaeological record suggests little growth during his reign, but under his successor, Solomon, it spread northward to encompass Temple Mount. Although the surface area perhaps quadrupled, much of this additional space was occupied by the Temple and the residences of the royal family.

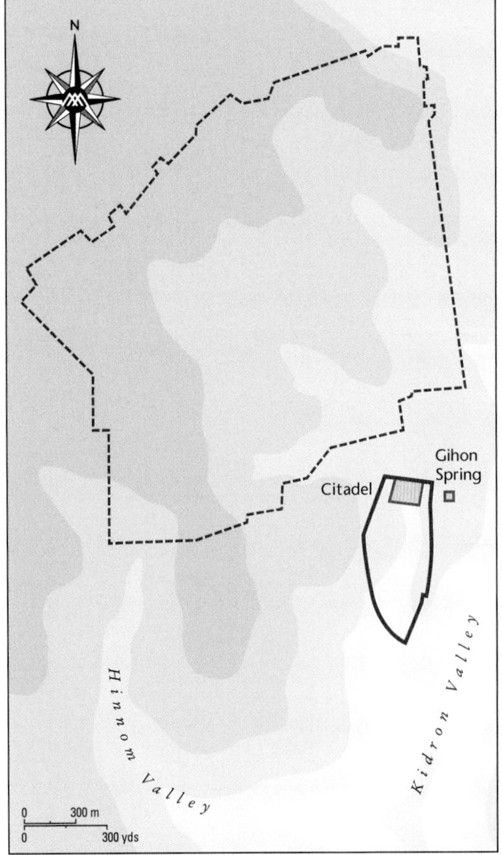

Jerusalem
1000 BCE
Old walled city as seen today

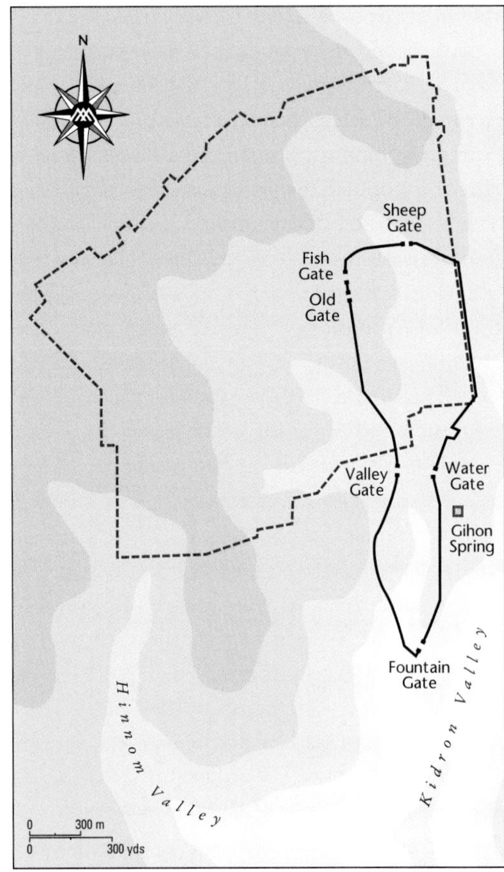

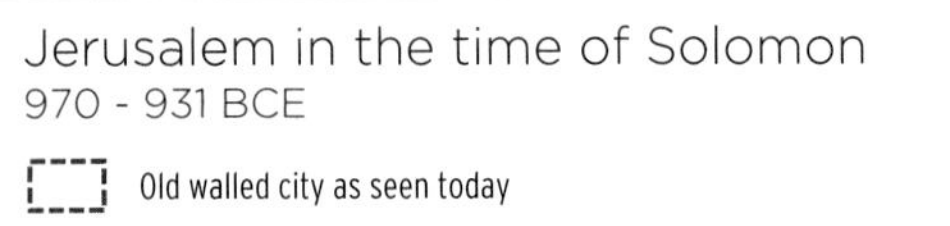
Jerusalem in the time of Solomon
970 - 931 BCE
Old walled city as seen today

Jerusalem's ambition and symbolism outpaced its political and economic footprint. From around 2,000 inhabitants in Solomon's time, the population swelled to perhaps 8,000 in the late 8th century BCE. Ironically, this growth was in part fueled by the loss of political power, as the loss of the northern kingdom of Israel halved its territory but sent a flood of refugees to the city. Thereafter, the city was ravaged by the siege of the Assyrian ruler Sennacherib (701 BCE), then decimated by the conquest and the mass deportation of its populace by the Babylonian Nebuchadnezzar. Then, with the Maccabean revolt (167–160 BCE), came resurrection. Independence brought native rule under the Hasmonean dynasty, expansion, and prosperity. The city's boundaries moved northward and westward and its population perhaps matched its pre-Assyrian peak by the ascension of King Herod in 37 BCE. Herod secured his position through Roman support in the ruthless suppression of a popular revolt. Unsurprisingly, he was widely despised by his subjects, but his adroit courtship of Rome kept the royal coffers full, and Herod devoted much of this wealth to a grandiose program of public works, including a wholesale renovation of his capital, Jerusalem. Apart from his own opulent palace, Herod commissioned a major reconstruction of the Temple and the building of the Antonia palace/fortress. The city's water supply was modernized, with new reservoirs such as the Serpent's Pool connected to the Gihon Spring by a network of aqueducts.

The general population remained deeply resistant to Herod's romanizing and hellenizing tendencies, for instance in the construction of theaters, amphitheaters, and hippodromes. The vindictiveness of his later years stoked this resentment further, and the widespread unrest that occurred upon his death foreshadowed the Great Revolt of 66–70 CE. However, by the death of Herod in 4 BCE, Jerusalem was a substantial city (population estimates range from 20,000–100,000) with, for the first time, an infrastructure to match its pretensions.

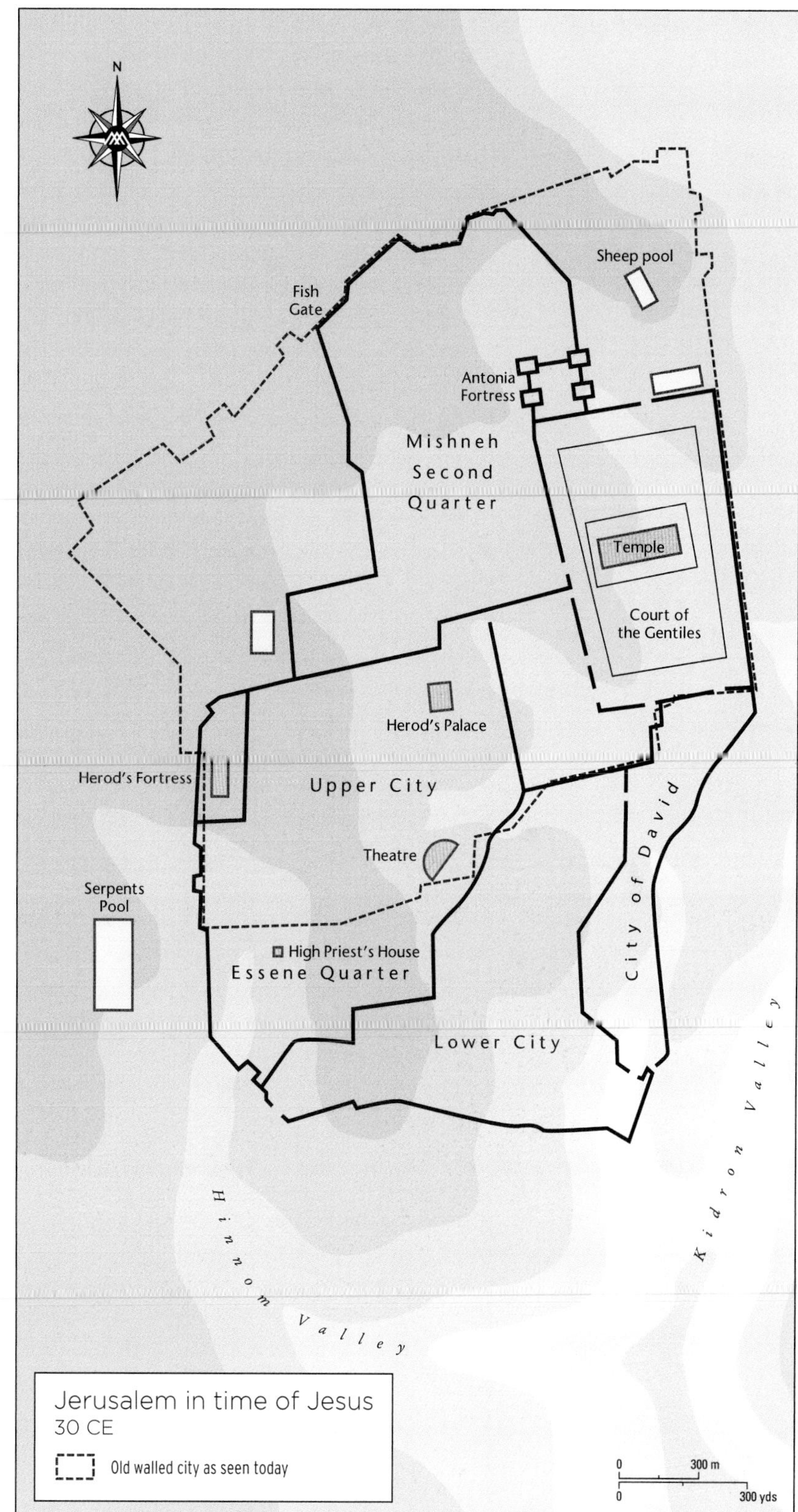

The Ministry of Jesus and Holy Land Sites

THE BUDDHA WAS OF ROYAL STOCK and spent 50 years traversing northern India after his enlightenment spreading his message to all levels of society. Muhammad established not just a faith but a military machine that would transport that faith over millions of square miles within a generation of the Prophet's death. By contrast, the ministry of Jesus, a man of modest background, seems an exquisite miniature: by tradition a mere three years in duration, and almost exclusively confined to the rural backwater of Galilee. He was ostracized by all levels of the political and religious establishment: to the Roman government he was an irritant, in a province with a tendency to instability; the religious hierarchy in Jerusalem conspired in his destruction; even the burghers of his hometown Nazareth twice rejected his teachings. Within days of his final visit to Jerusalem, as a respected teacher and prophet of recognized stature, he was tried and executed.

Jesus emerged, as if from nowhere – a carpenter from Nazareth – to be declared the Son of God on meeting with John the Baptist, possibly at Bethnabara a few miles south of the Sea of Galilee. On the rare occasions Jesus ventured outside his native region, his touch can seem unsure. In his initial exchange with the Canaanite woman begging him to heal her daughter he suggested that to do so would be like "casting his children's bread to dogs." It was only after her disarming rejoinder that "even dogs may eat the crumbs from the master's table" that he acceded to her request. On his way back to Galilee, he "cleansed" ten lepers – but only one bothered to thank him. In Samaria, his encounter with the woman at the well is, by contrast, a masterpiece of gentle persuasion.

At the time of this encounter, Jesus had already performed his first miracle, converting water into wine, and had already clashed with Judaism's dominant religious power-brokers. But miracles and pugnacity towards the status quo are staples of charismatic leaders and would-be messiahs, of which Israel had ample experience. The humility and directness of his seemingly humdrum encounters, often with women, is much more unexpected.

This humanity can be perceived in his repertoire of miracles, which are often interspersed with the telling of homespun parables. He did not part oceans, crumble city walls, or stall the progress of the sun (indeed he wearily rejected a demand from the Pharisees that he do the latter to prove his divinity) – although he did once calm a storm. One of his signature miracles is an act of outstanding hospitality – providing food for thousands of his hungry followers. If they came for the miracles, it seems likely they stayed for the teaching, often framed in the teasing, compelling, and unsettling stories that the tradition preserved and transmitted.

The site of the Transfiguration is disputed: it might be Mount Hermon on the Golan Heights, or Mount Tabor in the Jezreel Valley. Jesus also ventured off his normal path to Nain to raise a widow's son to life, an act presaging his subsequent revival of Lazarus at Bethany, a village on the outskirts of Jerusalem. In St John's telling, the raising of Lazarus was portentous: the last of the "seven signs" conclusively proving Jesus to be the Son of God, and, of course, prefiguring his own resurrection soon afterwards. As Jesus made a triumphal final entry to Jerusalem, the Sanhedrin (assembly) of the Jewish church elders had determined he must be eliminated, a resolve intensified by his violent expulsion of the money-changers from the Temple. He was tried and sentenced by Pontius Pilate and crucified by the Romans, perhaps in April of the year 30 CE. After his crucifixion at Golgotha, or Calvary, immediately outside the walls of Jerusalem, and the revelation of his empty tomb, the Gospel of Luke describes his encounter with two disciples on the road to Emmaeus, described as being 60 stadia (c. 8 miles) from Jerusalem.

The Christian holy day of Pentecost commemorates the disciples' meeting in Jerusalem 50 days after the resurrection, when the Holy Spirit descended on them. Endowed with the gift of tongues, they set out to preach the gospel: the inception of the Christian church.

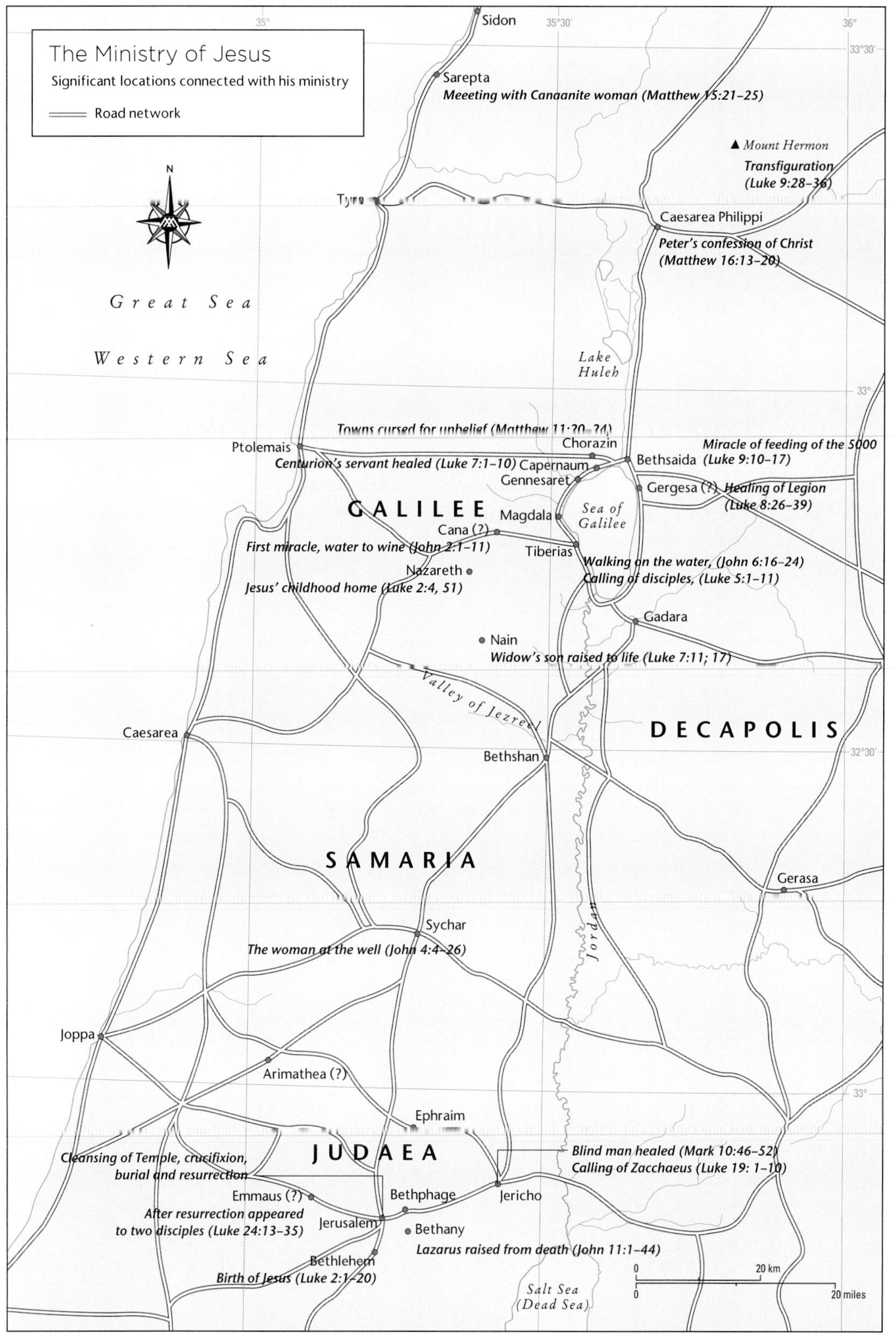

The Ministry of Jesus
Significant locations connected with his ministry
Road network
N
Great Sea
Western Sea
Sidon
Sarepta
Meeeting with Canaanite woman (Matthew 15:21–25)
Mount Hermon
Transfiguration (Luke 9:28–36)
Tyre
Caesarea Philippi
Peter's confession of Christ (Matthew 16:13–20)
Lake Huleh
Chorazin
Ptolemais
Centurion's servant healed (Luke 7:1–10)
Capernaum
Gennesaret
Bethsaida
Miracle of feeding of the 5000 (Luke 9:10–17)
Gergesa (?)
Healing of Legion (Luke 8:26–39)
GALILEE
Magdala
Sea of Galilee
Cana (?)
First miracle, water to wine (John 2:1–11)
Tiberias
Walking on the water, (John 6:16–24)
Calling of disciples, (Luke 5:1–11)
Nazareth
Jesus' childhood home (Luke 2:4, 51)
Gadara
Nain
Widow's son raised to life (Luke 7:11; 17)
Valley of Jezreel
Caesarea
DECAPOLIS
Bethshan
SAMARIA
Gerasa
Sychar
The woman at the well (John 4:4–26)
Jordan
Joppa
Arimathea (?)
Ephraim
JUDAEA
Cleansing of Temple, crucifixion, burial and resurrection
Blind man healed (Mark 10:46–52)
Calling of Zacchaeus (Luke 19: 1–10)
Emmaus (?)
Bethphage
Jericho
After resurrection appeared to two disciples (Luke 24:13–35)
Jerusalem
Bethany
Lazarus raised from death (John 11:1–44)
Bethlehem
Birth of Jesus (Luke 2:1–20)
Salt Sea (Dead Sea)
0 20 km
0 20 miles
35°
35°30'
36°
33°30'
33°
32°30'

The Age of the Apostles: St Paul's Journeys

The Age of the Apostles was the period from the start of the ministry of Jesus to the death of the last Apostle, John, in c. 100 CE. During this formative period early Christian communities evolved in Jerusalem, Antioch in Syria, and elsewhere, while the Apostles spread their message throughout the classical world: none more so than the man who in effect became Christianity's second founder.

Saul of Tarsus, born in Asia Minor, was both a Jew and a Roman citizen, who was brought up as a Pharisee. He responded to the emergence of the Jesus movement by becoming an enforcer of Pharisaic orthodoxy, traveling from synagogue to synagogue, preaching the persecution of Jews who believed Jesus to be a messiah. Traveling to Damascus on such a journey in c. 36 CE, Saul was struck blind and heard the voice of Jesus ask why he was persecuting him. This transformative experience made him a Christian, a transition he marked by changing his name to Paul. It also gave him a radical conviction of God's grace: if he, a persecutor, could be forgiven, anyone could be, Jew and Gentile alike.

A decade later, he began traveling to preach this message. Paul's first missions were in Syria, Cyprus, and Cilicia in the vicinity of his hometown of Tarsus. He had trained as a tent-maker, and used his trade to work his passage. He traveled extensively in Greece (including Athens, Corinth, and Philippi) and, Italy, reaching as far afield as Malta and Sicily. Hugely resilient, he attributed his survival of beatings, shipwrecks, and imprisonments to the power and grace of God. Paul exploited to the full the vastly improved freedom of travel and communication

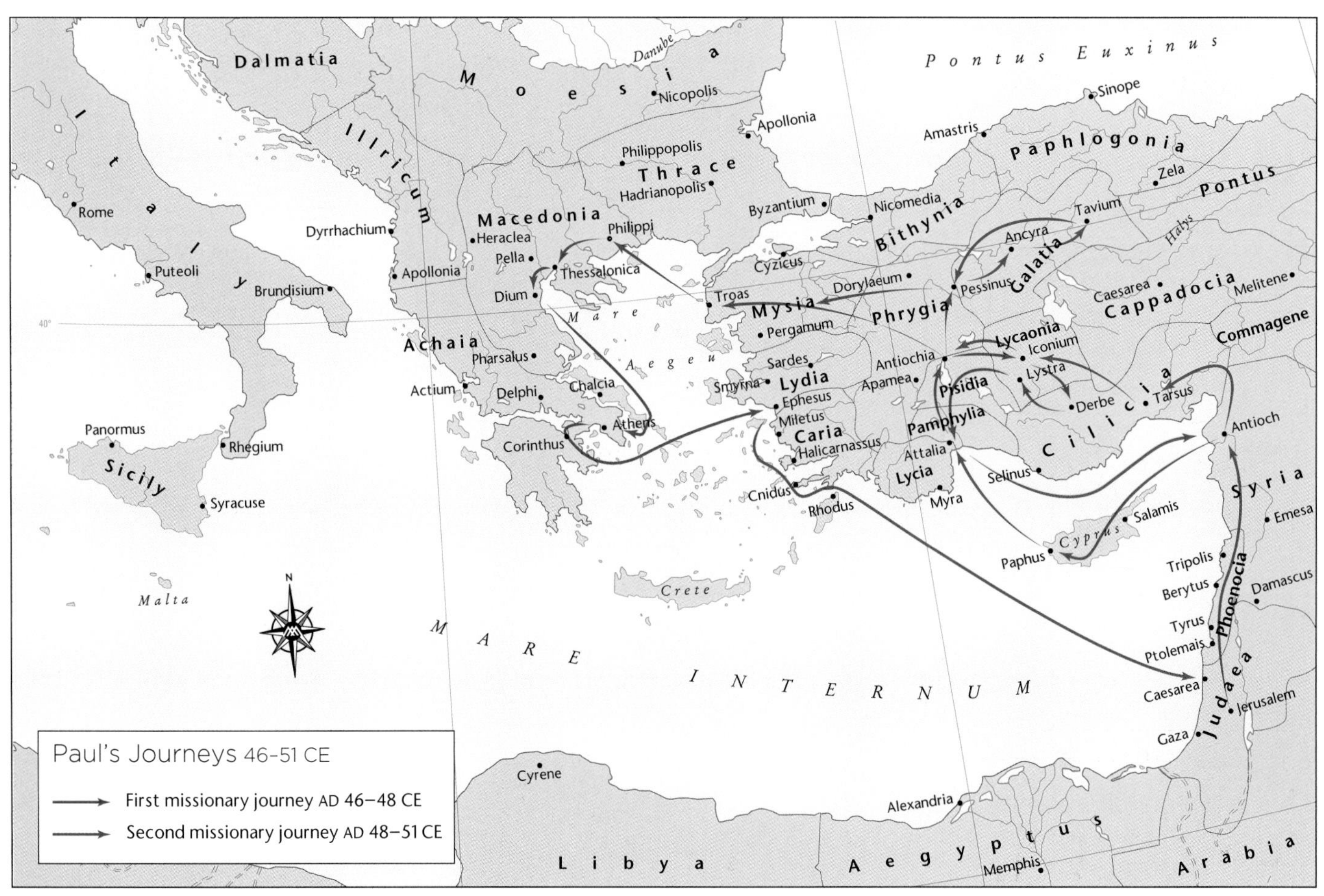

provided by the Pax Romana to seed a network of Christian outposts, and then nurture, encourage, and knit them together with his copious and impassioned correspondence.

His vivid letters to the embryonic Christian communities under his tutelary guidance prefigured the disputes that would later wrack the established church. Paul even accused Peter of hypocrisy in his letter to Galatians, sometimes clashed with other preachers on his travels, and criticized the wealthier patrons of the Corinthian community for eating apart from their humbler brethren.

After commencing his mission, he returned to Jerusalem a total of five times, and was frequently forced to assuage the criticisms of those who believed that Christianity should not be taught to Gentiles. He hammered out a bargain with Peter, who assumed responsibility for Jewish Christians, giving sanction to Paul's mission amongst the Gentiles. But on his final visit to Jerusalem, Paul was arrested, apparently for accompanying one of his converts into an area of the Temple forbidden to Gentiles. He was able to use his citizenship to persuade the Jewish authorities to transfer his case to Rome, and made his final journey there as a prisoner.

The circumstances of Paul's death remain a mystery. He was imprisoned in Rome in 64 CE, when the Emperor Nero purged Christians, holding them responsible for the Great Fire that had ravaged much of the city. Some accounts claim Peter was crucified and Paul beheaded during these reprisals; others, more speculative, that Paul managed a final mission to Spain before returning to Rome and execution.

The Early Christian Church to 200 CE

Persecution of Christians in the Roman Empire in the 1st and 2nd centuries was intermittent and localized, and much of the time they were relatively untroubled, but nevertheless they were widely regarded with suspicion if not outright hostility by both the authorities and the general population. The Bishop of Lyons was tortured to death with many of his flock in an outbreak of persecution (177 CE), and the influential Christian theologian Tertullian (c. 155–240) lamented that any natural calamity might lead to a call of "Away to the lions with the Christians!". As the Christian movement grew in the 3rd and early 4th centuries, it would face more sustained and systematic persecution, especially under the emperors Decius (in 250–51) and Diocletian (in 303–11).

By 200 CE the Christian movement was sizeable, with perhaps 150,000–200,000 Christians throughout the empire (and significant numbers beyond, with bishoprics in the Parthian Empire, for instance). Many of the missionaries were merchants, who spread the gospel during their commercial travels. Along with Rome, the major centers were Antioch and Alexandria. Jerusalem had been rebuilt as a pagan city by Emperor Hadrian after the Bar-Kokhba Revolt (132–135 CE); at this time the Christian base in the Holy Land was at Caesarea, with Jewish Christians moving across the Jordan to Pella in Decapolis. The greatest concentration of churches was in Asia Minor, where Paul devoted the bulk of his missionary activity and John the Apostle spent his final years at Ephesus. There were scattered bishoprics in the Western Empire, on the islands of the Mediterranean and an influential cluster in North Africa centred upon the bishopric of Carthage, which produced celebrated theologians such as Tertullian and Cyprian.

As the network expanded, the organization of the church began to be more formalized. During the 2nd century CE, a hierarchy of *episkopoi*, *presbyteroi*, and *diakonoi* (bishops/elders/administrators) began to be defined. At this time, particular reverence was accorded to Apostolic Fathers, those who had actually encountered and been taught by one or other of the original Apostles. Polycarp of Smyrna (d. 155 CE) and Ignatius of Antioch (d. c. 140 CE) were prominent within this group. By 200 CE

there were no Apostolic Fathers still living, but their authority persisted: when Bishop Victor of Rome (189–199 CE) tried to standardize Easter observance he was thwarted by an appeal to Polycarp's teachings. As this indicates, although the title "pope" is sometimes applied retrospectively to the early bishops of Rome, their primacy at this point was still tenuous.

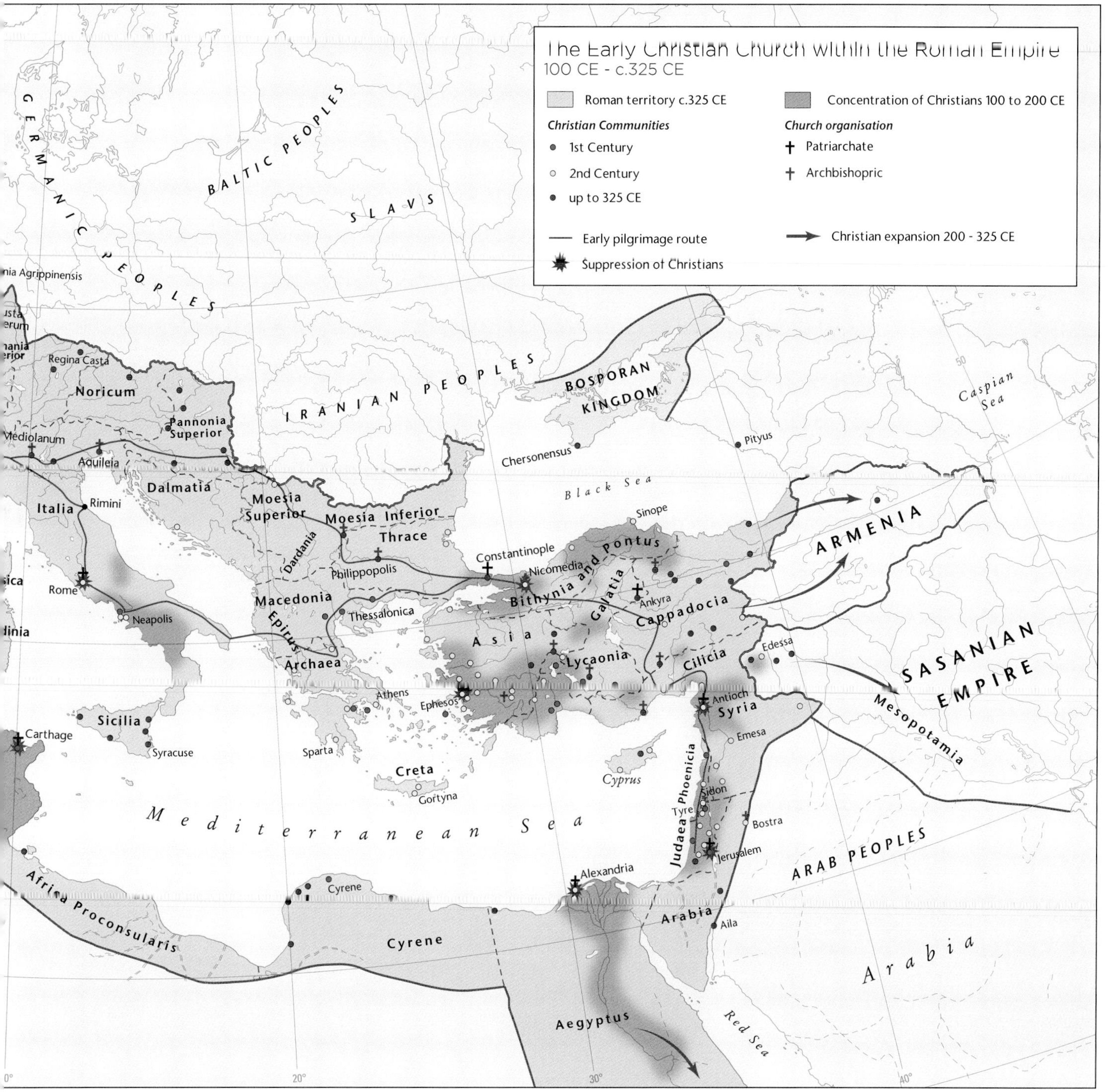

The Christianization of the Empire

The Chi Ro is one of the earliest forms of Christogram (a monogram that combines letters to form an abbreviation of the name Jesus Christ). It is formed by superimposing the first two letters (*chi* and *ro*) of the Greek word CHRISTOS. It was used by Emperor Constantine I (r. 306–337) as part of a military standard.

In its significance to the development of Christianity, Constantine's vison of the cross experienced on the night before the Battle of Milvian Bridge (312 CE) matches St Paul's vision on the road to Damascus. Constantine went on to win the battle, and and eventually to reunite the entire Roman Empire under his sole rule, a victory he attributed to the Christian God. Under the previous emperor, Diocletian, the most sustained persecution of Christians had been instigated (303–11 CE). He had also, before he abdicated in 305, divided the empire into eastern and western halves, each with its own emperor. The rolling civil war that ensued lasted for almost two decades.

Constantine achieved a decisive victory over Maxentius (the western emperor from 306–12 CE) at the Milvian Bridge but was forced to confront an even more powerful rival, the eastern emperor, Licinius. During the course of a brief rapprochement, the two rivals still standing were able to grant legal status and official tolerance to the Christian religion in the Edict of Milan (313 CE). The Edict of Milan granted Christianity legal status, but did not make it the state church of the Roman Empire.

Licinius was eventually vanquished in a series of engagements in 324 CE, culminating in the Battle of Chrysopolis. In the same year, Constantine would found an eastern capital for his empire, turning the ancient Greek city of Byzantium into a new, Christian Rome, called Contantinople. While Constantine refrained from being baptized until he was on his deathbed in 337 CE, he did enact a series of policies beneficial to the religion. These included the restoration of goods and properties confiscated during the persecution and fiscal and other privileges for clergy. The church received financial endowments, and Constantine commissioned the building of new places of worship including the Church of the Holy Sepulchre. He also ended the use of crucifixion as punishment.

Constantine did not merely protect the church: he asserted his authority over it, in particular by convening the Council of Nicaea (325 CE) which ruled against Arianism (although he would later display sympathy with Arian teaching). He also adjudicated in the disputes over Donatism, and gave precedence to Christian observances when they conflicted with prior

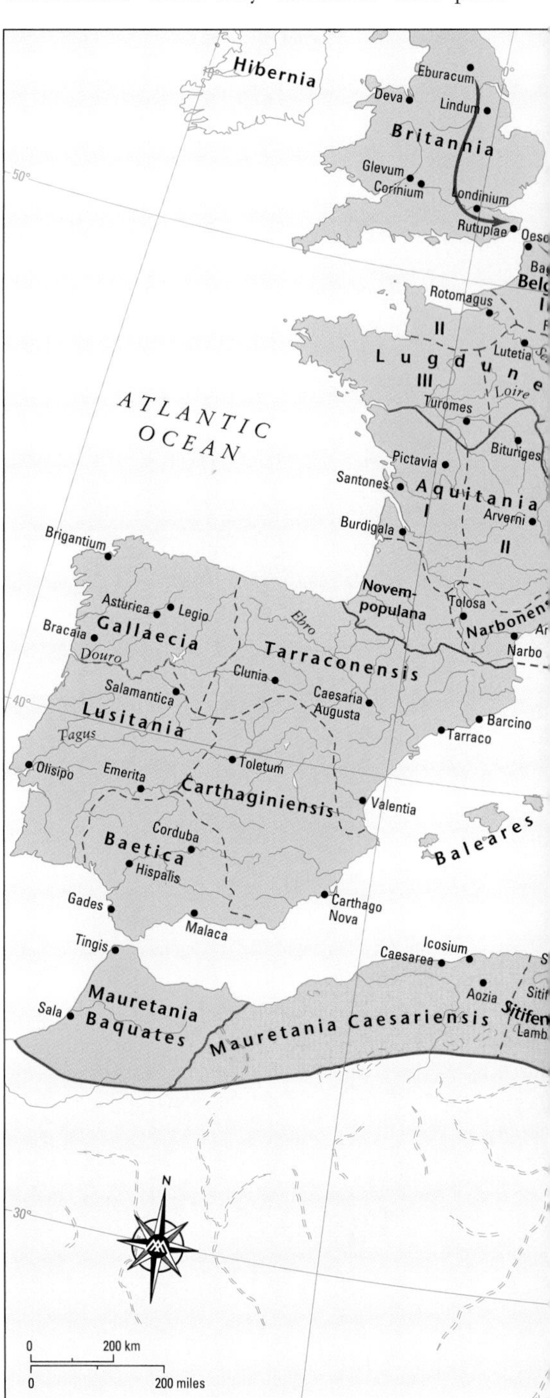

Judaic practice. Constantine, as an autocrat, favored centralized authority in the church, endorsing the church's efforts to uphold dogma and eradicate perceived heresies. Upon his death, Constantine was buried in the Church of the Holy Sepulchre: in less than three decades Christianity had been transformed from a hunted minority to a state religion. He is revered as a saint and *isapostolos* (equal-to-the-apostles) in various Orthodox denominations.

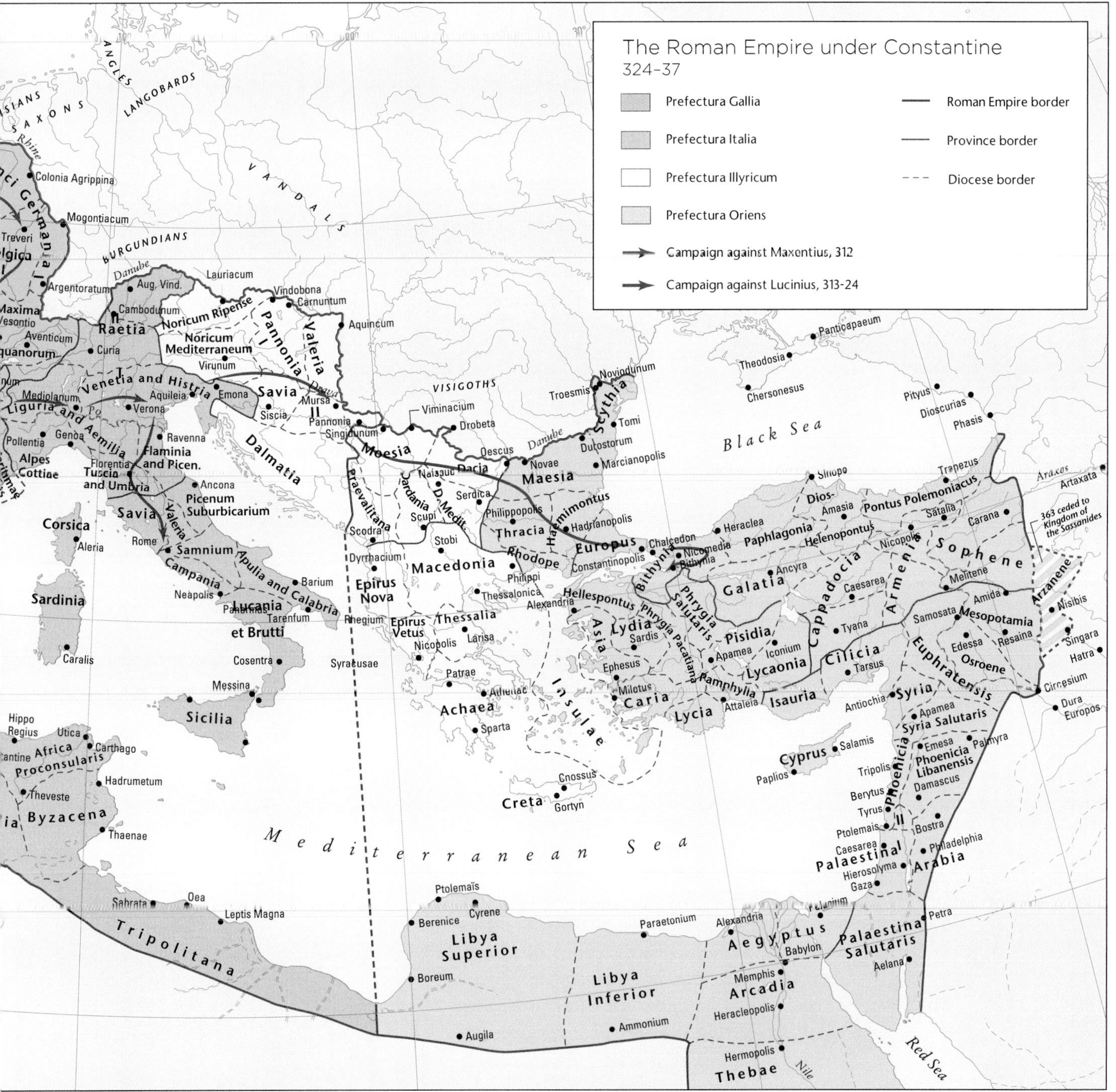

Early Christian Sects

Major religions have phases of exuberant diversification, with the exploration and occupation of new theological niches, followed by intense competition – and extinctions. Early Christianity's empire-wide network of bishops prevented it from fragmenting entirely, but the community remained highly fissiparous and many local Christian movements ended up being condemned and expelled by the "catholic" or "universal" church – which was itself, arguably, simply the largest and most enduring of the Christian sects.

The Ebionites, descendants of the original Jewish Christians, regarded Jesus Christ as the Messiah but rejected the doctrine of his divinity and the virgin birth. They were expelled from Judea in the aftermath of the Bar Kokhba Revolt (132–135 BCE) and the Ebionites dwindled into obscurity. The Sabellian challenge revolved around a divergent interpretation of the Godhead, propounding a singular divinity expressed in three forms rather than a Trinity. First advanced in Rome, the movement gained a foothold in North Africa. Marcion originated in Asia Minor: he was a dualist who entirely rejected Christianity's Jewish heritage, including the Hebrew Bible.

Gnosticism was a dualistic movement that emerged from Platonism, Zoroastrianism, and Christianity. *Gnosis* refers to knowledge based on personal experience or perception, through direct participation with the divine. Early theologians, such as Irenaeus, rejected it as a heresy, which denied the authority of the Apostolic succession and the gospel.

The most enduring of the dualistic movements were the Manichean followers of the 3rd-century Persian prophet Mani, whose radical opposition between matter (evil) and spirit (good) profoundly challenged Christian orthodoxy, but was nevertheless deeply appealing to many Christians for centuries to come.

The rigorous perfectionism of the Donatists, and their rejection of clergy they deemed to be compromised, provoked a schism in the church in Carthage in the early 4th century CE. The Donatists were extinguished when the "barbarian" Vandals invaded North Africa in 455 CE. The Vandals were Christians of a sect whose bid to define "Catholic" orthodoxy was particularly powerful and long-lasting: Arianism.

Arius's easily comprehensible doctrine maintained, simply, that Jesus Christ could not be "coeternal" and of the "same essence" as God the Father, because "if the father begat the son ... it is evident that there was a time when the Son was not." Arianism flourished despite being rejected by the Councils of Nicaea (325 CE) and Constantinople (381 CE). Even so, it remained a strong presence, especially among some Germanic tribes.

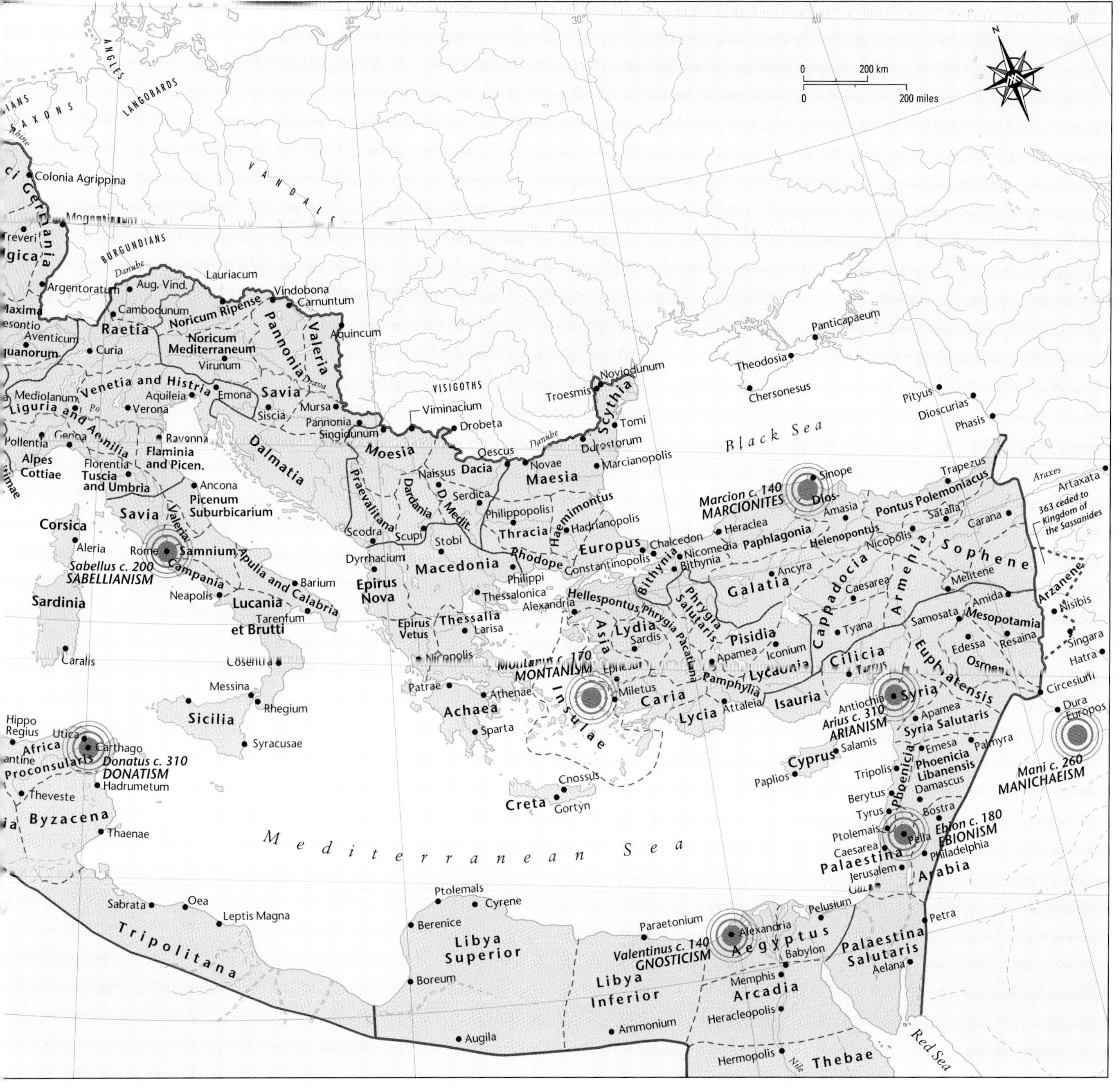

The Council of Chalcedon 451 CE

THE ESOTERIC THEOLOGICAL DEBATES that dominated the series of ecclesiastical councils culminating in Chalcedon took place against a backdrop of hordes of Goths, Huns, and Vandals despoiling and dismembering the remnants of the Western Roman Empire.

In the 4th-century councils commencing at Nicaea, an agreed official churchwide position had eventually been hammered out regarding the nature of the Trinity; that there were three divine persons combined in one essence. This construction, formally adopted at Constantinople (381 CE), focused renewed debate upon the nature of Christ. These apparently hairsplitting debates were in fact profoundly important: how God and man met and (perhaps) were united in Christ prefigured how all humanity might ultimately relate to God. Nestorius, Patriarch of Constantinople (428–31 CE) taught that Christ's human and divine natures were separate, and that the Virgin Mary was, therefore, not a "*Theotokos*" (God-bearer), having given birth to the human Christ. Nestorius was roundly condemned at the First Council of Ephesus (431 CE), expelled from his office and his views anathematized. The downfall of Nestorius was a victory for Alexandria's theologians, and for its then patriarch, Cyril. The dispute between Alexandria and Constantinople came to a head in 449 CE, when the bishop of Constantinople, Flavian, exiled a monk, Eutyches, who had accused various church officials of Nestorianism. The new patriarch of Alexandria, Dioscoros, backed Eutyches, calling a Second Council of Ephesus, from which the delegates of Pope Leo I were excluded, and Flavian was so badly beaten he died three days later.

Chalcedon was Pope Leo I's riposte. The Council deposed and exiled Dioscoros and the bishops who supported him. It was confirmed that Christ was both perfectly divine and perfectly human, except free from sin. It endorsed the doctrine that Christ had two natures in one person, rather than two distinct natures (Nestorius), or the single nature held to be implicit in the teaching of Eutyches. The Council laid down a set of clarifying institutional rules, and Leo's delegation returned to Rome triumphant.

The triumph was an illusion, and not only because Rome was sacked by Arian Vandals

four years later. The Council's decrees created a debilitating three-way split that endures in various forms to the present. The "Catholic" world accepted Chalcedon's definitions. But Nestorianism dominated the churches to the east of the Roman world, and "monophysite" or "miaphysite" churches following Eutyches' views were, and remained, dominant in northeast Africa.

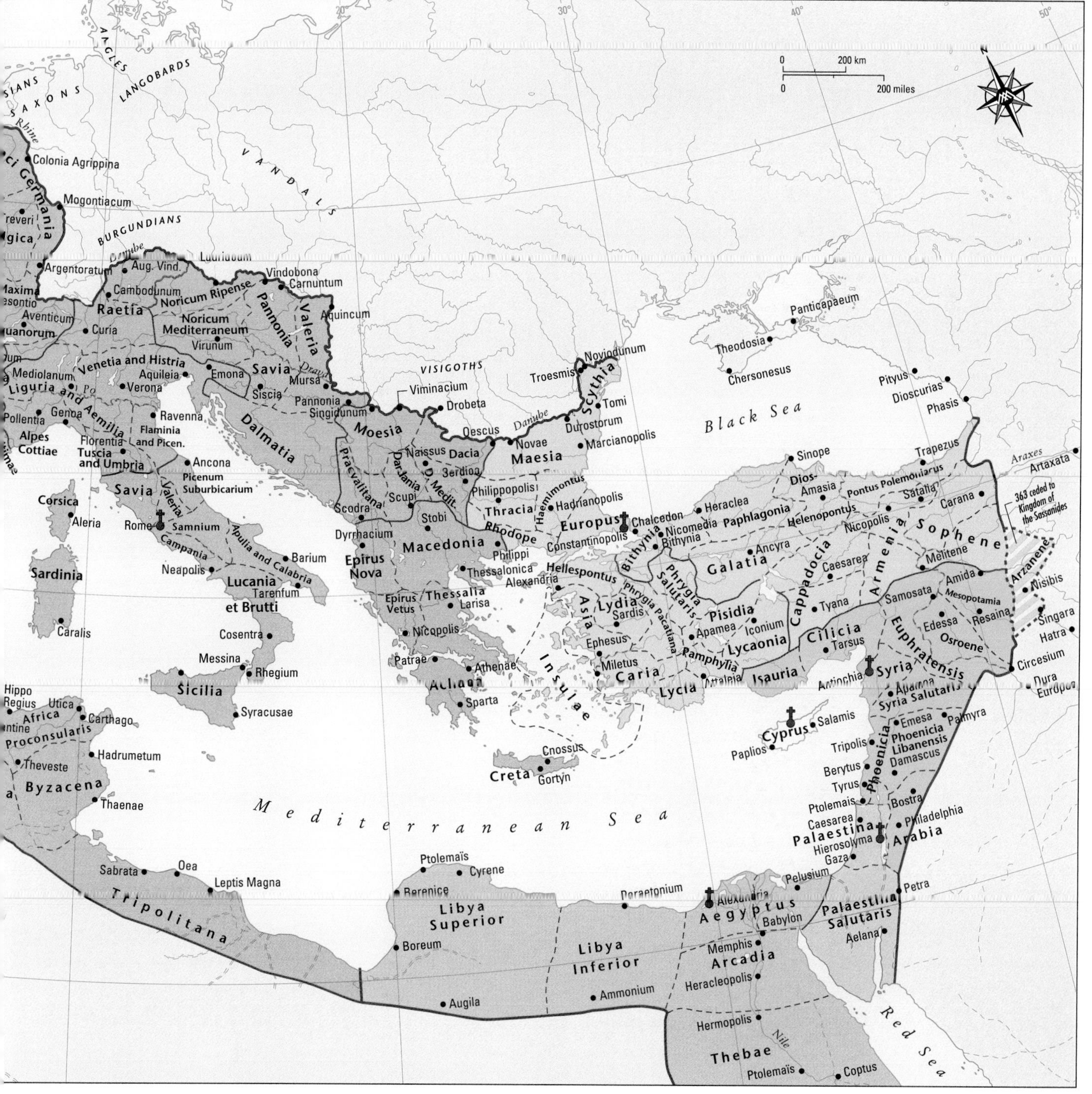

The Fall of the Empire in the West

The attempts of Diocletian (286–305 CE) to reduce the empire's increasing unmanageability by splitting it in two were initially successful, but then the invasion of Europe's eastern European plains by the Huns in the mid-4th century displaced Goths who fled for sanctuary to the Moesian borders, igniting a migratory chain-reaction that would prove disastrous for Rome.

Fleeing the Huns, "barbarian" incursions mounted, but the empire descended into a new series of civil wars. Britain was left exposed to Pictish marauding when Magnus Maximus recruited its garrisons to support his ill-fated bid for the purple, while Christianity became the unchallenged state religion when the last imperial claimant supporting polytheism was killed at the Battle of the Frigidus (395 CE). A lieutenant of the emperor during this victory was a Gothic nobleman, Alaric. Disappointed that his contribution was not rewarded with a senior command, Alaric turned renegade and began to plunder northern Italy, eventually laying siege to Rome twice before seizing and sacking the city (410 CE). Alaric died soon afterwards, but any chance of a Roman recovery was effectively terminated when another imperial pretender, Jovinus, overran Gaul with Burgundian and Alan allies, while Spain fell to the Visigoths and Sueves. When Carthage fell to the Vandals (439 CE), Rome had virtually no food supply or tax base. The Roman general Aetius, commanding largely barbarian mercenaries, turned the tide and defeated the fearsome invader, Attila, at the Battle of the Catalaunian Plains (451), only to be stabbed to death by a paranoid emperor.

Rome, defenceless, was sacked again by the Vandals in 455 CE, but was briefly resurgent under the Emperor Majorian (457–67 CE). Majorian was murdered through the treachery of Ricimer, his chief of staff, and three more puppet emperors succeeded before the Ostrogoth Odoacer performed the last rites when he bloodlessly deposed the last Roman emperor, the 16-year-old Romulus Augustulus, in 476 CE.

The Goths were the earliest barbarian adopters of Christianity; they had been converted by Ulfilas, who had been sent to them by the Arian emperor, Constantius II, and was appointed

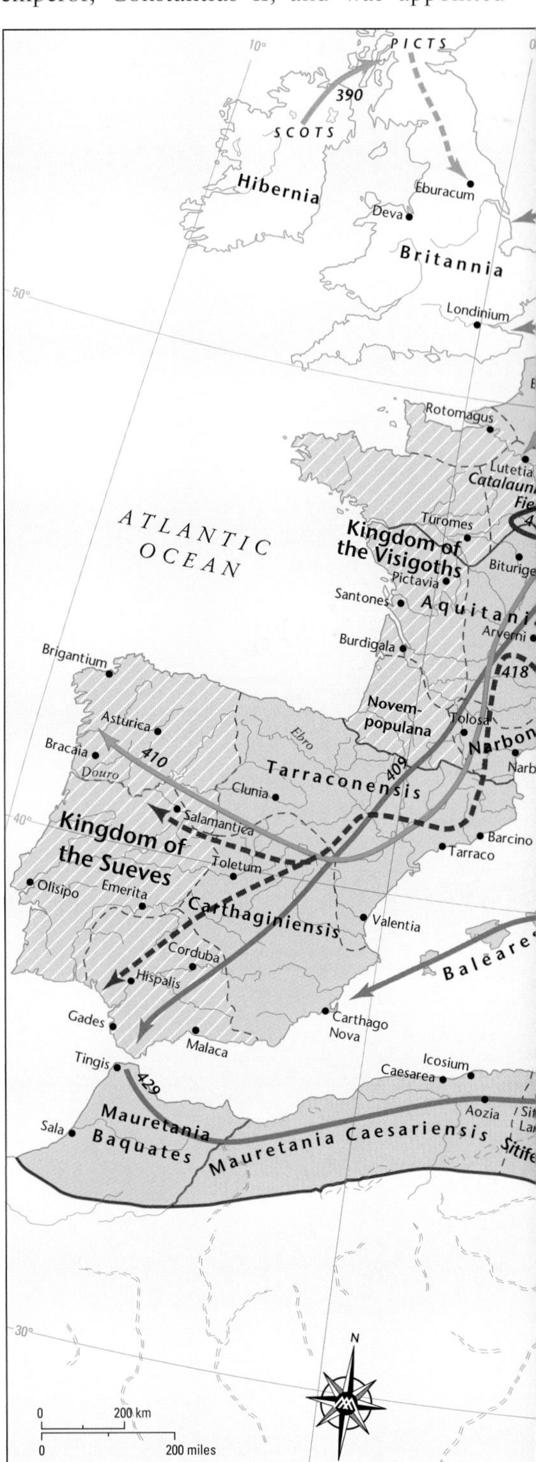

their first bishop in the 340s. For the most part, barbarians converted to Christianity, predominantly Arianism, after they crossed the borders of the Roman Empire, rejecting paganism in favor of a religion that appeared to be intrinsic to the civilization they were appropriating.

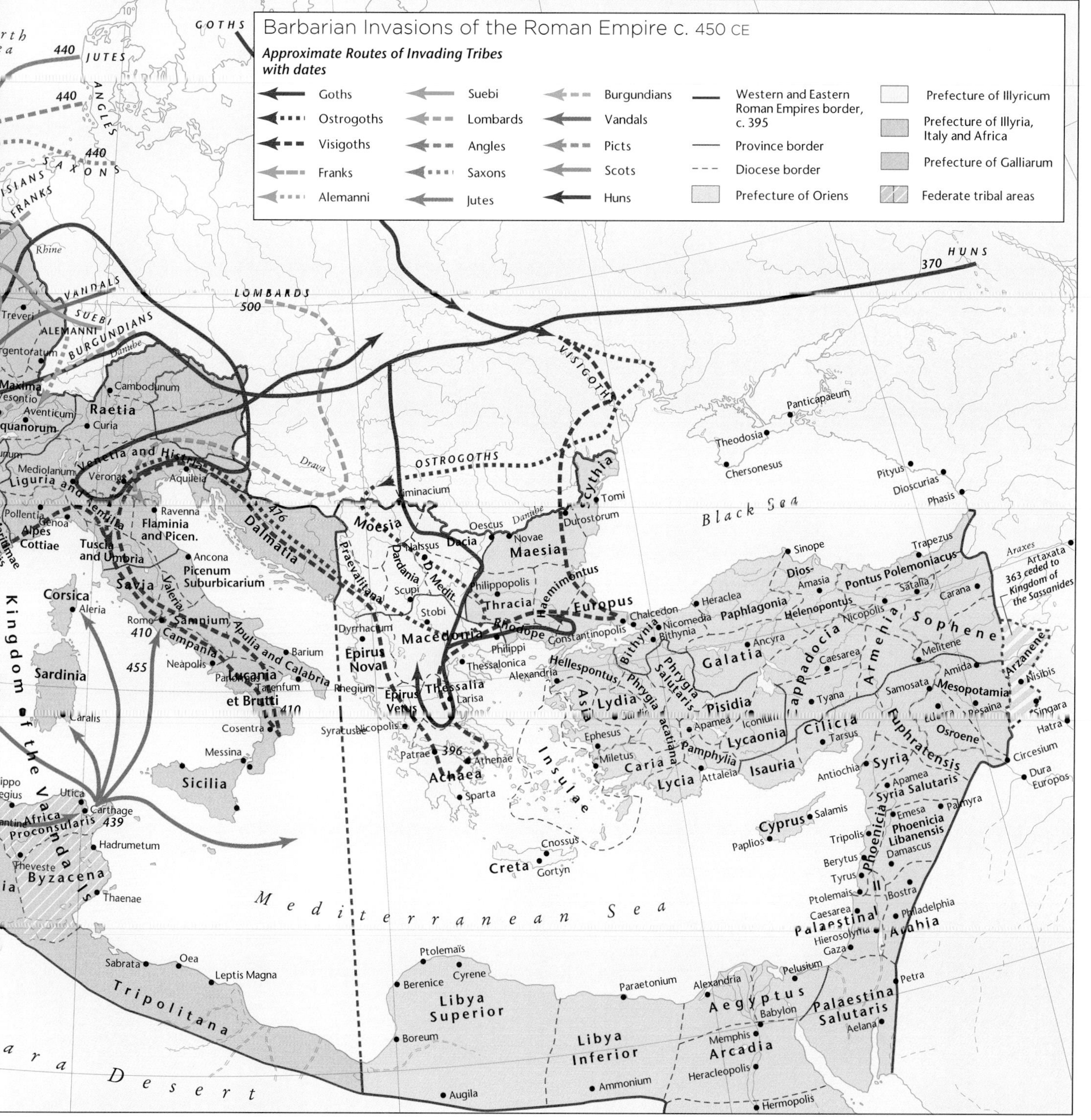

Creeds and Controversies

Ulfilas (311–83 CE) was a prodigious missionary: for 40 years he preached the gospel in Moesia and Dacia (Bulgaria and Romania), even devising a Gothic alphabet to produce a Bible in the language of his converts. Ulfilas was an Arian Christian and, at the time of his departure, this doctrine, with the backing of Emperor Constantius II, appeared to be in the ascendancy in the church. But, after decades of furious debate and politicking (a Roman commentator drily observed that, at this time "the highways teemed with galloping bishops"), the Council of Constantinople (381 CE) asserted Nicene orthodoxy, anathematizing Arianism.

Visigoths and Ostrogoths, warlike nomads who traveled vast distances to plunder and occupy the decaying empire, tended to disregard the latest conciliar decrees and it was Ulfilas's now heretical brand of Christianity that took root amongst many of the peoples whom Rome called "barbarians." Alaric the Visigoth, and Genseric the Vandal, who sacked Rome in 410 and 455 CE respectively, were both Arians. Ricimer, the romanized Sueve general who orchestrated the murders of four successive Roman emperors from 456–72 CE, was also Arian. And the final demise of the Western Empire in 476 was executed by the Goth Odoacer, yet another Arian. Pope Symmachus eked out a precarious existence under the rule of Theoderic the Great, the Arian King of the Ostrogoths (r. 493–526). Beyond Theoderic's empire extended the kingdoms of the Sueves and Burgundians, also with Arian rulers. Even the Gepids, who displaced the Huns in the central European plains, had aristocratic converts. But there were two chinks of light for the embattled papacy.

First, the Frankish warlord Clovis (481–511) united the Frankish tribes then drove the Arian Visigoths out of Gaul. At the urging of his wife, Clotilde, he converted to Catholicism. The Merovingian dynasty established by Clovis proved durable, despite frequent partition owing to Frankish laws of inheritance; it also stubbornly adhered to Catholicism, prefiguring the successor Carolingian dynasty and the Holy Roman Empire, established by Charlemagne.

Second, most barbarian leaders treated religious conversion as a form of everlasting life insurance rather than agonizing over the metaphysical detail, and were therefore tolerant of other strains of Christianity (in a way the church itself was not). Accordingly, the sway of Arianism in the west was broad but shallow, while the

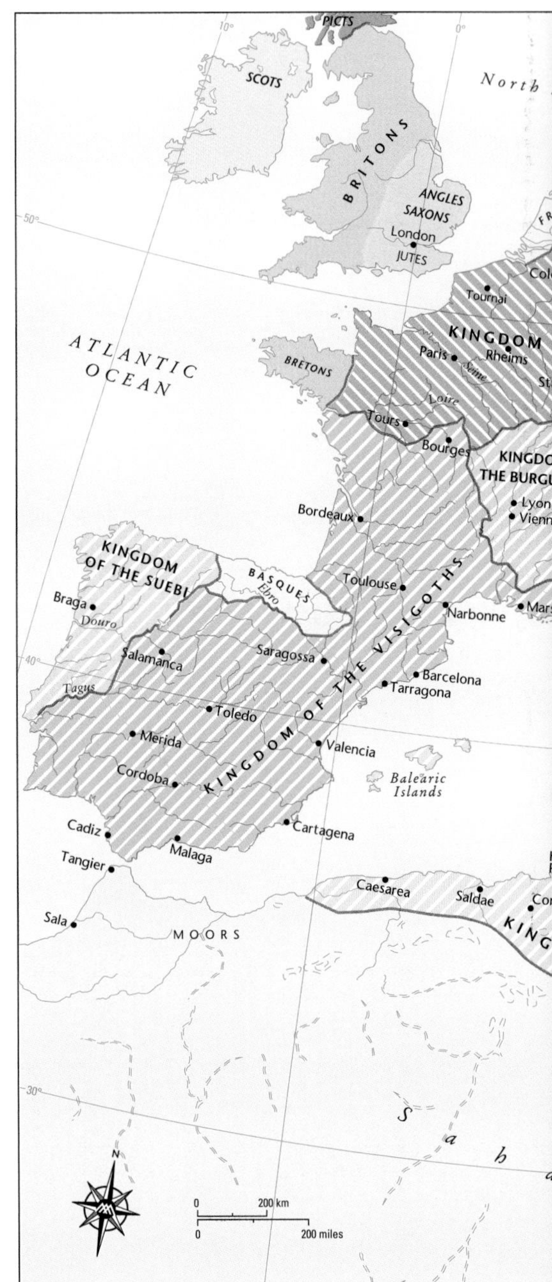

Eastern Empire, which remained largely intact, was resolutely Chalcedonian. The 5th-century popes, who were painfully aware of their lack of access to temporal power, asserted papal primacy. This curdled relations with the East, where a revisiting of the Chalcedonian settlement sparked the Acacian Schism (484–519 CE), in which the pope excommunicated Acacius, the patriarch of Constantinople, for producing an edict judged at variance with Chalcedon. The persistent feuding irritated Theoderic. While his counterpart in the east, Emperor Justin I, resolved the Acacian dispute, he also began to repress his Arian subjects. Theoderic contemplated countermeasures against Catholics but died before they could be enacted.

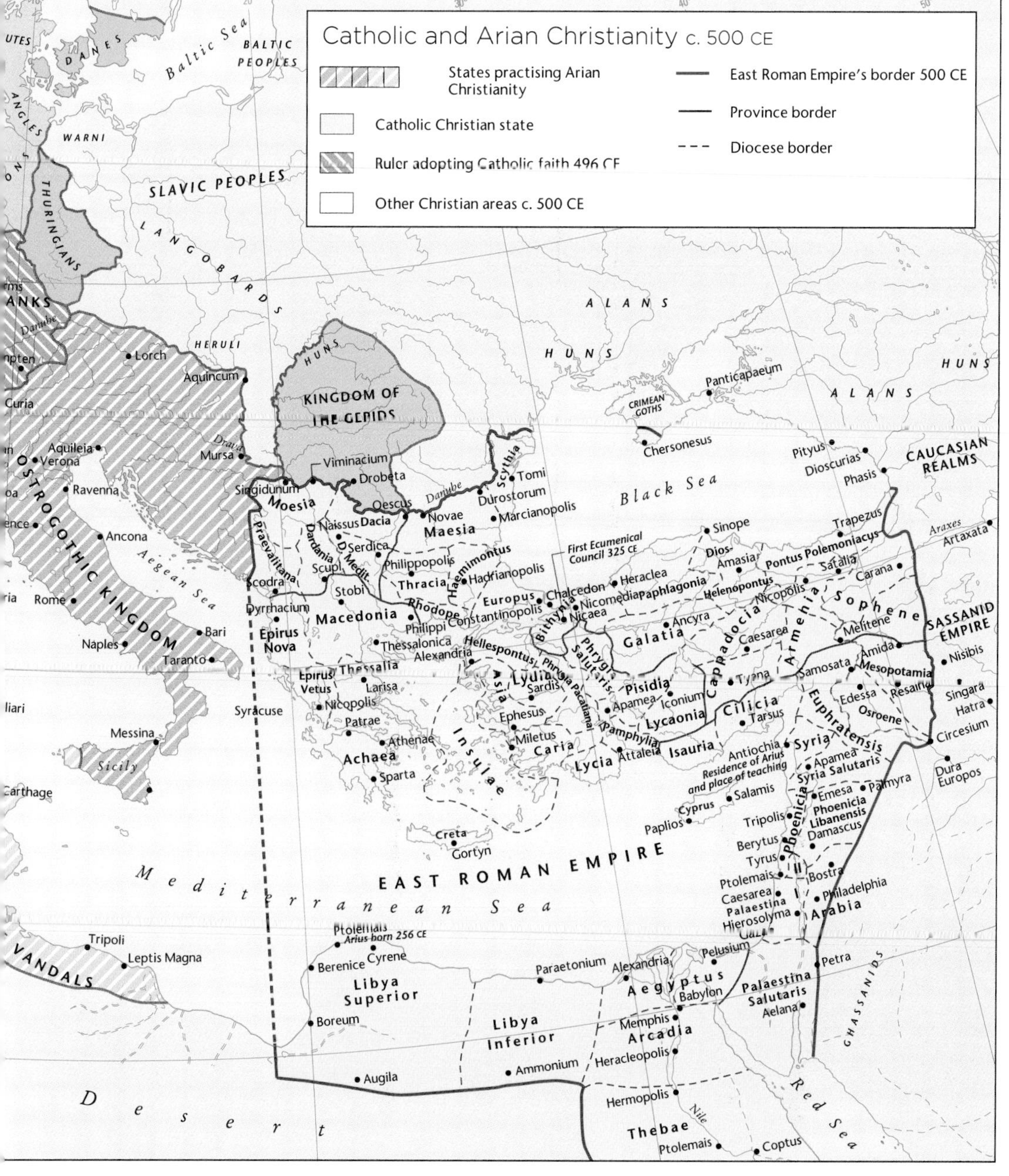

The Consolidation of Christianity to 600 CE

The eastern Roman Emperor Justinian I (527–65 CE) unwittingly delivered the *coup de grâce* for western Roman civilization. His general, Belisarius, recovered most of Italy and North Africa from the Goths and Vandals, but their territories were laid waste in the process. Out of the wreckage, the papacy in Rome eventually emerged, strengthened and renewed. Justinian would hold Pope Virgilius captive for eight years until he submitted to the imperial position in the theological dispute of the "Three Chapters" (a 145-year schism would ensue), but by the end of the century Pope Gregory the Great had reasserted Rome's spritual, although not political, primacy.

With the old empire now united in acknowledging papal authority, the monastic movement was free to flourish, often lavishly endowed by royalty and aristocracy seeking divine providence. The solitary Christian hermits who had withdrawn to the deserts of North Africa to live lives of ascetic contemplation were drawing together into communal monasteries by the 3rd century, originally in Egypt and then throughout the eastern Christian world. Western monasticism owed its origins to St Benedict of Nursia (c. 480–560 CE), who established his order in Italy in around 530 CE. His Benedictine Rule specified a monastic family with the abbot as father and monks as brothers, and established highly organized timetables with canonical hours set for services, prayer, spiritual reading, and labor.

As monasteries proliferated throughout western Christendom they became the guardians of the civilization that had been crushed by the barbarian invasions. In practical terms, monks were skilled agriculturalists, who introduced new crops and farming methods, such as irrigation. They were experienced metallurgists and glassworkers and their technical know-how pervaded Europe, forestalling a reversion to barbarism. More profoundly for the future of Christianity, they were assiduous copiers and preservers of ancient manuscripts, who rescued and nurtured a world of classical learning.

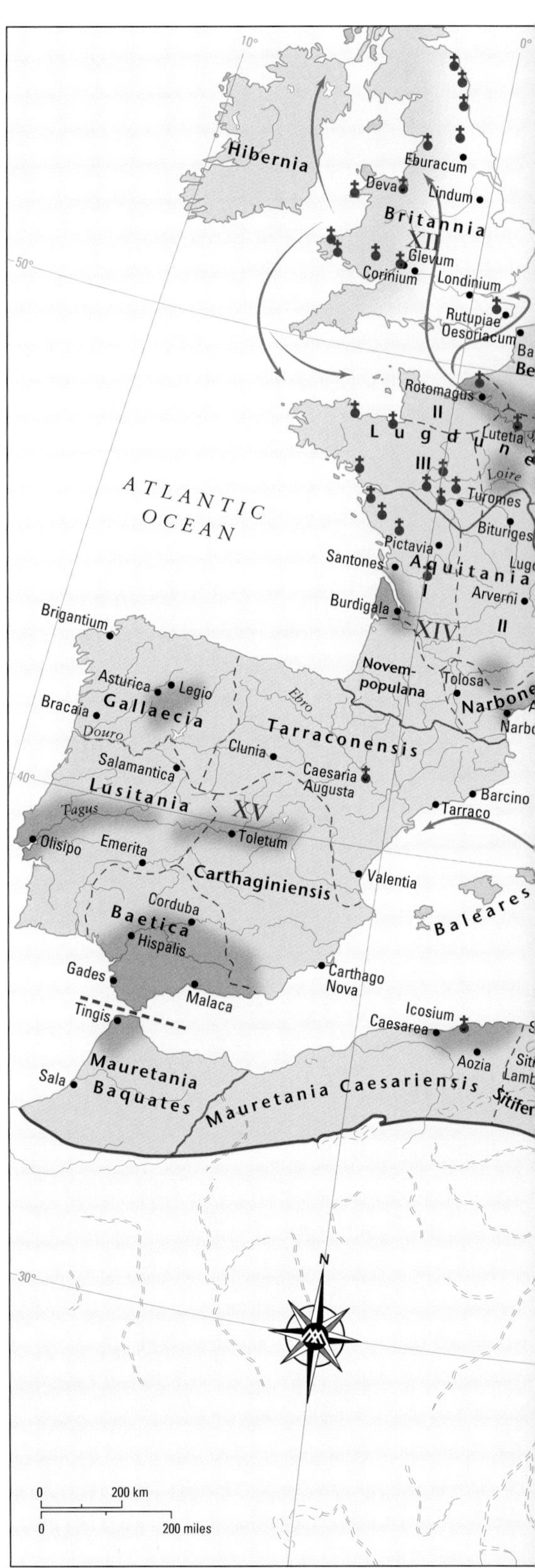

The Spread of Christianity to 600 CE
Extent of Christianity c. 400CE
Extent of Christianity c. 400-600CE
Expansion of monasticism
Monastic community
Western and Eastern Roman Empires border, 395
Province border
Diocese border
I Egypt
II Orient
III Pontica
IV Asia
V Thracia
VI Macedonia
VII Dacia
VIII Pannonia
IX Italia Annonaria
X Italia Suburbicaria
XI Africa
XII Britannia
XIII Gallia
XIV Seven Provinces
XV Hispania
Christianity expanding into Caucasus and Mesopotamia.
SAXONS
ANGLES
LANGOBARDS
VANDALS
BURGUNDIANS
VISIGOTHS
Colonia Agrippina
Mogontiacum
Treveri
Argentoratum
Aug. Vind.
Lauriacum
Vindobona
Carnuntum
Aquincum
Raetia
Curia
Noricum Ripense
Noricum Mediterraneum
Virunum
Pannonia I
Valeria
Savia
Emona
Siscia
Mursa
Pannonia II
Singidunum
Venetia and Histria
Aquileia
Verona
Mediolanum
Liguria and Aemilia
Pollentia
Genoa
Alpes Cottiae
Ravenna
Flaminia and Picen.
Tuscia and Umbria
Florentia
Ancona
Picenum Suburbicarium
Corsica
Aleria
Sardinia
Caralis
Rome
Valeria
Savia
Samnium
Campania
Apulia and Calabria
Barium
Neapolis
Lucania et Brutti
Panormus
Tarentum
Cosentia
Messina
Sicilia
Dalmatia
VIII
Utica
Proconsularis
Hadrumetum
Byzacena
Thaenae
XI
Sabrata
Oea
Leptis Magna
Tripolitana
Mediterranean Sea
Moesia
Praevalitana
Dardania
Dacia
Naissus
VII
Serdica
Scupi
Scodra
Stobi
Dyrrhachium
Epirus Nova
Macedonia
VI
Thessalonica
Philippi
Rhegium
Epirus Vetus
Thessalia
Larisa
Nicopolis
Patrae
Achaea
Athenae
Sparta
Insula
Creta
Cnossus
Gortyn
Viminacium
Drobeta
Oescus
Danube
Novae
Moesia
Durostorum
Marcianopolis
Troesmis
Noviodunum
Scythia
Tomi
Philippopolis
V
Thracia
Haemimontus
Hadrianopolis
Rhodope
Europus
Constantinopolis
Chalcedon
Nicomedia
Bithynia
Hellespontus
Alexandria
Black Sea
Panticapaeum
Theodosia
Chersonesus
Pityus
Dioscurias
Phasis
Trapezus
Sinope
Amasia
Paphlagonia
Heraclea
Helenopontus
Pontus Polemoniacus
Satala
Nicopolis
Carana
Artaxata
Araxes
Sophene
Melitene
Arzanene
Armenia
Galatia
Ancyra
III
Cappadocia
Caesarea
Tyana
Phrygia Salutaris
Phrygia Pacatiana
Asia
Lydia
Sardis
IV
Pisidia
Apamea
Iconium
Lycaonia
Ephesus
Caria
Miletus
Pamphylia
Lycia
Attaleia
Isauria
Cilicia
Tarsus
Antiochia
Syria
Apamea
Syria Salutaris
Euphratensis
Samosata
Amida
Mesopotamia
Edessa
Resaina
Osroene
Nisibis
Singara
Hatra
Circesium
Dura Europos
Palmyra
Cyprus
Salamis
Paphos
Tripolis
Phoenicia
Phoenicia Libanensis
Damascus
Berytus
Tyrus
Ptolemais
Caesarea
Palaestina
Hierosolyma
Gaza
Bostra
Philadelphia
Arabia
Petra
Pelusium
Palaestina Salutaris
Aelana
Alexandria
Aegyptus
Babylon
Memphis
Arcadia
Heracleopolis
Hermopolis
Thebae
Nile
Ptolemais
Coptus
Diospolis Magna
Red Sea
Paraetonium
Libya Inferior
Ammonium
Ptolemaïs
Berenice
Cyrene
Libya Superior
Boreum
Augila

Ireland: Churchmen and Scholars

Pope Celestine I (422–32) saw his mission as the preservation of religious orthodoxy by the rooting out of "profane novelties." When he learned that one such novelty, Pelagianism (which denied original sin, and emphasized human free will), was rife in Britain, from which the Roman army had recently withdrawn, he ordained a dual mission to "keep the Roman island Catholic, and make the barbarous island Christian." He despatched Bishop Germanus to Britain in 429. Two years later, Palladius, the newly appointed bishop of Ireland, was sent to tend to "recent converts" and to root out Pelagianism. Both were trained at the theological powerhouse of Auxerre, which would become a factory for missionaries to the hinterlands of the decaying Roman Empire.

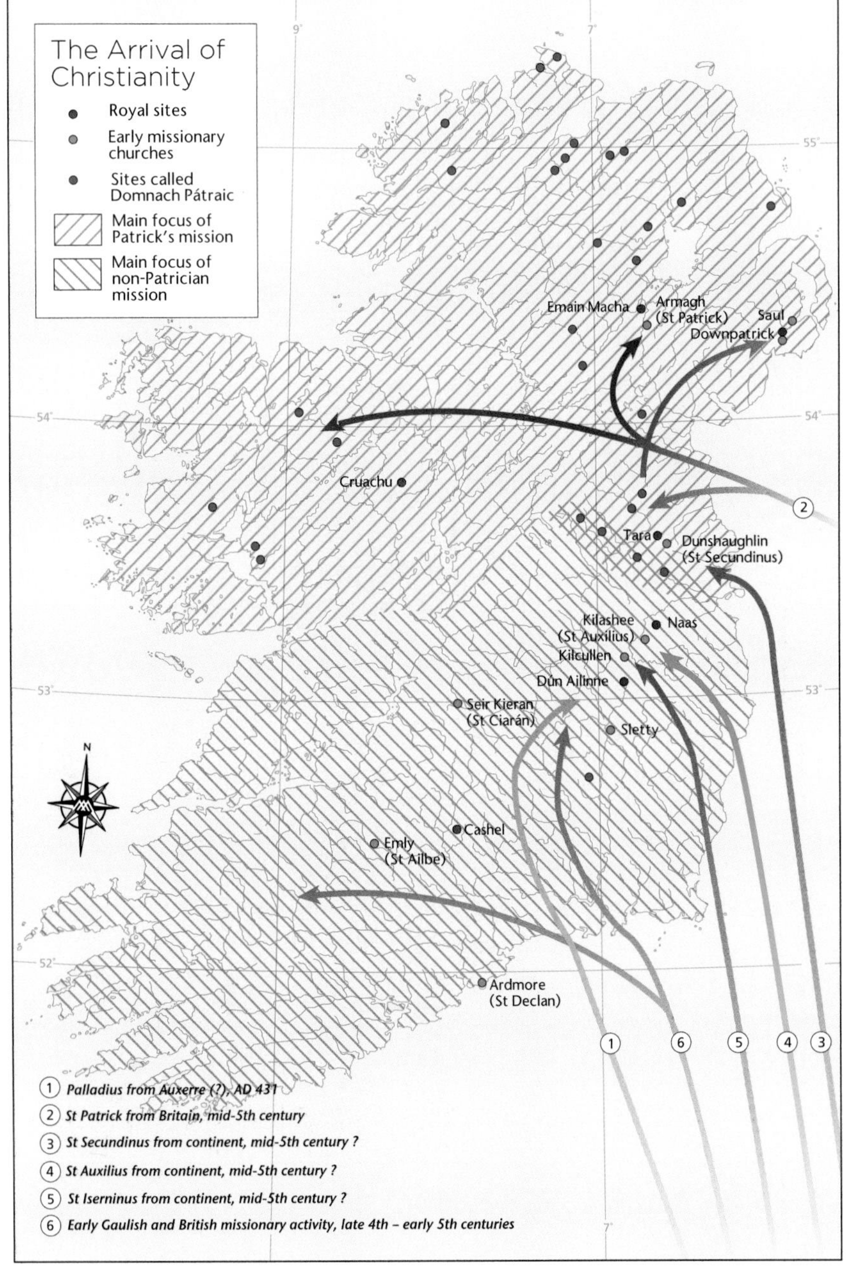

Ireland had never been under Roman rule, and was a hotchpotch of warring tribal chieftains with neither the habit nor the memory of centralized authority. The "recent converts" were probably a mixture of traders, escaped slaves, and refugees from the war-torn continent, although earlier missions may have occurred: St Ailbe of Emly and St Declan of Ardmore possibly pre-dated Celestine's emissaries.

Palladius was banished soon after his arrival by the King of Leinster, but hard on his heels came St Patrick, once more from Auxerre. Patrick was soon able to augment his traveling companions, Secundinus, Auxilius, and Iserninus, by recruits from the kin of the chieftains he was able to convert, such as Benignus, Odran and Fiacc. While Patrick concentrated his efforts in the north of the island, his traveling companions each established monastic communities in Meath, Killashee, and Kilcilliers. The foundation of monasteries proved key to the perpetuation of Christianity in Ireland: it created urban communities, and centers of written learning, where none had existed before, and a connective network that transcended tribal faultlines. Distinctive monastic and spiritual traditions evolved here: wilderness, isolation, and ocean served a similar role to the desert for the early Egyptian monastic fathers. The remote outpost was ready to export Christianity back eastward.

The Irish monk St Ninian was reputed to have established a mission, the "Candida Casa" at Whithorn in Galloway, in the early 5th century: it became a place of further education for a number of Irish missionaries to the mainland, before being eclipsed by Colum Cille's monas-

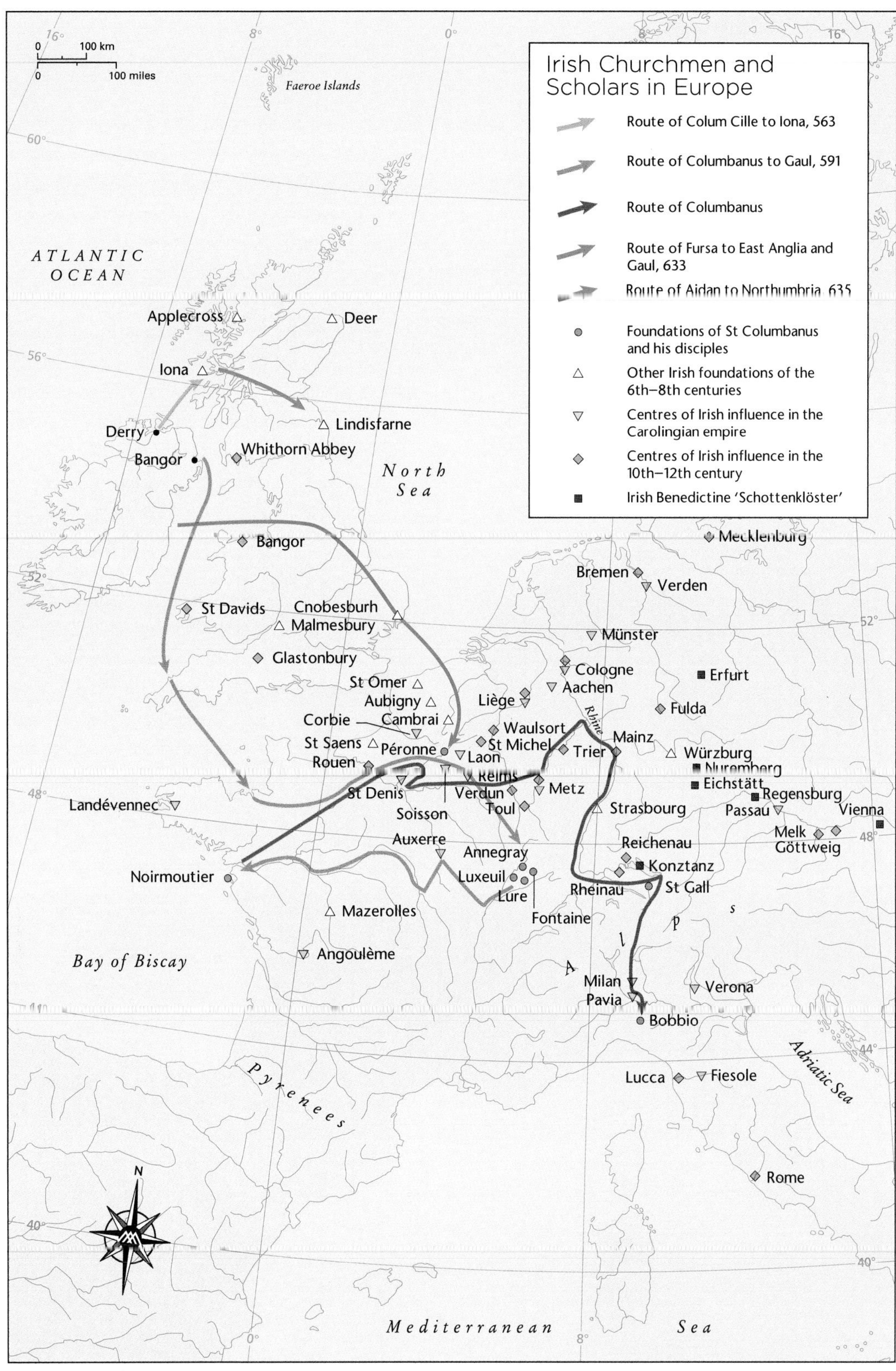

The monasatery of Iona in Scotland, founded by St Columban (Columbanus) became origin and way-station for missions to Britain and the continent. St Fursey (Fursa) did much to establish Christianity throughout the British Isles, particularly East Anglia. Columbanus worked to convert pagan enclaves in the Frankish Empire, reaching Bobbio in northern Italy, from 590–615. *Schottenklöster* were Irish monastic communities that appeared in Germany in the 11th and 12th centuries.

tery on Iona (founded 563). Aidan was an alumnus: he went on to found Lindisfarne monastery and convert the rulers of Northumbria, who, by defeating the last major Anglo-Saxon king, Penda of Mercia (655), effectively achieved the Christianization of England.

The Empire under Justinian 527–565

When Justinian I (527–65 CE) became emperor in Constantinople, the last emperor to speak Latin, he resolved to restore the old Roman Empire. Instead he helped to create something substantially new: an Eastern Roman Empire (as it continued to call itself) that survived for nearly another thousand years but with an increasingly distinct, Greek identity, which historians call the Byzantine Empire.

His general, Belisarius, first reclaimed North Africa from the Vandals (533–34 CE), before moving into Italy. He there found a formidable adversary in the Ostrogothic King, Totila. The ensuing Gothic Wars (535–54 CE) swung back and forth, laying waste to the Italian pensinsula and the city of Rome. After Totila's death, Belisarius' successor Narses was finally able to complete the conquest of Italy. In 552 CE, a Byzantine expeditionary force reconquered a portion of southern Spain from the Visigoths: this would prove to be the territorial high watermark of the Byzantine Empire.

Justinian reformed the legal code, purged administrative corruption and instituted efficient systems of tax collection. Buoyed by these achievements, he attempted to reconcile the doctrinal disputes that had riven the church since the Council of Chalcedon (or indeed, since Nicaea). His Three Chapters constituted a denunciation of three eminent theologians of the Antiochene School, Thomas of Mopsuestia, Theodoret of Cyrus, and Ibas of Edessa, who had propounded the separate divine and human natures of Christ. Justinian intended to appease the Monophysites (holding Christ had one divine nature), a position championed by the Alexandrian School. The influential Antiochenes were enraged; teachers they revered had been condemned, both the pope and the patriarch of Constantinople were unhappy that the careful compromise crafted at Chalcedon had been overturned, while for the Monophysites it was unsatisfactory, because it stopped short of endorsing their position. At the Council of Constantinople (553 CE), Justinian bullied the recalcitrant clerics into confirming the Three Chapters, imprisoning Pope Virgilius until he gave his assent. The resulting schism was not resolved for almost 150 years – Justinian's attempts to impose religious unity on his subjects by forcing compromise left many unsatisfied.

Despite all his restless achievements, the event of greatest long-term impact in Justinian's reign would be the massive plague epidemic of 541–42 CE, of a scale comparable to the Black Death in the 14th century. Some estimates have

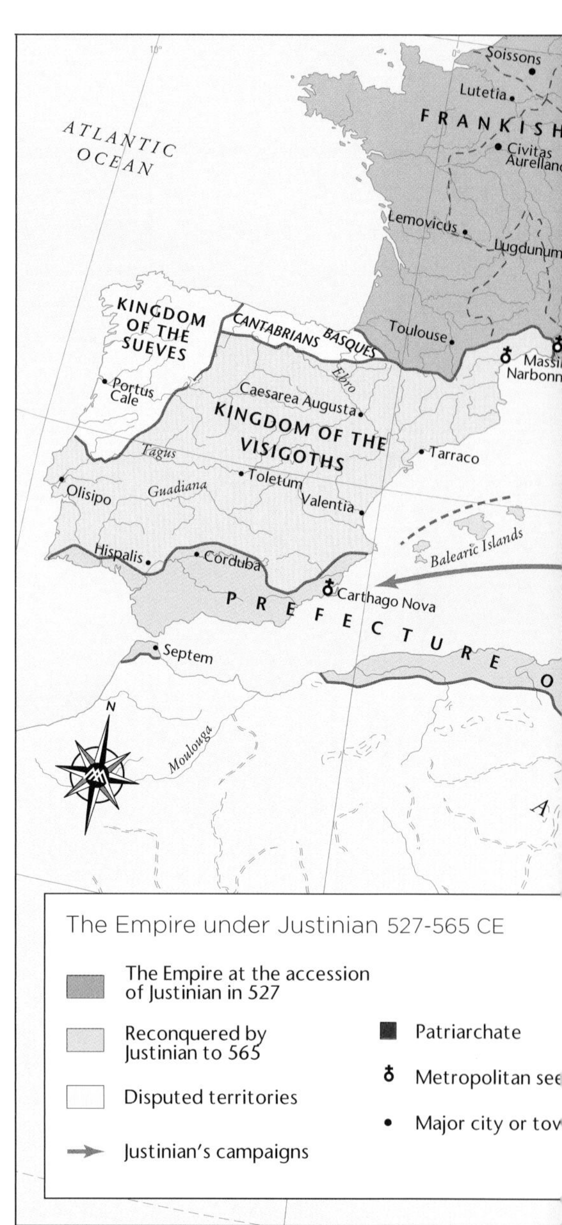

put the number of dead at 25 million; Justinian himself was infected, but recovered. Death rates were disproportionately high in the more densely populated territories of the empire, and thus tilted the balance of power toward the nomadic and semi-nomadic tribes on its borders. In 558–59 CE, the Hunnic Gepids, with other tribes, crossed the frozen Danube: the depleted empire had to bribe the tribes to fight amongst themselves until they finally dispersed. The laborious 20-year reconquest of Italy was blown away within three years of Justinian's death by a Lombard invasion. At the end of his reign, the octogenarian Justinian became drawn to the Monophysite-leaning sect of Aphthartodocetism, which held that the body of Christ was always incorruptible. He exiled the patriarch of Constantinople for opposing the doctrine, and was preparing to enact his beliefs across the empire when he died.

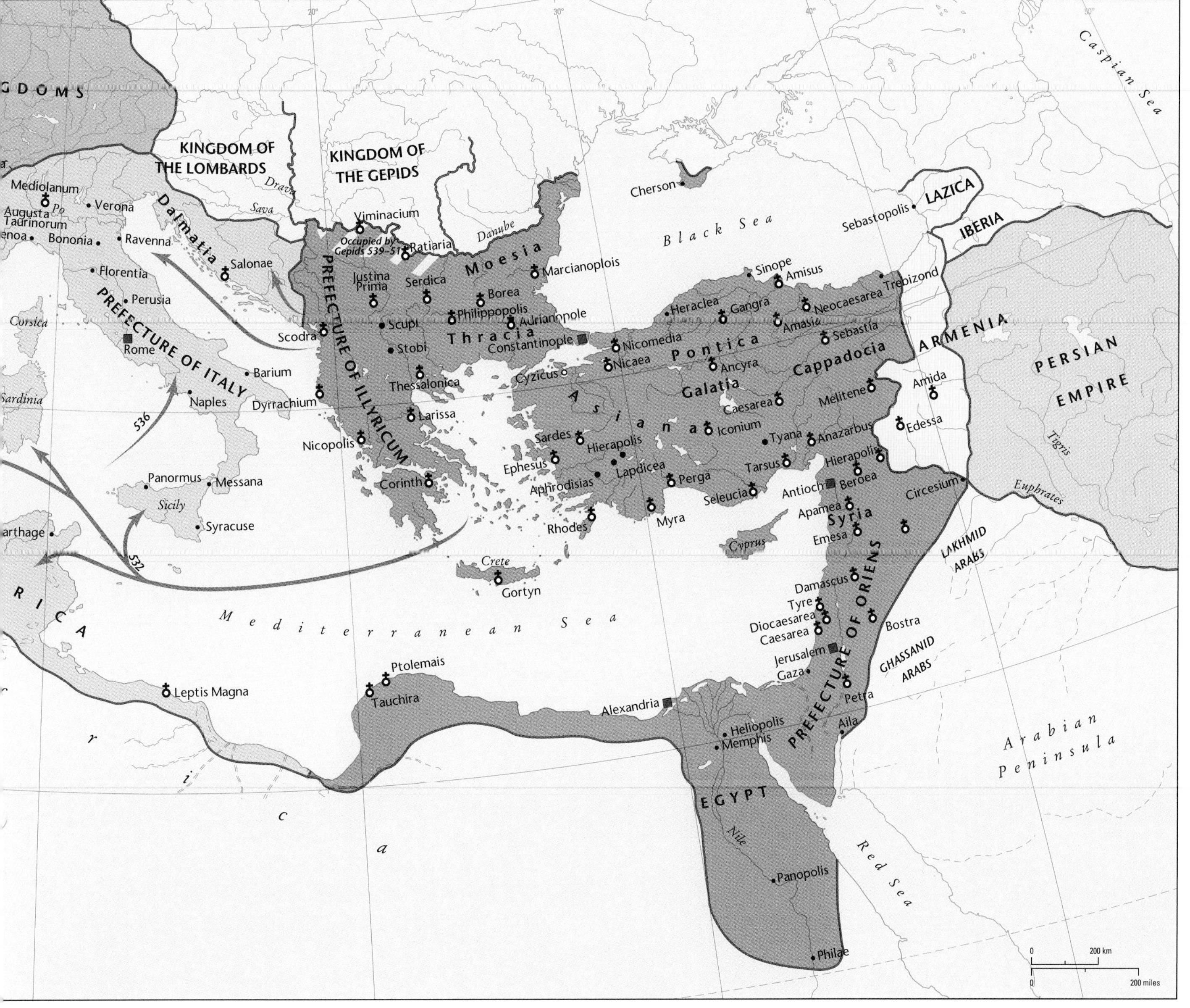

Nestorianism, the Church of the East

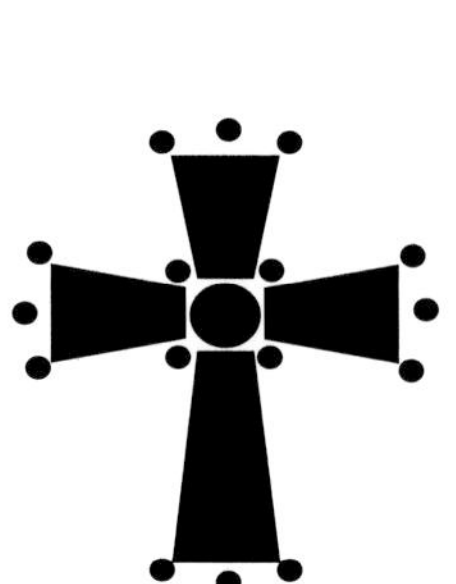

The Nestorian cross is composed of a Maltese-style cross, surrounded by dots representing the orders of ministry within the church.

THE SASANIAN EMPIRE dominated the Middle East from the 3rd century until the rise of Islam. The religion of its ruling class was Zoroastrianism. At its peak its rule stretched from the Mediterranean to India and encompassed a significant number of Christian communities. Yazdegerd I (399–421 CE) adopted a tolerant stance towards Christians, but his successors began to view them as potential fifth columnists for the Roman Empire to their west. Under intense political pressure, the Persian church declared its independence from the Roman church (424). Four years later, Nestorius was appointed patriarch of Constantinople and soon provoked a doctrinal storm by challenging the established Church position that Mary was a Theotokos (God-bearer), declaring that Christ's two natures (divine and human) meant he should be seen as having two persons, the divine Word and the fully human Jesus.

In 431 CE at the First Council of Ephesus, these positions were anathematized, and Nestorius was deposed and exiled. The resulting schism saw many of his supporters fleeing to Sasanian territory, and on the principle that an "enemy's enemy is one's friend," the ruling class encouraged Nestorianism in its Christian communities (although there were aberrations: thousands of Christians were massacred in Kirkuk in 446 CE). In 462 BCE Nestorians were protected against persecution and the Nestorian theological School of Edessa was permitted to move to the Persian city of Nisibis (489 CE).

The Nestorian-inspired Church of the East went through its own schism in the 6th century, but was restored by the efforts of one of its most eminent theologians, Babai the Great (551–628 CE) who followed the teachings of Theodore of Mopsuestia, mentor of Nestorius. Babai revitalized the church's monastic movement, and Nestorian missionaries traveled far and wide in Asia. Two Nestorian monks reputedly smuggled silk-worm eggs out of China in 551 CE and gave them to the Emperor Justinian I, enabling the Byzantines to monopolize the silk industry in the west. Prior to this mission, the monks had apparently been preaching in India, where, according to tradition, the Christian community along the Malabar Coast was founded by Thomas the Apostle in 52 CE.

Under the Sasanians, the patriarch of the Church of the East (or "Catolicos") was based in Ctesiphon, moving to Baghdad after the conquest by Islam. Enjoying broad tolerance under Islamic rule, the Church of the East had 15 sees within the caliphate by the 10th century, and a further five beyond its borders. They remained a pervasive presence in Asia until modern times.

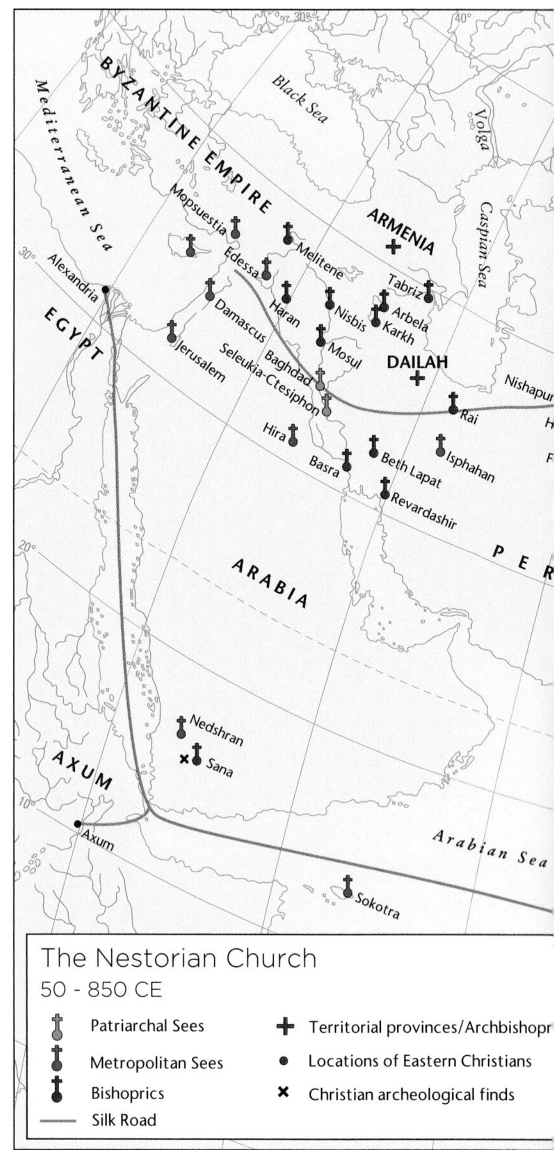

The other branch of Christianity to emerge from the Chalcedonian schism, the Oriental Orthodox churches, has played an important role in Egypt, Ethiopia, Armenia, Syria, and India. They accepted the ecumenical councils of Nicea (325), Constantinople (381), and Ephesus (431), but in 451 Pope Dioscorus I of Alexandria and 13 Egyptian bishops rejected the Chalcedonian and Nestorian dogma that Christ had two natures, divine and human, proposing that divinity and humanity are equally present within the single nature of Jesus Christ. They were called "monophysites," although they prefered the label "miaphysites." The refusal of the dissenting bishops, including the patriarchs of Alexandria and Antioch, to accept the Chalcedonian dogmas led to the first schism in the Christian church, in the early 6th century.

Depite centuries of persecution, they played an important role in the expansion of Christianity beyond the Byzantine Empire, taking the Christian faith from Alexandria and Ethiopia down to Africa, from Armenia to the north, from Antioch to the Far East.

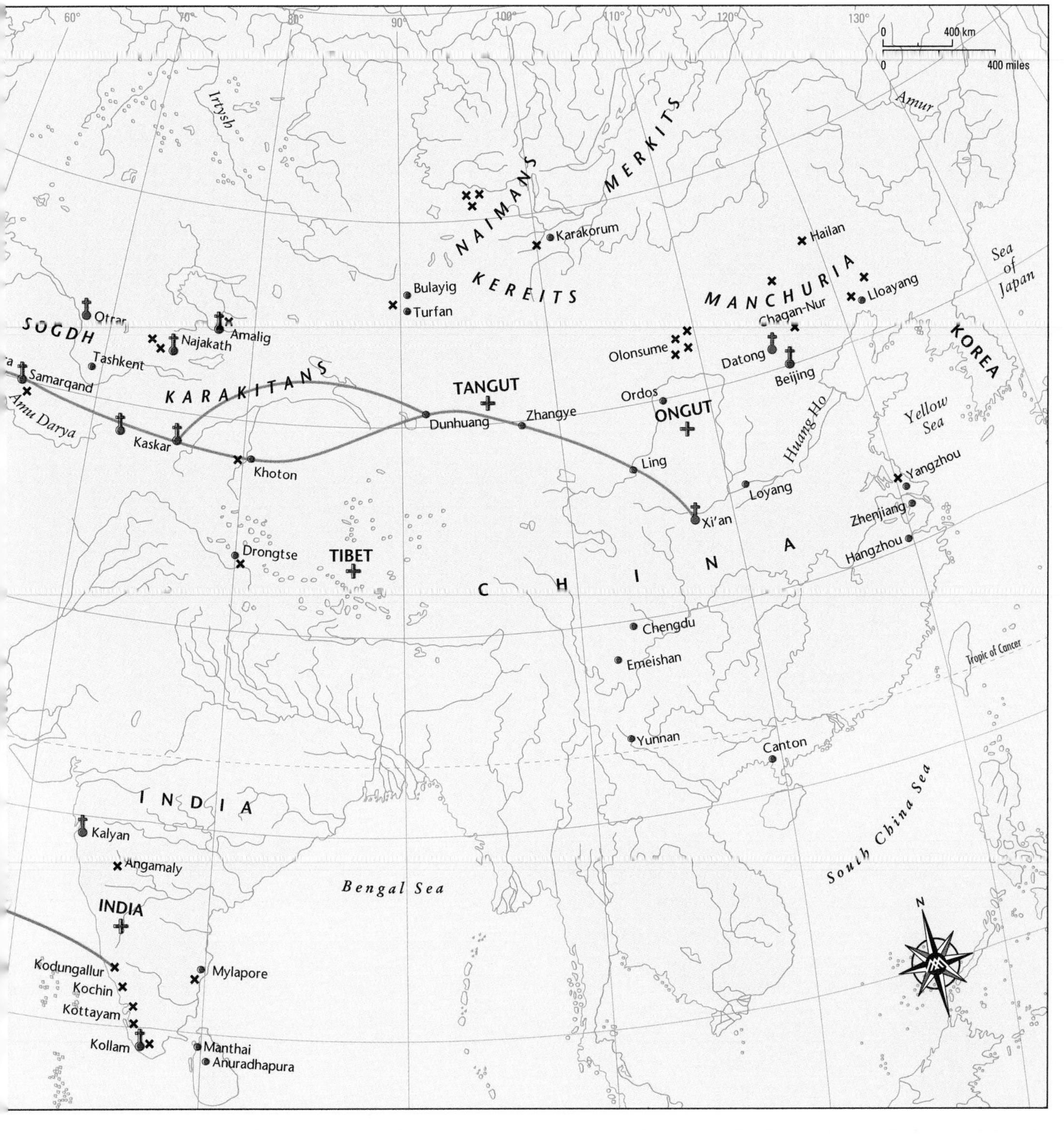

Nestorian missionaries traveled far and wide. They journeyed down the Arabian peninsula to Yemen and Arabian Christians apparently adopted Nestorian practice until the arrival of Islam, which eclipsed Christianity in Arabia. Missionaries also exported their beliefs along the Silk Road to distant China. Although Nestorian Christianity was persecuted during the reign of the Tang Emperor Wuzong (814–846) a resurgence occurred during the Mongol invasions of the 13th century, The Mongols had been prosleytized since the 7th century and a substantial minority, some of them very powerful warlords, were Nestorian Christians, However, the rise of the Ming dynasty in the 14th century led to the expulsion of Christians from China.

The Emergence of Islam

MUHAMMAD (570–623 CE), the visionary founder of Islam, is regarded by Muslims as the last and greatest of all the Prophets, and his revelation is recorded in the central text of Islam, the Quran. During his lifetime he laboriously united the quarrelsome nomadic tribes of Arabia, but the explosive expansion of the faith he founded would be largely posthumous. Muslim armies were bent on conquest, not conversion, and for the Christians of North Africa and the Middle East, aloof Muslim overlordship could be less strenuous than the peremptory theocracy of Constantinople, which often anathematized the strands of Christianity espoused in Antioch, Alexandria, and Carthage.

The Arab invasions seemed like a thunderbolt from a clear blue sky, but the Arabian peninsula, crisscrossed by caravan routes, and girt by the Red Sea, Persian Gulf, and Indian Ocean, was far from a backwater. Frankincense and myrrh were harvested from trees in the mountains of Yemen and Hadramaut. Arab merchants, like Muhammad, traveled far and wide, and Arab warriors learned the tactics of the military superpowers of the day, as mercenaries and auxiliaries in their wars.

The timing of the Islamic expansion was fortuitous. After a century of near constant warfare, the East Roman (Byzantine) and Sasanian empires were both economically crippled, and the latter, after defeat at the Battle of Nineveh (627), teetering on the edge of collapse. Their subject peoples had suffered military depredation and ruinous taxation, and were receptive to any alternative rule. After initial sorties met little resistance, the first great Islamic general, Khalid ibn al-Walid, meted out a series of crushing defeats on both the Byzantines (notably at Yarmouk in 636) and the Sasanians, capturing their capital at Ctesiphon (637). The Muslim leadership were adept in siege and naval warfare, with their victory in the Battle of the Masts (652) conferring mastery of the eastern Mediterrranean and enabling repeated and protracted sieges of Constantinople itself (672–78 and 717–18).

The Islamic invasions did much to define Christian Europe, by showing it what it was against. The swift advance of Islam across Christian northern Africa effectively extinguished Christianity there and the Mediterranean Sea became a border between two distinct

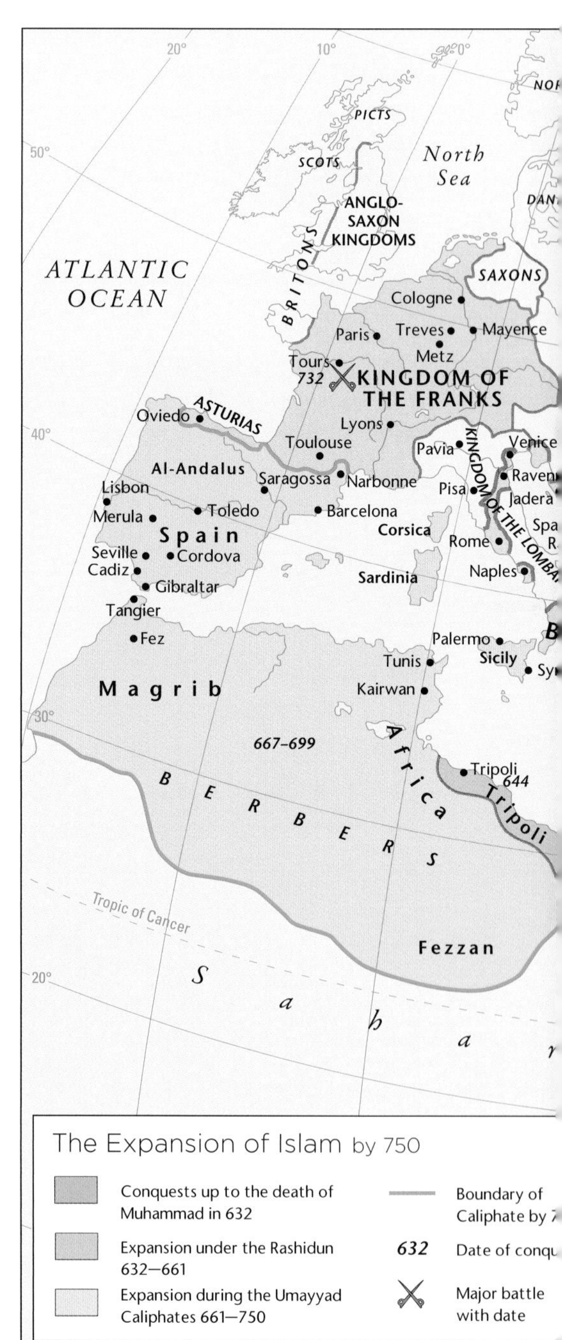

worlds, rather than a unifying feature. That maritime border was breached by the Berber and Arab invasion of Iberia in 711, a shocking incursion into western European Christian territory that was halted by the Franks at the Battle of Tours in 732.

There is no evidence of mass conversion to Islam after the conquests although other religions had a subordinate status. Conquered Christians and Jews ("People of the Book") were allowed to maintain churches and synagogues in exchange for paying the *jizya* (poll) tax.

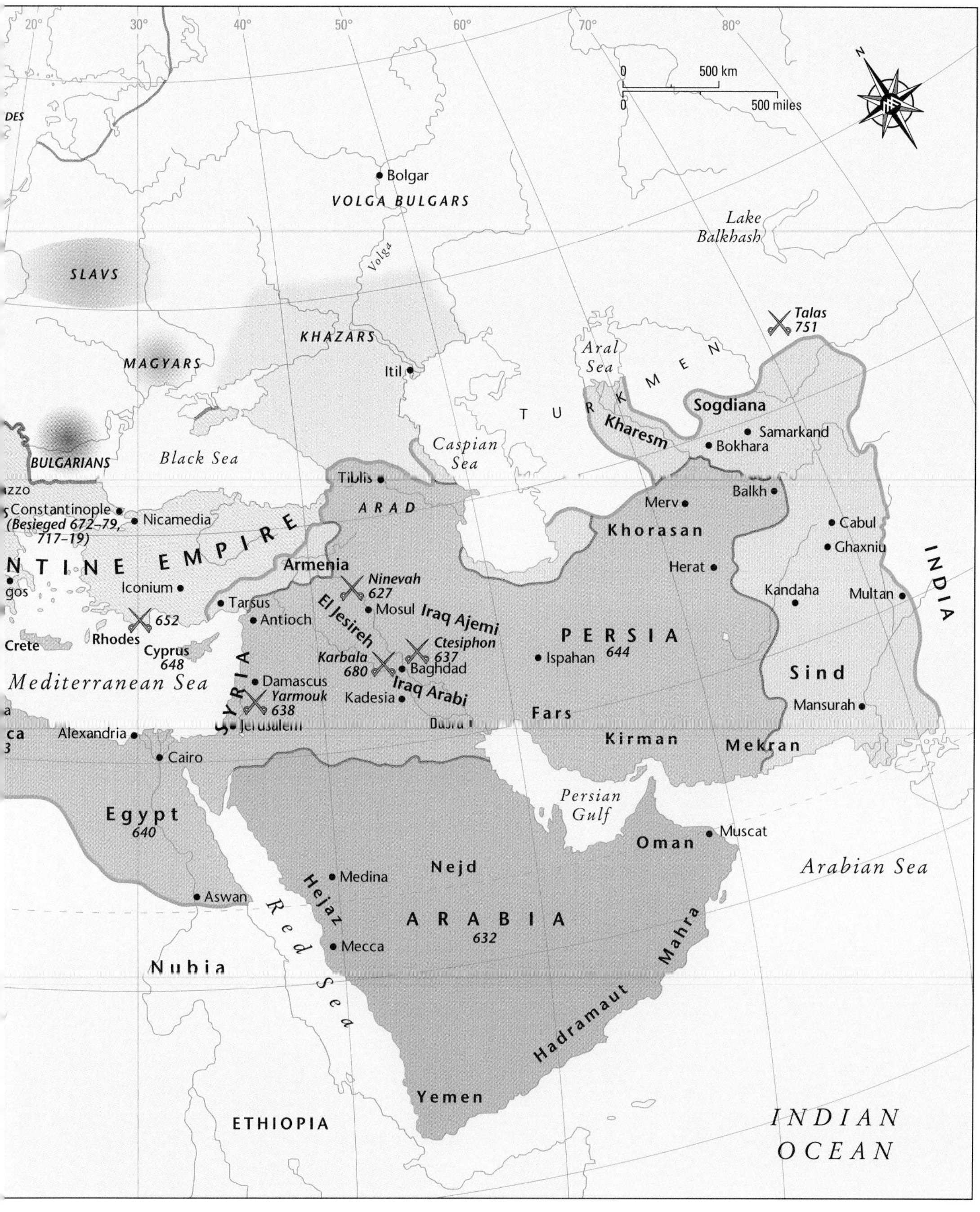

The Christian World c. 700–1000

The Church of the East became the national church of the Sasanian Empire in 410. When the Council of Ephesus condemned Nestorius (386–451) an exodus of his supporters reached the empire, which eventually adopted the doctrine of Nestorianism. The monasatery complex of Mar Bernam in eastern Syria, which dates to the 4th century, was blown up by Isis militants in 2015.

In 626 the Christian world appeared to be all-conquering, but the Islamic invasions were imminent and Christian hegemony was soon to face a serious challenge. In June 626 Byzantium confronted a massive amphibious assault by a combined force of Sasanid Persians and pagan Avars, who laid siege to the city while the Emperor Heraclius was a thousand miles away campaigning in Mesopotamia. The siege was repulsed after a series of naval victories, then in December 627 Heraclius crushed the Persian army at the Battle of Nineveh, reputedly dispatching their general in single combat. He returned in triumph, bearing the relic of the True Cross that the Persians had looted from Jerusalem. The Sasanian Empire collapsed, but within a decade the tide turned: a wave of Islamic invaders surged from the south, driving back the Byzantines to Asia Minor, and, establishing an empire under the Umayyad Caliphate (661–750) that stretched from Spain to Afghanistan.

The Islamic conquest helped to crystallize the underlying rifts in doctrine between Rome, Constantinople, and churches under Islamic control. The Monophysites (Miaphysites) established a separate Coptic church headquartered in Alexandria, and a Syriac church led from Antioch. The Nestorian Christians became *dhimmi* (a minority afforded legal protections) under the caliphate, and prospered: by the 10th century they had 15 metropolitan sees within the caliphate and a further five beyond its borders. Independent of, but isolated by, the caliphate, the already ancient churches of Armenia and Ethiopia developed distinctive forms of Miaphytism. The Christians of India's Malabar coast were organized as a province of the Church of the East by Patriarch Timothy I (780–823).

In Christianity's European heartlands the impact of the Islamic empire moved Christendom's center of gravity northward and westward. With the Byzantines increasingly preoccupied with the Islamic threat (Constantinople would be besieged six times before the millennium, by Muslims, Vikings, and Bulgars), the Frankish kingdom emerged as the main bulwark of Christendom. Charles Martel, king of the Franks in all but name, halted the Islamic armies' advance at the Battle of Tours (732 CE), and came to the attention of the Catholic church in Rome, but Charles resisted any formal alliance with the papacy, refusing its request for military assistance against the emperor in Constantinople, when the church was involved in a dispute over the authority of the emperor and the papacy. His achievement was eclipsed by the conquests of his grandson Charlemagne, who was crowned Holy Roman Emperor by the pope on Christmas Day 800 CE. He took on the mantle of a Christian ruler, oversaw a program of church reform and embraced the rooting out of paganism.

Meanwhile, Christianity advanced steadily northward. Mainland Britain was caught in a pincer of Celtic missionaries from Ireland, who founded churches and abbeys as far afield as Switzerland in the 6th century, and the "official" delegation from Rome initiated by St

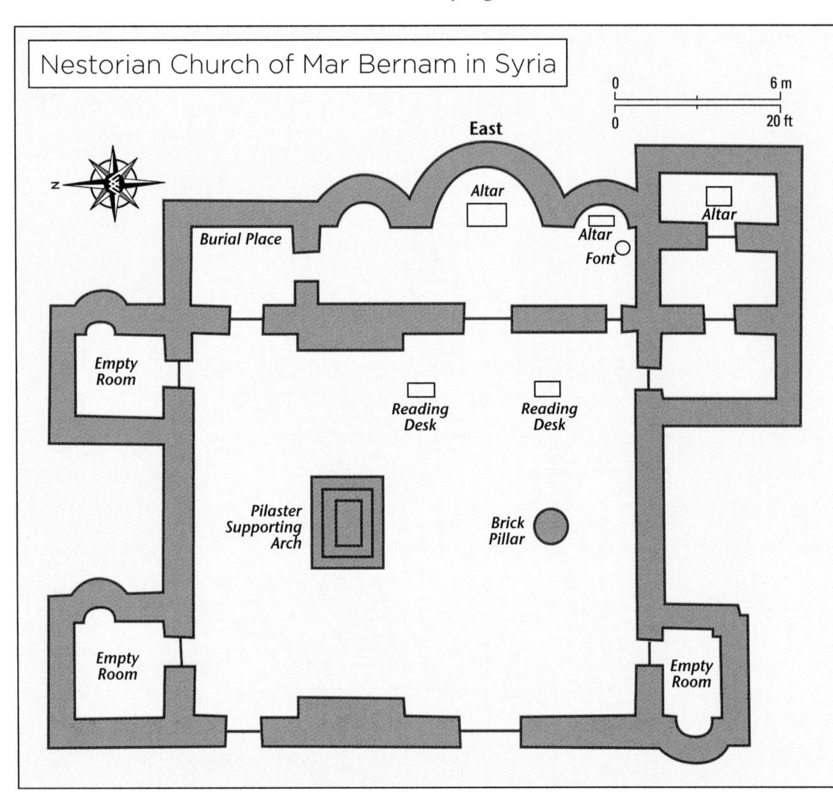

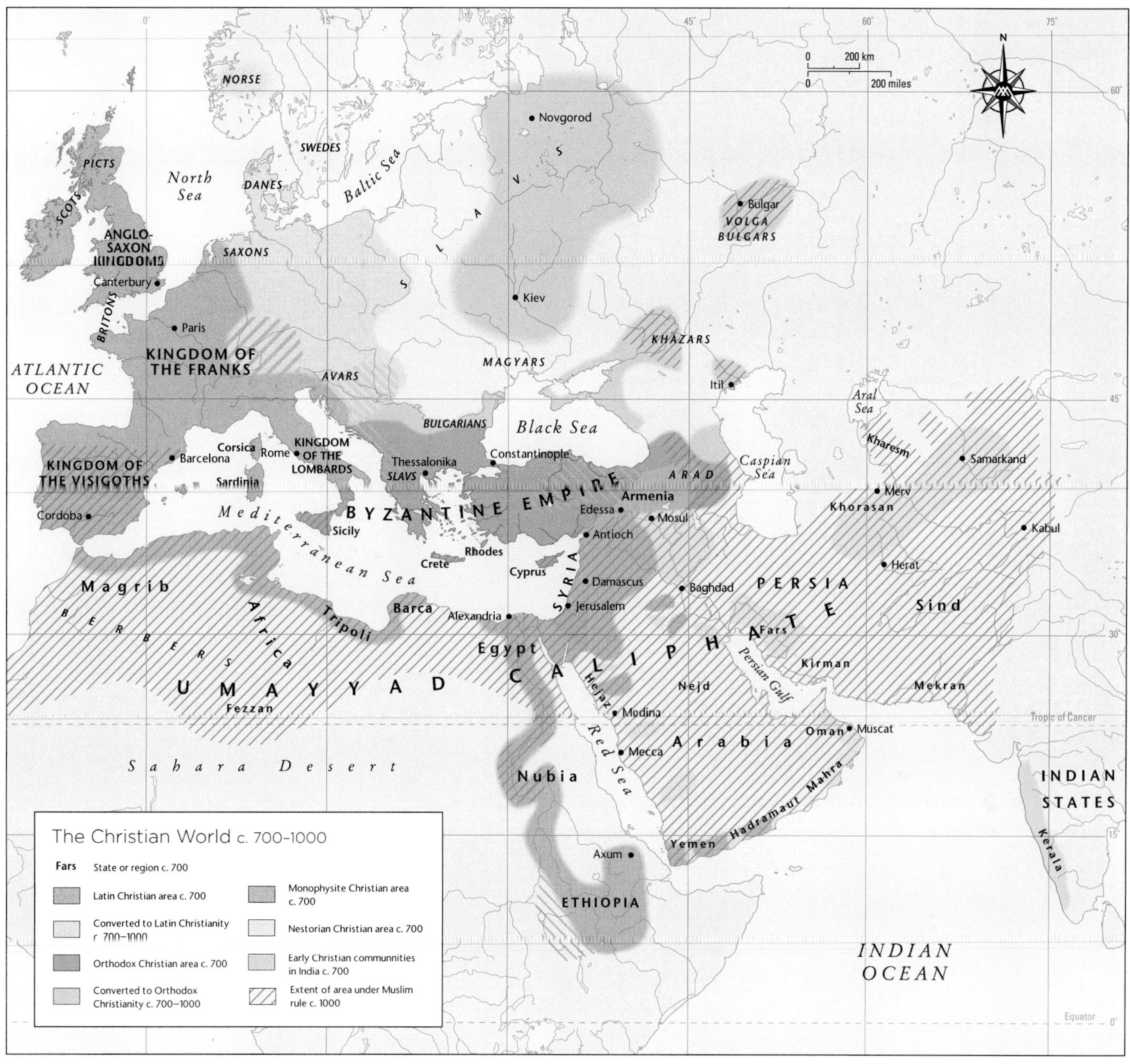

Augustine. Its last major pagan holdout, King Penda of Mercia, was slain in battle in 655 CE, and while Norse invasions from 793 onward reintroduced paganism, the invaders and ultimately the peoples of Scandinavia itself would eventually embrace Christianity too. After the Bulgar Empire converted in 863 CE, Viking conversions carried the religion to most of Scandinavia and western Russia.

While this expansion of Christendom continued apace, the papacy descended into its own *saeculum obscurum* (Dark Period) from c. 850–1050, when popes were essentially the puppets of first Frankish rulers and then powerful Italian families. Despite a vacuum in leadership, the monastic movement was radically rejuvenated by the Cluniac Reform initiated from 910 CE by St Odo, renewing their commitment to learning and caring for the poor; many also became important centers of agricultural production and, as sources of credit, helped to fuel the feudal economy.

MP
ΘΥ
IC XC

Christianity
IN THE MIDDLE AGES

Icon of Our Lady of Tikhvin, 15th–16th century CE

The Spread of Christianity in Europe

As the Western Roman Empire began to fail Christianity began to spread beyond the borders of the former empire. Christianity had spread from Roman Britain to Wales and Ireland and here a unique culture developed, which was in turn disseminated by Irish missionaries to Scotland and the continent.

The Anglo-Saxons who had invaded the former Roman colony of Britannia had reintroduced paganism and it took several hundred years for Christianity to re-root on English soil. Eventually Anglo-Saxon missionaries, such as Wilfrid, Willibrord, and Boniface, would travel abroad to convert their Saxon relatives in the Low Countries and Germany.

The Gallo-Roman inhabitants of Gaul had been overrun by pagan Germanic Franks in the 5th century. The Frankish king Clovis I converted to Roman Catholicism in 496 and his newly established kingdom became a bastion of Christianity in the early Middle Ages. The tensions between Rome and Constantinople, which originated over doctrinal issues and Rome's claim of primacy, ultimately led to a schism between Western (Latin) and Eastern (Greek) branches in 1054. This breach was deepened after the sacking of Constantinople during the Fourth Crusade in 1204 and the establishment of the Latin Empire in the east, which was seen as an attempt to supplant the Byzantine Empire.

The evangelization of Scandinavia began as early as the 9th century, though it met with only partial success and it was over 200 years before most of the Baltic region was Christianized. Religious military orders, especially the Teutonic Knights, who acted with papal sanction, played an important role in these campaigns.

The Eastern Orthodox church continued to send out missionaries to eastern Europe, most notably the conversions spearheaded by Cyril and Methodius to the southern and eastern Slavs, Serbia, and Bulgaria. In 988 Vladimir of Kiev was converted to Eastern Orthodoxy and married the sister of the Byzantine emperor, Basil II, marking the beginning of the conversion of Russia.

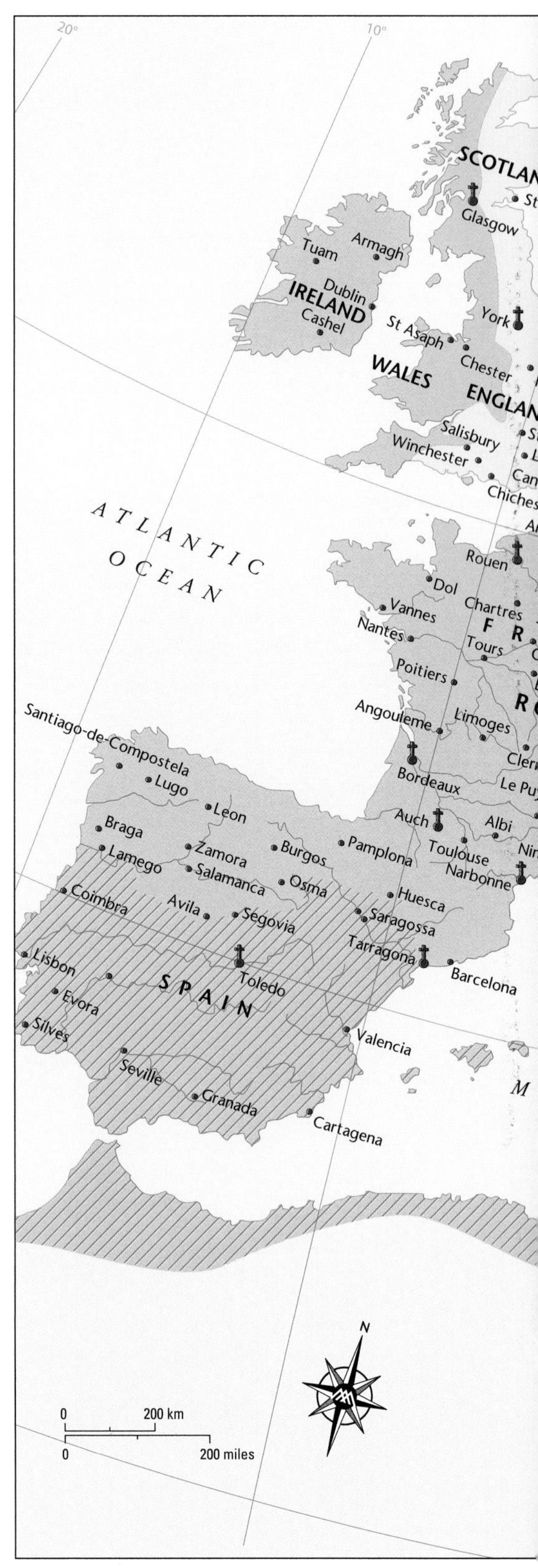

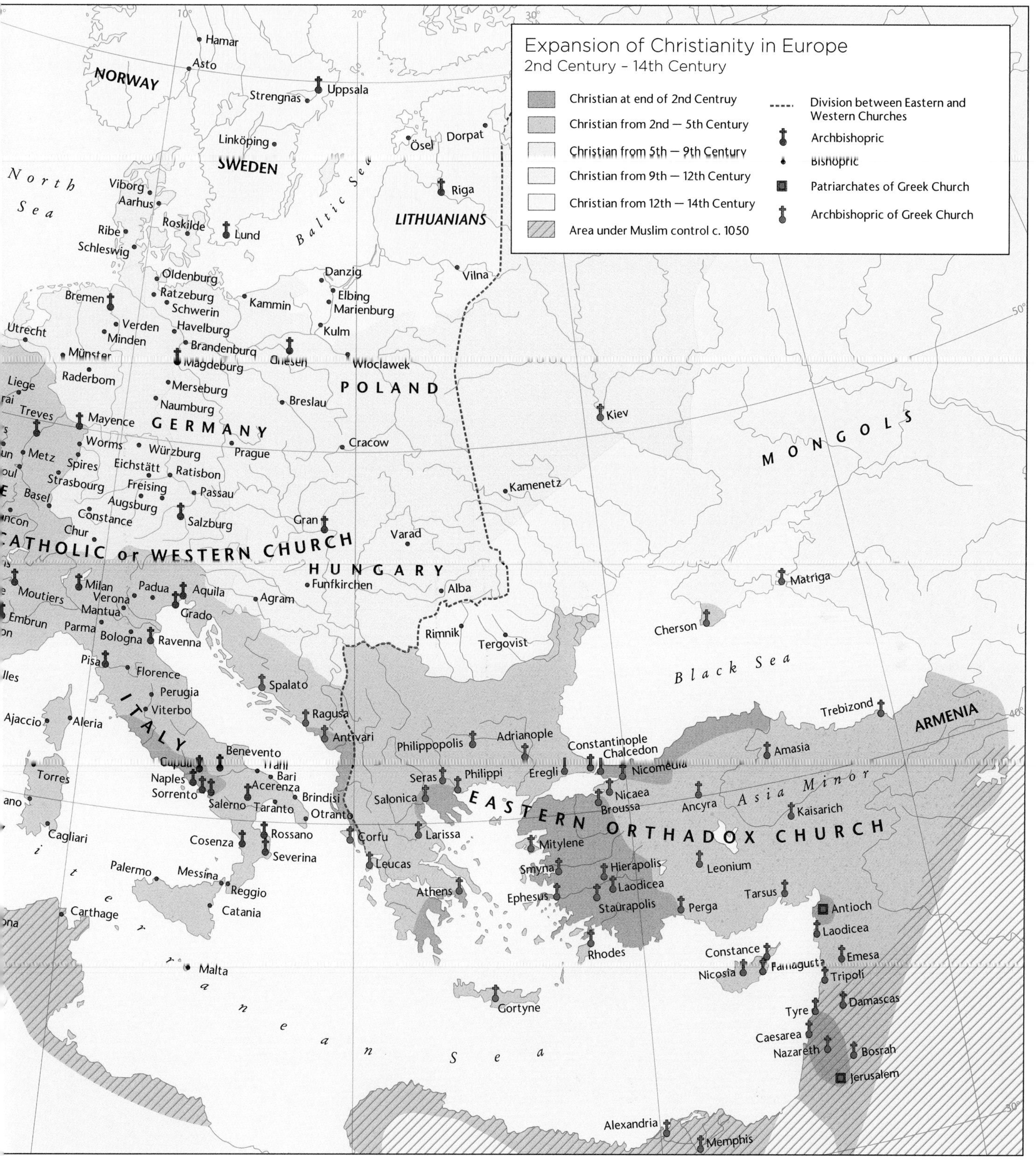
Expansion of Christianity in Europe
2nd Century - 14th Century
Christian at end of 2nd Centruy
Christian from 2nd — 5th Century
Christian from 5th — 9th Century
Christian from 9th — 12th Century
Christian from 12th — 14th Century
Area under Muslim control c. 1050
Division between Eastern and Western Churches
Archbishopric
Bishopric
Patriarchates of Greek Church
Archbishopric of Greek Church
NORWAY
SWEDEN
North Sea
Baltic Sea
LITHUANIANS
POLAND
GERMANY
HUNGARY
CATHOLIC or WESTERN CHURCH
ITALY
MONGOLS
Black Sea
ARMENIA
Asia Minor
EASTERN ORTHODOX CHURCH
Mediterranean Sea
Hamar
Asto
Uppsala
Strengnas
Linköping
Ösel
Dorpat
Riga
Viborg
Aarhus
Roskilde
Lund
Ribe
Schleswig
Oldenburg
Ratzeburg
Schwerin
Kammin
Danzig
Elbing
Marienburg
Vilna
Bremen
Verden
Minden
Havelburg
Kulm
Utrecht
Münster
Brandenburg
Magdeburg
Gnesen
Wloclawek
Liege
Raderbom
Merseburg
Naumburg
Breslau
Kiev
Treves
Mayence
Worms
Würzburg
Prague
Cracow
Metz
Spires
Eichstätt
Ratisbon
Strasbourg
Freising
Passau
Kamenetz
Basel
Augsburg
Constance
Salzburg
Gran
Chur
Varad
Milan
Verona
Padua
Aquila
Agram
Funfkirchen
Alba
Matriga
Moutiers
Mantua
Grado
Embrun
Parma
Bologna
Ravenna
Rimnik
Tergovist
Cherson
Pisa
Florence
Perugia
Viterbo
Spalato
Ajaccio
Aleria
Ragusa
Antivari
Trebizond
Philippopolis
Adrianople
Constantinople
Chalcedon
Amasia
Benevento
Capua
Trani
Torres
Naples
Bari
Seras
Philippi
Eregli
Nicomedia
Sorrento
Acerenza
Salonica
Nicaea
Broussa
Ancyra
Kaisarich
Salerno
Taranto
Brindisi
Otranto
Cagliari
Cosenza
Rossano
Corfu
Larissa
Mitylene
Severina
Leonium
Palermo
Messina
Leucas
Smyrna
Hierapolis
Laodicea
Tarsus
Reggio
Athens
Ephesus
Staurapolis
Perga
Antioch
Carthage
Catania
Laodicea
Rhodes
Constance
Emesa
Nicosia
Famagusta
Tripoli
Malta
Gortyne
Tyre
Damascas
Caesarea
Nazareth
Bosrah
Jerusalem
Alexandria
Memphis

Eastern Christianity and Iconoclasticism

In the 8th century Eastern Christianity, reeling from the Islamic assault and in a crisis of self-confidence, experienced the convulsion known as Iconoclasm, which was officially promulgated by Emperor Leo III (717–41), who had been born a shepherd in Thrace, on the Byzantine Empire's precarious western borders. Icons are works of religious art, commonly depicting Christ, the Virgin Mary, and the saints and angels, which date back to the early 3rd century. Leo's edicts against the veneration of these images may have been inspired by Islamic influence – Islam repudiates the worship of images – and, on a pragmatic level, may have been motivated by a desire to appease non-Christians within his empire. His iconoclastic edicts were strenuously opposed by both the pope, Gregory II, and the patriarch of Constantinople. Leo simply deposed the patriarch, and used the destruction of icons as a pretext for seizing church property and valuables. When his subjects in the Exarchate of Ravenna joined an armed uprising in 727 Leo sent a large fleet to subdue his critics; when it was badly damaged in a storm, the issue was decided. His subjects had successfully defied his edicts and the Exarchate of Ravenna became detached from the empire and Rome, and hence the pope was no longer under Byzantine rule.

Leo's son Constantine V (741–75) had the theological sophistication to create an intellectual framework to support iconoclasticism. The Council of Hieria (754), convened by Constantine, hammered out this framework. The Council was without representation from the sees of Antioch, Alexandria, and Jerusalem, which were under Muslim control, and from the papacy, which was violently opposed. Nevertheless, its proceedings and resolutions were a concerted attempt to ground iconoclasm in both scripture and the rulings of previous ecumenical councils on the nature of Christ. A total of 338 bishops assembled at Hieria declared: "If anyone shall endeavour to represent the forms of the Saints in lifeless pictures with material colors which are of no value (for this notion is vain and introduced by the devil), and does not rather represent their virtues as living images in himself... let him be anathema."

It was argued that any true image of Jesus must be able to represent not only his human nature but also his divine nature (which is impossible, because it cannot be seen or encompassed). By making an icon of Jesus, one is either separating his human and divine natures, since only the human can be depicted, and thus committing the Nestorian heresy; or one is confusing the human and divine natures, considering them one, and thus guilty of Monophysitism. The only acceptable religious image would be an exact likeness; "graven" (ie carved) images were prohibited by the Second Commandment. By a process of elimination, the only acceptable "representation" of Christ could be the holy sacraments of the Eucharist, since this is his actual body and blood.

While iconophile theologians, such as John of Damascus, and Theodore the Studite, fought

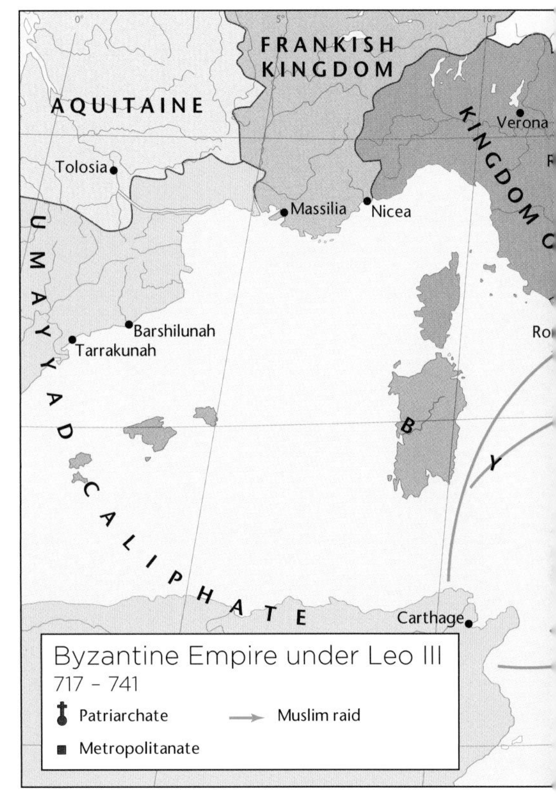

an eloquent rearguard action, Constantine embarked upon a systematic campaign to eliminate iconography, and to a considerable extent succeeded. In 766 the patriarch of Constantinople, an iconophile champion, was accused of plotting against the emperor and executed. However, with Constantine's death, the impetus behind iconoclasm diminished. When in 780 an infant Constantine VI became emperor, his mother, Empress Irene, became regent. An iconophile, she convened a Second Council of Nicaea (787), to which papal representatives were invited. This Council pronounced that the more images are contemplated "the more they move to fervent memory of their prototypes. Therefore, it is proper to accord to them a fervent and reverent adoration, not, however, the veritable worship which, according to our faith, belongs to the Divine Being alone – for the honor accorded to the image passes over to its prototype, and whoever adores the image adores in it the reality of what is there represented."

And so might matters have rested, but for the depredations of the pagan ruler of the Bulgars, Khan Krum, who laid siege to Constantinople in 813 after inflicting a series of humiliating defeats on Byzantine armies, killing one emperor, and forcing two others to abdicate in quick succession. In June, a mob of demoralized soldiers broke into the imperial mausoleum and prised open the tomb of Constantine V, who had been a scourge of the Bulgars as well as the arch-iconoclast, and begged him to rise from the dead and rescue the empire. Following this desecration, Leo V (813–20), prudently opted to reimpose iconoclasm. But this second episode lacked Constantine's zeal. In 843, a second empress regent to an infant emperor, Theodora, once more mobilized the iconophile lobby to repeal iconoclasm, for a second, and final, time. The entire chapter had helped to cement the difference between the West and the East, with its very distinctive culture in which icons now held an unassailable devotional importance.

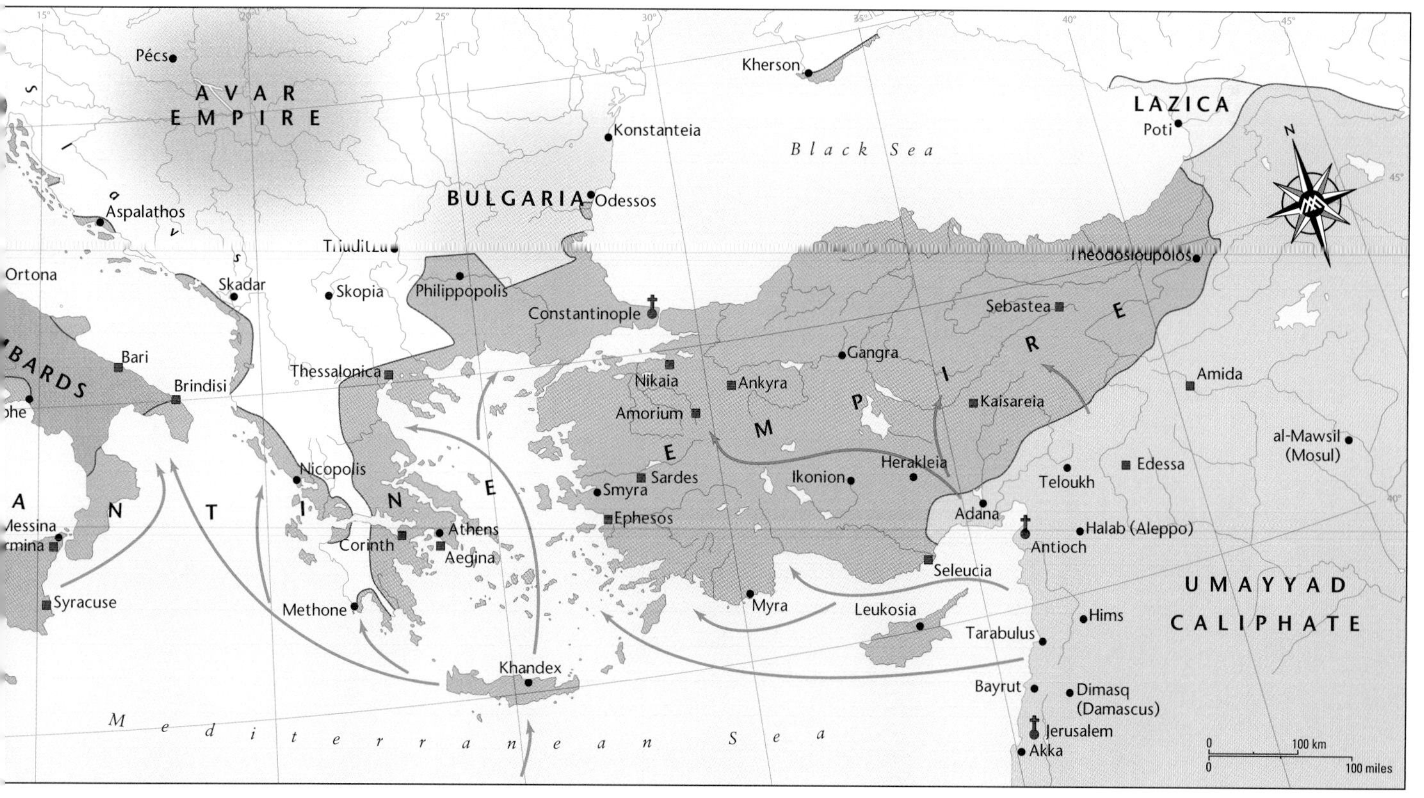

Carolingians and the "Holy Roman Empire"

Relations between the papacy and Constantinople were already strained by the ongoing Byzantine policy of iconoclasm. Since 781 the papacy had been dating its documents by reference to Charlemagne's reign rather than that of the Eastern emperor. Charlemagne's capital at Aachen became the center of a cultural renaissance, the "new Athens," while Charlemagne himself was hailed as the "new David" and "Constantine," the latter a galling reference for the Byzantines to the ruler who had first moved the imperial hub eastward.

The Catholic Merovingian dynasty had been kings of Francia since the early 6th century, but by the 8th, the Merovingians were reduced to figureheads, with real power increasingly wielded by the hereditary mayors of the palace. One such mayor, Charles Martel, won a decisive victory against Islamic armies at the Battle of Tours (732). His son Pepin "the Short" perfected the Frankish military machine, based on heavy cavalry, and waged successful campaigns against the Umayyads, Gascons, and Saxons. In 751 Pepin seized the throne from the last Merovingian king, a move which his ally Pope Zachary legitimized. The papacy's reward was Pepin's Donation of several Lombard cities, the nucleus of the future papal states. At Pepin's death in 768, his realm was split between his sons Charles and Carloman; Carloman's death in 771 reunited Francia under Charles, known to history as Charles the Great, or Charlemagne.

A formidable military leader, Charlemagne emerged victorious from a series of brutal and grueling campaigns against the Saxons, Lombards, Slavs, and Avars. After an initial expedition into Muslim Spain ended disastrously, his armies returned to capture Barcelona and establish a buffer Spanish march beyond the Pyrenees. An uninterrupted flow of war booty swelled the royal coffers and enabled him to cement the loyalty of his nobility, as well as maintain cordial relations with the papacy.

He rescued Pope Adrian I from the Lombards (773) and provided refuge to his successor Leo III after an assassination attempt (799). Returning with Leo to Rome, he adjudicated in the pope's favor in a case brought against him by his attackers, to be rewarded with a heavily choreographed coronation as the new "Emperor of the Romans" on Christmas Day 800. This recognized Charlemagne in place of the first ever empress regnant, Irene, in Constantinople. The clergy within his dominion hailed him as the "rector of a new Israel." In ecclesiastical matters Charlemagne exerted his centralizing power, sowing the seeds for the seismic conflicts between the empire and the church.

Charlemagne held a total of six synods during his reign, regularizing the internal organization of the church, standardizing liturgical practice, and both restoring old, and establishing new, archbishoprics. Controversially, his Council of Aachen (809) confirmed the addition of the "Filioque" clause to the Nicene Creed, representing a Western view of the nature of the Holy Spirit, but one which had never been accepted or approved by the Eastern church.

Charlemagne's reign marked a fundamental shift – both westward and northward – in Christendom's center of gravity. Yet Charlemagne remained an admirer of, and borrowed heavily from, the culture of his eastern rival. His celebrated Palace Chapel at Aachen was modelled on the Byzantine church of Ravenna. In the new lands he conquered, Charlemagne cemented his military control with conversion to Christianity, first by missionaries, then by the endowment of monasteries; it has been argued that unified religious belief was central to his efficient imperial governance of the disparate, newly conquered peoples. In the tribal borderlands of the Saxon marches, monasteries promoted urbanization and urbanity, acting as centers for both learning and commerce. His binding together of the growing empire's religious and political mission was reflected in Charlemagne's *missi dominici*, the royal agents-at-large, through whom Charlemagne transmitted his instructions to, and gathered intelligence from, his sprawling dominions: each *missi* would be jointly headed by one lay lord and one church official.

Charlemagne's longevity (he died in 814, at the age of 71), enabled him, inadvertently, to avoid the traditional disintegrator of Frankish empires, the divided inheritance. Two of his sons predeceased him, leaving Louis "the Pious" as sole heir. The Carolingian Empire would disintegrate after Louis' death, but the idea of a new, papally endorsed "Holy" Roman Empire would be revived in the 10th century and would endure in various forms before finally being dissolved in 1806 by the Enlightenment's Charlemagne, Napoleon Bonaparte.

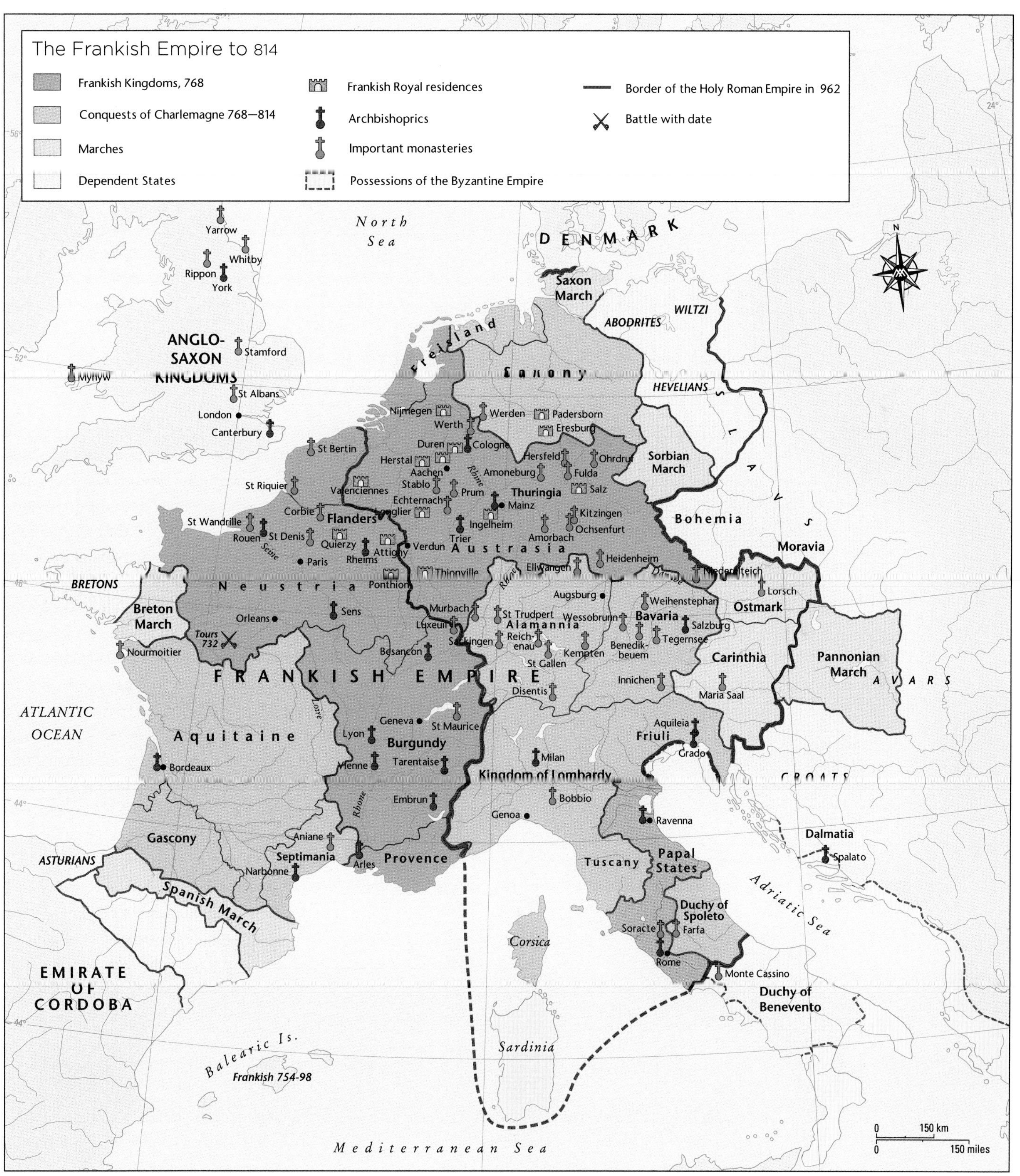
The Frankish Empire to 814
Frankish Kingdoms, 768
Conquests of Charlemagne 768–814
Marches
Dependent States
Frankish Royal residences
Archbishoprics
Important monasteries
Possessions of the Byzantine Empire
Border of the Holy Roman Empire in 962
Battle with date
North Sea
DENMARK
Saxon March
ABODRITES
WILTZI
HEVELIANS
SLAVS
Sorbian March
Bohemia
Moravia
Ostmark
Pannonian March
AVARS
Carinthia
Friuli
CROATS
Dalmatia
Spalato
Adriatic Sea
Yarrow
Whitby
Rippon
York
ANGLO-SAXON KINGDOMS
Stamford
St Albans
London
Canterbury
Freisland
Saxony
Nijmegen
Werth
Werden
Padersborn
Eresburg
Duren
Cologne
Herstal
Aachen
Hersfeld
Ohrdruf
Fulda
Amoneburg
Stablo
Prum
Thuringia
Salz
Echternach
Mainz
Kitzingen
Ochsenfurt
Ingelheim
Trier
Amorbach
Verdun
Austrasia
Heidenheim
Ellwangen
Niederaltaich
Lorsch
St Bertin
St Riquier
Valenciennes
Corbie
Flanders
St Wandrille
Rouen
St Denis
Quierzy
Attigny
Rheims
Paris
Thionville
Ponthion
BRETONS
Breton March
Neustria
Orleans
Sens
Tours 732
Nourmoitier
Murbach
Luxeuil
Säckingen
Besançon
St Trudpert
Alamannia
Reichenau
St Gallen
Kempten
Augsburg
Wessobrunn
Weihenstephan
Bavaria
Salzburg
Tegernsee
Benedikbeuern
Innichen
Maria Saal
Aquileia
Grado
Disentis
FRANKISH EMPIRE
ATLANTIC OCEAN
Aquitaine
Bordeaux
Geneva
St Maurice
Lyon
Burgundy
Vienne
Tarentaise
Milan
Kingdom of Lombardy
Bobbio
Embrun
Genoa
Ravenna
Gascony
Aniane
Septimania
Narbonne
Arles
Provence
Tuscany
Papal States
Duchy of Spoleto
Soracte
Farfa
Rome
Monte Cassino
Duchy of Benevento
Corsica
Sardinia
ASTURIANS
Spanish March
EMIRATE OF CORDOBA
Balearic Is.
Frankish 754-98
Mediterranean Sea
150 km
150 miles

The Missions of Saints Cyril and Methodius

Cyril and Methodius were brothers born in Thessalonica in the early 9th century. Cyril (826–69) proved a brilliant linguist, and had an early missionary posting to Samarra (in modern day Iraq). In 860, the khan of the Khazars in the Caucasus requested a missionary who could "converse with both Jews and Saracens," and Cyril seemed the obvious choice. The Khazars were not pagan: bizarrely, they had converted to Judaism a century earlier, and proved resistant to Cyril's Christian preaching. Undaunted, Cyril set about converting the pagan population of Phoulloi on the Crimean coast, but was expelled ignominiously when he chopped down a sacred oak tree.

Fortunately, Methodius (815–85) possessed the diplomatic skills the learned Cyril seemed to have lacked. A sound administrator, he had risen to become abbot of a monastery, a significant figure in the ecclesiastical politics of Constantinople. When Prince Ratislav of Great Moravia (r. 846–70) requested a missionary for his subjects, Photius, the patriarch of Constantinople, shrewdly judged that the brothers would be more effective working as a team.

The Slavs of Moravia had already been converted to Christianity by Latin missionaries, sent by the Frankish empire to the west. Louis II, the king of East Francia, had engineered Ratislav's ascent to the Moravian throne, but Ratislav now sought to preserve his independence by attracting Byzantine patronage – hence the overtures for missionaries. Photius had already intervened in an attempt by Boris, the khan of the Bulgars, to form an alliance with Louis; the mission to Moravia was an extension of these ecclesiastical geopolitics. For Cyril, underpinning their work with a written Slavic language became an all-consuming vocation. His Glagolitic alphabet (the Slavic for "sound") would be used for far more than transliteration; he devoted immense effort to creating an abstract Slavic vocabulary capable of expressing the metaphysical elements of Christian doctrine. His proficiency in, and respect for, their native language impressed the Slavs and contributed to a highly successful mission, so much so that it attracted the resentment of rival Frankish clergy, who insisted upon the Latin liturgy. Aware of the growing controversy, Cyril and Methodius set out for Rome in 868 to entreat Pope Hadrian's sanction for their native liturgy. Armed with the gift of a relic of one of the earliest popes, St Clement, the brothers received a warm reception and papal approval for their mission. A diplomatic compromise was reached; the brothers were permitted to use the native vernacular, provided that the service was first conducted in Latin. Cyril died during the visit to Rome, but Methodius was consecrated as an archbishop by Hadrian, with jurisdiction over Great Moravia, Pannonia, and Serbia.

Ratislav was overthrown by his nephew, Svatopluk, soon after Methodius returned from Rome. Although Svatopluk followed Latin rites, Methodius managed to garner the new ruler's patronage and survived a new summons to appear before Pope John VIII in Rome in 880, which was provoked by further complaints about his native liturgies from German clergy. Methodius tried to strengthen his position in the Eastern church by visiting Constantinople in 882. However, when Methodius died in 885, his ecclesiastical enemies rushed to Rome to denounce his teaching to Pope Stephen V and their complaint was upheld. The arch-accuser of Methodius, Bishop Wiching of Nitra, was appointed his successor, and Methodius' band of loyal disciples were either exiled or enslaved.

Thereafter the Western Latinists maintained their authority in the territories that constituted Great Moravia and Pannonia, which would eventually adhere to the Catholic church. Cyril's Glagolitic alphabet also proved too esoteric to gain lasting currency. However, the more user-friendly Cyrillic alphabet created by St Naum of Preslav and St Clement of Ohrid, which is used to this day throughout much of eastern Europe and named in his honor, would prove enduring, and go on to underpin a tradition of native language liturgy that would become the established practice throughout the Greek Orthodox church.

FINNIC PEOPLES
Norwegian Sea
Hladir
NORWAY
SWEDEN
Uppsala
Birka
Kaupang
Staraya Ladoga (Aldeigjuborg)
Novgorod (Holmgard)
ILMEN SLAVS
KRIVICHS
North Sea
DENMARK
Roskilde
Lund
Baltic Sea
BALTIC PEOPLES
VYATIHS
NORTHUMBRIA
York
Danelaw
Hedeby
RADIMICHS
Bremen
DREGOVICHS
SEVERIANS
Rhine
WESSEX
London
POLAND
Kiev
KHAZARS
Aachen
Cologne
Cracow
VOLHYNIANS
POLANS
Frankfurt
BOHEMIA
ULICHS
Normandy
Paris
EAST FRANKISH KINGDOM (GERMANIA)
MORAVIA
NITRA
Nitrava
Orléans
Lorch
TIVERIANS
WEST FRANKISH KINGDOM (FRANCIA)
Besançon
UPPER BURGUNDY
PANNONIA
Mosapurc
HUNGARY
Black Sea
Lyon
Milan
KINGDOM OF ITALY
Bordeaux
LOWER BURGUNDY
Venice
CROATIA
Danube
Presov
Bayonne
Avignon
Genoa
Nice
PAPAL STATES
Adriatic Sea
Serbia
Nish
BULGARIA
NAVARRE
ARAGON
Fraxinetum
Philippopolis
Adrianople
Constantinople
MUSLIM STATES
Barcelona
Corsica
Rome
Barium
Thessalonica
Tarragona
Naples
BYZANTINE EMPIRE
Aegean Sea
Balansiyah
Pr. of Benevento
Sardinia
Smyrna
Balearic Is.
Mediterranean Sea
Cartagena
Panormus
Sicily
Sétif
Tunis
Malta
Kairawan
RUSTAMIDS
ABBASIDS (AGHLABIDS)
The Missions of Saints Cyril and Methodius to the Slavs, 9th Century
1 Mission to the Khazars
2 Mission to Moravia
3 Cyril's journey to Rome
4 Christian missionaries from Rome

Christendom and the "Barbarians"

THE SO-CALLED "BARBARIANS" were migratory peoples who had launched attacks on the more settled societies of the Old World since Roman times. In the 9th century new marauders preyed upon Christendom, drawn by the wealth accumulated by religious establishments and centers of commerce. Ultimately they would be conquered by assimilation and conversion.

The Vikings were audacious and ingenious maritime marauders, even pretending to be Christians to assist their raids, as was the case in 860 when the Viking leader Bjorn gained entry into the Italian town of Luna by claiming that he had undergone a deathbed conversion, then turned the tables on the Christian defenders. After pillaging the town, the Vikings sailed homeward, only to be ambushed by Saracen pirates at the Straits of Gibraltar, losing 40 ships.

The Magyars, a confederation of nomadic tribes who settled in the Hungarian plains, became arch-exponents of the long-range cavalry raid, penetrating as far as Muslim Spain and the heel of Italy. They repeatedly defeated Frankish armies in battle and reached the walls of Constantinople in 937.

Charlemagne encircled his new empire with "marches," a buffer zone of client states, but internal conflict after his death left the borders undefended. The empire's maritime *cordon sanitaire* proved inadequate against Saracen corsairs, who sacked and raided in the Balearics and southern France, and established coastal bases at Monte Garigliano, Tarentum, and Bari, from which they launched attacks all around Italy, including three raids on Rome. The forces of Christendom began to fight back: the Saracen fortress on the Garigliano was captured by a papal coalition (915), and Otto the Great decisively defeated the Magyars at Lechfeld (955).

But the Vikings proved more durable, establishing a permanent powerbase in Normandy from the late 9th century, and a vast riverine empire in Russia, the Kievan Rus. In England, Viking invasion became Danish settlement and led to the eventual conversion of the settlers and the emergence of a unitary kingdom of England.

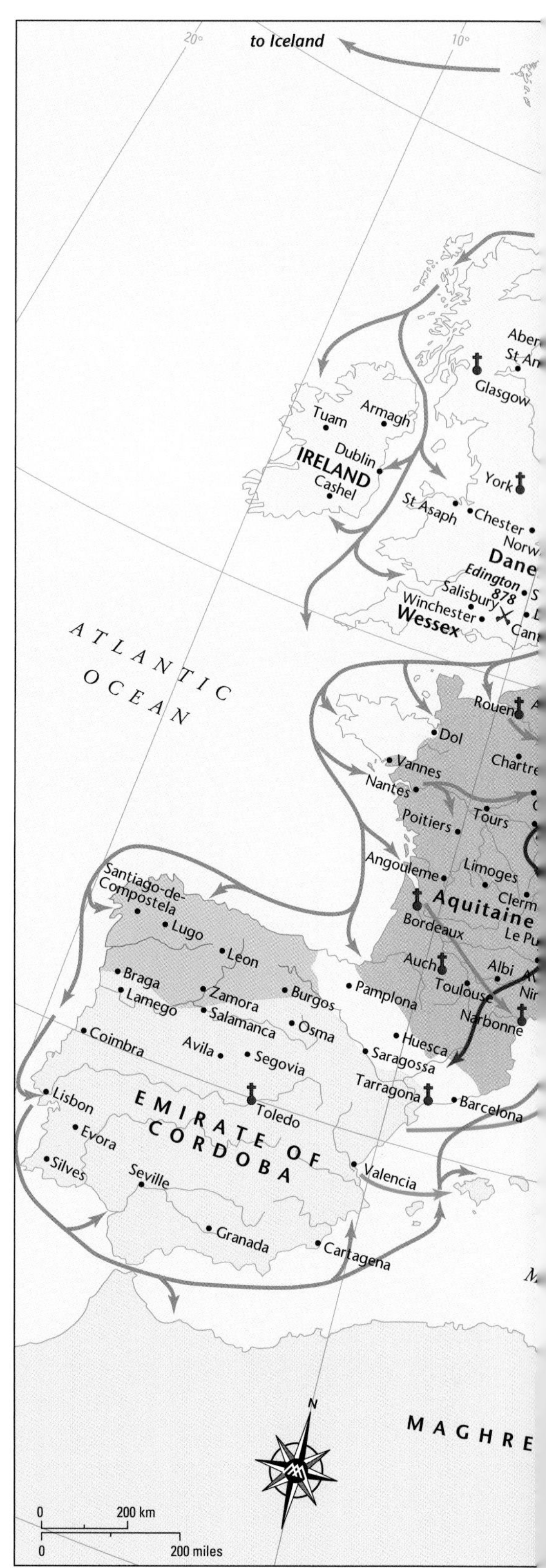

Christendom and the Barbarians
in the 9th Century
Viking raid routes
Magyar raid routes
Saracen raid routes
Main battle with date
Archbishopric
Bishopric
Patriarchates
Archbishopric of the Greek Church
NORWEGIANS
SWEDES
DANES
BALTS
POLES
KIEVAN RUS
BULGARS
PECHENEGS
KHAZARS
MAGYARS
BYZANTINE EMPIRE
ARMENIA
ABBASID CALIPHATE
Saxony
Baltic Sea
Black Sea
Mediterranean Sea
Uppsala
Strengnas
Linköping
Hamar
Asto
Viborg
Aarhus
Ribe
Roskilde
Lund
Schleswig
Oldenburg
Bremen
Schwerin
Ratzeburg
Kammin
Danzig
Elbing
Marienburg
Kulm
Gnesen
Dorpat
Ösel
Riga
Polotsk
Vilna
Kiev
Kamenetz
Bolgar 966
Sarkel 965
Itil 965
Matriga
Cherson
Tergovist
Dorostolon 971
Trebizond
Amasia
Kaisarich
Ancyra
Chalcedon
Nicomedia
Nicaea
Broussa
Eregli
Constantinople
Philippopolis
Adrianople
Seras
Philippi
Salonica
Larissa
Corfu
Leucas
Athens
Mitylene
Smyrna
Ephesus
Hierapolis
Laodicea
Staurapolis
Rhodes
Leonium
Perga
Tarsus
Antioch
Laodicea
Emesa
Tripoli
Damascas
Tyre
Constance
Nicosia
Famagusta
Gortyne
Utrecht
Minden
Verden
Münster
Havelburg
Brandenburg
Magdeburg
Riade 933
Merseburg
Raderborn
Eisenach 908
Naumburg
Liege
Breslau
Treves
Mayence
Worms
Würzburg
Praque
Cracow
Metz
Spires
Eichstätt
Ratisbon
Strasbourg
Freising
Augsburg
Passau
Pressburg 907
Basel
Lechfeld 955
Eisenach 908
Salzburg
Gran
Chur
Varad
Alba
Rimnik
Moutiers
Milan
Padua
Aquila
Verona
Grado
Mantua
Parma
Agram
Bologna
Ravenna
Florence
Perugia
Viterbo
Spalato
Ragusa
Antivari
Aleria
Ajaccio
Torres
Cagliari
Benevento
Capua
Trani
Naples
Sorrento
Bari
Acerenza
Garigliano 915
Brindisi
Salerno
Taranto
Otranto
Cosenza
Rossano
Severina
Messina
Reggio
Palermo
Catania
Carthage
Malta

The Rise of the Papal States

The "Donation of Constantine" appeared with mysterious and suspicious serendipity in the late 8th century during the bitter doctrinal quarrel between Rome and Constantinople over iconoclasm. It purported to be a letter from Constantine, the first Christian emperor, to Pope Sylvester I, where, in thanks for his baptism and conversion (and curing of his leprosy), he conferred on the pontiff primacy over the universal church and temporal dominion over

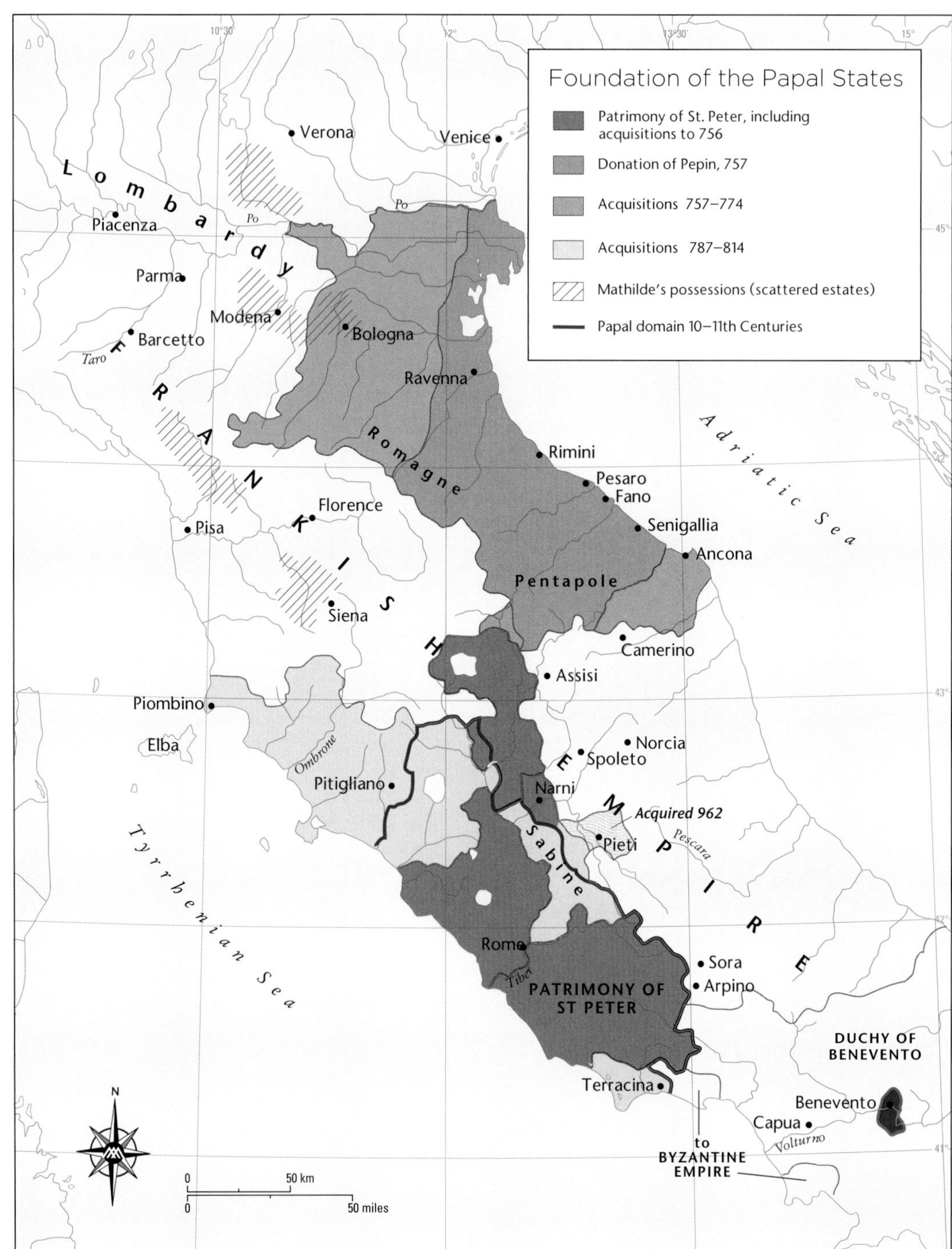

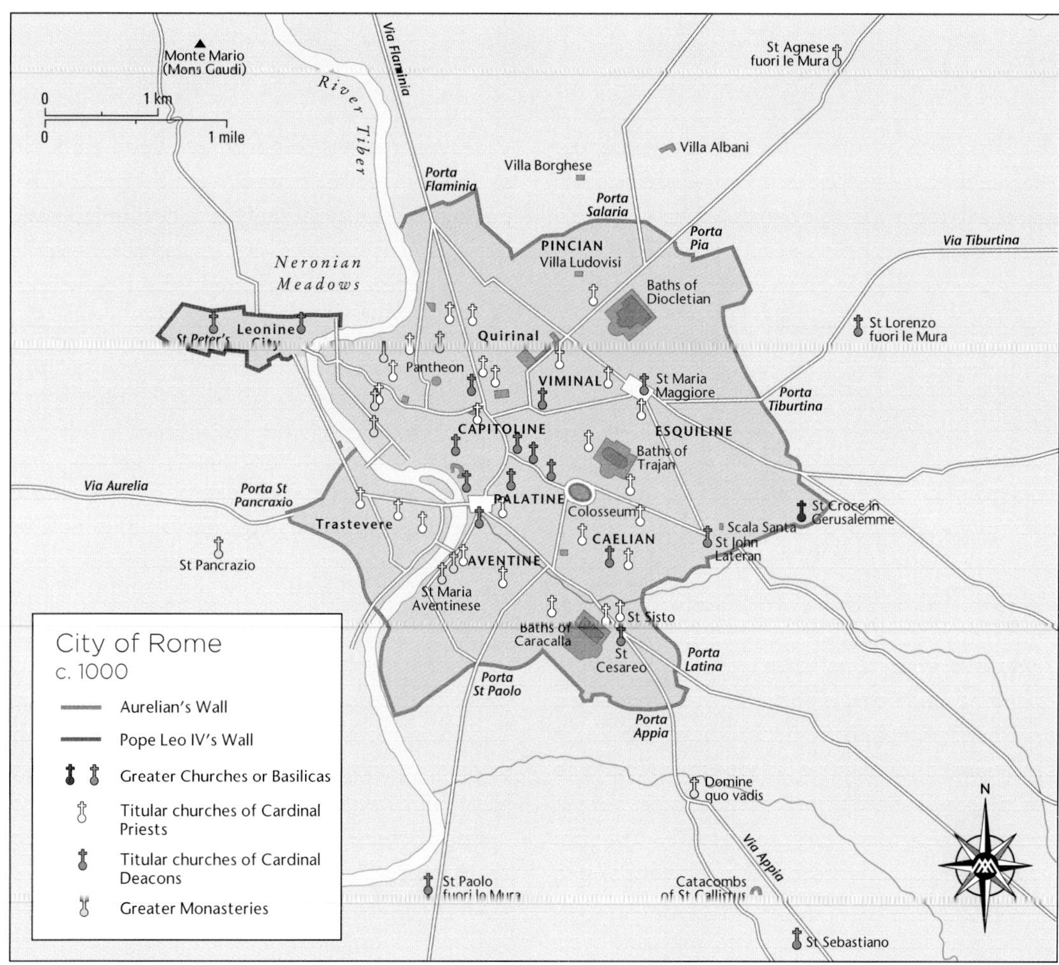

the Western Roman empire. The realization of the Donation's prerogatives was never remotely feasible, but citing it proved valuable when preaching against the rival in the east.

At the time of the Donation's emergence, the "Patrimony of St Peter" consisted of a jumble of far-flung estates bequeathed to the papacy by wealthy Romans in the twilight of the empire. Many of these provided highly lucrative revenues, but by the 750s only those adjacent to Rome, the duchy of Rome, remained, after the Byzantine emperor confiscated the papal estates in southern Italy, Sicily, and Illyricum during the iconoclast schism. When the Lombards, under their king Aistulf, drove the Byzantines from Italy in 751, Rome itself was threatened, and Pope Stephen II hurried across the Alps to beseech aid from the Frankish king, Pepin the Short. Pepin delivered handsomely, soundly defeating Aistulf and making a generous gift of captured Lombard territory to the papacy.

The Donation of Pepin (757) provided a legal basis for the erection of the papal states and revitalized the papacy as a temporal power, and included – to the mortification of Constantinople – the territory of the Exarchate of Ravenna, which had been the seat of Byzantine power in Italy until the Lombards intervened: Pepin was rewarded with the title of Patricius of the Romans. Pepin's son and successor Charlemagne was even more generous; after once more rescuing Rome from the Lombards (774) he made a series of further land donations and then provided sanctuary for Pope Leo III after aristocratic enemies drove him from Rome. His reward was to be crowned Roman Emperor in 800, but the status of the territory he bequeathed to the papacy remained ambiguous: was the Pope's temporal authority supreme, or was he a de facto administrator of a province in the Frankish Empire? This would become a vexed issue as relations between emperors and popes soured.

Ottonian Germany and Conflict with the Pope

IN THE 10TH CENTURY, the papacy fell under the control of first the Theophylacti, then the Crescentii, rival aristocratic families in Rome with a propensity for thuggery. Initially, the main external threat to the families' control came from the kings of Italy (at the time purely regional rulers in the north of the peninsula), but towards the middle of the century, a powerful new ruler emerged in East Francia, Otto I.

After first consolidating his power in Germany, Otto waged successful wars against the Slavs and Magyars, and established alliances with West Francia, Burgundy, Bohemia, and the Byzantines. Now domestically secure, Otto I invaded Italy, and had himself crowned king of the Lombards (951). The Italian king, Berengar II, displaced but not overthrown by Otto, sought territorial recompense by invading the papal states in 960. The pope at this time was John XII, notoriously dissolute, and a member of the Theophylacti clan. John appealed to Otto for help. Otto delivered, driving out Berengar and guaranteeing (with provisos) the integrity of the papal states in the Diploma Ottonianum. In return, John crowned him Holy Roman Emperor. The Diploma freshly guaranteed the land grants to the papal states of the earlier Carolingians.

Otto had increasingly seen the Catholic church as a way of legitimizing his rule, asserting his "divine right," and strengthening the ecclestiastical authorities, such as bishops and abbots, at the expense of the nobility, whom he saw as a threat to his power. He ensured that the ranks of the episcopate were populated by loyal members of his own family.

But Pope John XII sought to counter Otto's power by seeking alliances with Byzantium and the Magyars. Otto took umbrage and marched on Rome: John died suddenly while fleeing with the contents of the papal treasury. Otto appointed Leo XII as the papal successor, but the Roman populace objected, appointing Benedict V in his stead. On hearing of this, Otto once again marched on Rome and lay siege to the city in June 964, compelling the citizens to accept his choice of papal candidate, Leo XII.

Once again rebellion broke out in Italy, led by the son of Berengar II, Adalbert. Otto dispatched his loyal supporter, the Swabian ruler Burchard III, to stamp out the rebellion. When Leo died the church elected, with Otto's approval, John XIII as the new pope in 965. But the Roman populace were alienated by his arrogant behaviour and took him into custody. John escaped and sought help from Otto, who embarked on his third Italian expedition. Otto thenceforth asserted his control by ruling from Rome, waging campaigns to wrest much of southern Italy from Byzantine control by the time of his death in 973.

He was succeded by his son Otto II, who asserted his authority over the papacy by holding court in Rome, making the city his imperial capital, where he received potentates and rulers from all over Europe. He continued his father's policy of expanding the influence of the church wihin the empire, stressing the importance of monasteries and monasticism. He campaigned against the Byzantines in southern Italy, whch brought him into conflict with Muslim forces. The Muslims inflicted a severe defeat on the empire in 982, and the empire effectively lost control of southern Italy.

Following his father's sudden death from malaria Otto III was crowned king of Germany at the age of three, in 983. On attaining his majority he marched to Rome to claim his titles of king of Italy and Holy Roman Emperor, seeking to strengthen imperial control over the Catholic church through a series of papal appointments. When he died suddenly in 1002, without an heir, Italy began to break away from German control. Otto was succeeded by the duke of Bavaria, Henry II, who turned his attention to territory north of the Alps, although he sent three expeditions to Italy to assert his authority and challenge the Byzantine Empire. He cultivated personal and political ties with the Catholic church to strengthen imperial rule, using the church as a powerful force to counter the power of the German nobility, and proclaiming himself the protector of Christendom.

The Holy Roman Empire under Ottonian Rule
919–1024
Boundary of the Holy Roman Empire
Papal States
Marcher States of the Empire
North Sea
KINGDOM OF DENMARK
Rügen
County of Holstein
Billung March
Hamburg
Bremen
Verden
Friesland
Duchy of Saxony
Brunswick
Northern March
Brandenburg
POMERANIA
Pomerelia
Elbing
PRUSSIA
Stettin
Kulmerland
Mazovia
Great Poland
KINGDOM OF POLAND
Breslau
Cracow
County of Holland
Duchy of Brabant
Paderborn
Bruges
Antwerp
Cologne
M. of Lausitz
M. of Merseburg
M. of Meissen
Dresden
Duchy of Lower Lorraine
Bonn
L. of Thuringia
March of Zeitz
County of Hainaut
County of Vermandois
Luxembourg
Mainz
Frankfurt
Duchy of Franconia
Worms
Prague
Duchy of Bohemia
Moravia
Verdun
KINGDOM OF GERMANY
Metz
County of Champagne
Duchy of Upper Lorraine
Strasburg
Ratisbon
Augsburg
Duchy of Bavaria
Eastern March
Vienna
KINGDOM OF FRANCE
Duchy of Swabia
Salzburg
Buda
Pest
Duchy of Burgundy
County of Burgundy
Zurich
Innsbruck
Carinthian March
KINGDOM OF HUNGARY
KINGDOM OF ARLES
Geneva
Trent
Friuli
M. of Carniola
Slavonia
Grenoble
County of Savoy
Milan
March of Verona
Venice
Lombardy
Turin
M. of Istria
Croatia
Alessandria
Romagna
Bosnia
Bologna
Ravenna
Genoa
KINGDOM OF ITALY
Dalmatia
County of Provence
Arles
Nice
Pisa
Pentapolis
Ancona
Spalato
Rama
Marseilles
Tuscany
KINGDOM OF SERBIA
Ragusa
Adriatic Sea
Elbe
Mariana
Duchy of Spoleto
Aquila
Corsica
Papal States
Rome
Oslia
Principality of Benevento
P. of Capua
Benevento
Bari
0
100 km
100 miles
Bonifacio
Torris
Sardinia
Naples
D. of Amalfi
Principality of Salerno
Taranto
Otranto
Tyrrhenian Sea
BYZANTINE EMPIRE
Palermo
Reggio
EMIRATE OF SICILY
Syracuse

The Development of the Monastic Orders

The Benedictines, or "black monks," date their foundations to the 6th century, and the monastic rule generated by St Benedict of Nursia was the most common model for the monastic communities of the early Middle Ages. The Cluniac movement, founded at Cluny at Saône-et-Loire in France in 910 by the monk Berno, believed that monastic rule had become too lax and was determined to adopt stricter religious practices and spend more time in prayer. The Cluniacs were also champions of clerical reform, including the elimination of simony (the buying and selling of ecclesiastical privileges) and concubinage. The impetus that lay behind these reforms was secular interference in monasteries, which were often set up under the patronage of a feudal lord, who then demanded rights and privileges in contravention of the rule of St Benedict and interfered with the running of the monastery.

By the 12th century there were 300 Cluniac monasteries, all subordinate to the abbot of Cluny, and the Cluniac movement was one of the largest religious forces in Europe. Ultimately, the Order fell victim to its own success, wielding great political power and achieving great wealth through estate revenues and control over the pilgrimage site of Santiago de Compostela.

In 1098, a small group of monks established the "New Monastery" at Cîteaux, near Dijon. They also sought a more stringent use of the Rule of St Benedict. The Cistercian order, as it came to be known, reinforced rigor in observance with systematic organization and founded new monasteries in the uncultivated wilderness, away from the corrupt enticements of urban life. The Cistercians codified strict rules of observance, which were reinforced by the network that bound individual houses of the Order together.

Houses within the network propagated new "daughter houses," which they oversaw, while overall uniformity in conduct and practice was upheld through Annual General Chapter meetings, which the abbots of all monasteries in the Order had to attend. The Chapter meetings monitored compliance with the Rule, exercising discipline on houses and monks who failed to observe the required standards. The mechanism for enforcement was the Order's Constitution, the *Carta Caritatis*, the Charter of Love.

The Cistercians strove to mirror their austere lifestyles in their architecture. Monasteries were built insofar as was possible to a standardized design. A church was situated at the north of the complex, with the two cloisters nested either side of the south transept. The main dormitories were situated to the west, while the infirmary and lodgings for aged monks and novices were clustered around the smaller cloister. The abbot's lodging commanded the entrance to the monastic complex, while, separated from it by a dividing wall, were stables, accommodation for lay-brothers and artisans. Sustenance was derived from gardens and fish ponds within the complex. Sizeable estates were used for harvesting grain and animal husbandry.

The Cistercians were often innovators in their lay endeavors. They became master iron-founders, using the phosphate-rich slag to fertilize their fields. They also developed a knack for hydraulic engineering to exploit and control water power for their mills and sanitation in remote mountain locations. Cistercians were also major wool producers: their undyed woollen habits led them to be called the White Monks.

The Cistercian model proved highly successful; Orderic Vitalis (1075–1142), writing less than 40 years after the founding of the order, describes "a swarm of cowled monks [spreading] all over the world." Leading lights of the early order were St Robert of Molesme, St Stephen Harding, the first abbots of Cîteaux, and St Bernard of Clairvaux, its most influential early theologian. The Cistercians saw themselves as "desert monks" who sought out "lonely wooded places," but ended up cultivating and civilizing them and gathering new settlements around themselves. By the end of the 13th century there were over 500 Cistercian houses across Europe, many at its wild frontiers in Scandinavia, Scotland, and eastern Europe. >>

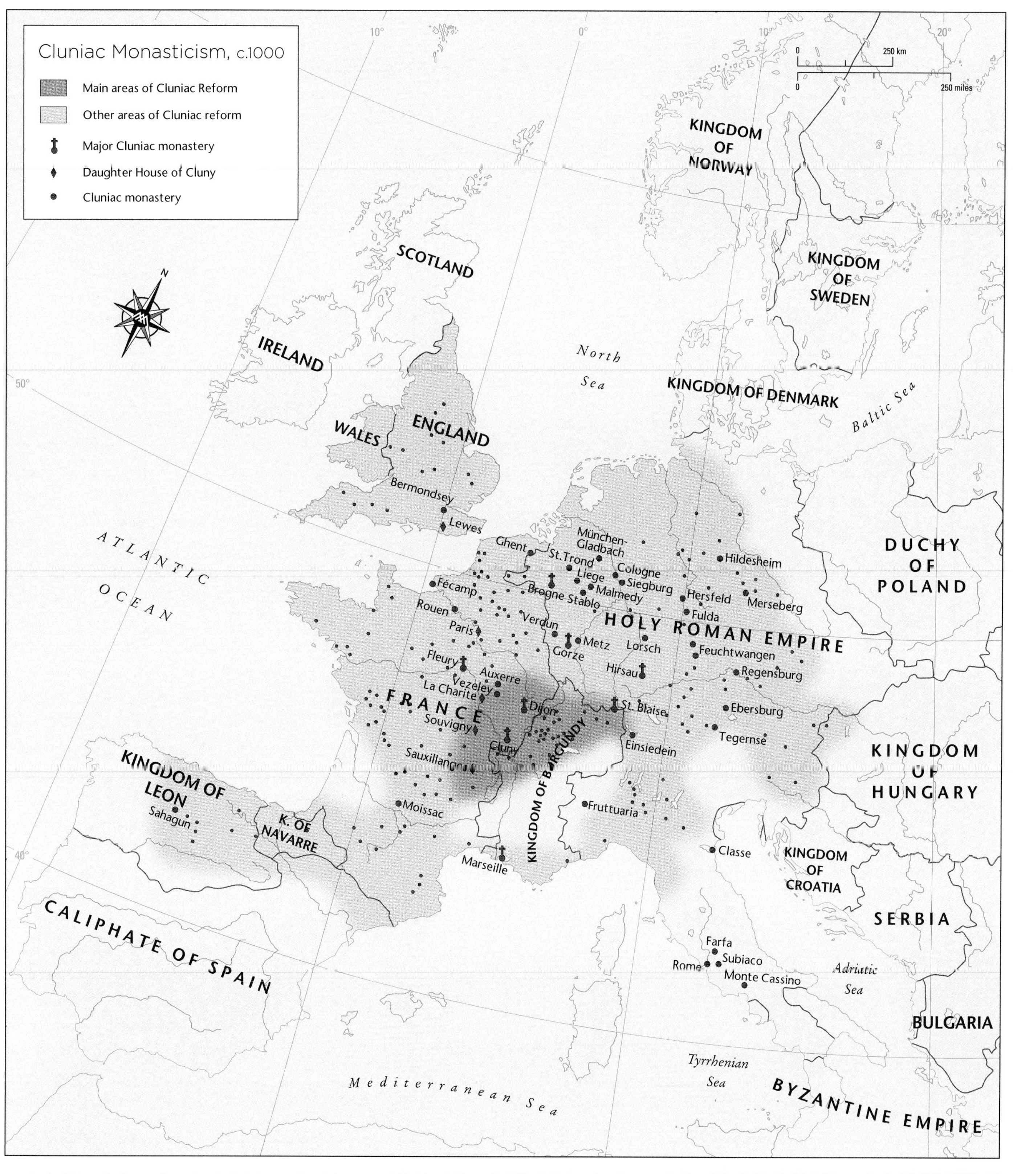
Cluniac Monasticism, c.1000
Main areas of Cluniac Reform
Other areas of Cluniac reform
Major Cluniac monastery
Daughter House of Cluny
Cluniac monastery
0 250 km
0 250 miles
KINGDOM OF NORWAY
KINGDOM OF SWEDEN
SCOTLAND
IRELAND
North Sea
KINGDOM OF DENMARK
Baltic Sea
WALES
ENGLAND
Bermondsey
Lewes
ATLANTIC OCEAN
DUCHY OF POLAND
München-Gladbach
Ghent
St.Trond
Cologne
Hildesheim
Liege
Siegburg
Fécamp
Brogne Stablo
Malmedy
Hersfeld
Merseberg
Fulda
Rouen
Verdun
HOLY ROMAN EMPIRE
Paris
Metz
Lorsch
Gorze
Feuchtwangen
Fleury
Hirsau
Regensburg
Auxerre
Vezeley
La Charite
FRANCE
Dijon
St. Blaise
Ebersburg
Souvigny
Tegernse
KINGDOM OF BURGUNDY
Einsiedein
Cluny
KINGDOM OF HUNGARY
KINGDOM OF LEON
Sauxillanges
Sahagun
K. OF NAVARRE
Moissac
Fruttuaria
Classe
KINGDOM OF CROATIA
Marseille
SERBIA
CALIPHATE OF SPAIN
Farfa
Subiaco
Rome
Monte Cassino
Adriatic Sea
BULGARIA
Tyrrhenian Sea
Mediterranean Sea
BYZANTINE EMPIRE

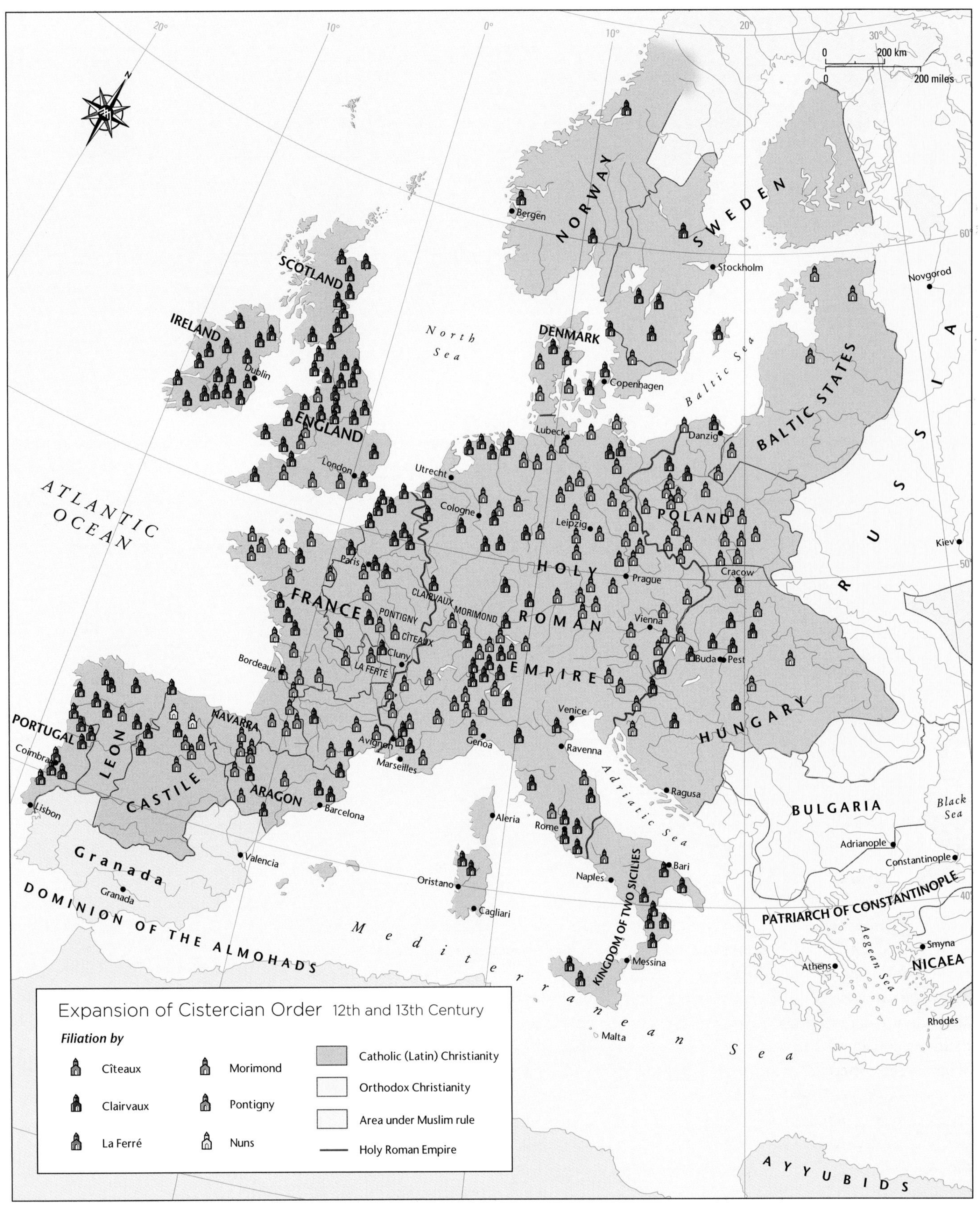
Expansion of Cistercian Order 12th and 13th Century
Filiation by
Cîteaux
Clairvaux
La Ferré
Morimond
Pontigny
Nuns
Catholic (Latin) Christianity
Orthodox Christianity
Area under Muslim rule
Holy Roman Empire
0 200 km
0 200 miles
ATLANTIC OCEAN
North Sea
Baltic Sea
Adriatic Sea
Mediterranean Sea
Black Sea
Aegean Sea
IRELAND
SCOTLAND
ENGLAND
NORWAY
SWEDEN
DENMARK
BALTIC STATES
RUSSIA
POLAND
HOLY ROMAN EMPIRE
FRANCE
HUNGARY
PORTUGAL
LEON
CASTILE
NAVARRA
ARAGON
Granada
DOMINION OF THE ALMOHADS
KINGDOM OF TWO SICILIES
BULGARIA
PATRIARCH OF CONSTANTINOPLE
NICAEA
AYYUBIDS
Bergen
Stockholm
Novgorod
Copenhagen
Dublin
London
Lubeck
Danzig
Utrecht
Cologne
Leipzig
Paris
Prague
Cracow
Kiev
CLAIRVAUX
MORIMOND
PONTIGNY
CÎTEAUX
Cluny
LA FERTÉ
Vienna
Buda
Pest
Bordeaux
Venice
Ravenna
Genoa
Avignon
Marseilles
Coimbra
Lisbon
Barcelona
Valencia
Granada
Ragusa
Aleria
Rome
Oristano
Cagliari
Naples
Bari
Messina
Malta
Adrianople
Constantinople
Athens
Smyna
Rhodes

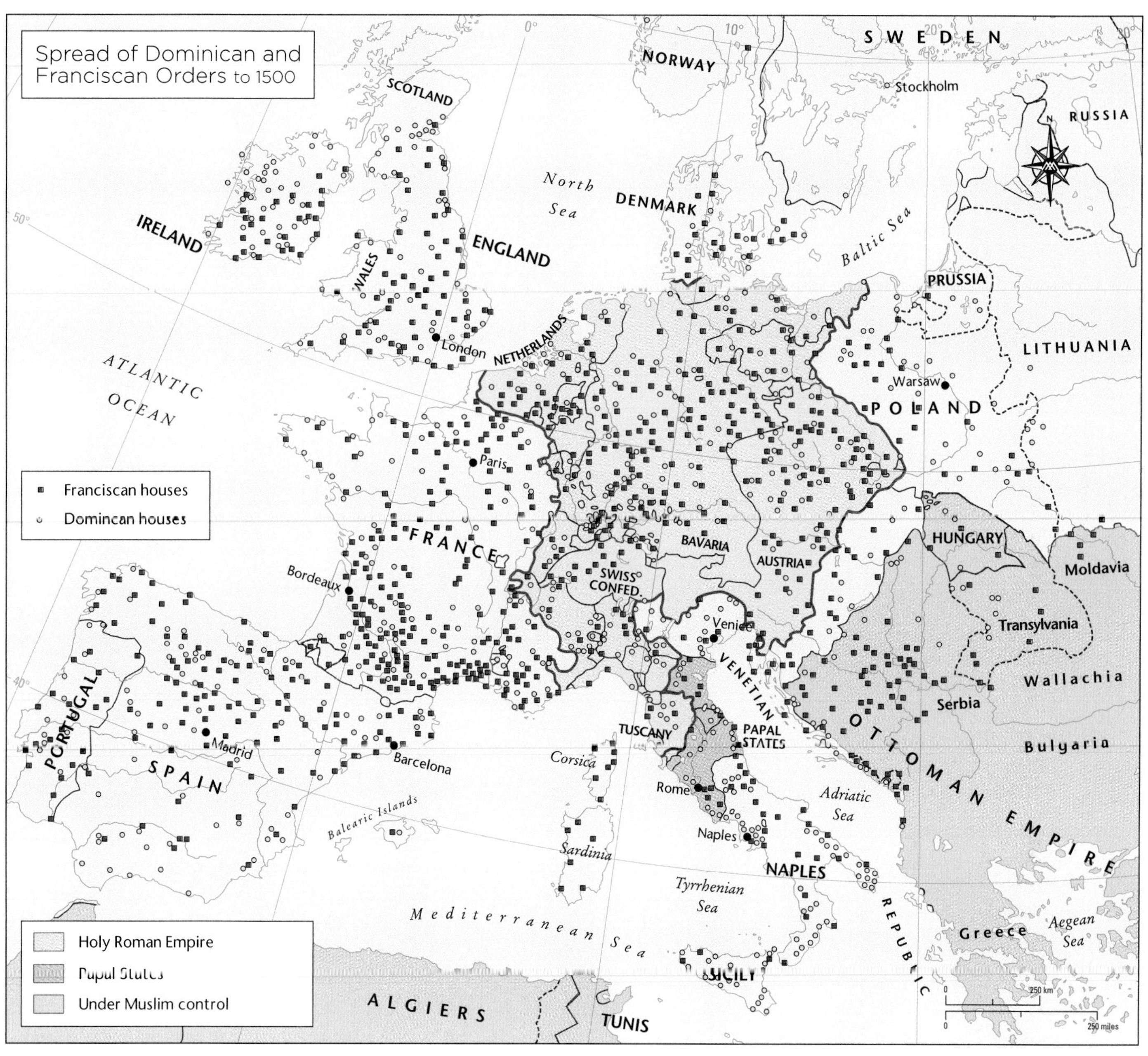

By the 13th century, Cistercian discipline had relaxed and rival orders emerged. The Franciscans, Dominicans, Carmelites, and Augustinians were mendicant orders, deliberately embracing an apostolic poverty that left them dependent on the charity of the faithful. Whereas the Cistercians had withdrawn into the wilderness, these "friars" chose to base themselves in towns, amongst the people to whom they ministered. Following the inspiration of their founding fathers, St Dominic (1216) and St Francis of Assisi (1223), they took a vow of poverty, renouncing worldly possessions, land, and income, whether as individuals or as communities. High intellectual standards were demanded of these friars, who became dominant figures in the universities. The Dominicans, following their founder's mission to the Cathars, stressed preaching and were also the administrators of the Inquisition. The Franciscans stressed "perfect poverty," which was hard to maintain; they eventually split into "Spirituals" and "Conventuals," the latter taking a more pragmatic interpretation of Francis' daunting ideals.

Even though the idea of poverty, embraced by the mendicant orders of the 13th century, ultimately proved unattainable, this "active," as opposed to the traditional "contemplative," mission became increasingly prominent in the Catholic church in the later medieval period.

The Formalization of Christian Architecture

House Church at Dura-Europos, Syria
3rd Century CE

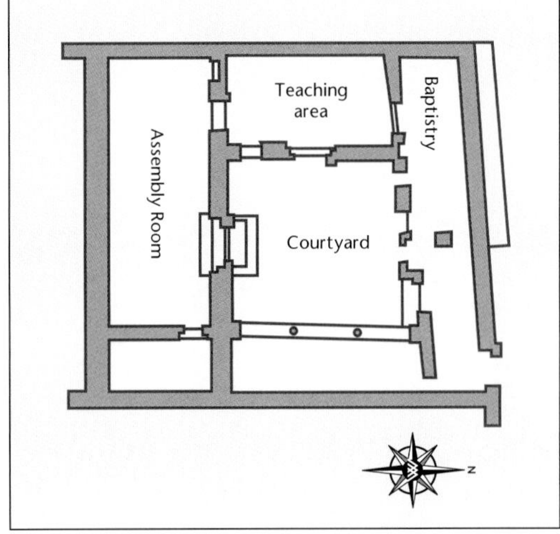

The conversion of Constantine produced a transformation in Christianity's status within the Roman Empire. Less than a decade after the persecution of Diocletian, it was not merely tolerated but the religion of state. Until this time, Christian places of worship had been modest affairs, even where and when authorities showed indulgence. Under persecution, believers had to practice their faith in privacy and secrecy. Now, cloaked in imperial approbation, Christians had the sanction to construct public – and ostentatious – religious architecture.

Universally, the form of that architecture avoided emulating the designs of the pagan temples the Christians supplanted. Roman temples were not designed to house congregations; their official business was conducted out front, with propitiatory sacrifices performed at an open-air altar. Temples varied in form, both over the empire, and through time, but the default model had a rectangular floor plan with a porticoed entrance topped by a triangular pediment. The initial church construction that followed Constantine's conversion (much of it commissioned by the emperor himself), was architecturally diverse. Many were shrines to martyred saints, with the body of the church used as an indoor graveyard for believers. Often these shrines were circular in floorplan (for instance, the building for pilgrims to Christ's tomb in Jerusalem) but the shrine for St Lawrence in Rome was U-shaped: there was no convention.

The classic cruciform design was apparently first hit upon by accident. The church Constantine dedicated to St Peter in Rome originally only consisted of the T-portion of the cross design; the massive nave with two aisles either side was added later to increase capacity. This happy accident soon became a standard, both proving functional and acting as a concrete representation of the faith's primary symbol.

In reality, the basilica was an adaptation of a building common in Roman secular architecture – in government buildings and law courts, where the presiding magistrate would be seated in a semi-circular extension or *exedra*. The long nave suited the processional nature of Christian worship, while the lateral aisles seated the congregation, with alcoves for shrines. At the head of the cross, a semi-circular apse (adopted from the *exedra*) for the altar was fronted by a *bema*, or raised dais for the clergy. In the early church, the entry tended to be at the eastern end of the basilica, but in the 7th and 8th centuries, the altar was generally situated to the east.

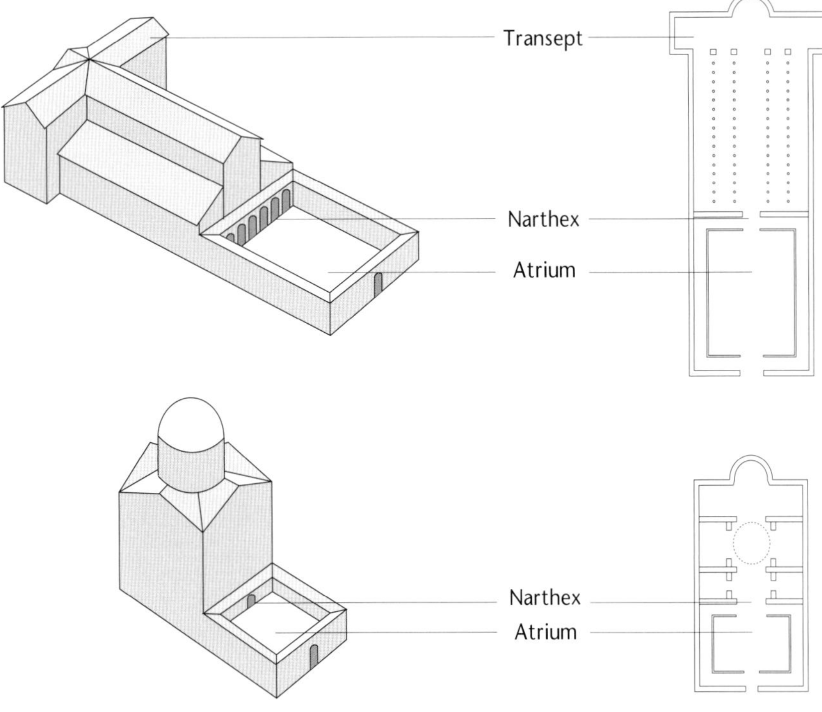

The cruciform design also diverged between the Byzantines, who commonly adopted the Greek (square) cross, and the Romans, who opted for the Latin (T-shaped) cross floor-plan. In a borrowing from Roman mausolea, churches frequently crowned the intersection of the arms of the cross with a dome: a spectacular example was commissioned by Justinian the Great in Hagia Sofia in Constantinople, which Paul the Silentiary described as "a great helmet, bending over on every side, like the radiant heavens... like the firmament that rests upon air." Hagia Sofia was so awe-inspiring that it attracted Islamic as well as Christian imitators.

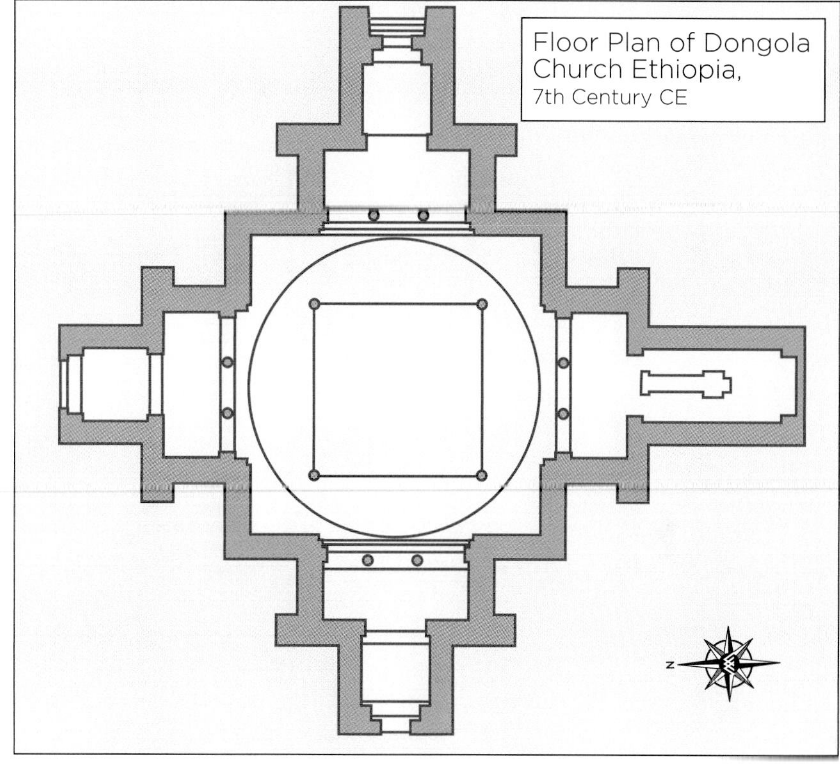

Floor Plan of Dongola Church Ethiopia,
7th Century CE

Romanesque architecture, with its arches, barrel vaults, and massive walls, was current in Europe in the 11th and 12th centuries. Its key influence was the architecture of the Byzantine Empire; the palace complex of Charlemagne at Aachen was influenced by the Byzantine church of St Vitale in Ravenna, Italy, and Romanesque architecture evolved from the buildings that were constructed during Charlemagne's reign. The Romanesque style also amalgamated elements of Roman architecture, appropriating the rounded Roman arch. This was a time when monasticism was expanding and when pilgrimages to the shrines of saints were becoming increasingly popular. Substantial churches needed to be built to accommodate this influx of pilgrims. The Romanesque abbey church at Cluny (*below*) was completed in 1130 and was at that date the largest church in Europe.

The new churches of the Romanesque period were built of stone, not wood. Because their walls were extremely thick, the windows were comparatively small to avert the danger of collapsing. The ground level of the nave was surrounded by arcaded arches, with bulky piers or columns, which were topped by second and third levels of smaller arches. Decorative elements were simple, using geometric shapes such as squares or lozenges. Early Romanesque roofs were wooden, but in time this evolved into stone roofs that were supported by barrel vaulting (semi-circular) or cross vaulting. Cluny is one of the most famous barrel-vaulted churches. >>

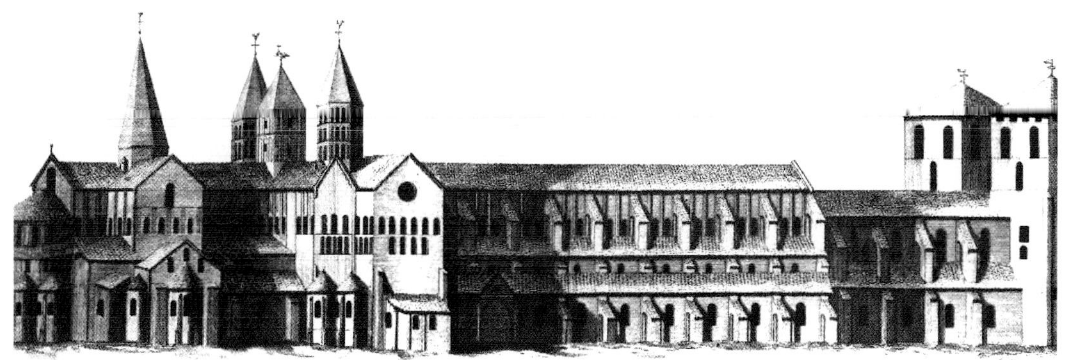

The Romanesque abbey church at Cluny after the third phase of construction, completed in the early 12th century.

In England the Romanesque style was known as Norman, after William the Conqueror who introduced the style following the Norman invasion in 1066. The 7th-century minster at Winchester was replaced by a Norman cathdral (below left), which was consecrated in 1093. Substantial rebuilding, in the Gothic style, took place in the 14th and 15th centuries (below right).

From the 12th century, economic growth led to increasing urbanization, and a renaissance in the construction of cathedrals as the visible expression of the increasing importance of cities as the hubs of political and religious authority. The Gothic style developed in northern France and evolved into a riot of both structural innovation and ornamental embellishment in its *Rayonnant* ("radiant") and *Flamboyant* Gothic phases in the High Middle Ages. Although it originated in France, the Gothic style can be found all over Europe, with outstanding examples in Spain, England, Italy, and throughout northern Europe.

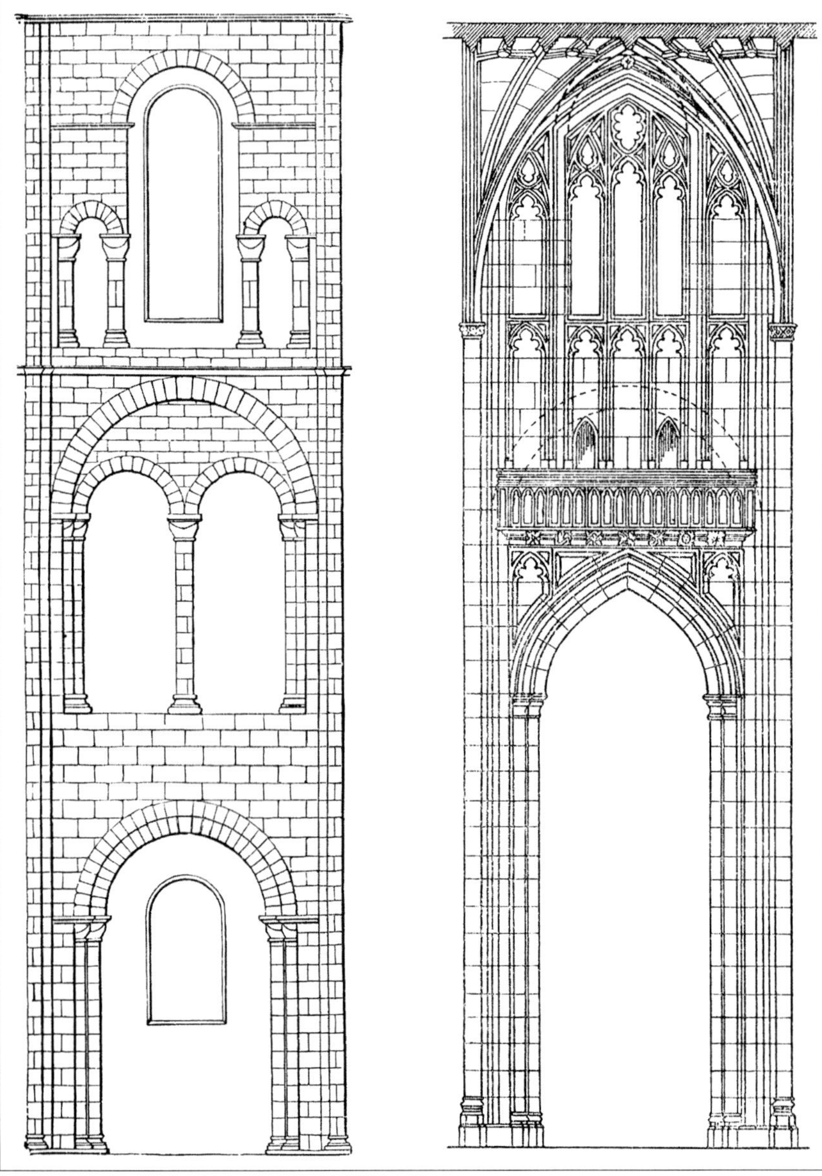

The Gothic style is believed to have been popularized by Abbot Suger (c. 1085–1151), whose innovative renovations of the eastern end of the Abbey of Saint-Denis in Paris both increased the height of the abbey and filled it with light. These design features became characteristic of the Gothic style. The most fundamental element of Gothic style is the pointed arch, which relieved some of the thrust, and therefore the stress, on other structural elements, making it possible to reduce the size of supporting columns and piers. In contrast to rounded Romanesque arches, pointed Gothic arches added to the impression of soaring height. As well as being aesthetically pleasing they could carry more weight than rounded arches. They became a dominant architectural feature, used in arcades, vaults, doors, windows, alcoves. The roofs of these increasingly tall buildings were supported by constructing rib vaults – a framework of diagonal arched ribs that extended across the ceiling. Flying buttresses, arches that extended out from the upper portion of the external walls, helped to push the weight outwards.

All these innovations allowed for larger windows and more light. Innovations in tracery, the stone framework that supports glass in the windows, meant that windows could become ever larger, with increasingly complex designs. Light flooded into the Gothic interiors and the extensive use of stained glass, especially through the revival of the medieval rose window, brought color into the interior.

The builders of Gothic cathedrals strove to make them prominent landmarks, visible for many miles around, and the towers, often topped by *flèche*, a spire of wood and coated with lead, were the last part of the cathedral to be constructed. In France and Spain it was the norm to construct two towers at the front of the building, whereas an English cathedral often also had an enormous tower at the crossing. Flying buttresses, rib vaults, stained-glass windows, and gargoyles all evinced an exuberance and flamboyance that was mirrored in the informal competition amongst medieval stonemasons to build the highest spire in Europe: two spires that achieved the accolade, Beauvais and Lincoln, subsequently collapsed.

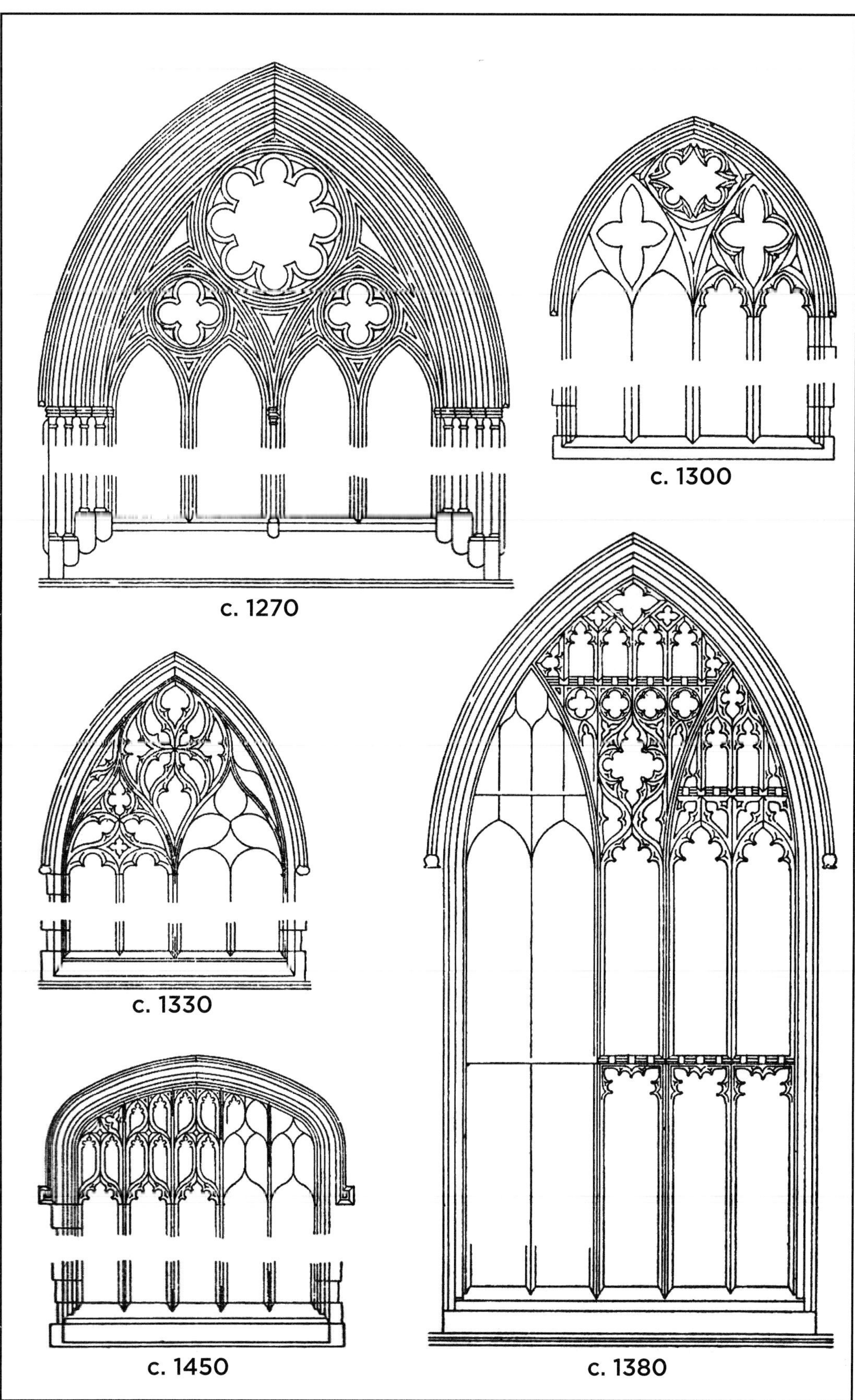

The delicate and ornate stonework that held the window – called tracery – became increasingly florid and exuberant as can be seen in these examples from English Gothic cathedrals.

The Great Schism of 1054

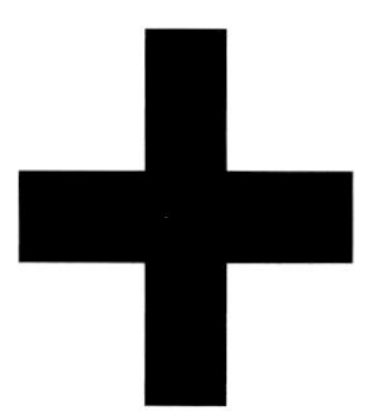

The Greek cross, or *crux imissa quadrata*, has four arms of equal length and is used by Eastern Orthodoxy. Its use can be dated to early Christians in the 4th century. The Latin cross, or *crux imissa*, has a longer vertical beam. The Latin cross began as a Roman Catholic emblem, but later became a universal symbol of Christianity.

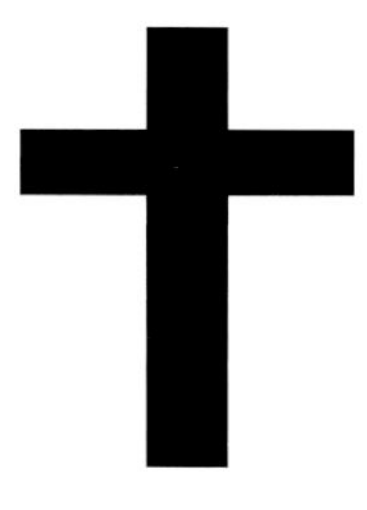

THE EASTERN AND WESTERN CHURCHES had become increasingly estranged from the 5th century onward. Doctrinal tensions had been caused by the unilateral adoption into liturgical practice by the Western church of the Filioque ("and through the Son") addition to the Nicene Creed. Doctrinal divisions were reflected in growing cultural divisions. The Byzantine church was *caesaropapist*, in which the head of state was also head of the church – irreconcilable with the independence (at least in aspiration) of the papacy.

In 1053, at the Battle of Civitate, Pope Leo IX led an army against the Normans, who were threatening to march on Rome. Defeated and taken captive, Leo wrote to Michael Cerularius, the patriarch of Constantinople, seeking common cause against the invaders. However, Leo also repudiated claims that the Western church was "judaizing" by using unleavened bread in holy communion, and cited the Donation of Constantine, which asserted the doctrinal supremacy of Rome.

By the time his legation arrived in Constantinople, Leo had died. Cerularius refused to meet the delegates, whereupon their leader, Cardinal Humbert of Silva Candida, melodramatically entered Hagia Sofia during the Divine Liturgy and left a Bull of Excommunication against the patriarch on the altar. In retaliation, a Byzantine synod anathematized the three legates.

The bull was invalid, as the legation's papal authority had expired with Leo, while the Byzantine anathemas were directed at just three individuals not the whole Western church. But the rift persisted, and subsequent events exacerbated matters further. In 1182 the "massacre of the Latins" in Constantinople outraged the Western church, and would help to precipitate the sack of Constantinople in 1204 by western crusaders, which left a bitter legacy..

Despite several attempts at rapprochement, the schism has not healed, although relations improved with the Second Vatican Council (1962–65), which recognized the validity of sacraments in the Eastern churches.

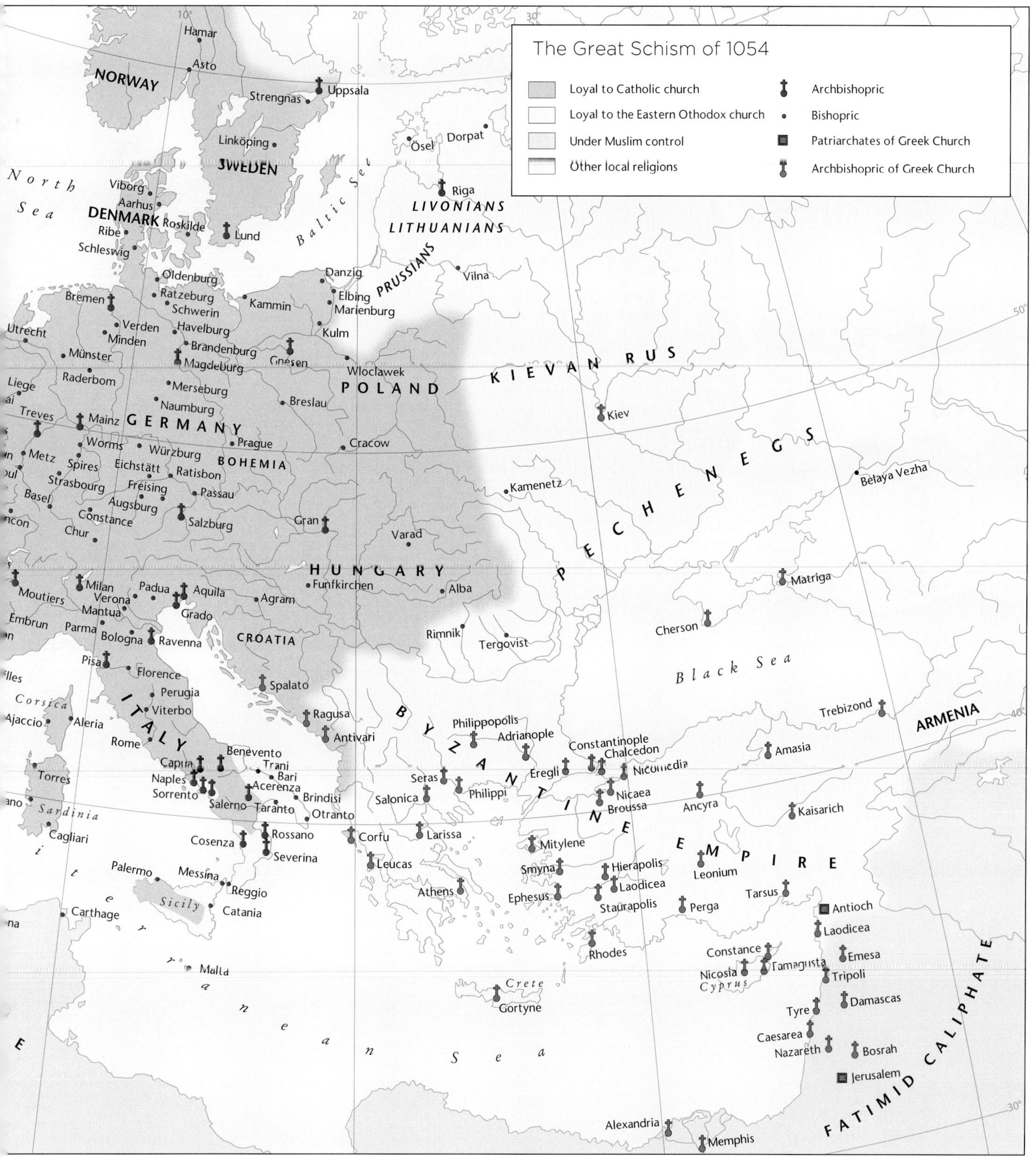
The Great Schism of 1054
Loyal to Catholic church
Loyal to the Eastern Othodox church
Under Muslim control
Other local religions
Archbishopric
Bishopric
Patriarchates of Greek Church
Archbishopric of Greek Church
NORWAY
SWEDEN
DENMARK
GERMANY
BOHEMIA
POLAND
HUNGARY
CROATIA
ITALY
PRUSSIANS
LIVONIANS
LITHUANIANS
KIEVAN RUS
PECHENEGS
BYZANTINE EMPIRE
ARMENIA
FATIMID CALIPHATE
North Sea
Baltic Sea
Black Sea
Mediterranean Sea
Hamar
Asto
Uppsala
Strengnas
Linköping
Viborg
Aarhus
Roskilde
Ribe
Lund
Schleswig
Ösel
Dorpat
Riga
Oldenburg
Ratzeburg
Schwerin
Bremen
Kammin
Danzig
Elbing
Marienburg
Vilna
Utrecht
Verden
Minden
Havelburg
Kulm
Brandenburg
Magdeburg
Gnesen
Münster
Raderbom
Wloclawek
Liege
Merseburg
Naumburg
Breslau
Treves
Mainz
Prague
Cracow
Worms
Würzburg
Metz
Spires
Eichstätt
Ratisbon
Strasbourg
Freising
Passau
Basel
Augsburg
Constance
Salzburg
Chur
Gran
Varad
Kiev
Kamenetz
Belaya Vezha
Moutiers
Milan
Verona
Padua
Aquila
Agram
Funfkirchen
Alba
Mantua
Grado
Embrun
Parma
Bologna
Ravenna
Rimnik
Tergovist
Matriga
Cherson
Pisa
Florence
Perugia
Spalato
Corsica
Ajaccio
Aleria
Viterbo
Ragusa
Antivari
Rome
Benevento
Trani
Capua
Bari
Naples
Acerenza
Sorrento
Salerno
Taranto
Brindisi
Otranto
Torres
Sardinia
Cagliari
Cosenza
Rossano
Severina
Palermo
Messina
Reggio
Sicily
Catania
Carthage
Malta
Philippopolis
Adrianople
Constantinople
Chalcedon
Nicomedia
Eregli
Seras
Philippi
Salonica
Nicaea
Broussa
Ancyra
Amasia
Trebizond
Kaisarich
Corfu
Larissa
Leucas
Mitylene
Smyrna
Hierapolis
Laodicea
Leonium
Athens
Ephesus
Staurapolis
Perga
Tarsus
Antioch
Laodicea
Rhodes
Constance
Famagusta
Nicosia
Cyprus
Emesa
Tripoli
Damascas
Crete
Gortyne
Tyre
Caesarea
Nazareth
Bosrah
Jerusalem
Alexandria
Memphis

The Rise of the University

Institutions devoted to higher learning existed in most of the major pre-Christian civilizations. The museum in Alexandria, the Buddhist centers in Taxila and Nalanda, and the Chinese state-run schools for the education of bureaucrats all had varied curriculums and attracted and accommodated students from a wide catchment area. In the Islamic Caliphate madrasas exhibiting many of the features of universities were flourishing in the 10th century, and education was more widely disseminated and literacy rates far higher than in Christendom.

The precursor to the development of universities in Europe was the reform program of Pope Gregory VII (1073–85), whose centralization of papal power and expansion of canon law led to a drive for the professionalization of the clergy. His 1079 papal decree regulated the formation of cathedral schools, some of which would evolve into the first universities. The process by which they formed was usually ad hoc, with students banding together into scholastic guilds, using their collective bargaining power to bulk purchase the services of academics and scriveners to support their education.

In Bologna (reputedly the oldest university, dating back to 1088), the student representative body controlled the hiring, firing, and rates of pay for their teachers – and the content of courses. If baulked, students would often strike to enforce their will. There were different operating models. The University of Naples, for instance, was founded by the Holy Roman Emperor Frederick II in 1224 specifically to train effective skilled bureaucrats for his administration, its ethos a deliberate antithesis to student-driven Bologna. Iberian universities such as Salamanca and Coimbra similarly owed their existence to royal patronage, while the independent colleges and halls that coalesced to form the universities of Oxford and (later) Cambridge were usually endowed by aristocratic benefactors. The University of Paris constituted a further model established by ecclesiastical patronage, and the church funded its teachers (the best paid in Europe). Pope Gregory IX issued a bull in 1231 that related to Paris, guaranteeing its institutional autonomy, which has been described as the Magna Carta of universities. Further bulls extended these privileges to other ancient universities, and generalized a principle first established in respect of the University of Toulouse (1233), that an academic once admitted to teach there was deemed fit to teach at any university without further qualification.

The typical entry age for students was 14–15 years (although older students were common at universities which specialized in medicine or law). The degree of Master of Arts commonly took six years to complete, and consisted of seven subjects, comprising an initial *trivium* (grammar, rhetoric, and logic) followed by a supplementary *quadrivium* (arithmetic, geometry, astronomy, and music theory). The syllabus later expanded to include physics, metaphysics, and moral philosophy. The range of approved texts was limited, with classical masters such as Cicero and Aristotle featuring prominently. Once the student completed their Masters, they could proceed to one of the higher faculties, and specialize in medicine, law, or theology.

In 1155, Emperor Frederick issued a decree, *Authentica Habita*, which extended to students at universities the same privileges enjoyed by the clergy, namely, the right to be tried in ecclesiastical rather than civil courts (or by university authorities), freedom of movement for the purpose of study, and immunity from the right of reprisal (whereby goods of persons of the same nationality could be confiscated in relation to the debts of a fellow national). Unsurprisingly, with such latitude, large numbers of young men living away from home for the first time frequently caused trouble; in 1229, when Paris students rioted, several were killed in a crackdown by the city guard. But the students "dispersed" (went on strike) in protest, and the pope himself, a Paris alumnus, stepped in to guarantee their rights. By the close of the Middle Ages, the possession of a university was a "must have" for any European territory that wished to assert its status in Christendom.

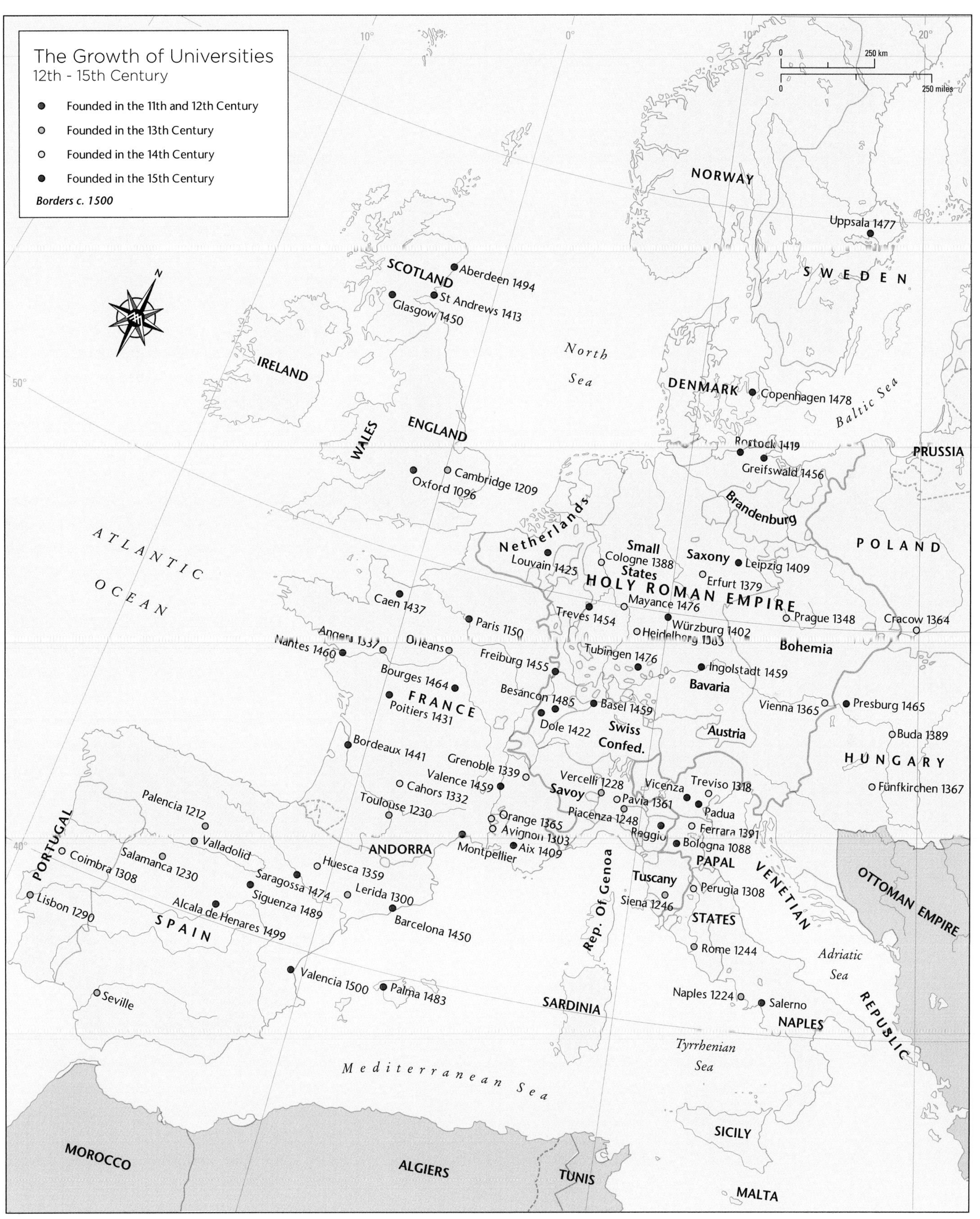
The Growth of Universities
12th - 15th Century
Founded in the 11th and 12th Century
Founded in the 13th Century
Founded in the 14th Century
Founded in the 15th Century
Borders c. 1500
250 km
250 miles
NORWAY
Uppsala 1477
SWEDEN
SCOTLAND
Aberdeen 1494
St Andrews 1413
Glasgow 1450
North Sea
IRELAND
DENMARK
Copenhagen 1478
Baltic Sea
WALES
ENGLAND
Rostock 1419
PRUSSIA
Greifswald 1456
Cambridge 1209
Oxford 1096
Brandenburg
Netherlands
ATLANTIC OCEAN
Small States
Saxony
Leipzig 1409
POLAND
Cologne 1388
Louvain 1425
Erfurt 1379
HOLY ROMAN EMPIRE
Mayance 1476
Caen 1437
Treves 1454
Prague 1348
Cracow 1364
Paris 1150
Würzburg 1402
Heidelberg 1385
Angers 1337
Orleans
Nantes 1460
Bohemia
Tubingen 1476
Freiburg 1455
Ingolstadt 1459
Bourges 1464
Bavaria
FRANCE
Besancon 1485
Basel 1459
Vienna 1365
Presburg 1465
Poitiers 1431
Dole 1422
Swiss Confed.
Austria
Buda 1389
Bordeaux 1441
HUNGARY
Grenoble 1339
Vercelli 1228
Treviso 1318
Valence 1459
Vicenza
Fünfkirchen 1367
Cahors 1332
Savoy
Pavia 1361
Palencia 1212
Toulouse 1230
Padua
Piacenza 1248
Orange 1365
PORTUGAL
Valladolid
Avignon 1303
Reggio
Ferrara 1391
ANDORRA
Aix 1409
Bologna 1088
Coimbra 1308
Salamanca 1230
Montpellier
PAPAL
VENETIAN
OTTOMAN EMPIRE
Huesca 1359
Saragossa 1474
Tuscany
Lisbon 1290
Siguenza 1489
Lerida 1300
Rep. Of Genoa
Perugia 1308
Alcala de Henares 1499
Siena 1246
STATES
SPAIN
Barcelona 1450
Rome 1244
Adriatic Sea
Valencia 1500
Palma 1483
Naples 1224
REPUBLIC
Seville
SARDINIA
Salerno
NAPLES
Tyrrhenian Sea
Mediterranean Sea
SICILY
MOROCCO
ALGIERS
TUNIS
MALTA

The Christian Call to Arms

IN 1095 TWO-THIRDS of the ancient Christian world, including the holy city of Jerusalem, was in Muslim hands. The Islamic world was divided between the Sunni Abbasid caliphate, based in Baghdad, and the Shi'ite Fatimids, based in Cairo. The Seljuks were Turkish nomads, recent converts to Sunni Islam, who swept into the Islamic world from their homeland near the Aral Sea. By the 1070s the Seljuk Empire had reached its zenith, with the Seljuk sultans controlling most of the Byzantine Empire and ruling from Nicaea in western Turkey.

In March 1094 an embassy to Rome sought the help of Pope Urban II against the Seljuk Turks; the Byzantine capital, Constantinople, was under threat. The pope resolved to enlist the help of knights in the West in defending the Christians of the East; this would provide a good opportunity to move closer to the Orthodox church and heal the schism that had been in place since 1054. A crusade to the East would also be a pilgrimage to Christianity's most holy site, Jerusalem, which had been in Muslim hands since 637. The military expedition he proposed would check the advance of Islam, and finally restore Christian access to the holy places of the Middle East. Enlisting the help of Europe's warrior elite would provide a *raison d'être* for an entire knightly class that had been disempowered by the break-up of the Carolingian Empire and were spoiling for a fight. In addition, the pope was involved in a power struggle with the German emperor, Henry IV (the Investiture Controversy), and the crusade was an effective way of enhancing the pope's standing.

Pope Urban II proclaimed the crusade at the Council of Clermont on 27 November 1095. There are five different reported accounts of the speech: but it is agreed that Pope Urban stressed the necessity of repudiating violence at home and maintaining the Peace of God, a movement led by the medieval church to protect ecclesiastical property, churchmen, women, and pilgrims from the endemic violence that was characteristic of the period. The pope also stressed the necessity of responding to the Byzantine Greeks, who needed help, and the value of an armed pilgrimage, which would bring both rewards in heaven and remission of sins for anyone who perished in the undertaking. One account of Urban's speech reports that the enthusiastic crowd responded with cries of "*Deus vult*!" (God wills it!).

During a year-long preaching tour of France, the pope stirred up the emotions of his audience and galvanized many into action. Over the next six years, perhaps as many as 130,000 men and women joined the armies that were heading for the East. Nobles and knights accounted for just 10 percent of the total fighting force; the rest comprised peasants or townspeople, who were caught up in the wave of enthusiasm. Tradition has it that every pilgrim took a vow to visit the Church of the Holy Sepulchre in Jerusalem and also received a cloth cross that was usually sewn onto their clothes.

The crusades were led by an army of knights and their retainers, drawn in the first instance from France's noble elite. The crusading ideal soon spread; marriage ties amongst the noble families of Europe meant that the crusading message permeated and spread beyond the French heartland, even though crusading was an expensive sacrifice, and many nobles were forced to sell or mortgage land at a time when Europe was suffering an agricultural crisis.

Yet the main purpose of the crusade was lost to many once they were on the way to the Holy Land. Armed and ready for violence, they mounted a series of brutal attacks on the infidels who were most immediately to hand – Europe's Jewish population – holding them responsible for the crucifixion of Jesus Christ. There were anti-Jewish riots at Rouen, in France, and in Bavaria and Bohemia. The worst anti-semitic violence occurred in the Rhineland, where the large and well-established Jewish population of Mainz was virtually annihilated in May 1096. Churchmen tried, with varying degrees of success, to stop these attacks. Nevertheless, every major crusading appeal during the 12th century set off fresh attacks against the Jews.

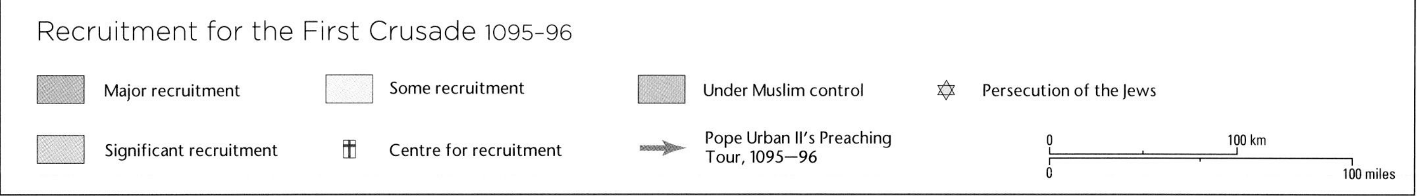

Recruitment for the First Crusade 1095–96

Major recruitment
Some recruitment
Under Muslim control
Persecution of the Jews
Significant recruitment
Centre for recruitment
Pope Urban II's Preaching Tour, 1095–96
0
100 km
0
100 miles
SWEDEN
SCOTLAND
Edinburgh
Aarhus
Lund
North Sea
IRELAND
Dublin
DENMARK
York
WALES
ENGLAND
Bremen
London
POLAND
Kanten
Cologne
Boulogne
Lille
Arras
Wessili
ATLANTIC OCEAN
Lorraine
KINGDOM OF GERMANY
Normandy
Beavais
Mainz
Prague
Rouen
Rheims
Trier
Worms
Champagne
Brittany
Chartres
Metz
Speyer
Regensburg
Etampes
Le Mans
Poitou
Angers
Blois
Vienna
Poitiers
Dijon
Maillezais
Nevers
Besancon
Aquitaine
Burgundy
HUNGARY
FRANCE
Lyon
Aquileia
Bordeaux
Trieste
Le Puy
Milan
Venice
Oveido
Gascony
Genoa
Nimes
Provence
Toulouse
St. Gilles
BYZANTINE EMPIRE
LEON AND CASTILE
Zara
NAVARRE
Marseille
Pisa
Florence
ARAGON
Ragusa
MUSLIM STATES
BARCELONA
Corsica
Barcelona
Rome
Bari
Naples
Salerno
Brindisi
Taranto
Valencia
Balearic Islands
KINGDOM OF BALEARES
Sardinia
DUCHY OF APULIA
ALMORAVID EMPIRE
Mediterranean Sea
County of Sicily
Algiers
Carthage
HAMMADID DOMINION

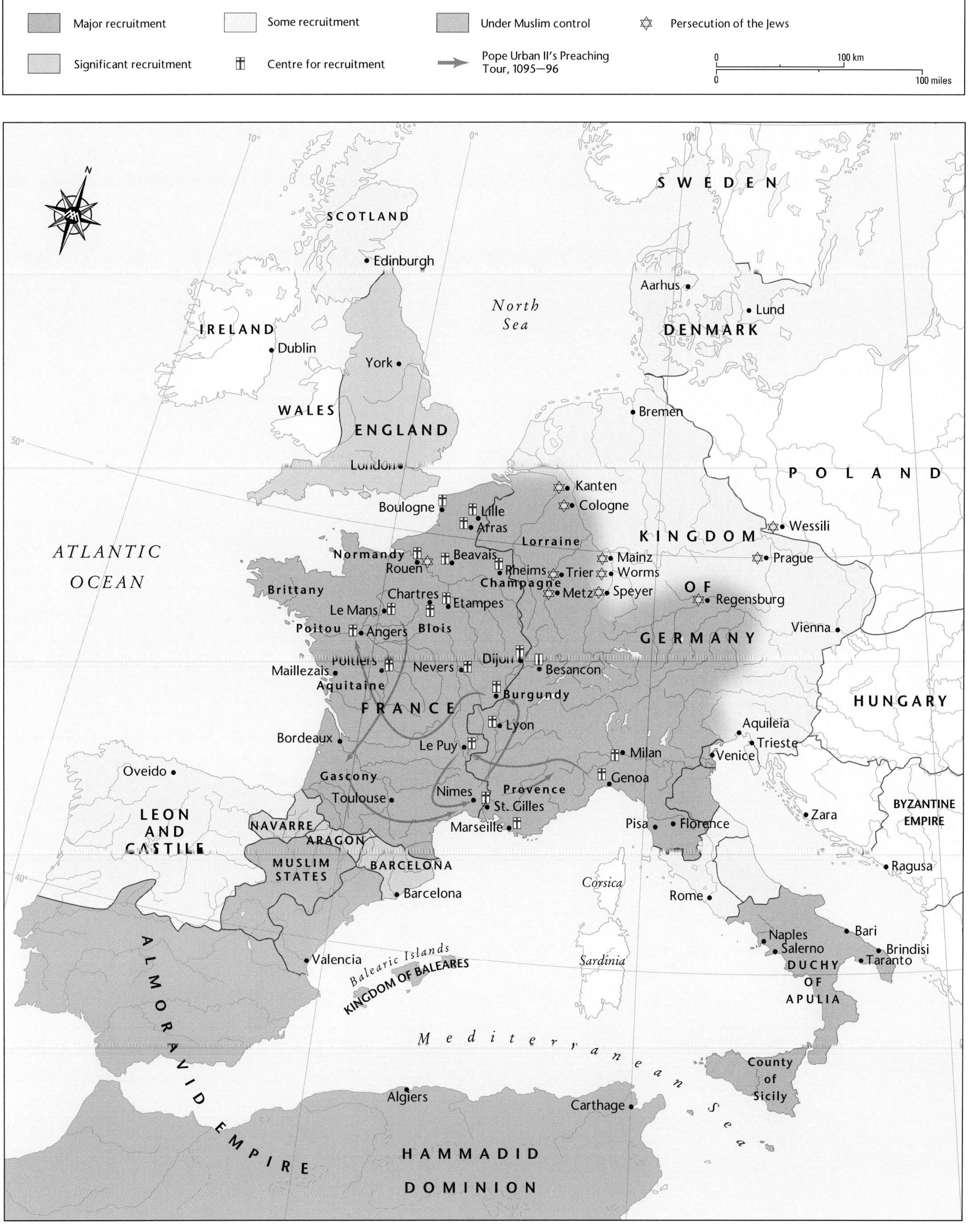

The First Crusade and Siege of Jerusalem

THE FIRST CRUSADERS FACED a daunting task. After a long and arduous journey through Europe, they passed through the Byzantine Empire, where they were met with a lukewarm welcome and some outright hostility. Once in Asia Minor they were isolated within enemy territory, with no regular supply points.

The crusaders left in three successive waves. The majority of the first contingent, which left early in 1096, never reached Asia Minor; only the crusaders under the command of Peter the Hermit reached their goal, where they were massacred by the combined forces of the Seljuks and Danismends (Anatolian nomads).

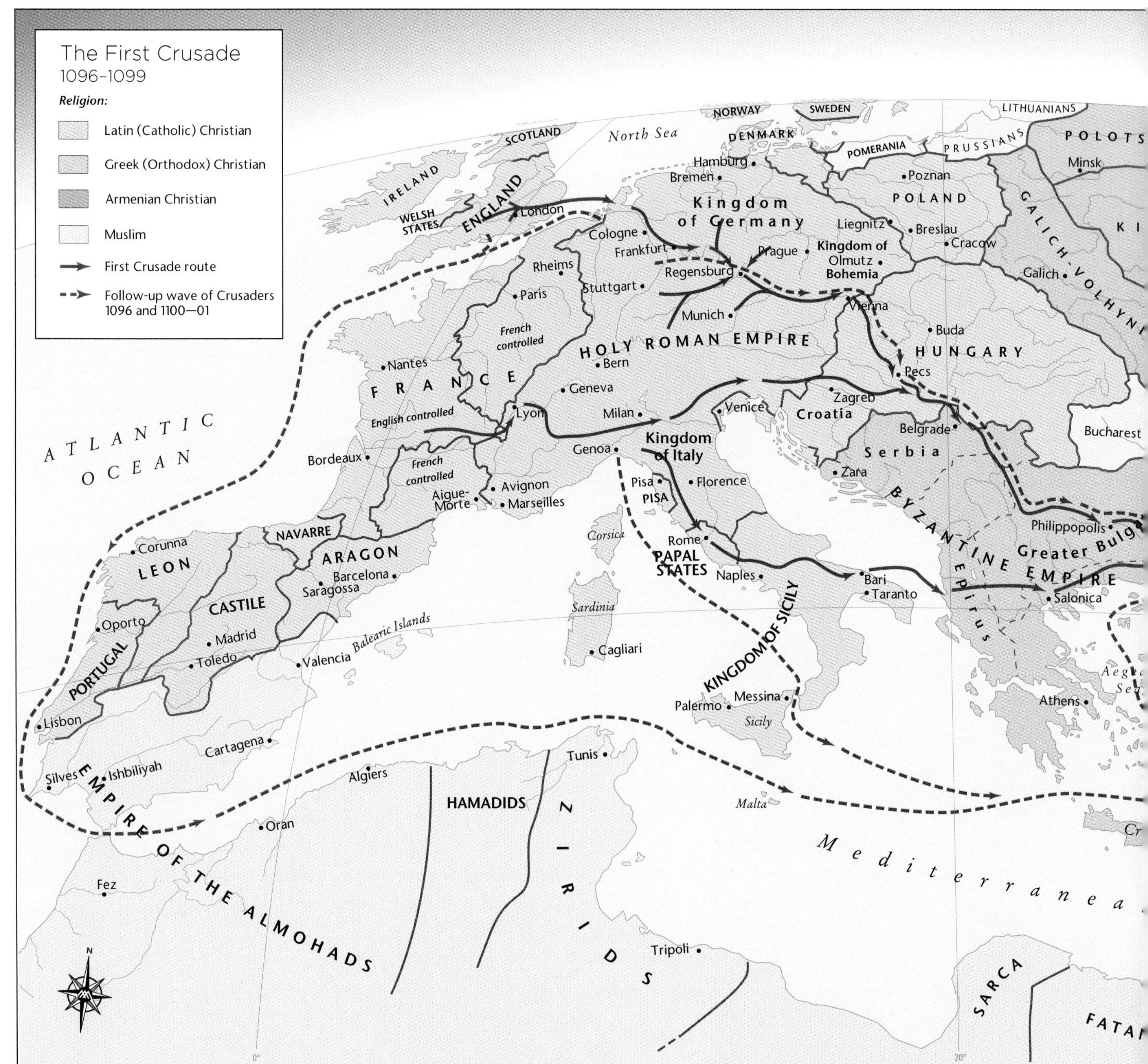

In June 1097 the second wave of crusaders captured Nicaea, the first major city to be taken from Muslim control. During that winter most of the army's pack animals died, and four out of five knights were left horseless as they traveled north to avoid the mountain passes, before sweeping down toward Antioch. Here they embarked on a siege that lasted seven and a half months, characterized by near-starvation – many knights had to forage as far as 50 miles away from the city – and increasing inertia.

But in March 1098 Baldwin of Boulogne captured the county of Edessa, establishing the first crusader state and setting up a buffer zone and supply point for much-needed provisions. The crusader states that were subsequently founded were outposts of Latin Christendom in the Levant, quasi-colonial enterprises surrounded by much larger and wealthier Islamic states.

The crusaders reached Jerusalem on 7 June 1099; their numbers by now were severely depleted and they had no appetite for a prolonged siege. After their first assault on the city was repulsed, they exploited the arrival of a contingent of Genoese mariners who stripped their ships to build effective siege engines. On 15 July 1099 the crusaders captured Jerusalem, and went on to defeat a large Egyptian army at Ascalon.

Isolated, depleted, and alienated, the crusaders viewed their victory as nothing short of miraculous. Their occupation of Muslim territory was brutal; they were determined to expel all the Muslims and Jews, leaving behind an indigenous Christian population that would, they hoped, soon be supplemented by western settlers.

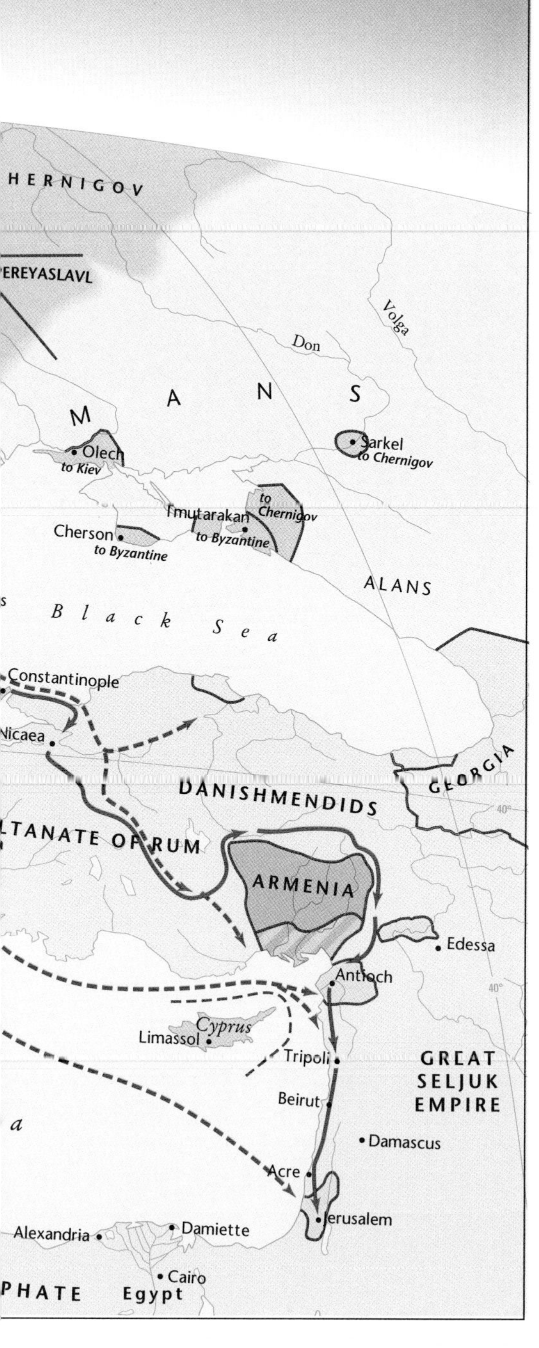

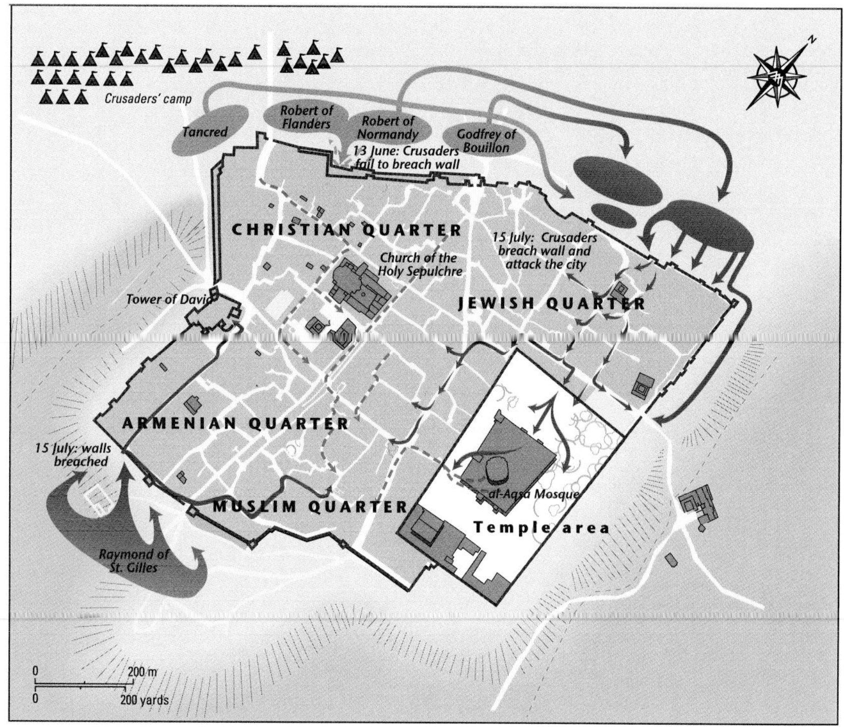

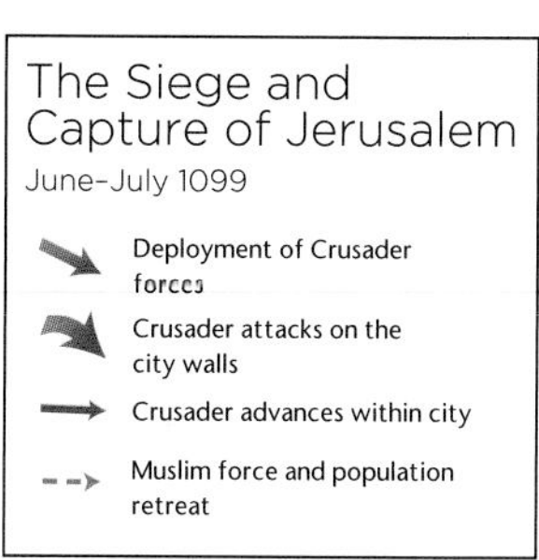

The Siege and Capture of Jerusalem
June–July 1099

The Second and Third Crusades

Galvanized by the Christian capture of Jerusalem, and outraged by the atrocities that were perpetrated by the Christian invaders, the Muslims formulated a strong military response and recaptured Edessa in 1144. Pope Eugenius called for a new crusade, enlisting Bernard, abbot of Clairvaux and major leader of the reform of Benedectine monasaticism, as the main preacher of the crusading ideal. He offered the knights an irresistible bargain; in return for taking the cross they would gain full remission for any unconfessed venial sins, allowing them to enter Heaven without passing through Purgatory. On Easter Day 1146 Louis VII and his nobles took the cross at Vézelay.

The two main forces were under the command of Louis VII of France and Conrad III of Germany, who reached Constantinople in the autumn of 1147, and headed to Edessa. Meanwhile other assorted crusaders made their own

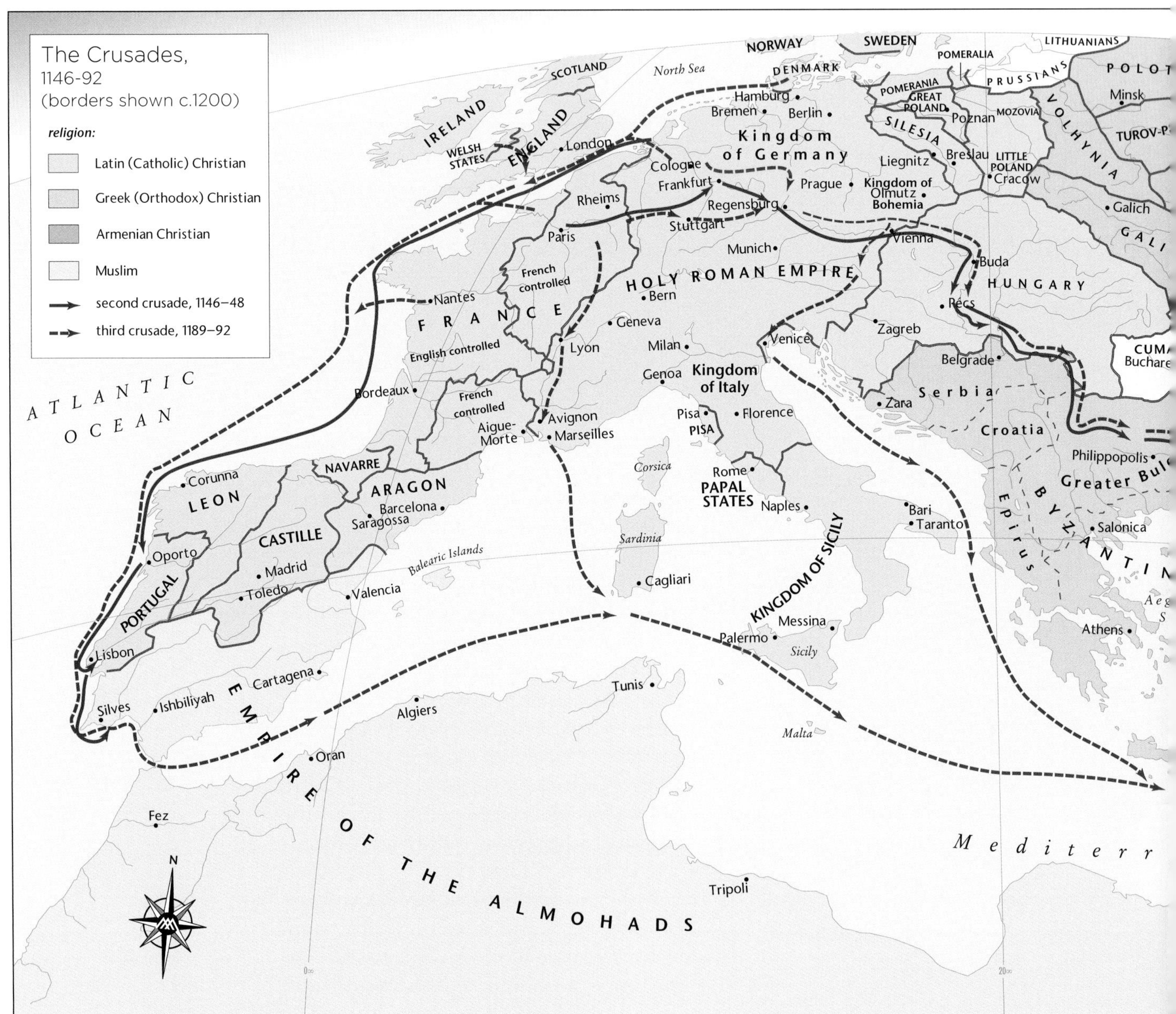

way directly to the Holy Land – some diverted en route to assist the King of Portugal capture Lisbon from the Moors in October 1147.

On arriving in Dorylaeum in Anatolia Conrad led his army into battle with the Turks in October 1147, but was heavily defeated. The remnants of his army joined up with the French, who were making their way along the coast to Adalia and Edessa. Agreeing that their disparate forces would combine to attack Damascus, they made an ignominious withdrawal when they found themselves under heavy attack. This debacle eroded crusading enthusiasm in the West and repeated calls for assistance were ignored over the next three decades.

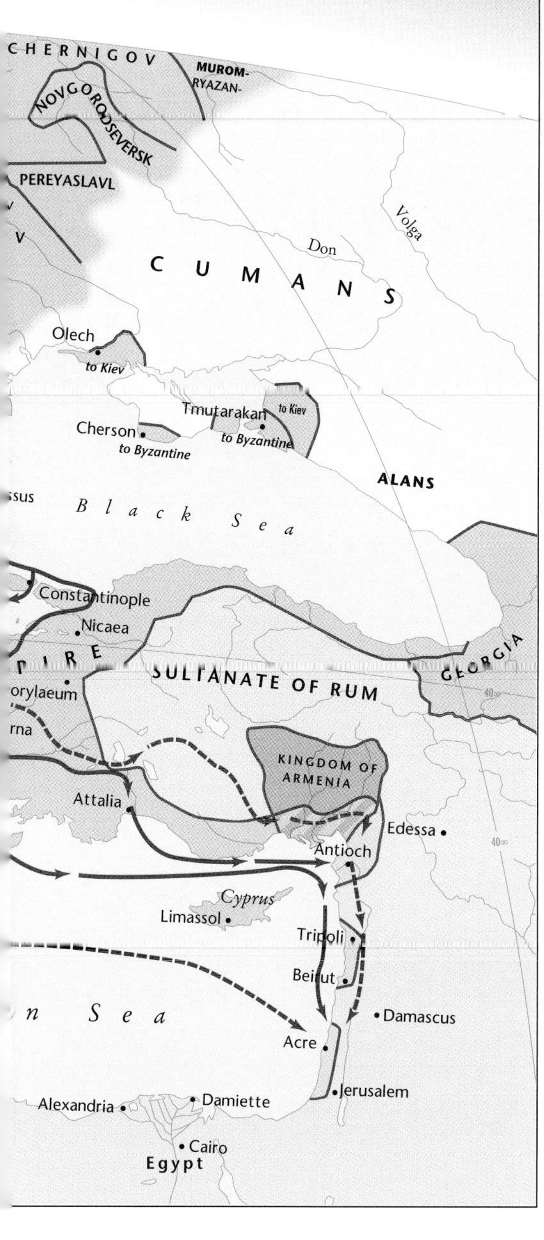

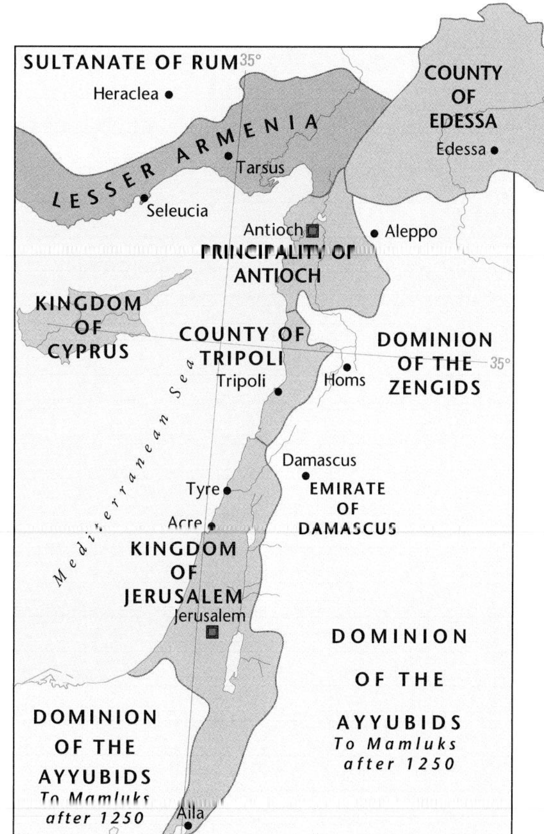

Crusader States to 1291

Latin Patriarchates

Although the Third Crusade failed in its main objective, Jerusalem, it did allow the Franks to retain a narrow coastal strip of crusader states, which could be used as a springboard for future expeditions.

In 1187 the Muslim leader Saladin wiped out a Christian army at Hattin, near Lake Tiberias, and swept through the Holy Land, driving out the crusaders from Palestine and Syria and recapturing Jerusalem, causing grief and outrage in the West. A further crusade, spearheaded by Richard of Poitou (later Richard I of England), headed to Acre in 1190. The German emperor, Frederick Barbarossa, at the head of a massive army, drowned in a river in Asia Minor on 10 June 1190. Richard took Acre in July 1191; over the next two years he marched twice to within a few miles of Jerusalem, but failed to take the city. On 2 September 1192 he signed a treaty whereby the Christians retained control of the coast between Acre and Jaffa, and were allowed to visit the Holy Sepulchre in Jerusalem.

The Apogee of Papal Power

THE INVESTITURE CONTROVERSY was a struggle between Pope Gregory VII and King Henry VI of Germany over Henry's assertion that he had the right to invest ecclesiastical officeholders with the symbols of power. Gregory's *Dictatus Papae* (1075) asserted the pope's place as the highest authority in the church and papal prestige was restored with the launch of the First Crusade in 1095. Innocent III (r. 1198–1216) was one of the most influential of the medieval popes, who claimed supremacy over Europe's temporal rulers and was ambitous to bring the papacy to the forefront of medieval politics. His boldest maneuvers were directed towards avoiding the encirclement of the papal states by the Holy Roman Empire. After asserting the papal prerogative to "anoint, consecrate and crown" any imperial candidate, he eventually saw his choice, Frederick II, prevail through force of arms at the Battle of Bouvines (1214).

His crusades against the heretical Cathars, spurred on by the assassination of a papal legate, were both ruthless and effective. He sponsored the Fourth Crusade, only for it to take a

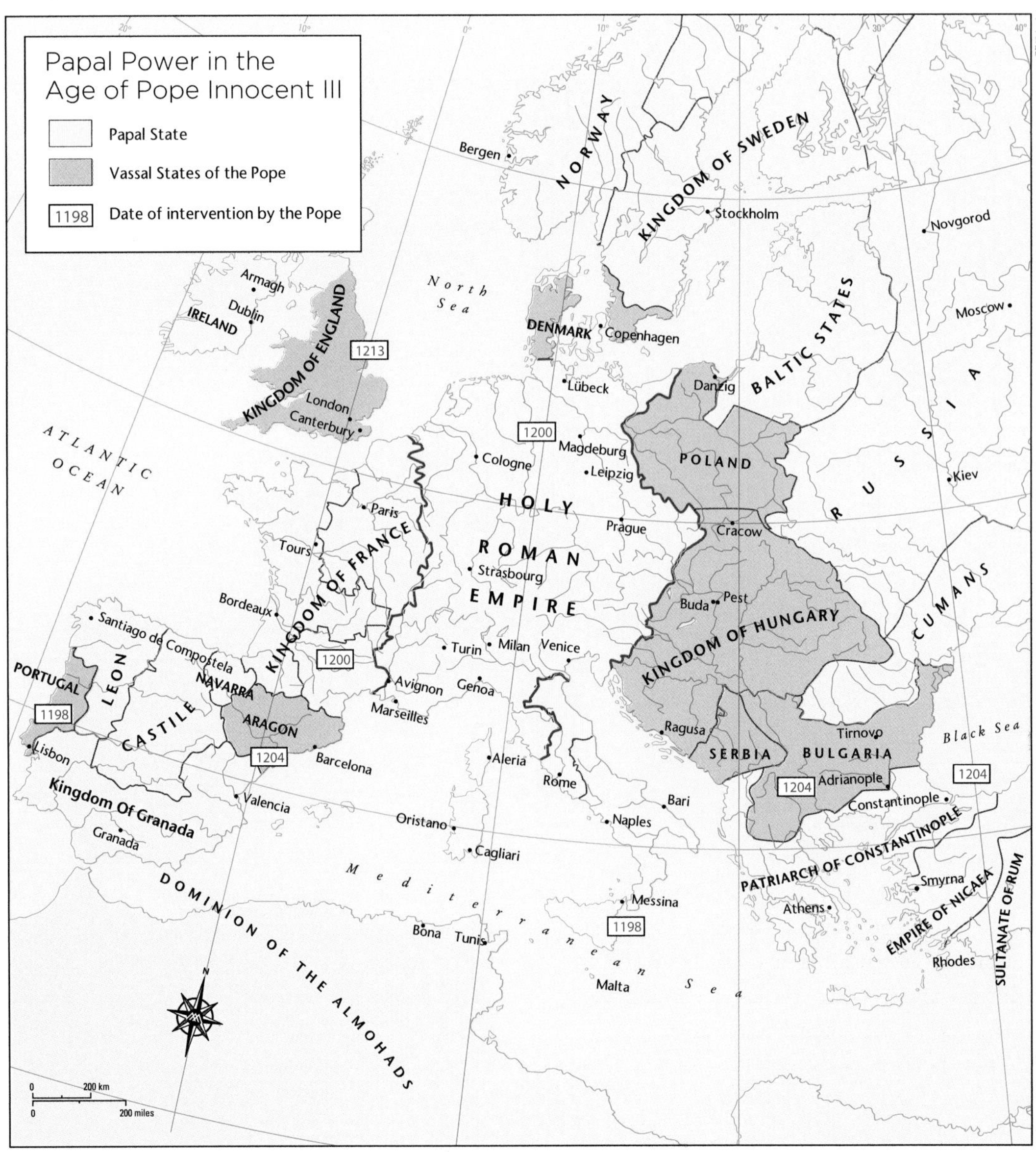

disastrous turn with the sacking of Constantinople by the crusading armies. Yet, he exploited this debacle to create the Latin Empire, extending his sway over the whole church.

He approved the foundation of the Dominican and Franciscan mendicant orders. At the Fourth Lateran Council (1215) far-reaching ecclesiastical reform was instituted, including the approval of the term "transubstantiation" to describe the eucharistic miracle, as well as new regulations aimed at bringing preaching and the sacrament of confession to the entire Christian population. Papally led reform was from now on going to reach into every parish in Christendom.

The Fourth Crusade: Siege of Constantinople

THIS MOST INFAMOUS CRUSADE (1202–04) saw another attempt to take Jerusalem, but ended up with the sacking of Constantinople, the greatest Christian city in the world. Called by Pope Innocent III in August 1198, the original destination was to be Egypt, the center of Muslim power in the Near East. The Venetian Republic agreed to provide the transport that would ship some 35,000 crusaders to Egypt. and the crusaders agreed to assist the Venetians in recovering Zara, on the Adriatic Sea, lost to Hungary in 1186. The pope repudiated their decision to attack a Christian city and excommunicated both them and their Venetian allies.

In January 1203 the crusaders entered into an agreement with the Byzantine prince Alexios

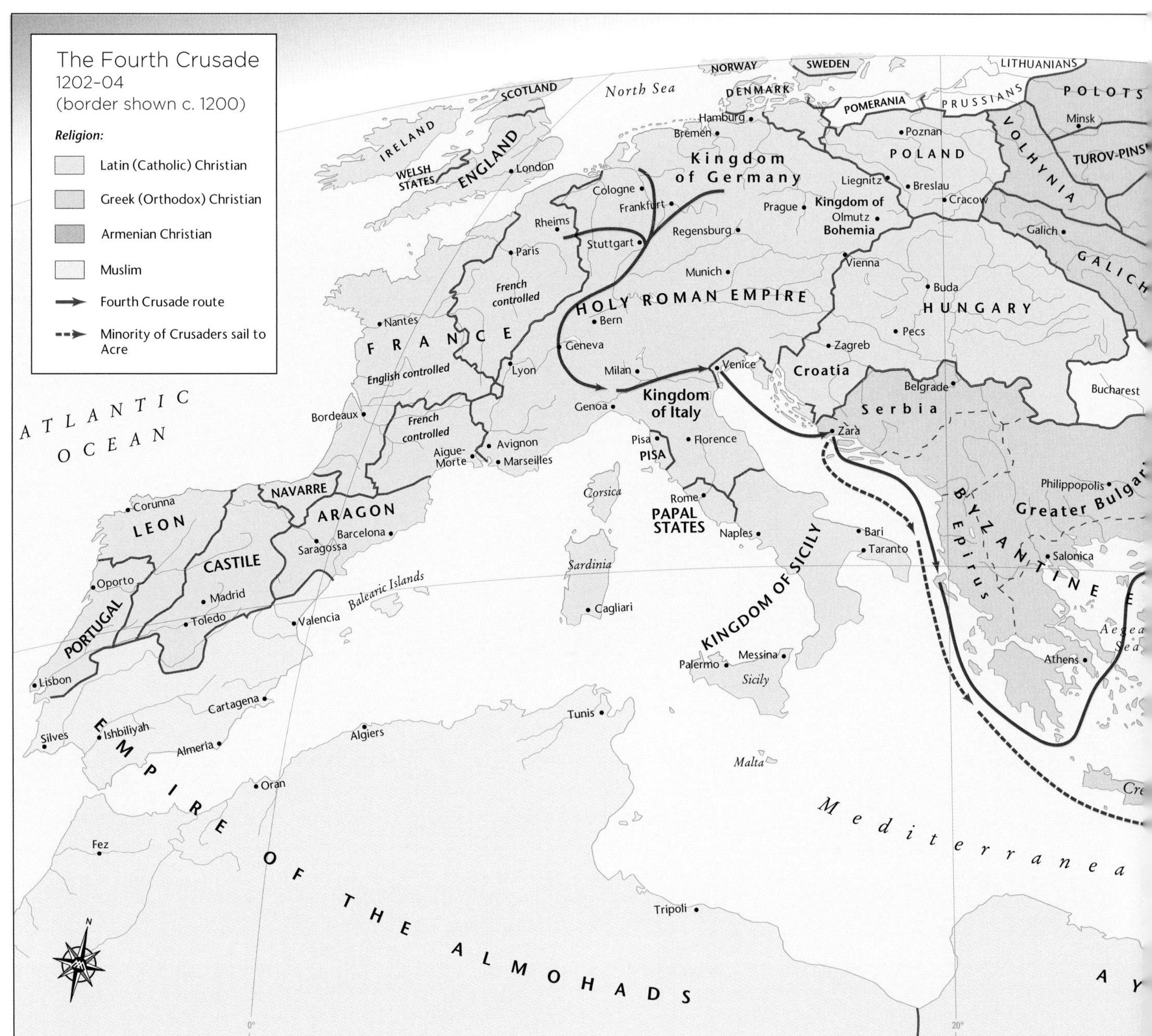

Angelos to divert to Constantinople and reinstate his deposed father on the throne, in return for a payment of 200,000 marks. On 17 July, following a general assault, Alexios IV was crowned co-emperor with his father. The people of Constantinople bitterly resented the terms of his agreement with the crusaders, who were still awaiting payment, and anti-western

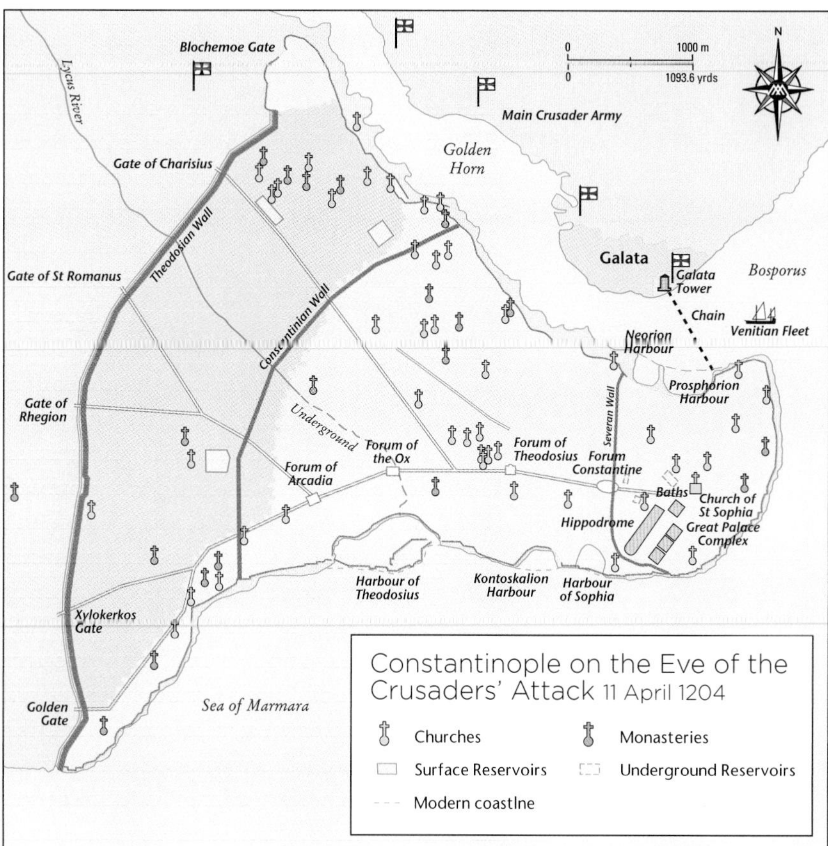

Constantinople on the Eve of the Crusaders' Attack 11 April 1204

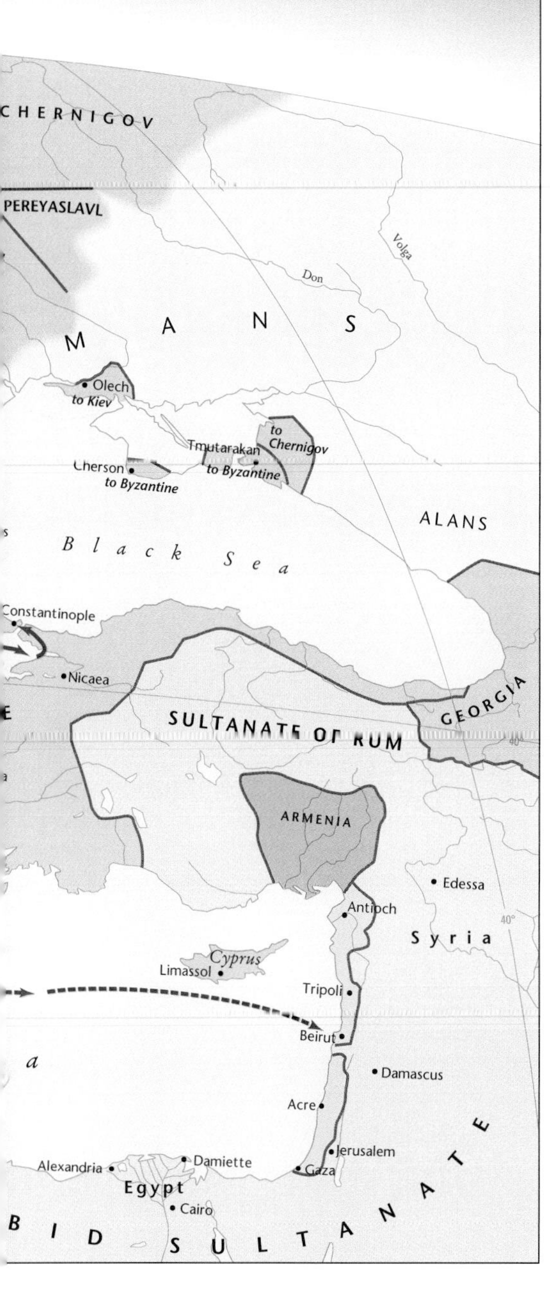

feelings erupted into rioting and street fighting. In January 1204 the co-emperors were deposed and murdered and the crusaders, unable to claim the money they felt was due to them, decided to take Constantinople for themselves. On 12 April they forced their way through the city's gates. and an orgy of terrible violence was unleashed, leading to the massacre of 400,000 of the city's defenders and inhabitants. After three days of looting and pillaging the city's cultural and religious artefacts, including the invaluable manuscripts housed in the library, Constantinople was in the cruaders' hands. They had dealt a crippling blow to the Byzantine Empire, which fragmented into three rump states, centered on Nicaea, Trebizond, and Epirus. The Latin Empire of Constantinople – a collection of new crusader states within former Byzantine territory – was established and Count Baldwin of Flanders was crowned the first Latin emperor.

The disastrous crusade left an enduring legacy of mistrust and betrayal amongst Greek Christians, reinforcing the schism between the churches in the East and West.

The Latin East

FOLLOWING THE FALL OF CONSTANTINOPLE in 1204 much of the Byzantine Empire was partitioned amongst newly created crusader states. The Latin emperors of the houses of Flanders and Courtenay controlled the territory around Constantinople itself. The newly founded kingdom of Thessalonika formed an arc around the northern Aegean. In Morea (the Peloponnese) Geoffrey of Villehardouin established the principality of Achaia.

At their capital, Andravida, in the northern Peloponnese, the Villehardouin family maintained a brilliant chivalric court. They ran their state on feudal lines, and the prince's chief vassals were the high barons, including the archbishop of Patras, many of whom built spectacular castles. Latin bishoprics, archbishoprics and abbeys were established in some of the Latin centers, but most of the Latin clergy were absentee and the majority of the local population adhered to the Greek Orthodox church. The prince of Achaia was overlord of other Latin rulers, including the lords of Thebes and Athens, the dukes of the Archipelago (the Aegean islands) and the Orsini family of Cephalonia.

Latin rule in the East was never secure, and some of that instability derived from the concessions that had been made to the Venetians in order to secure their assistance during the Fourth Crusade. The Venetians controlled a large part of Constantinople itself and occupied Crete from 1212, where they set up a colonial regime with Italian settlers. The dukes of the Archipelago, in the Aegean Sea, were a Venetian family, the Sanudos, who held their island territory as a fiefdom of the princes of Achaia.

Two surviving outposts of Byzantine rule, founded by Byzantine aristocrats who had fled Constantinople after the Fourth Crusade, remained: Nicaea and Epirus. In 1224 the des-

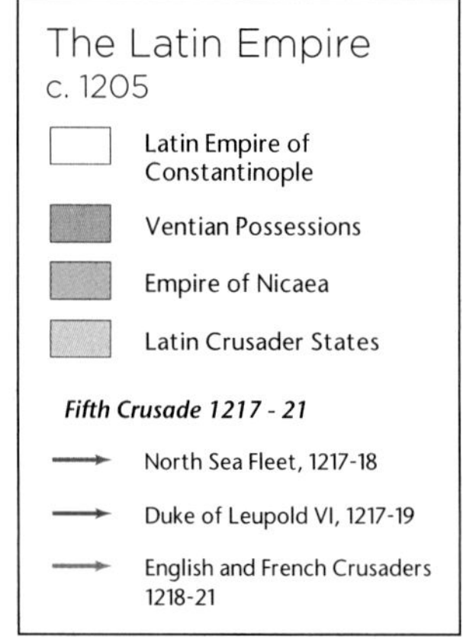

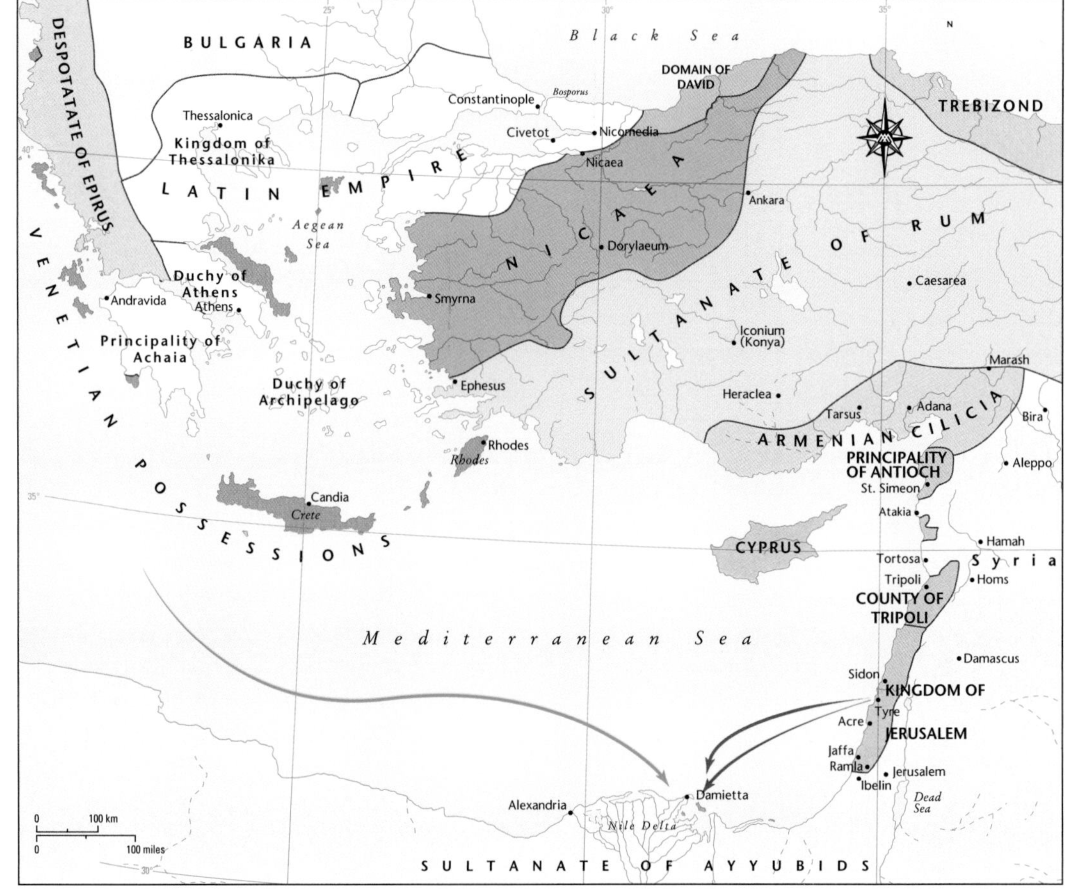

potate of Epirus conquered the Latin kingdom of Thessalonika. The empire of Nicaea began expanding its territory in 1225 under the leadership of John III Doukas Vatatzes. The first territories he acquired were ceded from the rival Latin Empire immediately to the north, following an unsuccessful coup against him, for which the Latin Empire had provided support. John III formed an alliance with the Second Bulgarian Empire over the next 20 years and gradually reduced the power of the Latin Empire, which held on to Constantinople until 1261.

As with all the Latin states, the Orthodox church was replaced by the Roman Catholic church, but not actually suppressed. A Catholic hierarchy was established under the dual authority of the archbishop of Constantinople and the papal legate. Western monastic orders, such as the Cistercians, Dominicans, and Franciscans, were established in the empire. While the Orthodox clergy retained their rites and customs, they were subordinate to the Catholic hierarchy.

To the west of the Latin Empire the short-lived kingdom of Thessalonika was annexed by the empire of Nicaea in 1246 after an internal power struggle, along with other territories in the region belonging to the Second Bulgarian Empire. Nicaea became increasingly powerful and assertive, defeating William of Villehardouin at the Battle of Pelagonia in 1259. The Seljuk Empire on Nicaea's eastern frontier was coming under attack from the Mongol Empire which allowed Nicaea to focus pressure on its western rivals and eventually reunite the former heartland of the Byzantine Empire in 1261 when the emperor of Nicaea, Michael Palaeologus, recaptured Constantinople, re-establishing the Byzantine Empire. Trebizond and Epirus remained independent Byzantine states. The principality of Achaia survived but when William died in 1275 it was passed on to his son-in-law, Philip of Anjou, the son of Charles I of Naples, and from this point on it was ruled from Italy.

Constantinople was once again the capital of the reinstated, but much weakened, Byzantine Empire, which embarked on a series of wars against the Latin states and Epirus. This left its eastern borders undefended against Turkish invasions, leading to the eventual fall of the Byzantine Empire to the Ottoman Turks in 1453.

The Crusader States and Military Orders

Cross of the Order of the Hospital of Saint John in Jerusalem, commonly known as the Knights Hospitaller. The Order arose in Jerusalem in the 11th century and in 1099, following the conquest of Jerusalem in the First Crusade, received a papal charter and was charged with the defense of the Holy Land,

FREDERICK II'S GAINS IN THE HOLY LAND, agreed in the Treaty of Jaffa (1229) were extended by the crusade of 1239–41, led by Count Thibald of Champagne and Earl Richard of Cornwall. Despite Thibald's defeat at Gaza, the ensuing negotiations left the kingdom of Jerusalem controlling more territory than at any time since 1187.

The ports of Acre and Tyre brought commerce and prosperity to the European settlers. In addition the crusader states extended to Cyprus and the Anatolian mainland. Richard I of England had invaded Cyprus in 1191 and, when it proved difficult to govern, he sold it to the Knights Templar in 1192. The crusader states also enjoyed relations with the Christian kingdom of Armenia, also known as Cilician Armenia, which was founded by Armenians fleeing the Seljuk invasion. The kingdom submitted to the papacy and was heavily influenced by western culture.

However, relations between the Christian states were always fraught with tensions. The royal family of Armenia and the princes of Antioch were related by marriage and contested for control for the principality of Antioch – in the 13th century the Armenians launched a series of invasions, briefly occupying Antioch in 1216. In the following decade civil war broke out on Cyprus, which was ruled by five Cypriot knights, the *baillis,* under the overlordship of Frederick II. In 1229 John of Ibelin, the crusader Lord of Beirut, invaded Cyprus and the struggle, which extended to the mainland, lasted for four years, ending with John's victory.

An increasingly important locus of power in the crusader states was the so-called military orders. Their emergence can be dated to the early 12th century, when a French knight called Hugh of Payns formed a small brotherhood to defend the pilgrim road to Jerusalem. The brothers were given part of the Temple enclosure as their headquarters in the holy city and were henceforth known as the Knights Templar. The Hospital of St John in Jerusalem had been founded as a charitable institution in the 11th century. The Hospitallers, or Knights of St John, began to assume military responsibilities in the 1130s. The members of the military orders were laymen, frequently titled knights. However, they cooperated closely with the clergy and in some instances took religious vows, such as poverty, obedience, and chastity. Templars and Hospitallers acquired extensive properties in the West and established convents that acted as recruiting centers for crusaders. The rulers in the Latin East, lacking manpower and resources, gave or sold strongholds to the orders, which were entrusted with the defence of frontier territory. The military orders exercised a powerful influence in military and political counsels.

Most of the military orders' castles in Syria had been lost in the aftermath of the Battle of Hattin (1187). But once the crusaders regained control of the Levant in the early 13th century the orders' holdings increased again. Some castles were recaptured as the Christians advanced; some were new constructions; some were passed on to the Christian orders by knights who could no longer defend them. A growing number of strongholds in the kingdom of Jerusalem passed under the control of the Knights Hospitaller and the Templars. The Knights Hospitaller would evetually extend their control to the Byzantine island of Rhodes, which they conquered in 1310, and Malta (1530).

The Teutonic Order was formed in Acre in 1192 to assist pilgrims in the Holy Land and to establish hospitals. After the loss of the Holy Land in 1291 the Teutonic Knights, who had already consolidated their position in pagan Prussia, Pomerelia, Neumark, and Livonia, become a powerful trans-European organization with their headquarters in Magdeburg.

The crusader states engaged in trade and diplomacy with their Muslim neighbors, but an attempt to intervene in Muslim politics by allying with the prince of Damascus against the sultan in Egypt led to the loss of Jerusalem and a defeat by the Egyptian army at La Forbie in 1244. After 1250 they would be faced with a new, more aggressive power, the Mamluks.

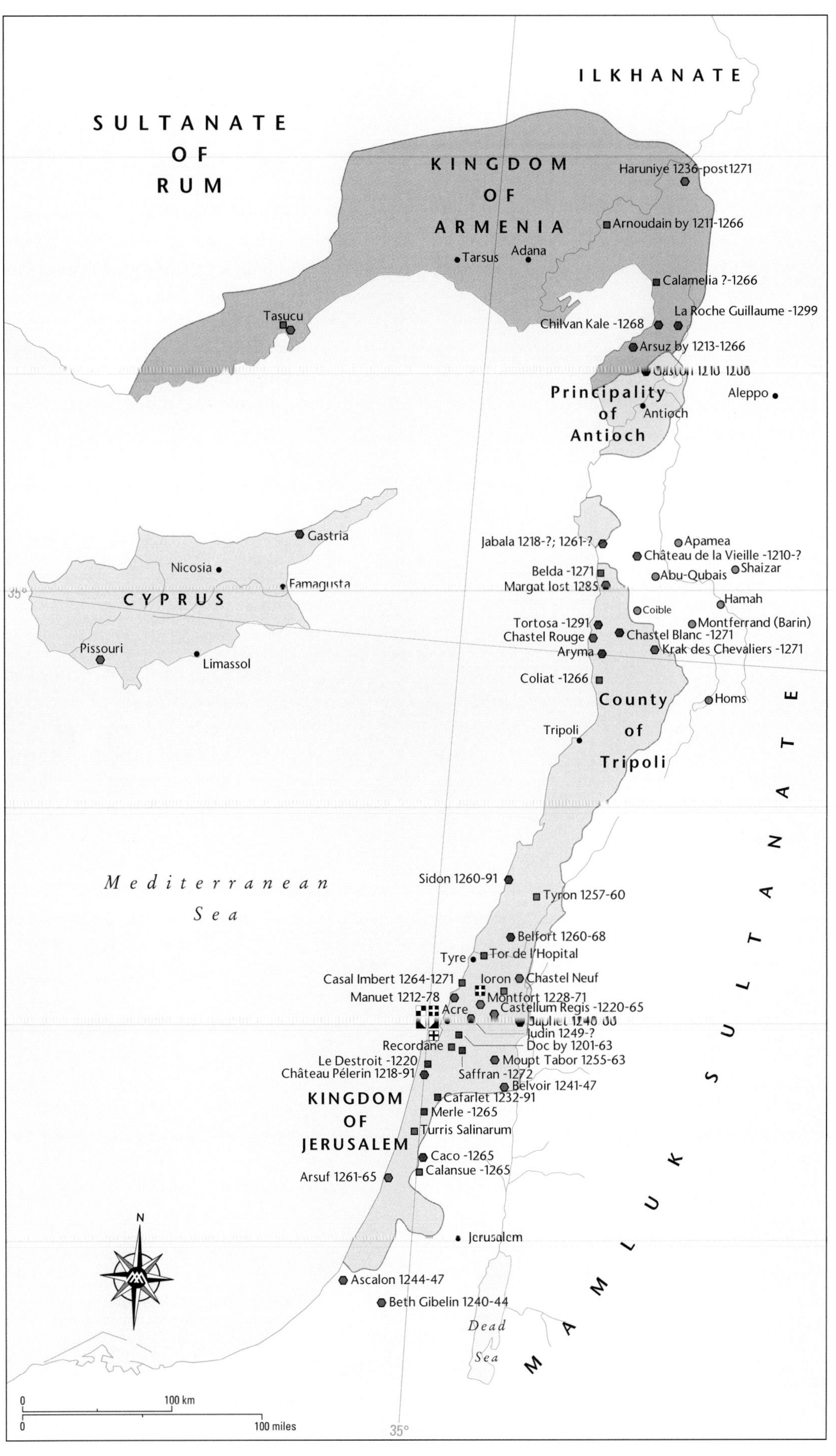

Military Orders in the Latin East, 1197-1291

The Final Crusades

By the 13th century holy war was becoming a flexible concept, allowing the church to act against its enemies on many fronts, with the rationale that Christians were being protected. Emperor Frederick II was already in conflict with the papacy over control of southern Italy and his refusal to join the Fifth Crusade (1217–21) earned him excommunication. Having married the heiress to the throne of Jerusalem, Frederick made his way there, and used his diplomatic and linguistic skills to negotiate the peaceful, although short-lived, restoration of the city to the Christians (1229–44), something the crusade had failed to achieve.

Louis IX of France (r. 1226–70), commonly known as St Louis, was canonized in 1297 for his services to the cross. A zealous and devout Christian, he spent four years preparing his crusade (1248–54) to recover Jerusalem. Many of the great nobles of France took the cross, taking retinues of lesser knights and peasants with them. The church paid a tenth of its ecclesiastical revenues for five years, covering two-thirds of Louis's expenses for this enormously expensive campaign. The successful mobilization in France was not matched elsewhere in Europe, where political rivalries minimized support, so Louis's army of some 15,000 men was mainly drawn from France, with some support from Lorraine, Italy, Scotland, and England.

Louis landed in Cyprus in 1248, where his army gradually mustered before setting off to the original goal of the Fourth Crusade, Egypt. Despite taking the Egyptian port of Damietta at the mouth of the Nile in 1249, they were eventually halted on their march to Cairo, and a large contingent was slaughtered at Mansurah (1250).

Louis's army, depleated and disease-ravaged, retreated to Damietta and, on 6 April, Louis was surrounded and forced to surrender. He was released just a month later after paying a huge ransom and sailed on to Acre, where he remained for four years. Here, he effectively took over the government and fortified the citadels at Acre, Jaffa, Caesarea, and Sidon. He finally left for France in April 1254.

In the 1250s the crusader states of the Holy Land were under threat from the Mongols, who established a garrison at Gaza and attacked Sidon in 1260. The Mamluk general (later sultan) Baibars was a ferocious exponent of *jihad* (holy war), who staged a fightback, driving the Mongols back to the Euphrates, capturing Caesarea and Arsuf, and the Knights Hospitaller

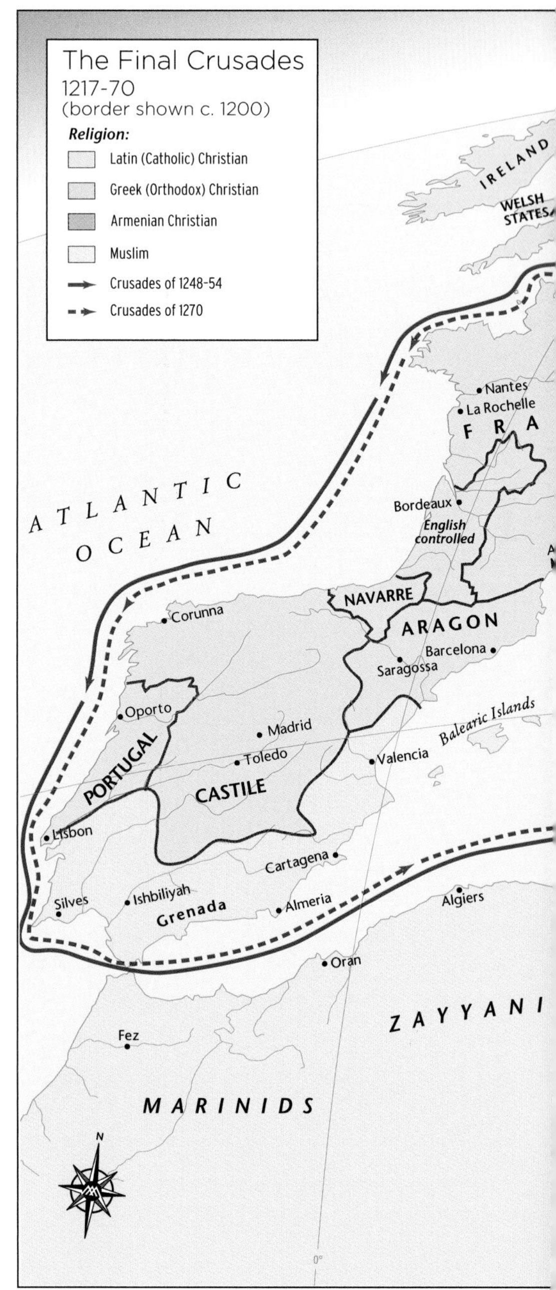

stronghold of Krak des Chevaliers.

On 24 March 1267 Louis took the cross again. Tunis, ruled by Emir Muhammad I, would be his destination, as it would provide a solid base from which to attack the Nile. On landing in Tunis in 1270 many of the crusaders were immediately struck down by dysentery; Louis died on 25 August, and the remaining crusaders negotiated a treaty with Muhammad I.

By this stage the Mamluks were ascendant in the Levant, and many European rulers were preoccupied by their own domestic battles, while the papacy was locked in conflict with the Holy Roman Empire over Siciliy and southern Italy. With the fall of Acre in 1291, the Latin East and crusading era effectively came to an end.

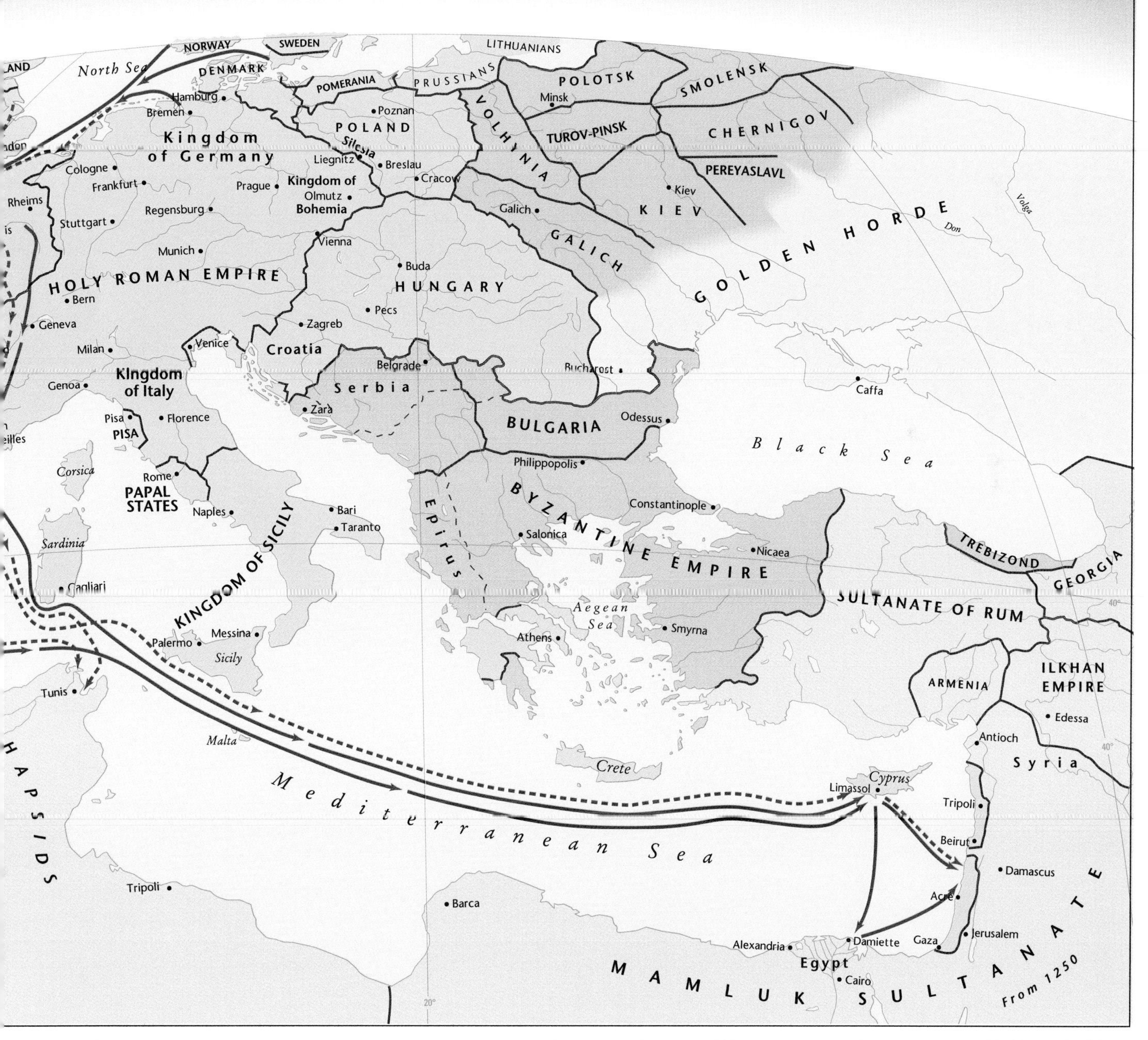

The Mongol Invasions

THE MONGOL TRIBES of northern China coalesced into the Mongol Empire, under the rule of Genghis Khan (?1167–1227) in 1206. He set in motion a series of invasions that would reverberate in Europe for the following 50 years.

The skill and mobility of Mongol horsemen was legendary; their archers and lancers were devastating. The tactics of the mounted Mongol archers owed much to nomadic hunting and herding practices.

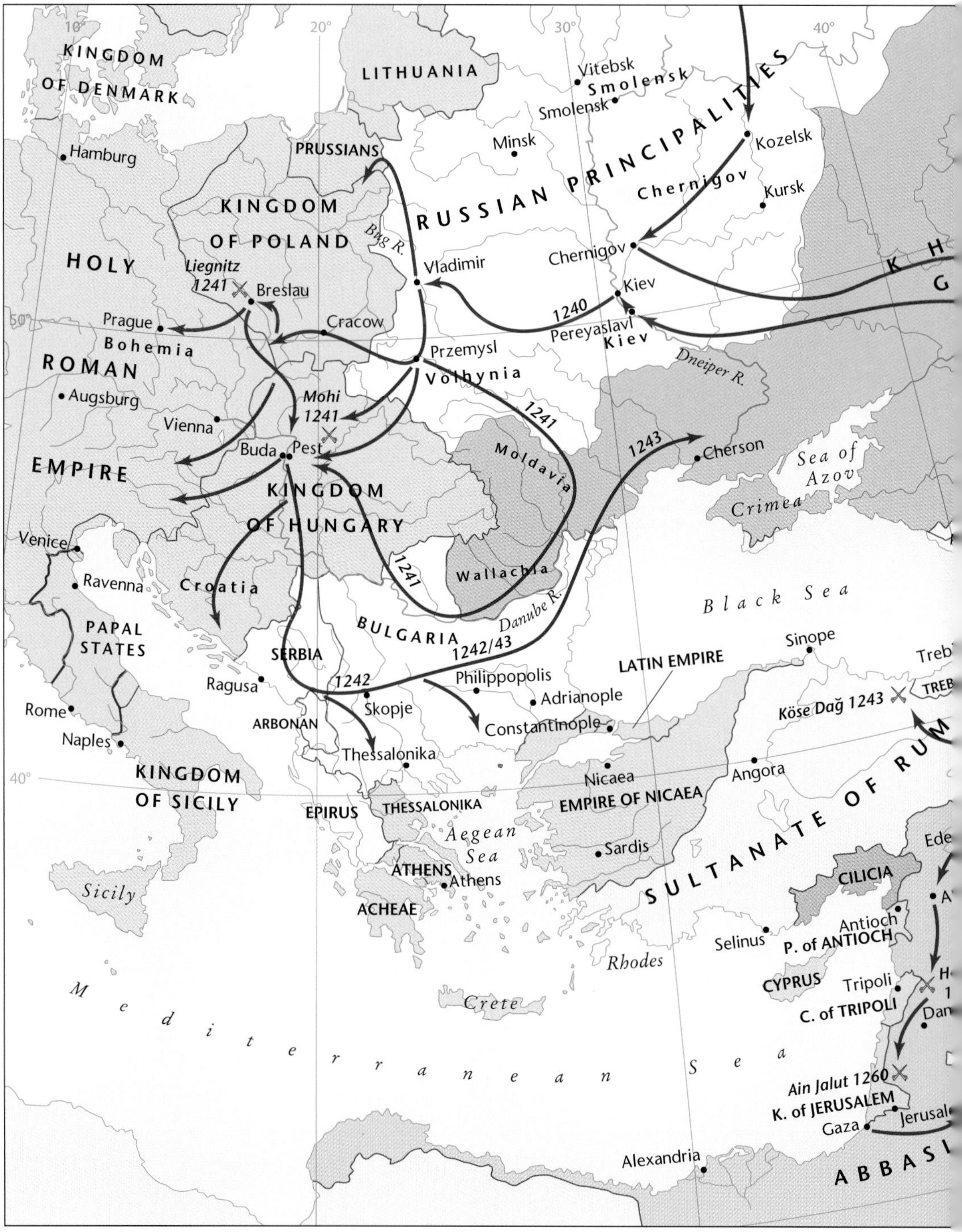

By the time of Genghis's death in 1227, his armies had conquered as far west as the Caspian, annihilating the Khwarizm Empire, and crushed the Chin and Xi Xia kingdoms of northern China. When one of his grandsons, Batu, invaded Russia and eastern Europe from 1236–42, the Mongols came into contact with Christian Europe for the first time. Following the Battle of the Sit River (1238), when the Russian forces were routed, Batu then split his forces, roaming south as far as the Crimea, subduing the principalities in turn. Unexpectedly leaving Novgorod untouched, the Mongol armies then advanced into eastern Europe, before the death of the Great Khan suspended operations. Crusades had been preached against them by a number of German bishops, followed by Popes Gregory IX and Innocent V, but little had come of them, and it was the withdrawal of Mongol forces, rather than the efforts of the crusaders, that gave eastern Europe a reprieve.

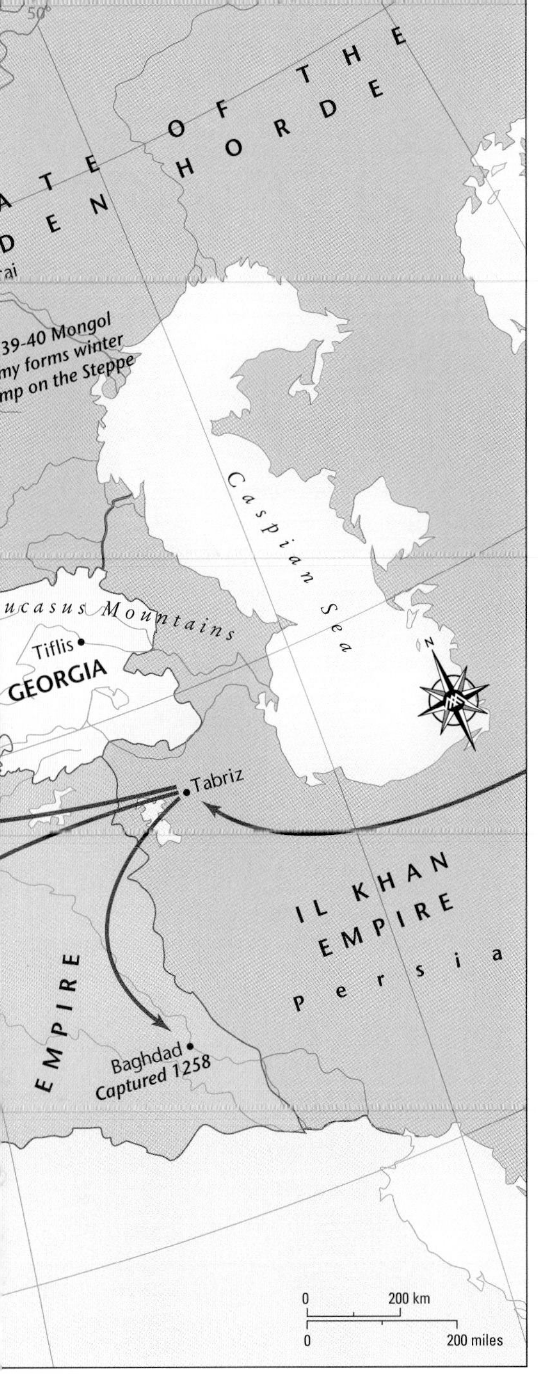

Another of Ghengis's grandsons, Hülegü, founded the Il-Khanid dynasty and took Baghdad in 1258, then turned his attentions to Syria, where he was defeated by the Mamluks at Ayn Jalut in 1260. The crusader states now faced a dilemma; the main enemy of the Mongols, the Mamluk sultanate, was also their foe, but they decided that the Mongols posed a greater threat, and adopted a policy of neutrality. The Mamluk army routed the Mongol aggressor in 1260 and Hülegü Khan was forced to retreat to Persia. Here he became embroiled in a civil war with his Mongol-Caucasian rival, Berke Khan.

From 1262 the Mongol Empire split into four separate khanates: the Great Khanate in China and Mongolia; the Chaghatai Khanate in Central Asia; the Golden Horde in Russia; and the Il-Khanate in Persia. When the Golden Horde formed an alliance with the Mamluks the Il-Khanate tried to combine forces with the Christians. Indeed, Franciscan and Dominican missionaries had traveled to Baghdad and founded many Christian convents within the Il-Khanate. But a military alliance with the Christians was never practicable and the Mongols of the Il-Khanate eventually converted to Islam, making peace with the Mamluks in 1322.

The Fall of Kievan Rus

Kievan Rus was a loose federation of Slavic lands that had coalesced from the 9th century. Under the rule of Vladimir (r. 980–1015) it became a loose federation of city-states, held together by the family bonds of the ruling princes, the Ruikovichi, who were descended from the Varangian chieftain Rurik. Vladimir ruled from the city of Kiev, and his twelve sons were the princes of the largest cities in Rus.

The Christian Varangians possessed their own church in Kiev by 944, but it was Vladimir who ordered the mass conversion of Kievan Rus to Christianity. Christianity co-existed with paganism for some time; people created Christian icon corners and shrines within their homes, while at the same time fearing household spirits, and venerating Nature. Finno-Ugric shamans continued to resent the new faith.

The Orthodox patriarch in Constantinople appointed a metropolitan bishop with his episcopal see in Kiev, and a bishop in each of the principalities, which became dioceses. Bishops had jurisdiction over crimes against religious law or church property, and were able to finance the church through the fines they levied. They also had licence to adjudicate upon family life and sexual behavior.

With Christianity came the practice of monasticism. A group of hermits living in caves above the Dnieper River formed the first monastery in Rus, evolving a model that combined asceticism, discipline, and communal living with social service within the community. The monks cared for prisoners, the poor, the physically disabled, and travelers. Monks and priests transcribed Byzantine texts and religious works, wrote hagiographies, histories and chronicles of the princely dynasties and cities, and produced texts that described pilgrimages to the holy places of the Near East.

New religious buildings, first in wood and then in stone, such as the Cathedral of St Sophia in Kiev, followed the precepts of Byzantine architecture. The construction of these buildings, along with the dissemination of religous texts and national histories by monastic communities all contributed to a strong sense of national unity in Kiev, which prospered as *entrepôt* and trading center between Novgorod and northern Europe, and Constantinople and the Near East.

The nomadic Mongols originated in the region of present-day Mongolia and when these various Turkic tribes were united under the outstanding military leadership of Genghis Khan, European peace and stability were threatened. The Mongols' first onslaught took them through the mountain passes between the Black and Caspian Seas to the southern steppes of Russia. Some of the Kievan princes joined forces with the Polovtsy, who dwelled in the area north of the Black Sea, to defend their territory against the Mongols, but were crushed at the Battle of Kalka River (1223). Genghis Khan's grandson, Batu, attacked the Volga Bulgars in 1236, crossing the Volga in 1237. For the next two years Vladimir-Suzdal was ravaged and many towns destroyed. Internal dissent between the various principalities weakened their defense, and by 1240 the Mongols had advanced deep into the heart of Russia, destroying Kiev.

The Kievan princes surrendered, along with the Republic of Novgorod, which was spared pillage because its prince had accepted Batu as his overlord. Batu had no interest in occupying Rus or directly ruling the Slavs; he allowed the ruling princes to govern in their territories, as long as they served his interests, for example by providing armies to fight on his behalf. The Russian princes had to provide tax or tribute to their Mongol overlords, who ruled in Russia for the next 200 years.

Invading Mongols had initially sacked and pillaged churches and monasteries, but the Mongols were tolerant in religious matters. Initially shamanist pagans, they eventually converted to Islam but remained tolerant toward Christianity. During the years of Mongol rule the Russian Orthodox church asserted itself as a beacon of national and religious identity. Exempted from taxation and protected by the Mongol authorities, the church became increasingly wealthy and powerful.

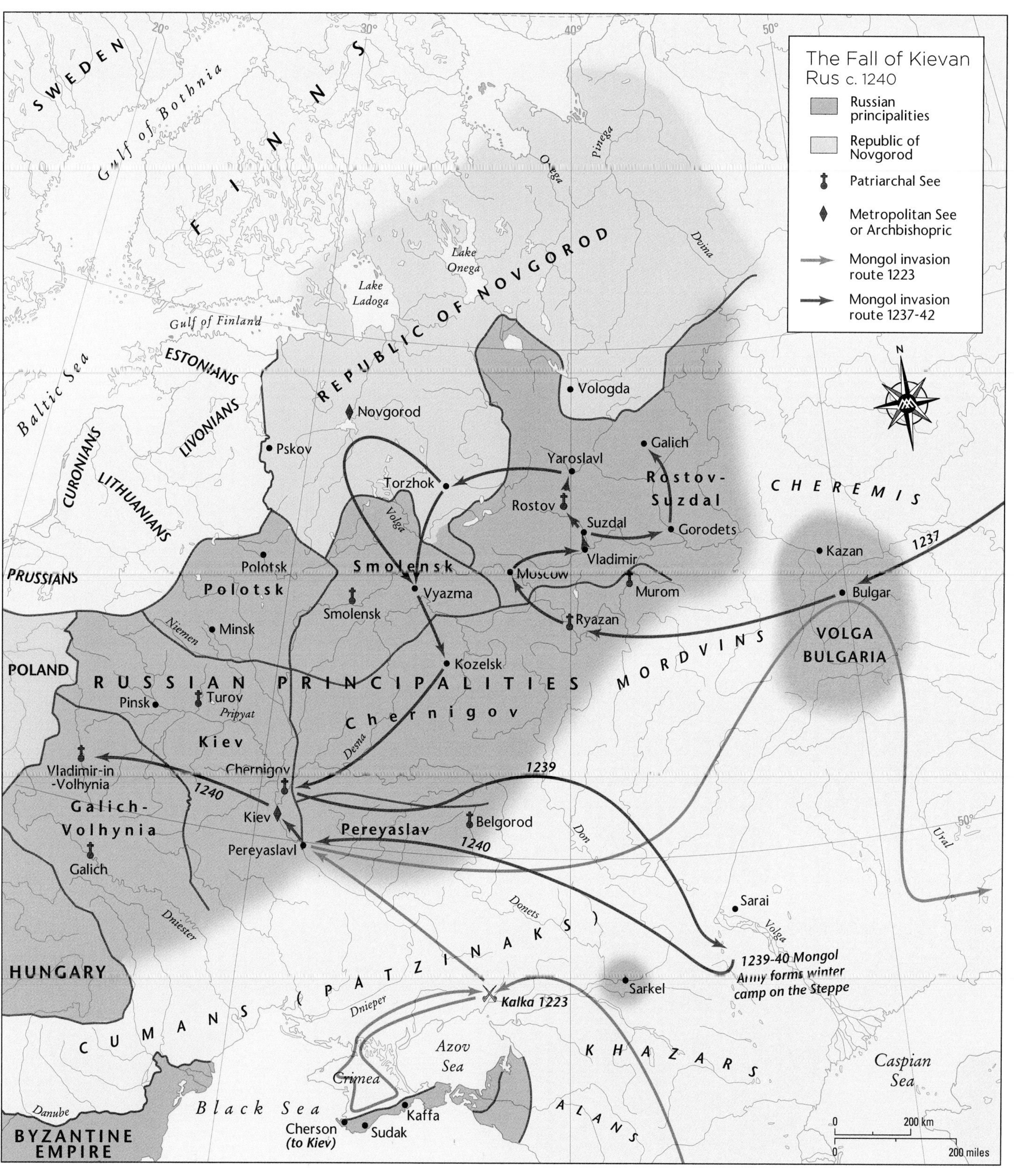
The Fall of Kievan Rus c. 1240
Russian principalities
Republic of Novgorod
Patriarchal See
Metropolitan See or Archbishopric
Mongol invasion route 1223
Mongol invasion route 1237-42
SWEDEN
Gulf of Bothnia
FINNS
REPUBLIC OF NOVGOROD
Lake Onega
Lake Ladoga
Gulf of Finland
Baltic Sea
ESTONIANS
LIVONIANS
CURONIANS
LITHUANIANS
PRUSSIANS
Novgorod
Pskov
Vologda
Galich
Yaroslavl
Torzhok
Rostov
Rostov-Suzdal
Suzdal
Gorodets
Vladimir
Moscow
Murom
Ryazan
Smolensk
Vyazma
Polotsk
Minsk
Kozelsk
POLAND
RUSSIAN PRINCIPALITIES
Turov
Pinsk
Pripyat
Kiev
Chernigov
Vladimir-in-Volhynia
Galich-Volhynia
Galich
Pereyaslav
Pereyaslavl
Belgorod
1239
1240
Desna
Niemen
Volga
Onega
Pinega
Dvina
CHEREMIS
Kazan
Bulgar
1237
VOLGA BULGARIA
MORDVINS
Don
Ural
Donets
Sarai
1239-40 Mongol Army forms winter camp on the Steppe
Sarkel
Kalka 1223
Dnieper
Dniester
CUMANS (PATZINAKS)
HUNGARY
Azov Sea
Crimea
Kaffa
Sudak
Cherson (to Kiev)
Black Sea
Danube
BYZANTINE EMPIRE
KHAZARS
ALANS
Caspian Sea
0 200 km
0 200 miles
20°
30°
40°
50°
N

The End of the Crusader States

THE MAMLUKS WERE A CLASS of soldier-slaves, captured as children in the south Russian steppes. They were taken to Egypt – then under Ayyubid rule – where they converted to Islam. The Mamluks murdered the Sultan and seized control in Egypt in 1250. Syria remained loyal to the Ayyubids, but fell prey to the invading Mongols. The decisive victory of the Mamluks over the Mongols at Ayn Jalut in 1261 ensured that the Mamluks now had ascendancy over the old Ayyubid Empire. They went on to create a centralized state that posed a far more formidable threat to the Latin settlements than the loose network of principalities that preceded them. Power was exercised through the military and provincial rulers, known as *naibs*, who reported direct to the sultan in Cairo. The citadels of Damascus and Aleppo had their own military governors as a means of safeguarding against provincial revolts.

Feeling that the Mongols posed a greater threat than the Mamluks, the Christian states chose to adopt a policy of neutrality towards the Mamluks. The leader of the Mamluk vanguard at Ayn Jalut had been a general named Baibars (Baybars). When Sultan Qutuz was assassinated Baibars succeded him as sultan of Egypt. In 1263 he turned his attention to the crusader states and launched the first of a series of destructive raids along the Mediterranean coast. These raids continued to be conducted annually, and were aimed at the economic infrastructure; strongholds were also eliminated. In 1265 Caesarea and Arsur fell to the Mamluks. In 1266 Baibars conquered Saphet, which became a base for operations against the Latins in the south. In 1268 Baibars besieged the city of Antioch, which fell after a comparatively weak defense, and thousands of its citizens were massacred. Krak des Chevaliers fell three years later.

A short breathing space followed for the crusader states when the Mamluks were involved in a succession crisis following Baibars' death and also dealing with a further Mongol invasion of Syria in 1280. The Hospitallers in the northern Levant had been ready to ally themselves against the Mongols and the new sultan, Kalavun, launched a renewed assault in 1285, attacking and destroying Tripoli in 1289.

The beleaguered settlers once again appealed for help from the West and in 1290 a fleet of 25 Venetian and Aragonese galleys arrived with crusaders from the north of Italy, but they did not stand a chance against the massive army, commanded by Kalavun's son and successor al-Ashraf Khalil, which set out from Egypt in March 1291, arriving in Acre on 5 April. The ensuing siege lasted for seven weeks and when the Mamluks finally breached the city walls resistance collapsed; many citizens were murdered, others managed to escape by sea. The seaside Templar fortress on the west of the city held out for ten more days. The Templar treasury was smuggled out to Sidon, before the fortress was eventually stormed. Khalil paraded captured crusaders and crusader standards through the streets of Damascus, and returned to Cairo with the gate of the Church of St Andrew in Acre, which was used in the construction of a mosque.

The Mamluk triumph effectively spelt the end of crusades to the Holy Land. Pilgrims, friars and Latin clergy were still granted access to Jerusalem. The main stronghold of Christianity within the east Mediterranean became Cyprus, which had been purchased in 1191 by Guy of Lusignan, the former king of Jerusalem. His dynasty was to rule the island until 1489. The island was strategically placed, economically stable and its capital at Nicosia became the most splendid city in the Latin East. After the fall of Acre both the Hospitallers and the Templars chose Cyprus as the location of their new headquarters. While there was an archbishop of Nicosia and suffragan bishops of Paphos, Limassol and Famagusta, the majority of the population remained loyal to the rites of the Greek Orthodox church, maintaining their own monasteries and building a new Orthodox cathedral in Famagusta. Following a period of Genoese rule and decline in the 14th century the Cypriots were finally forced to recognize the suzerainty of the Mamluks in 1426.

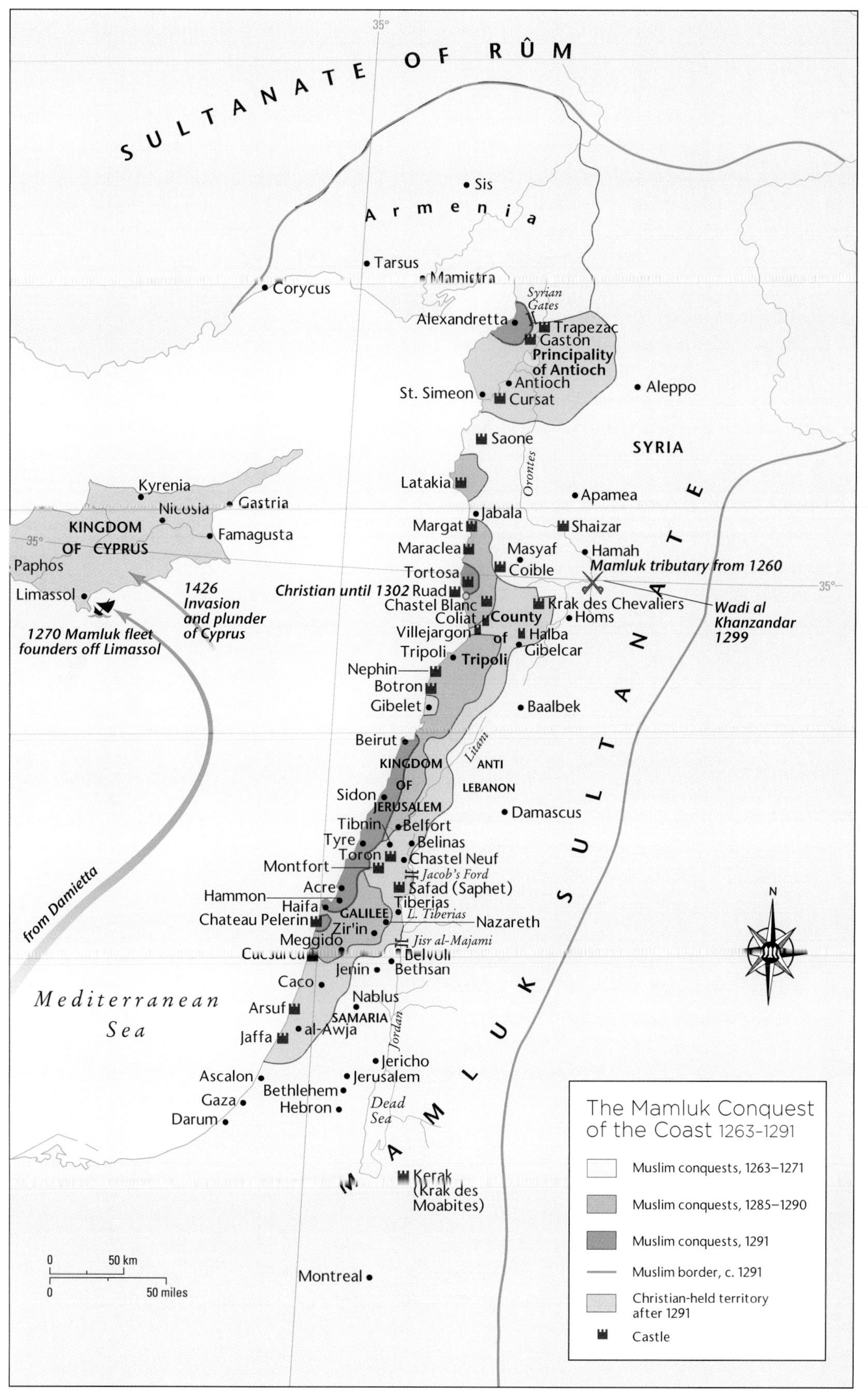
SULTANATE OF RÛM
Sis
Armenia
Tarsus
Mamistra
Corycus
Syrian Gates
Alexandretta
Trapezac
Gaston
Principality of Antioch
Antioch
St. Simeon
Cursat
Aleppo
Saone
SYRIA
Latakia
Orontes
Apamea
Kyrenia
Nicosia
Gastria
KINGDOM OF CYPRUS
Famagusta
Paphos
Limassol
Jabala
Margat
Shaizar
Maraclea
Masyaf
Hamah
Tortosa
Coible
Mamluk tributary from 1260
1426 Invasion and plunder of Cyprus
Christian until 1302 Ruad
Chastel Blanc
Krak des Chevaliers
Wadi al Khanzandar 1299
Coliat
County of Tripoli
Homs
1270 Mamluk fleet founders off Limassol
Villejargon
Halba
Tripoli
Gibelcar
Nephin
Botron
Gibelet
Baalbek
Beirut
KINGDOM OF JERUSALEM
Litani
ANTI LEBANON
Sidon
Damascus
Tibnin
Belfort
Tyre
Belinas
Toron
Chastel Neuf
Montfort
Jacob's Ford
Hammon
Acre
Safad (Saphet)
from Damietta
Haifa
GALILEE
Tiberias
L. Tiberias
Nazareth
Chateau Pelerin
Zir'in
Meggido
Jisr al-Majami
Belvoir
Jenin
Bethsan
Caco
Nablus
Mediterranean Sea
Arsuf
SAMARIA
Jaffa
al-Awja
Jordan
Jericho
Ascalon
Jerusalem
Bethlehem
Gaza
Hebron
Dead Sea
Darum
Kerak (Krak des Moabites)
MAMLUK SULTANATE
Montreal
0 50 km
0 50 miles
N
35°
The Mamluk Conquest of the Coast 1263-1291
Muslim conquests, 1263–1271
Muslim conquests, 1285–1290
Muslim conquests, 1291
Muslim border, c. 1291
Christian-held territory after 1291
Castle

Christian Pilgrimage in the Later Middle Ages

THROUGHOUT THE MIDDLE AGES Christians sought to engage in arduous physical travel to achieve a spiritual goal. If possible, they visited the actual places in the Holy Land where Jesus and the apostles had lived, or they ventured to Rome, the scene of Christian martyrdoms, which was endowed with holy relics that were believed to bring the pilgrim closer to sanctity.

After the Christian sites in the Holy Land fell under Islamic rule the pilgrimage maps were reorientated and Santiago de Compostela in Galicia, where bones believed to belong to Saint James were unearthed, became an important destination. Pilgrims often walked along the route barefoot, wearing a scallop shell, the symbol of Saint James. Pilgrim churches appeared along the routes to Spain. In France alone there were four main routes, and four cities on these routes – Le Puy, Arles, Paris, and Vézelay – became pilgrimage sites in their own right. Major sites became wealthy from pilgrim revenues, and competition for valuable relics was fierce. The relics displayed were often idiosyncratic: Canterbury sold phials of the "blood" of Thomas Becket; Walsingham Abbey held the "milk of the Virgin Mary," while several sites claimed a saint's finger, or a piece of the True Cross.

The military orders formed in conjunction with the crusades all assisted pilgrims. The Knights Templar provided security for pilgrims while traveling, safe custody for their possessions during their long absence, and offered letters of credit secured against their chattels: the genesis of modern banking. "Judicial pilgrimage" enabled criminals to expiate their offences – they were required to obtain clerical sign-off at all the pilgrim way-stations to attest completion of the journey. Wealthy individuals often paid substitutes to complete "vicarious pilgrimages" on their behalf.

All of these practices injected wealth into the pilgrimage networks, much of it to the laity who provided services to pilgrims. Pilgrimage routes became associated with a growing culture of mobility and travel during the period: this was a pious practice with major secular repercussions.

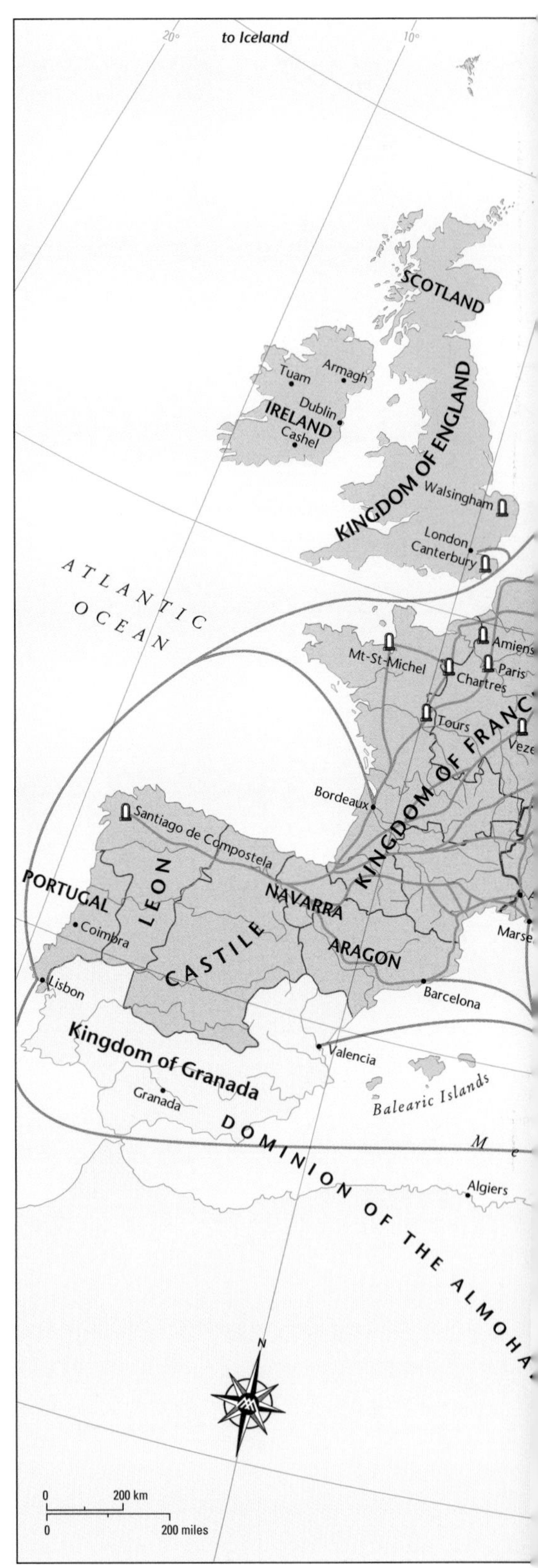

Christian Pilgrimage in the Late Middle Ages
Catholic (Latin) Christianity
Orthodox Christianity
Other Christianity
Community of Jacobite Christians
Community of Nestorian Christians
Community of Maronite Christians
Area under Muslim rule
Pilgrimage route to Jerusalem and Santiago de Compostela
Major shrine
Holy Roman Empire
NORWAY
KINGDOM OF SWEDEN
Bergen
Oslo
Stockholm
Novgorod
ORDER
Moscow
RUSSIAN PRINCIPALITIES
DENMARK
Copenhagen
TEUTONIC
Lübeck
Hamburg
Breman
LITHUANIA
Magdeburg
Cologne
Leipzig
POLAND
Kiev
HOLY ROMAN EMPIRE
Prague
Cracow
Nuremberg
MONGOLS
Vienna
Buda
Pest
KINGDOM OF HUNGARY
Cherson
Milan
Venice
Crimea
Caspian Sea
GEORGIA
Black Sea
Ragusa
Adriatic Sea
Aleria
Rome
BULGARIA
Trebizond
Adrianople
Bari
Durazzo
Constantinople
Naples
EMPIRE OF NICAEA
PATRIARCH OF CONSTANTINOPLE
SULTANATE OF RUM
Aegean Sea
Smyna
ARMENIA
CALIPHATE OF BAGHDAD
Arbela
Messina
Athens
Sicily
Antioch
P. of ANTIOCH
Baghdad
Rhodes
C. of TRIPOLI
Malta
Cyprus
Tripoli
Crete
Damascas
Tyre
KINGDOM of JERUSALEM
Tripoli
Jerusalem
Alexandria
DOMINION OF THE AYYUBIDS

The Christianization of the Baltic

The northern crusades, unlike the military campaigns in the Holy Land that were aimed at liberating former Christian lands from Muslim rule, were organized by popes and Christian rulers to convert pagans to Christianity. Pope Celestine III's call to arms in 1195 marks the beginning of the northern crusades, but the Catholic kingdoms of Scandinavia and Poland and the Holy Roman Empire were already conducting piecemeal campaigns against their non-Christian neighbors. Much of this conflict was directed at gaining economic ascendancy in the region and control of lucrative sea routes and trade networks, but the pope's call gave the sanction of the church to this conflict, and brought papal knights and armed monks to the region. Ostensibly an armed missionary campaign, the crusades provided the opportunity for territorial expansion and the acquisition of great wealth.

The Livonian Brothers of the Sword was a Catholic military order established by Albert, bishsop of Riga, in 1202, with the express purpose of converting the pagan Livs (Livonians), Letigallians, and Selonians living around the Gulf of Riga. By 1230 the Livonian crusaders had conquered Livonia (approximately the area of modern Latvia). Meanwhile the Danes who had been attacking the Baltic coast from Lübeck to Danzig conquered northern Estonia in 1220. In 1206 the Danish King Valdemar II and Andreas, the bishop of Lund, landed on the island of Ösel and attempted to establish a stronghold there. The attempt failed and the Öselians continued to raid the Estonian coast, wiping out the newly established Swedish stronghold of Leal (Lihula). Ösel did not submit to Christianity until 1220 when the papal legate, William of Modena, crossed the frozen sea and took the island's major strongholds. Meanwhile, to the north, the Swedes launched a series of campaigns against Finland, during which they clashed with the Russians.

Christianization of conquered popuplations was achieved by destroying the symbols of their native religion. Pope Alexander's III's Bull (1171 or 1172) called for crusaders against the Estonians to "spread the Christian religion with a strong arm," and there was no doubt that the Baltic Christians achieved conversions through the sword, backed by papal authority.

Between Livonia and Christian Germany there was still a swathe of pagan territory. Attempts to convert the pagan Prussians, aided by another small military order, the Knights of Dobrzyn, had failed, and Duke Conrad of Masovia, whose territories were under threat from the Prussians, called in the Teutonic Knights, an order founded in 1190 in Acre in Palestine. On arrival in Prussia the Teutonic Knights rapidly absorbed the Knights of Dobrzyn and once again began to carve out an independent Monastic State of the Teutonic Knights, disregarding the rights of their host Duke Conrad or the existing missionary church. In 1226 Frederick II's Golden Bull of Rimini granted Prussia to the Teutonic Order. In 1234 Pope Gregory IX took the Knights' territory under his protection as a papal fief. In 1236 the Knights also took over the Sword Brothers in Livonia, after they were defeated by the pagan Lithuanians. The Mongols were beginning to press on Europe's eastern borders and probably fears about the Order's ability to withstand this threat led to the granting of an extraordinary privilege in 1245, by which the Knights could grant plenary crusade indulgences, offering full remission of sins, to Germans who assisted them, without any papal authorization. By 1250 the Teutonic Knights had established an independent Baltic state and could wage a perpetual crusade to defend it. They worked to develop the region by building castles, bringng in Christian German peasants to settle unpopulated areas, and controlling trade. One-third of their conquered territory was given to the Catholic church. Along with the new German settlers came churches and monasteries (mainly Cistercian).

With the aid of the merchants of Lübeck and Bremen, supplemented by visiting crusaders, the Knights embarked on the conquest of the indigenous pagan tribes. As the Knights drove

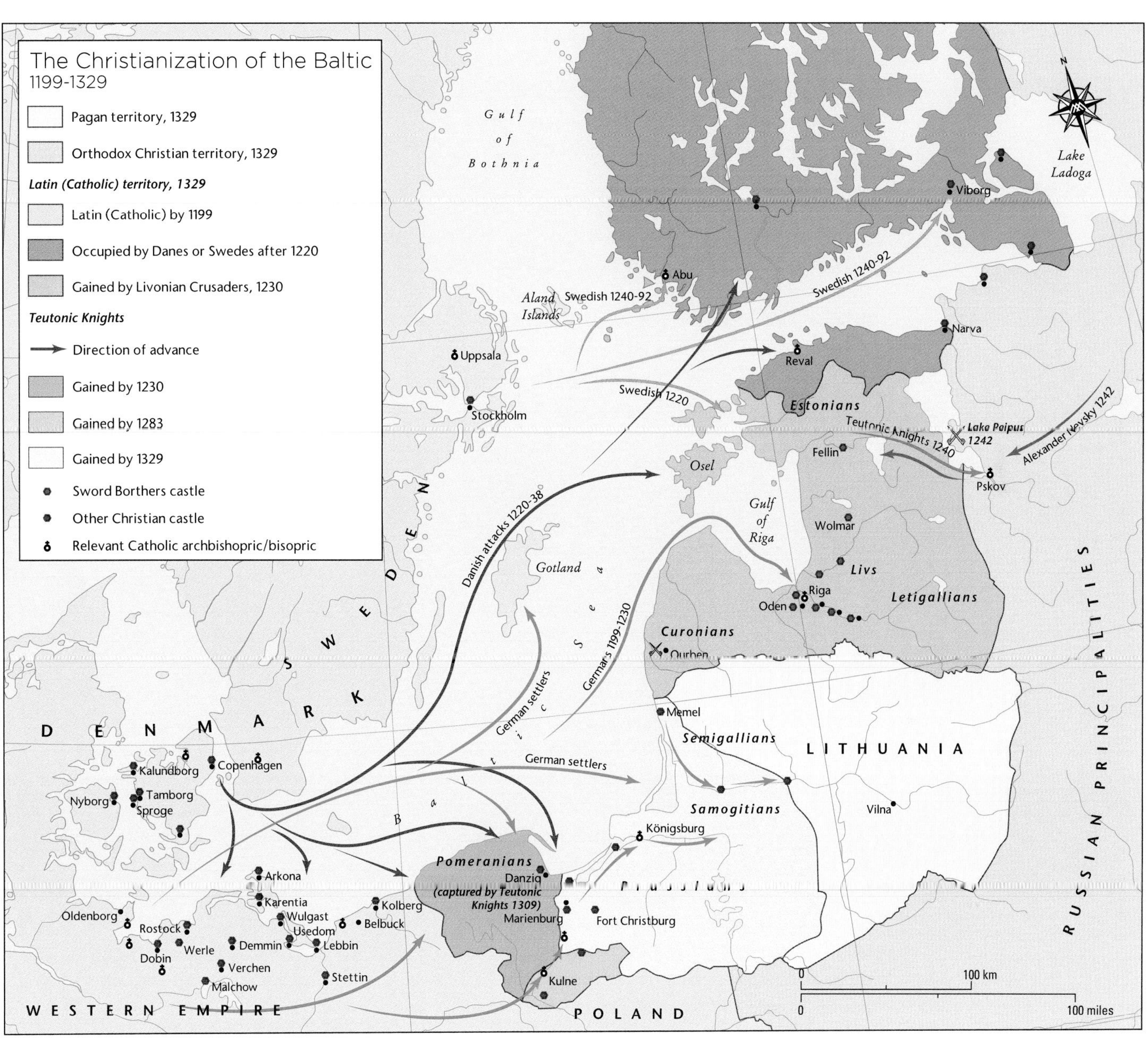

eastward they came into contact with Novgorod and the Russian principalities. Their eastward progress was finally halted by Prince Alexander Nevsky of Novgorod in the Battle of Lake Peipus (5 April 1242). This defeat marked the end of the crusaders' campaigns to invade Russia and convert the Eastern Orthodox population to Catholicism.

In Prussia itself the Knights' advance was inexorable, utilizing the threat of violence and the promise of rights and social status to those who accepted Christianity. In 1309 they conquered Danzig and eastern Pomerania and in 1346 they acquired northern Estonia from the Danish King Valdemar IV. Following the fall of Acre in 1291 the Order relocated its headquarters to Marienburg (1309), acknowledging the change in priorities and the true base of its power. By 1389 Lithuania, the last pagan state to withstand the crusaders, had converted to Christianity.

Medieval Heresies

MEDIEVAL CHRISTIANITY was riven by dissenting religious movements which the church under papal authority anathematised as "heresies." It aimed to counter them with means ranging from preaching against their errors, through judicial persecution, to crusading. Of all the medieval "heretical" groups, the Albigenisans, or Cathars, presented the most radical threat to Christian orthodoxy, believing that there were two Gods, the good God of the spiritual world and the evil God of the material world in which the soul was imprisoned. To free their souls the Cathars rejected worldly possessions and pleasures, and renounced the church.

This heresy took firm root in the remote, mountainous regions of southern France, with many Cathars amongst the region's noble families, and the papacy became alarmed. In 1208 a crusade was proclaimed and Béziers and Carcassonne were awarded to a northern baron, Simon of Montfort, who procceded to brutally suppress the Cathars. The movement persisted for a century more, and it was the Inquisition, not the crusaders, that finally broke it.

The Waldensian movement, which started in Lyon, took its name from Peter Waldo (1140–1270) who renounced his worldly goods and preached the gospel, which he had translated into Provençal. The Waldensians were declared heretics, mainly because in their communities, lay people, including women, were allowed to preach. They were excommunicated by Pope Lucius III in 1184 and persecuted by the church.

Also in 1184, the pope established the first formal Inquisition in Languedoc: a tribunal specifically empowered to seek out and to reconcile or punish heretics. By 1229 the Papal Inquisition was permanently established, staffed chiefly by friars of the newly founded Dominican Order. The tribunals stamped out the Cathars and drove the Waldensians and others to the margins, but the heresy-hunting bureaucracy ensured that, by the close of the medieval period, the church was highly sensitive to real or imagined doctrinal challenges, and less able to absorb and co-opt new religious movements.

The Cathar yellow cross was worn by repentant Cathars under the orders of the Roman Catholic church.

In addition to the Cathars and Waldensians, many other "heresies" thrived in Medieval Europe. The Lollards of England were followers of the theologian John Wycliffe in the 1370s, whose radical views prefigured the Protestant Reformation. In Bohemia followers of the Czech reformer Jan Hus, who was burnt at the stake in 1415, also adopted views that precipitated the Reformation. The Bogomils of the Balkans were dualists, who believed in a world within the body and a world outside the body. They did not build churches, considering the body to be their temple.

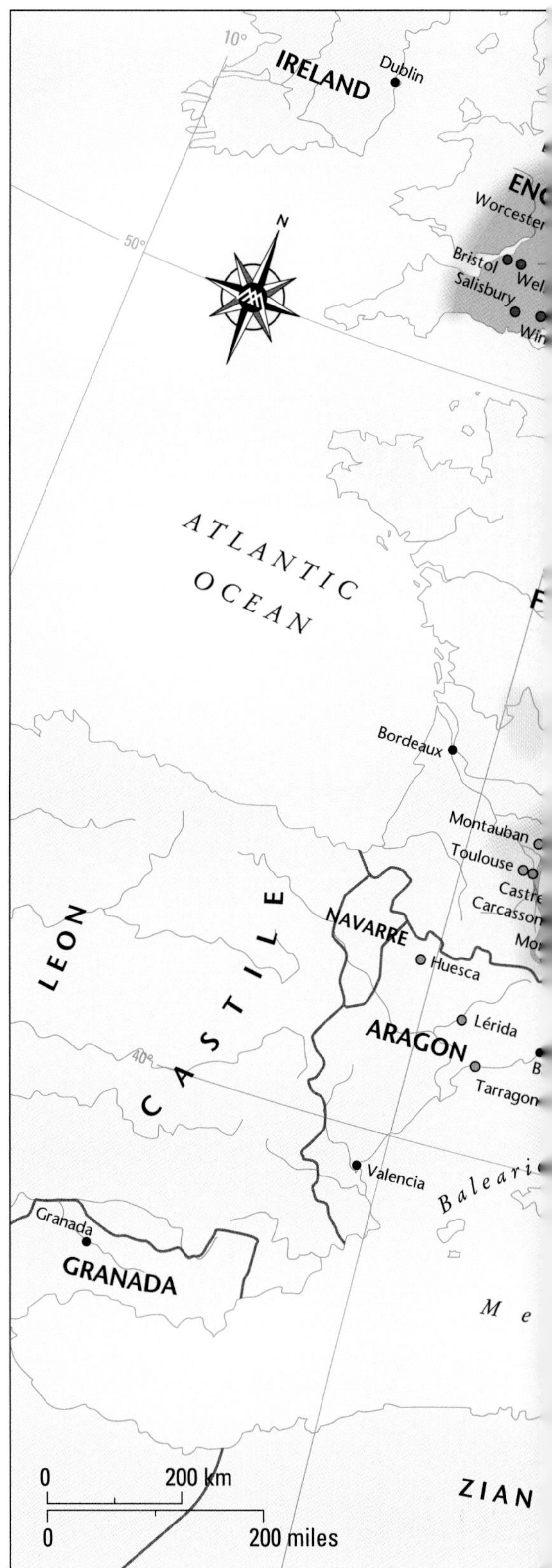

Medieval Heresy and Dissent
12th – 17th Century
Borders late 14th Century
Hussites and Hussite centre
Lollards and Lollard centre
Albigensians and Albigensian centre
Bogomils and Bogomil centre
Waldensians and Waldensian centre
Fraticelli and Fraticelli centre
Holy Roman Empire
North Sea
DENMARK
Copenhagen
Baltic Sea
Lubeck
Danzig
TEUTONIC ORDER
Ipswich
Canterbury
Dover
Utrecht
Deventer
Groonendaal
Berlin
Cologne
Liege
Leipzig
POLAND
Melnik
HOLY ROMAN EMPIRE
Trier
Metz
Toul
Prague
Cesky Brod
Bohemia
Kutna Hora
Tabor
Regensburg
Jonvelle
Pupping
Vienna
Sankt Oswald
Neustadt
Sankt Christophen
LITHUANIA
Moldavia
Besançon
Cluny
Buda
Pest
HUNGARY
Vienne
Valence
Montélimar
Avignon
Aix
Marseilles
Legano
Milan
Pavia
Turin
Bergamo
Verona
Venice
Parma
Genoa
Ferrara
Florence
Ravenna
Antibes
Pisa
Siena
Arezzo
Asciano
Croatia
Belgrade
Wallachia
Orvieto
PAPAL STATES
Adriatic Sea
Nish
SERBIA
BULGARIA
Black Sea
Viterbo
Aleria
Corsica
Ragusa
Sofia
Belyatovo
Philippopolis
Adrianople
Rome
BYZANTINE EMPIRE
Constantinople
Bari
Sardinia
Naples
ALBANIA
Thessalonika
Oristano
KINGDOM OF NAPLES
OTTOMAN TURKS
Cagliari
Aegean Sea
Smyrna
Athens
Athens
SELJUK SULTANATE
Messina
Sicily
Achaea
to Byzantine Empire
HAFASIDS
Rhodes

Monasteries in Russia 1200–1500

Vladimir, the Grand Prince of Kiev, converted to Christianity in 988, and a richly idiosyncratic branch of the Orthodox church came into being. Stressing their independence, the early rulers in Kievan Rus maintained dynastic and diplomatic links with the Latin West. In 1051 Yaroslav the Wise appointed Hilarion the first Slavic metropolitan (a diocesan bishop or archbishop of a metropolis). Hilarion had been living in a cave at the time of his elevation, an accommodation he inherited from St Anthony of Kiev, who founded the city's Monastery of the Caves. Based on his earlier experience as a hermit on Mount Athos in Greece, the monastery housed an idiorrhythmic community, where each member lived in separate cells and regulated his own religious practice. This would be adopted as a template in many Russian monastic communities: it was a frontier society, and in their restless pursuit of seclusion, monks often became the pioneer settlers of those frontiers. The ethos, liturgy, and *typicon* (governing precepts) of these monasteries were often inspired by ascetics like St Sabbas and St Eurhythmius, who built *lavras* (clusters of cells around a central refectory) in the Syrian desert.

The 12th century witnessed a wave of monastic establishment fanning out from Kiev, and also from the commercial hubs of Novgorod and Pskov in the northwest; however, the raiding of the nomadic Cumans eventually caused the disintegration of Kievan Rus, and by 1200, the duchy of Vladimir-Suzdal became the main sponsor of new monastic communities in a belt extending from Polotsk to Kostroma. In 1240 the Mongol invasion wreaked massive devastation, but having imposed their suzerainty, the Golden Horde proved relatively accommodating to Christianity, exempting the clergy from taxes (1270), and allowing the rulers of the Russian city-centered *appanages* (aristocratic estates) a large measure of autonomy – provided tribute was paid.

To the west, the Grand Dukes of Lithuania exploited the power vacuum to occupy the former territories of Kiev: most of the dukes were pagan, but Mindaugas (1251–63) converted before repudiating his faith, and his successor Vaisvilkas was actually a monk before his accession, and abdicated to return to his monastery. During the Lithuanian early flirtation with Christianity a number of monasteries were established including Vitebsk and Mstislavl.

In the Russian heartland, Moscow steadily gained ascendancy over the other Mongol vassal states during the 1300s. In 1331, Moscow annexed the principality of Rostov, and a young citizen of Rostov, Bartholomew of Radonezh, moved to Moscow and became a monk, adopting the name Sergius. Seeking solitude, he became a hermit in the forests north of the city, later becoming *hegumen*, or abbot, of a community of monks there, founding what would become the most celebrated monastery in Russia, Trinity-St Sergius Lavra. Around this nucleus, a *posad*, or trading outpost grew up. This pattern of development would become a trademark of Russian monasticism.

The disciples of St Sergius (1314–92) established more than 40 monasteries, many in remote areas, becoming the pioneers of the colonization of Russia's frontiers. For example, St Cyril and St Ferapontus founded Belozersk by White Lake in the wilderness of the Russian north in 1397. At the same time, St Stephen of Perm (1340–96) adopted a more conventional missionary role, spreading Christianity deep into the Russian interior, and cementing his conversion of the native Komi people by creating a written version of their language.

By the 15th century, the pioneering settlement program, coupled with royal and aristocratic bequests, made many monasteries wealthy landholders, with substantial rental income and lucrative concessions in fisheries, hunting, salt production, and the fur trade. In the 16th century a new ascetic movement emerged, which opposed ecclesiastical land-ownership, the "non-possessors", led by Nil Sorsky (1433–1508), who raised the question at the Moscow Synod of 1503. Ivan the Terrible would later side with the "possessors" and retain the status quo.

Monasteries in Early Russia 14th–15th Centuries
Roman Catholic rites
Eastern Orthodox rites
Under Islamic rule
Tatar settlement areas
Missionary activity of Stephen of Perm
Approximate boundary between Eastern and Western Christianity
Catholic missionary center
Principal Orthodox monastery
Norwegian Sea
Barents Sea
Arctic Circle
NORWAY
SWEDEN
White Sea
Solovki Monastery
ZYRIANS
Trinity
Finland
Siskoy
Ustvymsk
Valaam
Lake Onega
Konevitsky Rozhdestvensk
Lake Ladoga
Vyborg
RUSSIAN STATES
Veliky Ustiug
Mikhailo-Archangelsk
Gulf of Finland
Ladoga
Ferapontov
Kushensk
Reval
Belozersk
Nikitsk
Spaso-Kamenniy
PERMIANS
WENDS
Vologda
Vyatka
Perm
Gulf of Riga
Baltic Sea
Novgorod
Kornilev
Galich
Pskov
Borovichi
Krasny Kholm
Riga
Kostroma
Uglich
Yaroslavl
Makarev
TEUTONIC ORDER
Rostov
LITHUANIANS
Torzhok
Pereslavl
Tver
Suzdal
Danzig
Volokolamsk
Trinity
Vladimir
Nizhniy Novgorod
Kazan
PRUSSIANS
Polotsk
Vilna
Moscow
Ufa
Mozhaisk
Murom
Kulm
Borovsky Palnutiev
Smolensk
Bulgar
Serpukov
Ryazan
GREAT BULGARIA
Minsk
Kozelsk
Warsaw
Pustynsk
Penza
POLAND
LITHUANIA
KHANATE OF THE GOLDEN HORDE
Chernigov
Volhynia
Lvov
Kiev
Podolia
Ukraine
MOLDAVIA
New Saray
HUNGARY
Tana
Astrakhan
Sea of Azov
Crimea
WALLACHIA
Kuban
Cherson
Kaffa
Caspian Sea
0 100 km
0 100 miles
BULGARIA
Black Sea
GEORGIA
N

The Western Schism 1378–1417

The Avignon Papacy (1305–77) was a period, initiated by Pope Clement V, when the papal capital moved to Avignon in southern France. The seven Avignon popes were all French, as were most of the cardinals. The Avignon papacy gained a reputation for corruption and subordination to the French monarchy, which compromised its spiritual integrity. A likely precipitating factor in the return of the last of the Avignon popes, Gregory XI (1370–78), to Rome was the "War of the Eight Saints" (1375–78), which threatened a Florentine takeover of the papal states.

Gregory died soon after his return to Rome, provoking a fraught election. The Roman mob, incited by powerful aristocratic factions, wanted one of their own as pope. The College of Cardinals, still overwhelmingly French, were otherwise minded. On 8 April 1378 they came up with the compromise of the Archbishop of Bari, a Neapolitan, who took the name Urban VI. He promptly delivered a jeremiad denouncing the cardinals who had elected him, cardinals who were already in fear of the mob's reaction to the election of a non-Roman as pope. A group of them declared the election of Urban invalid because it was made under duress, appointing one of their number, Robert of Geneva, as pope – Clement VII – in his place. Clement repaired to Avignon to set up a rival papal court.

Mutual denunciations came thick and fast and the whole of Europe split along factional lines, with France leading the support for Clement, while the Holy Roman Empire stood behind Urban. Efforts to call an ecclesiastical council to resolve the crisis were paralyzed by the canon law requirement that such a council be convened by the pope, and neither claimant would agree to do so. Clement tried to break the impasse by bribing various French aristocrats to invade southern Italy; Urban died while campaigning against one of these invasions. He was succeeded by Boniface IX (1389–1404). Clement was succeeded by Benedict XIII in 1394.

Only after the successor to Boniface, Innocent VII, died in 1406, was a Roman pope, Gregory XII (1406–15), elected on the express condition that he be prepared to resign his office if Benedict could be persuaded to do likewise. It was agreed that a council would be held to resolve the dispute, but both papal claimants reneged on attending. In exasperation, the two factions of cardinals held a council in Pisa in 1409 regardless, deposed both popes and elected another pope, Alexander V, in their place.

Neither of the original papal claimants accepted the council's ruling: there were now three popes in contention. Alexander V died in 1410; his successor John XXII was supposedly based in Rome, but forced to flee by forces loyal to Gregory XII. Finally, John and Gregory agreed to a council at Constance (1414–18), which would resolve the issue, although Benedict remained defiant. As the Council proceeded, John became uncomfortably aware that proceedings were likely to end badly for him, and fled the deliberations disguised as a messenger. He was pursued and captured; upon his return the Council, overseen by Sigismund, the Holy Roman Emperor, threw the book at him. As Edward Gibbon drily observed, "The more scandalous charges were suppressed; the vicar of Christ was accused only of piracy, rape, sodomy, murder and incest."

Gregory XII stayed meekly to accept his deposition; he was at least recognized retrospectively as having been the true pope, and was rewarded with the sinecure of Bishop Cardinal of Frascati. John was imprisoned but eventually released after a ransom was paid by the Medici; by then, Gregory had died and John succeeded him as Bishop of Frascati. Meanwhile Benedict XIII had remained in Perpignan, stubbornly claiming to be the true pope despite having been deposed twice, declared a schismatic, and excommunicated. He spent his final years in Aragon, where his pontificate was still recognized. He even had a successor antipope, Clement VIII, who belatedly agreed to abdicate in 1429.

One major consequence for the church was the theory of conciliarism, which held that the church should be able to challenge, threaten, punish, or even depose, the pope. The reality was that the church's authority was permanently eroded; there was a marked decline in morality and discipline. The schism gave European laymen and women cause to look at exactly what was wrong with the church structure and they began to actively seek out their own ways to learn and interpret the faith and bring it out of the sole control of church officials, paving the way for the Reformation.

The Hussite Crusade

DURING THE CRISIS of the Western Schism, the only truly successful dissident movement in the Western Middle Ages was brewing in Bohemia. The Czech scholar Jan Hus, a onetime rector of the University of Prague, was inspired by the anti-papal doctrines of the condemned English theologian John Wycliffe (d. 1384), and appalled by the conflict between the rival popes of the schism. Hus condemned clerical corruption, and in particular, the sale of indulgences, but his most provocative action was to offer consecrated wine as well as bread to the laity during their Eucharist. This Utraquist ("in both kinds") sacrament was not considered heretical, of itself. But the church condemned the Utraquist contention that the sacrament *must* be offered in both kinds to achieve salvation. Hus was excommunicated, then lured to the Council of Constance (whose principal business was resolution of the Papal schism) under promise of safe conduct, purportedly to resolve his dispute with the church. Instead, on the principle that there was no obligation to honor a promise made to a heretic, he was imprisoned, condemned, and burned at the stake in 1415.

The consequences were explosive. Unrest broke out all over Bohemia. Its king, Wenceslas, and his brother, Sigismund, king of Hungary (the supposed guarantor of Hus's safety at Constance) attempted heavy-handed repression and the rebels responded with the "Defenestration of Prague," when royal and city officials were thrown from the upper windows of the town hall. Sigismund mounted his first "crusade" to subdue the rebellion, which should have been straightforward: his opponents were mainly peasantry with no formal military training. But the Hussites were under the command of a grizzled, one-eyed military genius, Jan Zizka (c. 1360–1424), who developed innovative tactics, including the first use of hand-held firearms in European warfare and circled wagons to blunt cavalry attacks. In all, five crusades were mounted, but the invaders, mostly composed of soldiers from the Holy Roman Empire and its allies, were repeatedly defeated by the Hussites. However, the movement would prove fissiparous. Various factions emerged, with, at either extreme, the ultra-radical "Taborites"(their base was a town built and named after the mountain of the Transfiguration of Jesus) and the moderate Utraquists.

After the death of Zizka from plague, the Hussites' own discipline relaxed, and they attracted enmity with their "Magnificent Rides," plundering expeditions that reached as far as

the Baltic Sea, aimed against the countries that supplied men to fight in the Hussite crusades. However, the *coup de grâce* was delivered from within the movement. At the Battle of Lipany (1434), the Utraquist Bohemian nobility defeated the Taborites decisively, and Zizka's successor, Prokop the Bald, died in the battle.

Utraquists nevertheless established dominance over Bohemia for the rest of the century – the only really successful revolt against Rome for the whole of the medieval period. The remnants of the Taborite radicals reformed as the *Unitas Fratrum* (the Unity of Bohemia Brethren) during the Protestant Reformation, only to be brutally repressed during the forcible recatholicization of Bohemia after the Protestant defeat at the Battle of the White Mountain (1620) in the Thirty Years' War. Their underground survivors ("the hidden seed") would emerge in the 1720s in Herrnhut as the Moravian Brethren.

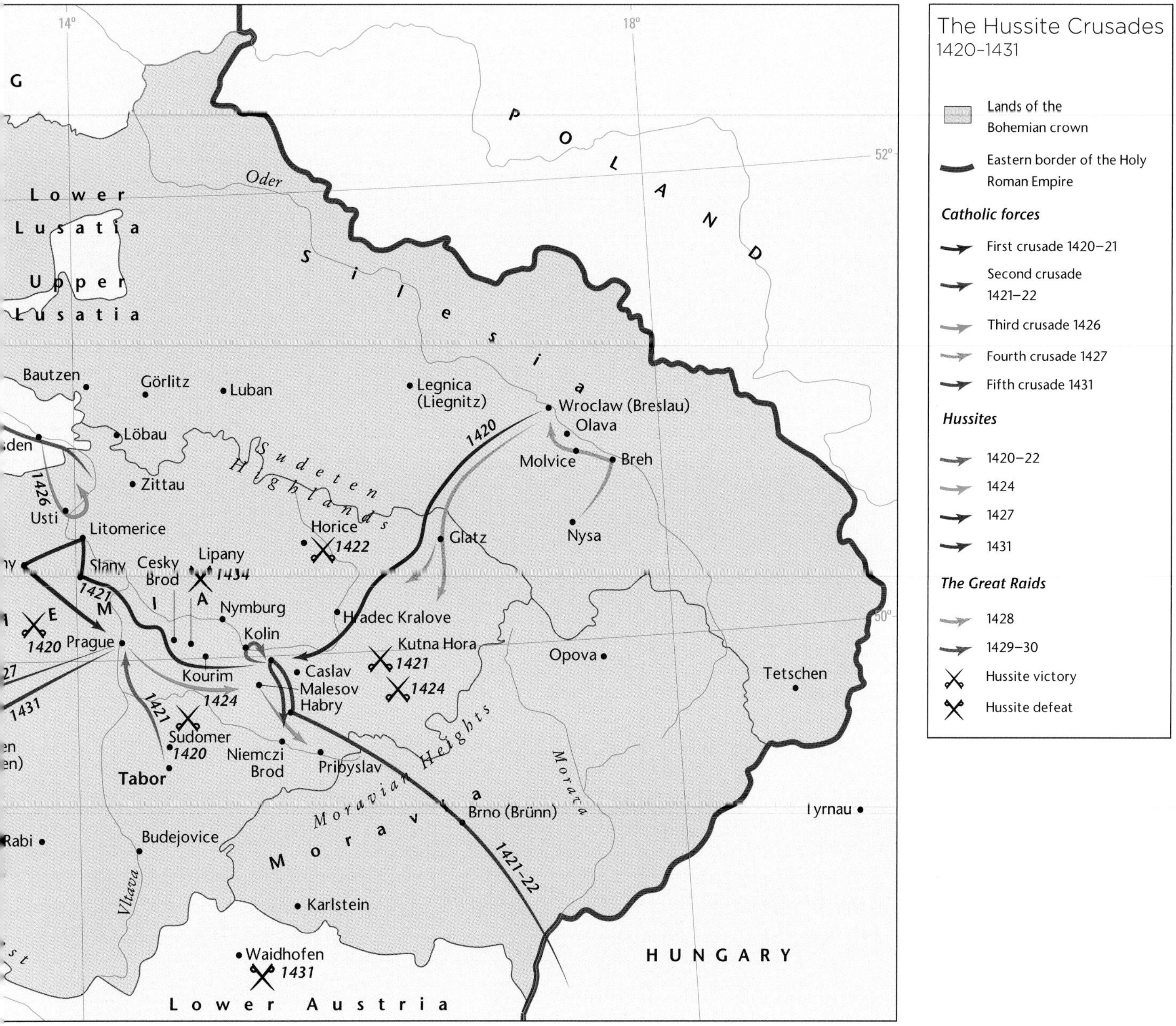

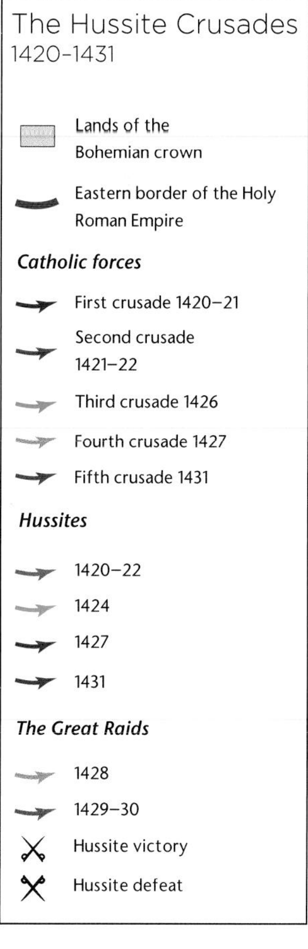

The Fall of Byzantium, 1453

The last papally proclaimed crusade came to a disastrous conclusion at the Battle of Nicopolis (1396). A huge multinational crusader army, built around contingents from France, Hungary, and Burgundy with naval support from the Venetian fleet, was decisively defeated by the Ottoman forces of Sultan Bayezid I. Constantinople now appeared doomed – but Bayezid soon after suffered a shocking defeat at the hands of the Mongol warlord, Tamerlane, and died in captivity. The subsequent Ottoman civil war granted Constantinople a brief reprieve, but under Murad II (1421–51) the Ottomans resumed their westward advance. Eastern European rulers on the frontline organized two further crusades in the 1440s, both spearheaded by the Hungarian general John Hunyadi. These campaigns also ended in defeat at Varna (1444) and Kosovo (1448) but temporarily halted the Ottoman progress. In 1451, a new Sultan, Mehmet II, decided to mount a concerted attempt to take Constantinople.

By this time Constantinople was isolated within territories under Ottoman control, with a few lingering dependencies in Peloponnesian Greece and on the Black Sea. In the hope of securing military aid from the West, Emperor John VIII Palaeologos and Patriarch Joseph II had, at the Ecumenical Council of Florence (1439) accepted the so-called "Filioque" clause, conceding the Latin Christian view that the Holy Spirit proceeds from the Son as well as from God the Father. Given that this clause had been disputed for close to a thousand years, this was a major

concession, permitting the Pope, Eugenius IV, to proclaim the union of the church under his primacy in a triumphal bull, *Laetentur Caeli* ("let the Heavens Rejoice"). However, Mark, bishop of Ephesus, refused to agree to the change, or the assertion of the Catholic doctrine of purgatory, and on his return to Constantinople he rallied both ecclesiastical and popular opposition to the Union. The Russian metroplitan, Isidore, gave his assent in Florence, but was promptly deposed on his return to Moscow, setting Russian Orthodoxy on the road to autocephaly (self-rule).

As Mehmet II tightened his stranglehold upon the city, the act of Union remained unsigned and inoperative, and the aid sent by the West proved paltry. Two ships and 800 men arrived from Venice, but promises of further reinforcements were so delayed that the Ottomans were able to impose a naval blockade, sealing the city off. This was cemented when Mehmet ordered the building of a fortress on the Bosphorus, which he nicknamed the "throat-cutter". Inside the city, the population had been depleted by disease and years of attrition. The once mighty Byzantine navy now consisted of just 26 vessels, while a total of perhaps 5,000 defenders guarded a population reduced to about 50,000. The Walls of Theodosius, a defensive line four miles long, were the greatest bastion in the medieval world. The siege lasted six weeks, during which the defenders withstood a massive artillery bombardment, rendered all the more effective by the unprecedented use of gunpowder weapons. Finally, on May 29, the third wave of assaults, spearheaded by the Sultan's elite guard of Janissaries, managed to enter the city and open the main gates. Three days of destruction ensued. The last Emperor, Constantine XI, was amongst those killed.

When Constantinople fell, Christendom reverberated with the shock – then swiftly moved on. Mehmet converted the Hagia Sofia into a mosque, and Constantinople into the imperial capital. He advanced further into Europe, and the eastern Mediterranean and Black Sea were soon under Ottoman control as Byzantium's last outposts in Morea, Trebizond, and Crimea were mopped up. The Ottomans entered a Golden Age with Constantinople adorned by new palaces, mosques, mausoleums, and bridges.

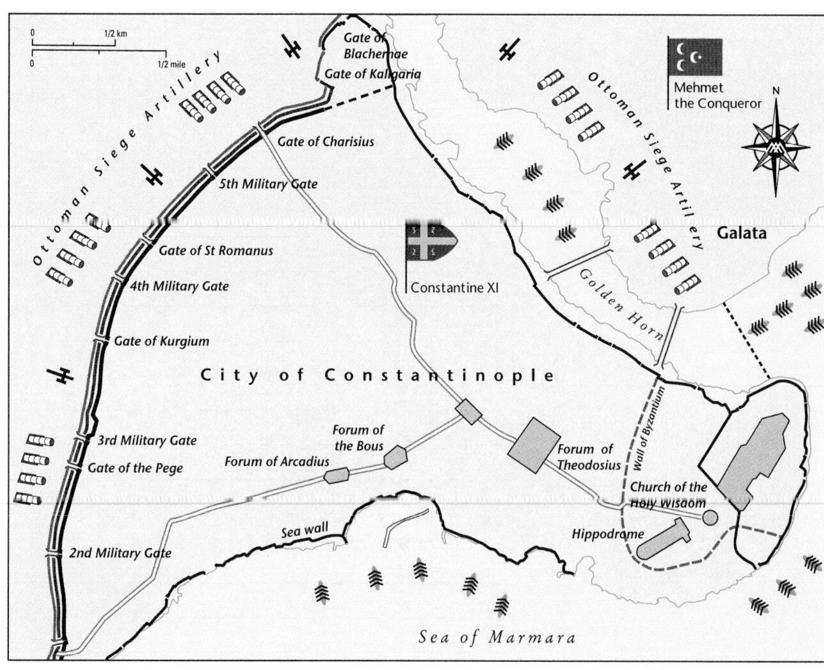

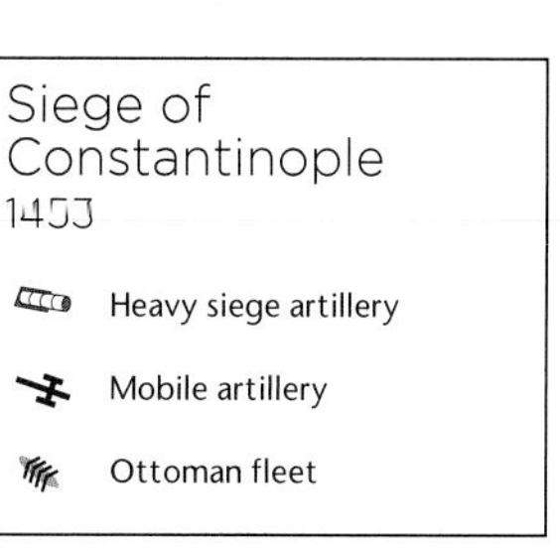

Under the Ottomans, Christianity was generally tolerated, and the patriarch of Constantinople was actually endowed with greater authority than he held under the Byzantines, becoming ethnarch with both political and ecclesiastical responsibility for all Christians within the empire. However, the authority was at the whim of the Sultan, and could disappear very rapidly.

The fall of the Byzantine Empire led to population movements and shifts in the balance of power. The Ottomans had moved against the Venetian and Genoese colonies, ousting them from the eastern Mediterranean. Many Greek scholars found refuge in the Italian city-states, bringing with them the knowledge of the Greco-Roman tradition that would propel the Renaissance. The Orthodox church had now lost its ancient sees of Jerusalem, Antioch, Alexandria, and Constantinople, and as a consequence its center of authority shifted to eastern Europe and Russia over the following centuries.

Renaissance Humanism in Europe

An important feature of central and northern Italy in the Middle Ages was the development of urban communes, which broke away from control by local bishops and counts. The rise in trade, and the growing wealth of these cities, led to a decline in feudalism and a rise in wealthy families and a mercantile class, who took almost complete control of the government of the city-states. It was in this atmosphere that innovative thought and new ideas about statecraft flourished.

The Renaissance began as a secular scholarly project to rediscover the knowledge, art, and literature of the classical world unfiltered by the clerical lens that had constrained intellectual inquiry during the Middle Ages. It became known as *studia humanitatis*, or the study of the "humanities," as opposed to the classical medieval emphasis on the study of divinity: hence the label "humanism." The crucible for this movement was northern Italy, politically tempestuous and economically vibrant, with a concentration of independently minded universities. The commercial empire of Venice conferred access to the learning of the Islamic world, and in the region's libraries, archives, and monasteries, vast troves of classical literature awaited, ready to be brought into the light.

Petrarch (1304–74), often termed the "Father of Humanism," was educated at the universities of Bologna and Montpelier, and traveled widely in western Europe, unearthing many classical texts along the way. Politically, he advocated a return to the Roman republic, and railed against the corruption and ostentatious opulence of the Avignon papacy, the "Babylon of the West." Trained as a priest, he nevertheless believed the injection of classical virtues could underpin a reinvigoration of the church. Petrarch's friend and contemporary, Boccaccio, was a literary pioneer. His *Decameron* presents a startling challenge to clerical sensibilities both in its vernacular Tuscan dialogue and earthy content. Boccaccio acted as a diplomat on behalf of several Italian cities, and later in life was ordained and served as a legate for Pope Innocent VI.

Petrarch had advocated the study of *literae humaniores*, and, with its dissemination through universities, humanism became intrinsic to the education of the governing classes. Its pervasiveness would culminate in the election of two outstanding humanists as pope: Nicholas V (1447–55) and Pius II (1458–64). The fall of Constantinople made available to humanist scrutiny a flood of original Greek religious documents salvaged by fleeing Byzantine savants. Lorenzo Valla and other classical scholars were able to demonstrate errors in St Jerome's Latin translations of the original Greek and Hebrew source texts. Humanist scholarship was beginning to gnaw at the foundations of papal and ecclesiastical authority: their academic pursuit of objective truth, unmediated by the religious establishment, would find its spiritual parallel in the Protestant Reformation.

But the humanist zeal for inquiry would next challenge church doctrine from a new and unexpected direction. Nicolas Copernicus, the son of a prosperous Polish copper merchant, received an extended and comprehensive humanist education at the Universities of Cracow and Padua. He qualified in canon law, but his vocation was astronomy, and was influenced by earlier humanists' re-examination of the work of the Greek philosopher Ptolemy. His treatise "On the Revolutions of the Heavenly Spheres," published soon after his death in 1543, theorized that the Earth rotated daily on its axis, and revolved yearly around the Sun, completely upending church dogma that the Earth was stationary and the Sun and Moon its satellites. The church fought to suppress what it viewed as an outrageous heresy, and it was over a century before the cumulative efforts of Kepler, Galileo, and Newton (amongst others) forced acceptance of heliocentrism as conventional wisdom.

The quintessential Renaissance humanist scholar, Erasmus, cultivated a network of patrons, colleagues, and acolytes in his unceasing travels. He was frequently excoriating in his criticism of the Catholic church and monastic orders in particular. Accordingly, he was accused of being the catalyst for Protestantism. But while sympathetic to many elements of Luther's moral critique, he disavowed his doctrinal radicalism, while Luther jeered at Erasmus' scholarly propensity to "compare everything and affirm nothing." A more pronounced antithesis to Erasmian scepticism might be found in the much darker humanism of Nicolas Machiavelli's *The Prince* (1513), an exploration of the unfettered pursuit and exercise of power divorced from its moral and religious framework.

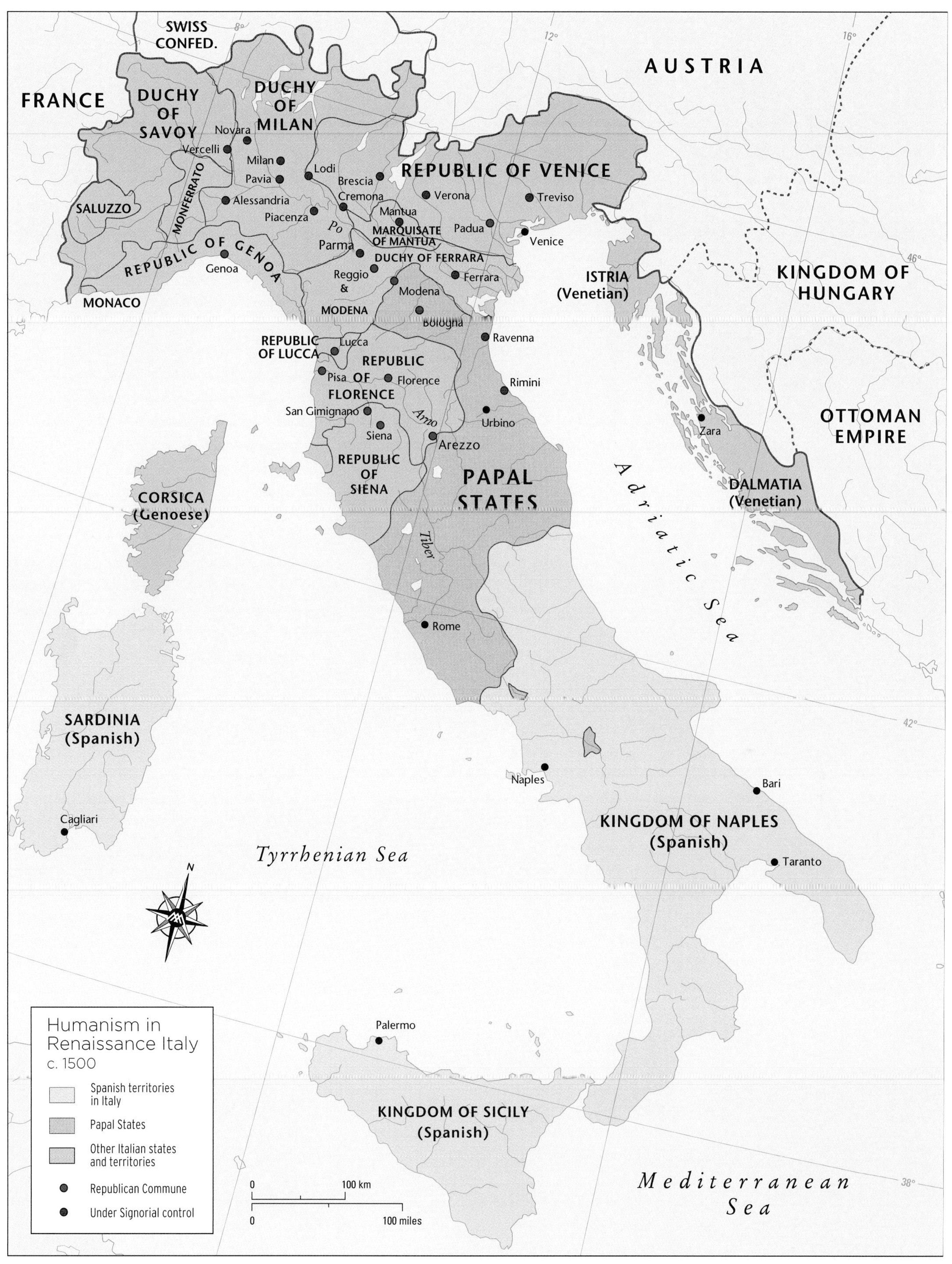
SWISS CONFED.
FRANCE
DUCHY OF SAVOY
DUCHY OF MILAN
AUSTRIA
REPUBLIC OF VENICE
SALUZZO
MONFERRATO
REPUBLIC OF GENOA
MONACO
Novara
Vercelli
Milan
Pavia
Lodi
Brescia
Cremona
Verona
Treviso
Alessandria
Piacenza
Mantua
Padua
Venice
Po
Parma
MARQUISATE OF MANTUA
DUCHY OF FERRARA
Genoa
Reggio & MODENA
Modena
Ferrara
Bologna
ISTRIA (Venetian)
KINGDOM OF HUNGARY
REPUBLIC OF LUCCA
Lucca
Ravenna
REPUBLIC OF FLORENCE
Pisa
Florence
Rimini
San Gimignano
Arno
Urbino
Siena
Arezzo
Zara
OTTOMAN EMPIRE
REPUBLIC OF SIENA
PAPAL STATES
Adriatic Sea
DALMATIA (Venetian)
CORSICA (Genoese)
Tiber
Rome
SARDINIA (Spanish)
Naples
Bari
Cagliari
KINGDOM OF NAPLES (Spanish)
Tyrrhenian Sea
Taranto
N
Palermo
KINGDOM OF SICILY (Spanish)
Mediterranean Sea
Humanism in Renaissance Italy c. 1500
Spanish territories in Italy
Papal States
Other Italian states and territories
Republican Commune
Under Signorial control
0
100 km
0
100 miles
8°
12°
16°
46°
42°
38°

The Rise of Printing

JOHANNES TRITHEMIUS, the Abbot of Sponheim in Germany, who was variously a lexicographer, cryptographer and necromancer, wrote a treatise "In Praise of Scribes" in 1492, in which he asserts "he (who) scribes the great texts…is introduced little by little to the great mysteries… and his inmost soul is greatly illuminated." Trithemius was determined that his defense of the endangered art of scribing reached the greatest possible audience – so he had it printed. And as a knowledge-hungry polymath, Trithemius amassed in his abbey library a collection of over 2,000 printed works. The printing revolution overwhelmed even its most ardent detractors.

Trithemius was writing less than 40 years after Johannes Gutenberg, a goldsmith in Mainz, managed, after years of painstaking experiment, to perfect the manufacture of small metal movable type amenable to mass production. Gutenberg produced 200 copies of his revolutionary 42-line Bible in 1453 – then promptly went bust, after his backers sued to recover their investment. But the genie was out of the bottle. One of Gutenberg's creditors, Johann Fust, used the printing equipment he was awarded in court to set up a thriving business in 1457, producing the first, primitive, color printing. By 1461, a rival in Bamberg, Albrecht Pfister, had produced the first printed books in German, and the first with woodcut illustrations. By the end of the decade the new technology had crossed the Alps, to become an accelerant in the cultural and artistic conflagration of the Italian High Renaissance. While the courts of the Sforzas in Milan and Medicis in Florence were enthusiastic consumers and commissioners of printed materials, the epicenter of the new industry came to be its commercial capital, Venice.

As the number of printshops mushroomed, so did the variety of materials produced. From an early concentration on religious texts and homiletics, some publishers set out to disseminate classical learning. Aldus Manutius in Venice became a prolific producer of small, easily portable pamphlets or *enchiridia*: his vast and eclectic output included the scientific treatises of Aristotle, the comedies of Aristophanes, and the poetry of Petrarch. One of his primary patrons – and authors – was the great Dutch Renaissance humanist, Erasmus. As the industry expanded, the roles in the printing process became formalized, with a keen demand for skilled compositors, engravers, and pressmen. Different models for financing publication also evolved: publication syndication spread the risk amongst a group of investors, while subscription publishing allowed print runs to be tailored to demand for the product.

Counterfeiting appeared early on the scene, with pirate copies of popular works starting to do the rounds in the 1470s. And the unrestrained profusion and proliferation of printed matter soon revealed the capacity of the technology to subvert the status quo. Scribal publication had of necessity restricted access to knowledge to a small, mostly clerical elite. Now a cacophany of other voices, some outside the educated elites, could, and did, join the conversation.

Das Narrenschiff ("the Ship of Fools") published in 1494 by Sebastian Brant, satirized religious corruption. It featured a St Grobian, patron saint for the vulgar, and a pilgrimage to Narragonia, the Fools' Paradise. It rapidly sped through 13 editions in Latin, German, Dutch, French, and English. The church had been mocked before, but never to such a wide and diverse audience.

With the advent of the printing press an increasing number of books of a secular nature were published, and this had a profound effect on scientific investigation. Scholars could work on the same problem in different parts of Europe, share, and compare their results with a large number of other scholars. As printing grew more advanced, cartographers began to produce and circulate more advanced maps, greatly advancing geographical knowledge. All these developments would pave the way for the Scientific Revolution and the Enlightenment, which would bring about a radical alteration in the ways in which Europeans viewed the world and the universe.

Printing Presses of Europe
15th Century
Holy Roman Empire 1477
Major printing centre
City or town with printing press by 1500
SWISS. C Swiss Confederation
SCOTLAND
IRELAND
ENGLAND
Oxford
Westminster
London
North Sea
DENMARK
SWEDEN
Stockholm
Baltic Sea
TEUTONIC ORDER
Danzig
Kulm
POLAND
Wismar
Lübeck
Hamburg
Gouda
Delft
Zwolle
Deventer
Magdeburg
Bruges
Antwerp
Leuven
Cologne
Leipzig
Erfurt
THE HOLY ROMAN EMPIRE
Mainz
Bamberg
Breslau
SILESIA
Cracow
Prague
Speyer
Strasbourg
Nuremberg
Ratisbon
Brunn
MORAVIA
Ulm
Reutlingen
Augsburg
Basel
Memmingen
Vienna
Buda
KINGDOM OF HUNGARY
Gratz
ATLANTIC OCEAN
Rohan
Caen
Rouen
Paris
Rennes
Nantes
Orleans
FRANCE
Poitiers
Bergerac
Lyon
Geneva
SWISS. C
Brescia
Vecenza
Milan
Treviso
Pavia
Padua
Venice
Ferrara
Genoa
Bologna
Florence
PAPAL STATES
Adriatic Sea
Ragusa
OTTOMAN EMPIRE
Rome
K. OF NAPLES
Naples
Corsica
Sardinia
Messina
Sicily
Santiago
Oporto
PORTUGAL
Burgos
Pamplona
NAVARRE
Zamora
Valladolid
Salamanca
CASTILE
Madrid
Zaragoza
Lerida
Montauban
Toulouse
Lisbon
Toledo
ARAGON
Barcelona
Valencia
Faro
Seville
Granada
K. OF GRANADA
Balleanic Is.
Mediterranean Sea
MOROCCO
HAFSIDS

Islamic Spain and the Reconquista

The cross of St James, with flourished arms and surmounted by a scallop shell, the symbol of the saint, was the emblem of the 12th-century Spanish military Order of Santiago.

In the late Middle Ages, Spain would become Christendom's most reliable supplier of good news in the war against the infidel. The good news, however, had been a long time coming. The 8th-century invasion of the Umayyad Caliphate was resisted only by the toehold Kingdom of Asturias. The mighty Charlemagne established a trans-Pyreneean marchland of Septimania, but his empire did not long survive his death. Almanzor (978–1002), the most powerful of the caliphs of Cordoba, came close to driving the Christians out of the peninsula entirely, even pillaging the shrine of Santiago de Compostela. But in 1031, Cordoba disintegrated into a patchwork of warring statelets, the *taifas*. In the chaos, the Christian states of the north, Leon, Castile, Aragon, and Pamplona (later Navarre) were able to make inroads.

El Cid (1043–99) rose to prominence in this period, fighting for various Christian (and Muslim) rulers before carving out a principality of his own in Valencia. During the 12th century, a number of religious-military orders were established with papal authority to help prosecute the Reconquista, beginning with the Order of Alcantara (1164).

In 1212 a vast Berber army led by the Almohad Caliph, Muhammad al-Nasir, encamped in the Andalusian mountains poised to invade Christian Spain. To counter this threat, the kingdoms of Castile, Aragon, and Navarre had formed an alliance, and their forces were augmented by units from four military orders: Santiago, Calatrava, the Knights Templar, and the Knights Hospitaller. Outnumbered, the Christians badly needed to surprise their enemy, but the precipitous canyon of Puerto del Rey blocked their way. A local shepherd, Manuel Alhaja, was recruited as a guide, marking the narrow path through the defile with a cow's skull. The Christians followed the path and ambushed and routed the Almohad army at the Battle of Navas de Tolosa. Alhaja was rewarded with a jocular hereditary title of Cabeza de Vaca (Cow's Head) complete with an escutcheon emblazoned with bovine skulls.

After Navas de Tolosa, as the Christian kingdoms wrested the ascendancy, the military orders were able to acquire substantial landholdings in the marchlands ringing the shrinking Moorish domain. Spain also became a magnet for mercenaries and adventurers from across Europe attracted by the rich booty on offer. In 1147, King Alfonso of Portugal was able to make use of crusaders waiting to sail to the Holy Land to recapture Lisbon. During this period Christians, Muslims, and Jews lived together relatively peacefully and in Cordoba, for example, Christians and Jews played an important role in the intellectual life of the city

Between 1236 and 1248, Cordoba, Valencia, and Seville were taken by Christian forces, leaving the remnant emirate penned in Granada, a vassal state of the Kingdom of Castile. By 1482, Ferdinand II of Aragon and Isabella I of Castile – the "Catholic monarchs" whose marriage would create the unified kingdom of Spain – had formed an alliance with the sultan of Egypt against the Ottomans, leaving Granada isolated, and were ready to embark upon the final campaign of expulsion. The last emir, Boabdil, surrendered in January 1492 and was allowed to retire to a fiefdom in the foothills of the Sierra Nevada.

During the course of the Reconquista, persecution of the Jews had been extremely virulent (they had enjoyed privileges and tolerance under Muslim rule and were seen as collaborators), with large-scale massacres taking place in 1366 and 1391. In 1492, Ferdinand and Isabella ordered the wholesale expulsions of the Jewish population of their two kingdoms. The legacy of Al-Andalus, a diverse residue of Muslims and Christians of Jewish descent (*conversos*) and Christian Muslim converts, engendered paranoia in the new rulers, and the Spanish Inquisition had been instituted to root out potential heretics in 1483. Under direct royal authority (unlike classic medieval inquisitions), this tribunal rigorously enforced conformity to Christianity, executing 2,000 or more *conversos* for continued loyalty to their Jewish heritage.

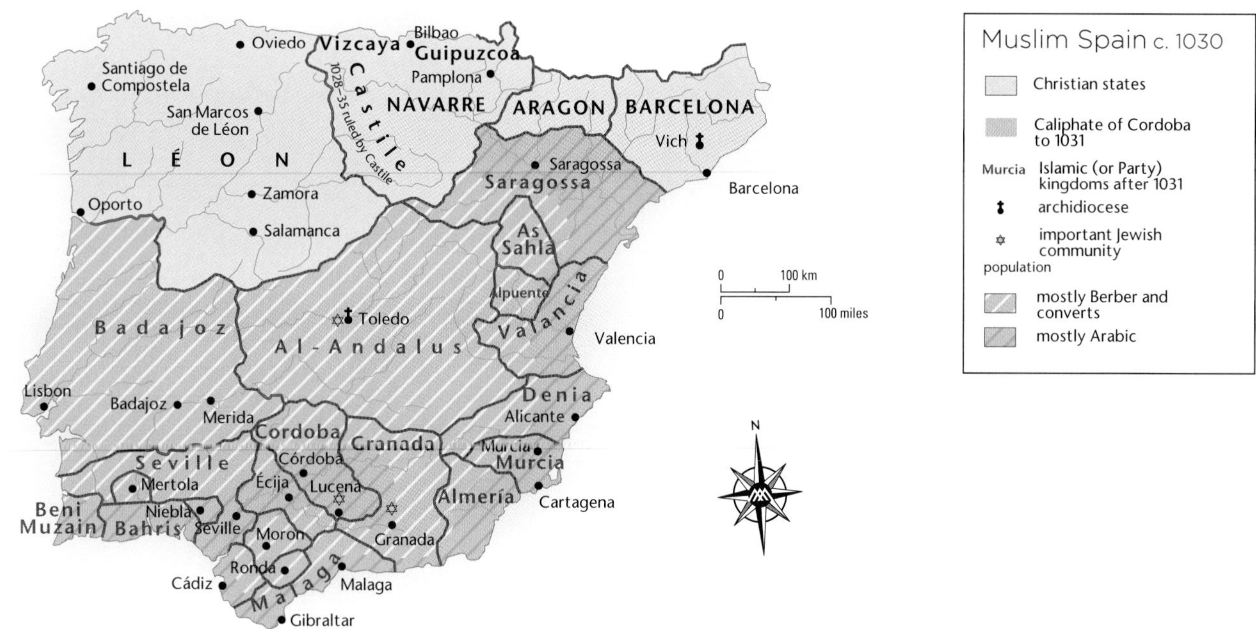

Muslim Spain c. 1030
Christian states
Caliphate of Cordoba to 1031
Murcia
Islamic (or Party) kingdoms after 1031
archidiocese
important Jewish community
population
mostly Berber and converts
mostly Arabic
Oviedo
Vizcaya
Bilbao
Guipuzcoa
Santiago de Compostela
Pamplona
Castile
1028–35 ruled by Castile
NAVARRE
ARAGON
BARCELONA
San Marcos de Léon
Vich
L É O N
Saragossa
Saragossa
Barcelona
Zamora
Oporto
Salamanca
As Sahla
Alpuente
Valencia
Toledo
Badajoz
Al-Andalus
Valencia
Lisbon
Badajoz
Merida
Denia
Alicante
Cordoba
Granada
Seville
Córdoba
Murcia
Murcia
Mertola
Écija
Lucena
Almería
Cartagena
Beni Muzain
Niebla
Bahris
Seville
Moron
Granada
Ronda
Cádiz
Malaga
Malaga
Gibraltar
0
100 km
0
100 miles
N

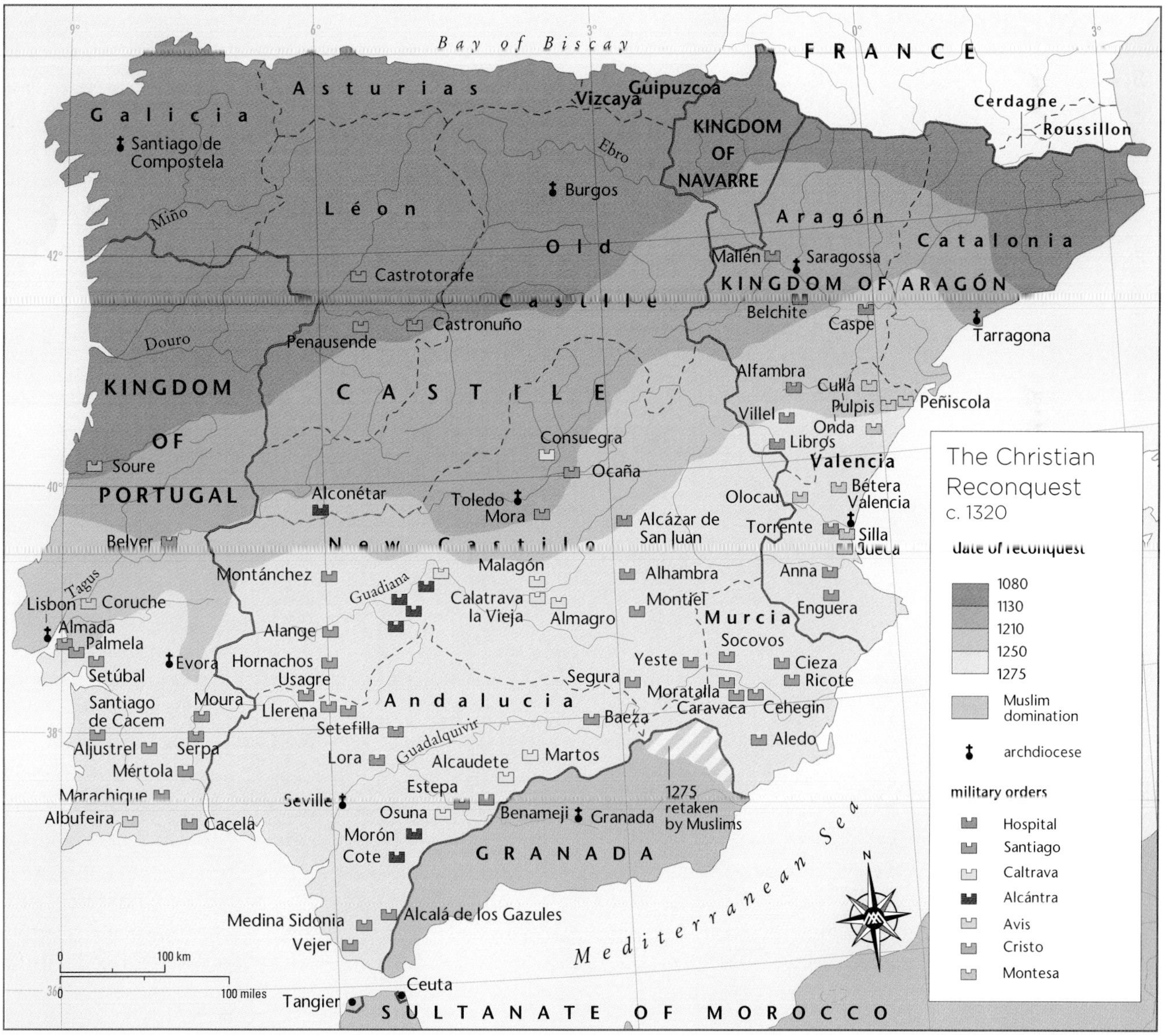
Bay of Biscay
FRANCE
Asturias
Vizcaya
Guipuzcoa
Cerdagne
Roussillon
Galicia
Santiago de Compostela
KINGDOM OF NAVARRE
Ebro
Burgos
Miño
Léon
Aragón
Catalonia
Old Castile
Mallén
Saragossa
Castrotorafe
KINGDOM OF ARAGÓN
Belchite
Caspe
Castronuño
Tarragona
Douro
Penausende
Alfambra
KINGDOM OF PORTUGAL
CASTILE
Culla
Pulpis
Peñiscola
Villel
Onda
Consuegra
Libros
Soure
Valencia
Ocaña
Bétera
Valencia
Alconétar
Toledo
Mora
Olocau
Alcázar de San Juan
Torrente
Silla
Sueca
Belver
New Castile
Malagón
Montánchez
Alhambra
Anna
Tagus
Guadiana
Calatrava la Vieja
Montiel
Lisbon
Coruche
Almagro
Enguera
Almada
Murcia
Palmela
Alange
Socovos
Evora
Hornachos
Yeste
Cieza
Setúbal
Usagre
Segura
Ricote
Santiago de Cacem
Moura
Llerena
Andalucia
Moratalla
Caravaca
Cehegin
Setefilla
Baeza
Aljustrel
Serpa
Lora
Guadalquivir
Alcaudete
Martos
Aledo
Mértola
Estepa
Marachique
Seville
Osuna
Benameji
Granada
1275 retaken by Muslims
Albufeira
Cacelá
Morón
Cote
GRANADA
Mediterranean Sea
Medina Sidonia
Alcalá de los Gazules
Vejer
0
100 km
0
100 miles
Ceuta
Tangier
SULTANATE OF MOROCCO
The Christian Reconquest c. 1320
date of reconquest
1080
1130
1210
1250
1275
Muslim domination
archdiocese
military orders
Hospital
Santiago
Caltrava
Alcántra
Avis
Cristo
Montesa
N

East African Christianity

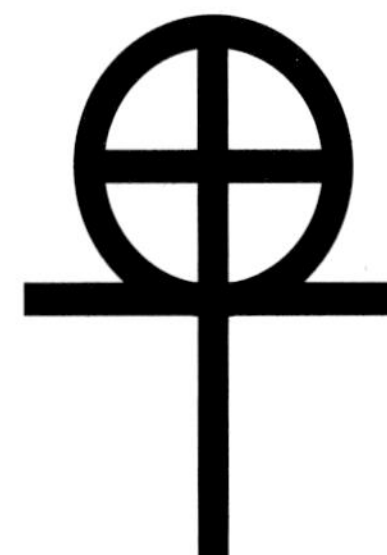

This cross, shaped like a letter T surmounted by an oval was originally the ancient Egyptian symbol for "life." It was adopted by the Egyptian Copts, and is known as the *crux ansata*, meaning "cross with a handle."

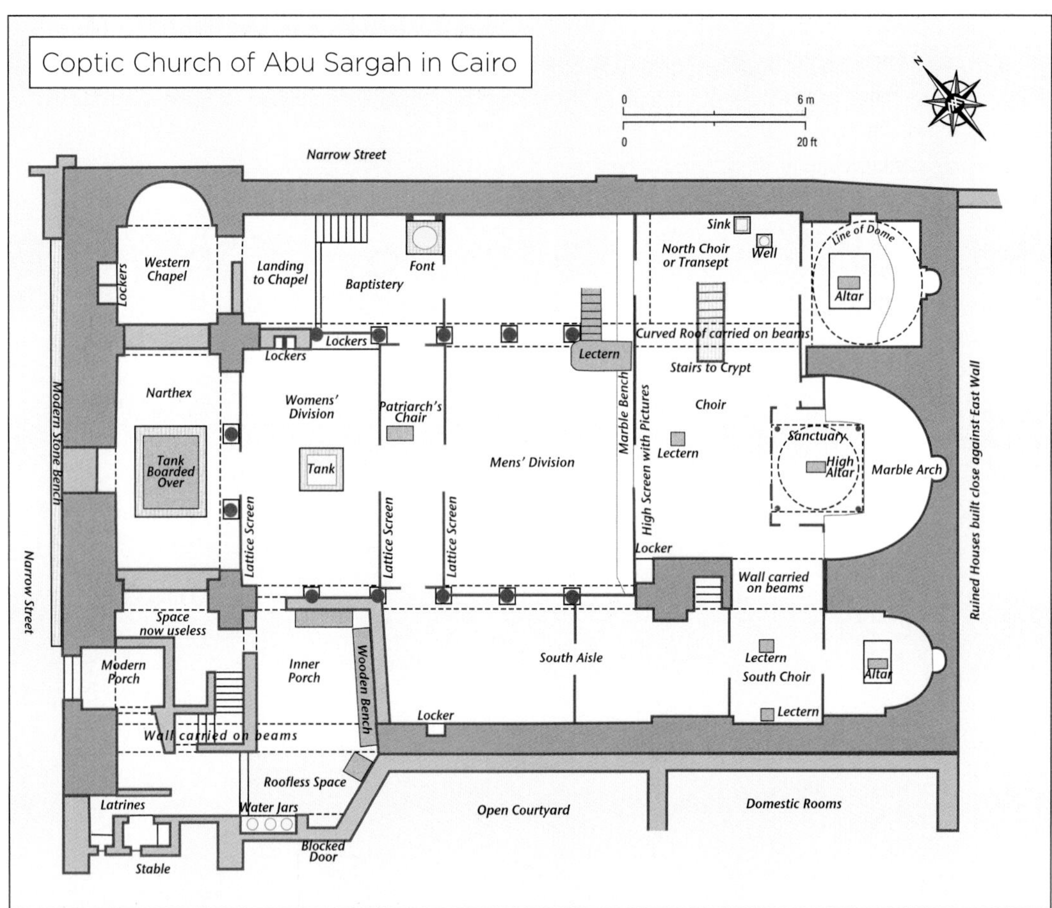

The Coptic Orthodox Church traced its foundation to the Apostle Mark, who is traditionally held to have brought Christianity to Egypt in the 1st century CE. The Copts were Miaphysites, who split from the broader Christian community in 451 following Patriarch Cyril's dictum that Jesus Christ's divine and human natures were "without separation, without mixture, without confusion, and without alteration," The Coptic Church is associated with a monastic tradition that dates to the 3rd century and Egypt is seen as the birthplace of Christian monasticism – by the 5th century there were thousands of monasteries, cells, and hermits' caves scattered across the Egyptian desert. Copts were persecuted by the Byzantines and subsequently by Muslim invaders. Under Muslim occupation they paid a higher rate of tax, which had a negative impact on church revenue, and were exempt from military service.

Saint Frumentius of Tyre converted Ethiopia's first Christian ruler, Ezana, in the 4th century. The *abun*, the Metropolitan Archbishop of the Ethiopian Orthodox Tewahedo Church, was appointed by the patriarch of Alexandria and shared the Coptic Church's Miaphysitism. The Ethiopian Church was part of the Coptic Orthodox church until 1959, when it was granted its own patriarch.

Yekuno Amlak of Ethiopia (r. 1270–85) conducted a succession of campaigns against the Muslim Mamluk rulers of Egypt, which led to the disruption of the succession of *abuns*. The hiatus would last until 1337, and in this period, a new reformist monastic movement sprang up, the House of Ewostatewos. Through its eponymous founder, the movement's keynote issue was celebration of both the Jewish and Christian Sabbath. The *abun* was restored in 1337, but the feud continued, threatening schism until the Negus (ruler) Zara Yakob held a synod in 1449, at which the abun, and by extension the Coptic patriarch, was persuaded to accept the local observance. Zara Yakob defeated the threatening Adal Sultanate at the Battle of Gomit (1445), but in his later years he became both more devout and more despotic.

Ethiopia entered a dark period in the 16th century. From 1528 until 1540, the armies of the Adal Sultanate conducted a jihad throughout the kingdom, leaving the Negus a fugitive. The invaders destroyed churches, libraries, and monasteries, and the capital eventually moved to Gondar. The kingdom had survived with the help of a Portuguese expeditionary force, but the military assistance came with strings attached. The Portuguese wished to see Ethiopia converted to Catholicism, and with that intent, Jesuit missionaries arrived in the kingdom in 1557. The Jesuits achieved considerable success, crowned by the conversion of the Negus Susneyos in 1621. However, when Susneyos attempted to impose his new faith on the population, he was forced to abdicate, and his son expelled the Jesuits in 1633.

Apart from the Italian invasion and occupation of Ethiopia (Abyssinia) from 1935–41 the line of Christian emperors remained unbroken until Emperor Haile Selassie was deposed in a *coup d'etat* in 1974.

Ethiopia was a bishopric under the Church of Alexandria and for many centuries the Coptic church consecrated the bishops that were to serve in Ethiopia, However, in the late 1940s Emperor Haile Seslasie began to negotiate reforms that woud lead to the Ethiopian church's independence and in 1951 Basilios became the first Ethiopian religious leader to be consectrated by the Ethiopian church. In 1959 it became an ecclesiastically independent, autocephalous, body.

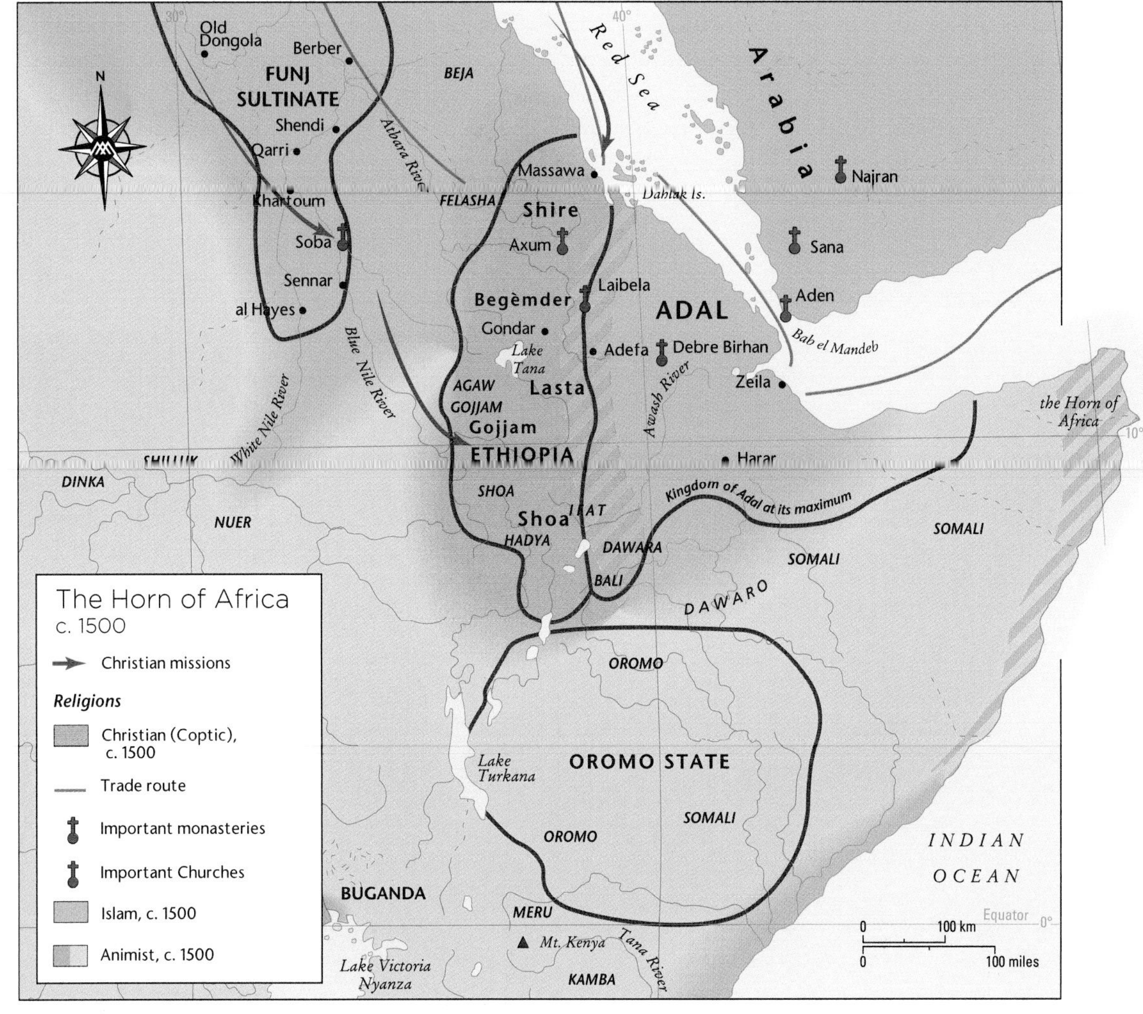

The Consolidation of Christian Russia

In the fall of 1492, as Columbus was first setting foot in the New World, the Christians of Muscovy were preparing for the end of the Old World. Their interpretation of the scriptures held that the apocalyptic event would occur in year 7,000 of their calendar (a millennium for each day of the creation). When the year passed without incident, Muscovites celebrated their deliverance with a church-building spree while their autocratic ruler Ivan III (r. 1462–1505) held it as divine endorsement of his imperial mission, with Moscow, his capital, a "Third Rome."

This ambition was hardly original in eastern Europe. The ruins of "Third Romes" littered the Balkans: Dusan the Mighty of the Serbs, and Simeon the Great of the Bulgars both made similar claims for Skopje and Tarnovo. During the reign of Ivan's grandfather, Vasily I, Moscow was just one of a number of jostling Russian states all under the yoke of the Golden Horde; the invasions of Timur Lenk distracted his overlords sufficiently for him to annex Nizhni Novgorod, Kaluga and Veliki Ustlug. His successor, Vasily II, was blinded in a vicious civil war before defeating Vasily the Cross-eyed to secure his son Ivan's patrimony.

However, Ivan and his successors would enjoy a crucial advantage over their Balkan predecessors: Moscow was beyond the grasp (and generally the interest) of the dominant power of the age, the Ottoman Empire. In 1453, Sultan Mehmet I had finally captured the "Second Rome," Constantinople, leaving Ivan free to style himself the champion of the Orthodox faith in its war with the infidel. Ivan was an insatiable acquirer of land, by any means available: military conquest, dynastic alliance, even legal subterfuge. In alliance with the Tatars of Crimea, he successfully campaigned against the Golden Horde, the nominal overlords of Muscovy for the first two decades of his reign. The climactic event of the conflict, the so-called "Great Stand of Ugra" (1480), was actually bathetically anticlimactic. The armies of Ivan and the Khan faced off on opposing banks of the Ugra River; Ivan's army, outnumbered, withdrew but the Tatars, inexplicably, chose not to pursue. Thereafter, Ivan ceased paying tribute to the Horde, leaving him a free hand to pursue his expansionist ambitions.

He picked off the rival city states of Yaroslavl, Rostov, Tver and finally Novgorod, with its substantial trade network in the Baltic. He defeated Lithuania at Vedrosha (1500), annexing large swathes of Ukraine, while his son Vasily III took control of the last surviving autonomous provinces of Pskov and Ryazan. Determined to safeguard his access to the Baltic, he had a huge fortress built at Ivangorod and, in alliance with Denmark, declared war upon Sweden (1495–97). The war ended ignominiously at the Swedish fort of Viborg, when the Russian besiegers fled in panic after the defenders detonated a massive explosion with gunpowder and barrels of tar.

Ivan's attitude to the church was both calculating and aggrandizing. He initially supported the monastic movement, because the foundation of monasteries in remote areas created convenient nuclei for the extension of his rule. However, he showed sympathy with the anti-monastic "Judaizer" movement – Christians who taught that it was necessary to adopt Jewish customs and practices. Ivan saw the potential in the movement's rejection of ecclesiastical hierarchy for cementing his own control over the church – and its copious assets. As the movement became progressively more radical – renouncing the Trinity and the divinity of Christ – Ivan's authoritarianism prevailed, and he sided with the ecclesiastical establishment, led by their chief inquisitor, Joseph Volotsky.

Ivan married the niece of the last Byzantine emperor, practiced elaborate Byzantine-style court rituals and adopted the cognomen "Tsar and Autocrat". Italian artists and craftsmen were hired for extravagant architectural projects, including an ornate extension of the Kremlin. However, for all Ivan's pretensions, and vast territorial gains, Muscovy had yet to be tested in combat against any of the major powers of the day. >>

Expansion of Muscovy
1462–1533
Expansion of Muscovy by 1462
Expansion of Muscovy by 1505
Expansion of Muscovy by 1533
Boundary of Muscovy by 1462
Boundary of Muscovy by 1505
Boundary of Muscovy by 1533
0
250 km
0
250 miles
N
LAPPS
Gulf of Bothnia
FINNS
SWEDISH EMPIRE
White Sea
Lake Onega
Lake Ladoga
REPUBLIC OF NOVGOROD
Olonets
Dvina
Veliki Ustiug
Kama
Perm Lands
Gulf of Finland
Reval
Ivangorod
Beloozero
Vologda
Viatka
Viatka Lands
Lake Peipus
Novgorod
TEUTONIC ORDER
Pskov
Riga
MUSCOVY
Kostroma
Yaroslavl
Rostov
Tver
Nizhniy Novgorod
Vladimir
Volga
Kazan
Moscow
Vilna
Vitebsk
Oka
LITHUANIA
Smolensk
Kolomna
KAZAN KHANATE
Minsk
Mogilev
Kaluga
Tula
Ryazan
Penza
Dnieper
Desna
POLAND
Pinsk
Orel
Novosil
Tambov
Novgorod-Seversk
Chernigov
Kursk
Kiev
Kharkov
ASTRAKHAN KHANATE
Don
Dnieper
Cherkassy
CRIMEAN KHANATE
Volga
Prutul
Jassi
Kishinev
MOLDAVIA
OTTOMAN EMPIRE
Azov
Astrakhan
Sea of Azov
Kerch
Black Sea
Kuban
Kuma

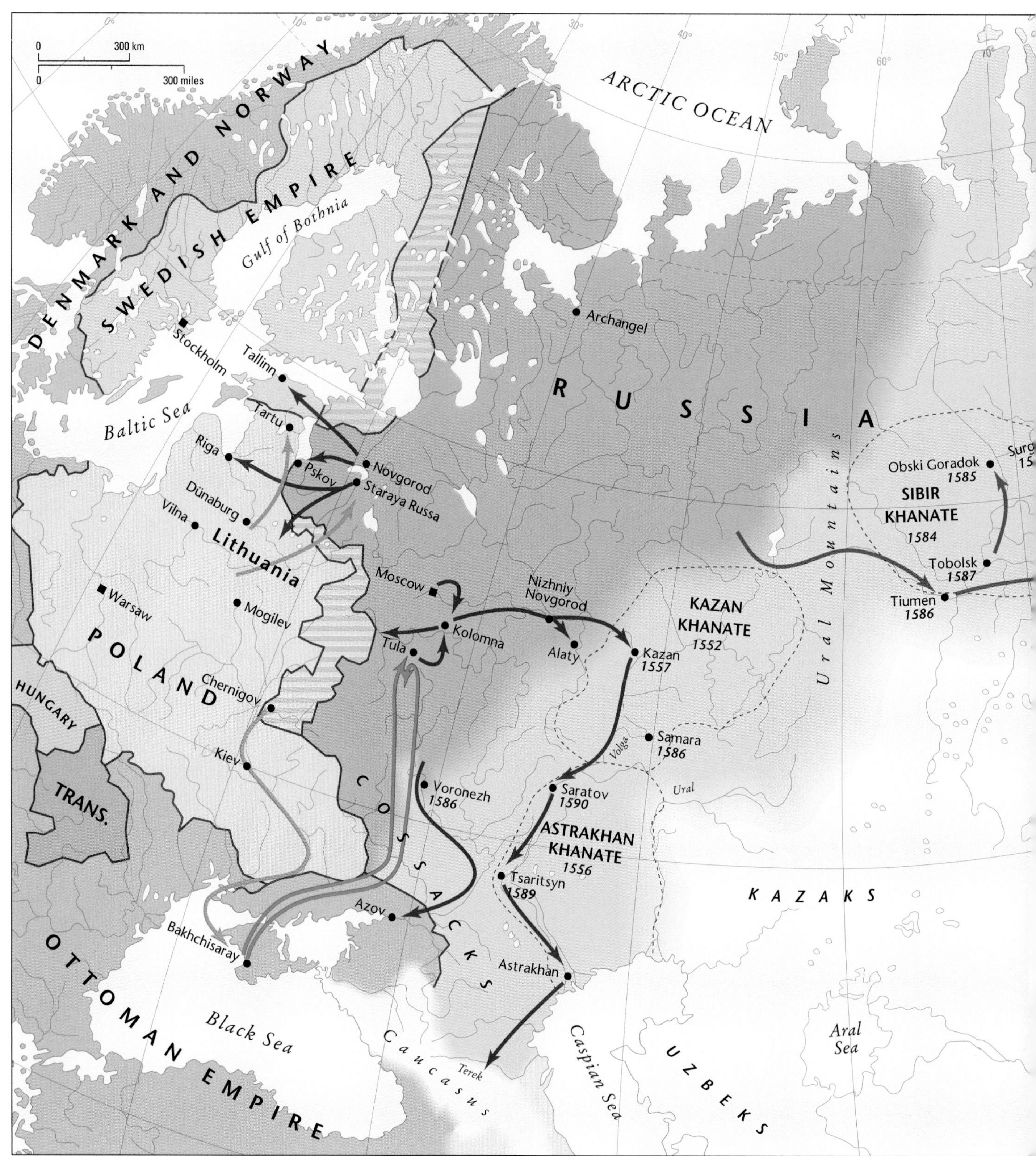
0 300 km
0 300 miles
ARCTIC OCEAN
DENMARK AND NORWAY
SWEDISH EMPIRE
Gulf of Bothnia
Stockholm
Tallinn
Baltic Sea
Tartu
Riga
Pskov
Novgorod
Staraya Russa
Dünaburg
Vilna
Lithuania
Archangel
RUSSIA
Moscow
Warsaw
Mogilev
POLAND
Kolomna
Tula
Nizhniy Novgorod
Alaty
Kazan 1557
KAZAN KHANATE 1552
Ural Mountains
Obski Goradok 1585
SIBIR KHANATE 1584
Tobolsk 1587
Tiumen 1586
HUNGARY
Chernigov
Kiev
TRANS.
Voronezh 1586
COSSACKS
Samara 1586
Volga
Ural
Saratov 1590
ASTRAKHAN KHANATE 1556
Tsaritsyn 1589
KAZAKS
Azov
Bakhchisaray
OTTOMAN EMPIRE
Astrakhan
Black Sea
Caucasus
Terek
Caspian Sea
UZBEKS
Aral Sea

The Stroganovs were descendants of the Pomors, hardy settlers on Russia's Arctic coast. They developed a sprawling commercial empire based on the mining of salt and iron, fur trading, and fisheries. In 1580, Ivan IV "the Terrible" (r. 1533–84) was being pummelled on his western borders by the allied forces of Sweden and Poland-Lithuania (he would ultimately lose most of Ingria and Livonia in the 1582 treaties concluding the war), and decided to salve his wounded pride with a punitive expedition against the Tatar Khan of Sibir. The Stroganovs were happy to oblige, and hired a Cossack ex-Volga river pirate, Yermak Timofeev, to lead the expedition. After defeating the Khan in battle, a victory that marked the beginning of the conquest of Siberia, Yermak's army fell victim to the Siberian winter, resorting to cannibalism before Yermak was killed in a Tatar ambush. But a trail had been blazed. By the century's end, the Tatars had been converted to Christianity, and missionaries, settlers, and gold prospectors fanned out around the fortress outposts of Tara and Tomsk.

Earlier in his reign, Ivan had waged a series of wars against the Tatar khanates on his southeastern borders, annexing both Kazan and Astrakhan. He celebrated by commissioning the eight-sided Red Square Cathedral of the Intercession to commemorate the eight victories of the campaign. The Crimean Tatars would prove more obdurate, repeatedly raiding Russian territory and even firing Moscow in 1571. Ivan retaliated with a decisive counter-attack, crushing the Tatars at the Battle of Molodi, 40 miles southeast of Moscow, in 1572.

Between these two victories, Ivan had initiated the programs of atrocities that would earn him his epithet. He created the *oprichnina*, a state-within-a-state outside the rule of law. Russia's first military police, the *oprichniki*, was a ruthless militia fuelled by lucrative grants of land and unbridled powers. Amongst the black-cloaked *oprichniki* who terrorized both the boyar aristocracy and the peasantry were Ivan's ever willing instruments, the Stroganovs.

Christianity

THE AGE OF REFORM
1500–1800

The Miracles of Saint Ignatius Loyola, Circle of Peter Paul Rubens, 1640

Catholicism in the New World

Jacques Gaspé planted a cross in Canadian territory in 1534 and claimed the new territory named "Canada" for King Francis I of France. Colonies established in the 16th century failed, but French fishing fleets visited Atlantic coastal communities and made contact with the First Nations. Following the arrival of Samuel Champlain and the foundation of Quebec City as the capital of New France in 1605, the Jesuits arrived in Canada in 1635 and became very active in the new colony.

One consequence of Pope Alexander VI's division of the world into Spanish an Portuguese zones of exploration in 1493 (the Treaty of Tordesillas) was that Brazil, which projects much further east into the Atlantic than any European realized at that time, fell into the Portuguese zone; it was duly claimed by Portugal and remains lusophone down to the present.

The colonization of the New World began with Christopher Columbus' discovery of Hispaniola in 1492. The Spanish began building an empire in the Caribbean, and conquistadors soon followed, penetrating deep into Central and South America, and southwestern North America, and conquering the great indigenous civilizations of Aztec Mexico (1519–21) and Inca Peru (1530s). The Portuguese arrived in Brazil as early as 1500.

The Hispanic colonies of Central and South America were completely dominated by the Catholic church. As early as 1493 Pope Alexander VI, in his papal bull *Inter caetera*, awarded colonial rights over the newly discovered lands to Spain and Portugal. A year later, by the Treaty of Tordesillas, the pope set up a demarcation line 370 leagues (1,185 miles) west of the Cape Verde Islands, which divided the world between the two Iberian claimants; no other nation ever accepted this papal disposition. Endorsed by the papacy, the Portuguese and Spanish colonists saw their actions as a religious crusade; they had received permission to seize the newly revealed land and claim it for Catholicism.

The Spanish and Portuguese monarchs were granted sweeping and unprecedented powers over the church in their colonial territories, giving them virtually total control over the appointment of clergy at all levels. Not only was the church the largest landowner in the colonies but it also aimed to control every aspect of its congregation's lives, from birth to marriage and death. The church sent out missionaries, who were responsible for converting the millions of New World natives to the Catholic faith, although often only in the most superficial sense. The church divided power and status by race, implementing a rigid social hierarchy, and enforcing its creed, sometimes with violence, threats, and enslavement. In this way the colonization of Latin America was reinforced by the notion of a Christianizing mission.

In 1511 the Dominican friar Antonio de Montsenos rebuked the church for its cruel and inhuman treatment of indigenous peoples, provoking an intense debate in 16th-century Spain about human rights. The *economida* system of forced or tenured labor, which dates to the beginning of the 16th century, effectively amounted to slavery. In 1524 Franciscan missionaries, known as the Twelve Apostles of Mexico, arrived in New Spain, followed by Dominicans in 1526 and Augustinians in 1533, while Jesuits arrived from the 1540s. In 1537 Pope Paul III issued the bull *Sublimis Deus*, confirming that American Indians were fully rational human beings who had the same rights to be baptized as the rest of humanity.

The Spanish *Requirimiento* was a legalistic proclamation that was read to local populations, demanding that they convert to Roman Catholicism on pain of slavery or death. It was a legal justification for the conquest of local peoples, on the grounds of their refusing the "legitimate" authority of the kings of Spain and Portugal, which had been granted by the pope.

The first wave of missionary efforts in South America were characterized by mass baptisms and conversions, accompanied by campaigns to eradicate indigenous gods and religous practices. Native workers built new, and increasingly impressive, churches, which it was believed would supplant old places of traditional worship. But little attempt was made to understand the culture, religious practices, or beliefs of the native peoples. It soon became clear that pre-Hispanic religious practices, such as Andean ancestor worship, persisted underground.

The Jesuits worked successfully on the fringes of sedentary societies, amongst the nomadic hunter-gatherers, and the goal was to create autonomous missionary societies, sometimes called *reducciones*, which became an increasingly important new world institution. But the missionaries also brought deadly diseases to which the natives had no resistance, and in new mission settlements natives were living in cramped spaces with poor hygiene, where diseases spread. The epidemics the missionaries introduced may have done much to persuade the natives of the power of the new faith.

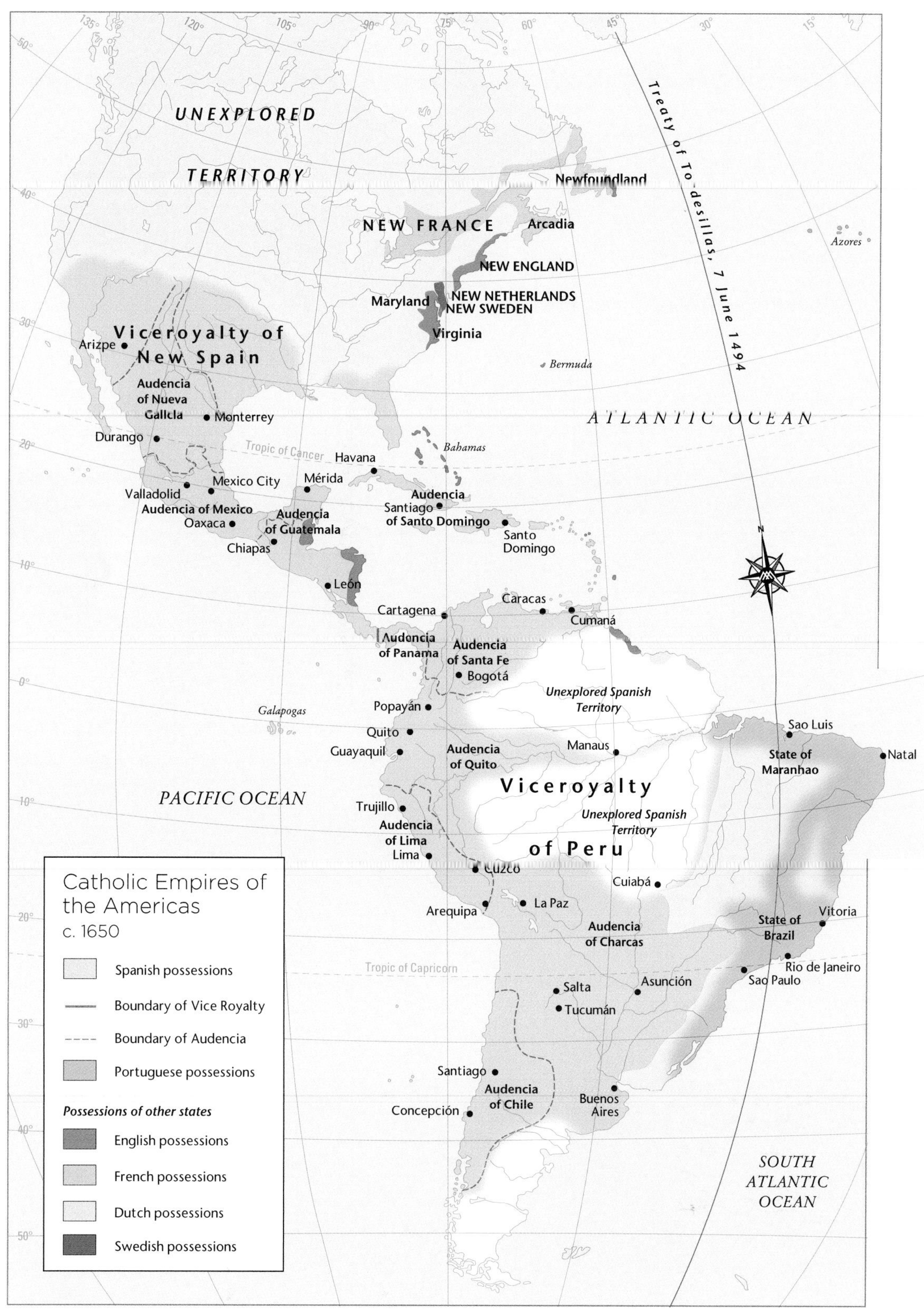
UNEXPLORED
TERRITORY
NEW FRANCE
Newfoundland
Arcadia
NEW ENGLAND
Maryland
NEW NETHERLANDS
NEW SWEDEN
Virginia
Treaty of Tordesillas, 7 June 1494
Azores
Bermuda
Viceroyalty of New Spain
Arizpe
Audencia of Nueva Galicia
Monterrey
Durango
Tropic of Cancer
Havana
Bahamas
ATLANTIC OCEAN
Mexico City
Mérida
Valladolid
Audencia of Mexico
Oaxaca
Audencia of Guatemala
Chiapas
Audencia
Santiago
of Santo Domingo
Santo Domingo
León
Caracas
Cumaná
Cartagena
Audencia of Panama
Audencia of Santa Fe
Bogotá
Unexplored Spanish Territory
Galapogas
Popayán
Quito
Guayaquil
Audencia of Quito
Manaus
Sao Luis
State of Maranhao
Natal
PACIFIC OCEAN
Viceroyalty of Peru
Trujillo
Audencia of Lima
Lima
Cuzco
Cuiabá
Arequipa
La Paz
Audencia of Charcas
State of Brazil
Vitoria
Rio de Janeiro
Sao Paulo
Tropic of Capricorn
Asunción
Salta
Tucumán
Santiago
Audencia of Chile
Concepción
Buenos Aires
SOUTH ATLANTIC OCEAN
Catholic Empires of the Americas
c. 1650
Spanish possessions
Boundary of Vice Royalty
Boundary of Audencia
Portuguese possessions
Possessions of other states
English possessions
French possessions
Dutch possessions
Swedish possessions

Catholic Missions in the Old World

Having conquered the last Muslim occupiers of the Iberian peninsula in 1492, the Spanish and Portuguese, who were embarking on projects of global maritime exploration even before Columbus' discovery of a sea route across the Atlantic the same year, began to extend Western Christendom beyond the boundaries of Europe.

The Portuguese had begun their colonial adventures in Ceuta in North Africa in 1415, and were soon pushing southward down Africa's Atlantic seaboard. Early conquistadors were always accompanied by at least one chaplain, and in 1482 Diogo Cão came into contact with large villages in Kongo; the king and his wife were eventually baptized in 1491. The Portuguese rounded the Cape of Good Hope and reached India by 1498. Having gained a foothold on new territories, they set about missionary projects to convert indigenous populations, with varying degrees of persuasion and coercion. Once Christianized, Portuguese subjects in these territories came under the Inquisition's authority. The Inquisition also claimed oversight of indigenous Christian populations, such as the Syriac Nestorians of India, who date their beliefs to the 1st century CE. Yet Portuguese colonial holdings were precarious footholds, coastal trading ports that did not have the resources or manpower to penetrate further inland, or undertake a program of Christian proselytization.

In 1493 Pope Alexander VI had authorized a compromise in which Spain and Portugal divided the non-Christian world into distinct zones of exploration: in its final form, this deal drew a meridian down the Atlantic and another down the western Pacific, with Spain claiming rights to settle the western hemisphere and Portugal

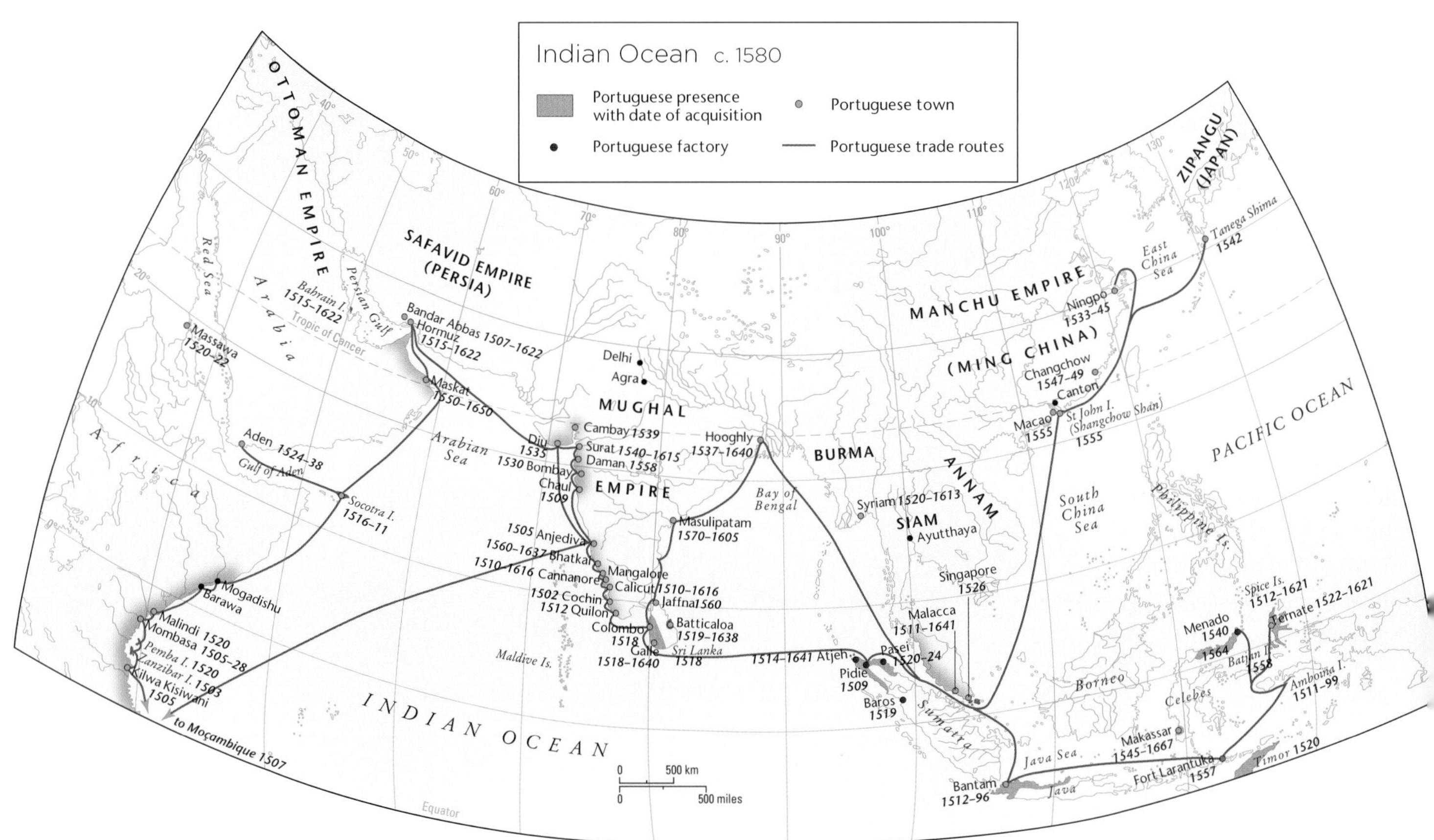

the eastern. It soom became apparent that the world was much larger than originally supposed. This move effectively protected Portugal's new trade routes around the African coast, and into Asia. As a result, Portugal quickly grew rich from the monopoly on the eastern trade route to India and the Spice Islands.

Pope Julius II (r. 1503–13) granted the Portuguese the *Padroado*, near-absolute authority over the church in their new territories, effectively abdicating papal authority within their domains. But Portugal's colonial adventures were bringing it up against powerful Asian empires that had already experienced contacts over several centuries with Europe and were therefore not susceptible to obliteration by new diseases, as was the case in Latin America, and which could easily match the military and economic sophistication of the Europeans. It was only in small enclaves, such as Goa, that the Portuguese could indulge in untrammelled promotion of their Catholic faith – it was in Goa that they built St Catherine's, the largest Catholic cathedral in Asia.

As everywhere in the Catholic world, the mainstays of the mission were the religious orders, in particular the Franciscan friars and the newly founded Society of Jesus, or Jesuits. The Jesuit mission to the East, which was pioneered by Francis Xavier from 1542 onward, was distinguished by its cultural creativity, as Jesuit missionary theologians such as Alessandro Valignano reached well beyond European colonial territories and tried to build forms of Christianity that respected and adapted to indigenous languages, cultures, social structures and even to religious norms.

In southern India an Italian Jesuit named Robert de Nobili (1577–1656) adopted the dress of an Indian holy man and gained the status of a guru amongst the lower castes. The Portuguese furiously opposed him, but lost their case against him in Rome in 1623. Conversions to Catholicism in the Tamil regions were predominantly due to the efforts of Nobili and his Italian successors.

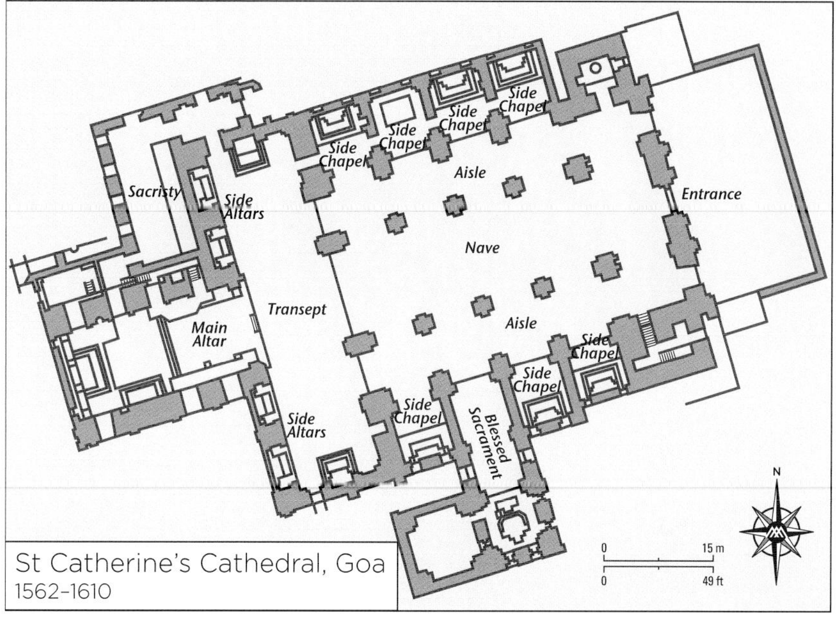

St Catherine's Cathedral, Goa
1562–1610

The Portuguese arrived in Ceylon (Sri Lanka) in 1505, and intervened in a number of succession struggles in small local kingdoms, converting many princely rulers to Catholicism, and controlling most of the island with the exception of the Central Highlands and the east coast. Franciscan missionaries established centers from 1543 onwards, and Dominicans and Augustinians arrived by the end of the 16th century. The Portuguese used their powers of patronage and preference to promote Christianity, which became well established amongst the landed aristocracy. Many coastal communities, especially in the region around Colombo, underwent mass coversions and Catholic churches and schools were built all over the country. In 1658 the Dutch East India Company displaced the Portuguese. The Dutch were Calvinists and expelled all Catholic priests from the island, but made only limited efforts actually to convert the Catholic population and none at all to win over Hindus or Buddhists. Many Catholics remained loyal, settling in the independent Kandyan kingdom, beyond Dutch control. No priest worked on the island until Joseph Vaz, a member of the Oratory of Goa, arrived secretly in 1687 to begin reorganizing the church. >>

The Portuguese sailed through Indonesian waters in 1511, seeking sandalwood and spices from the Spice Islands. Catholic communities were soon established in the Moluccas, Amboine, and Ternate. From 1546–47 St Francis Xavier spent 14 months in what is now Indonesia and founded a minor seminary in Ternate, and Dominicans also settled in the region, establishing a seminary in Solor, the hub of the sandalwood trade, in 1596. By the end of the 16th century there were more than 22,000 Catholics in Indonesia. As Dutch control expanded in the East Indies the Dominicans moved eastward, eventually reaching the coast of East Timor in the late 18th century. The Dutch East India Company moved to suppress the Catholic missions in the Spice Islands because they supported their Portuguese trading rivals, but carried out little missionary activity, being concerned to avoid disputes with the local Islamic authorities that might disrupt trade. However, some Catholics under Dutch rule converted to Protestantism, or to Islam, notably along the coast of Solor and Flores. In 1615 the first Protestant Church was established in Ambon.

China was one of the world's most powerful empires and was resistant to any contact with foreign countries, even for mercantile purposes. The Jesuits decided that they must espouse the customs of their hosts and when the Italian Matteo Ricci, the first Jesuit to enter Beijing, arrived in 1582 he adopted the costume of a Buddhist monk, which he quickly changed to a Confucian scholar, realizing that he would gain much more respect from people in authority. He had learnt Chinese in Macao and he lived peaceably in the predominantly Buddhist province of Guangdong for more than a decade. The Jesuits were able to impress the Chinese scholarly class with their knowledge of mathematics,

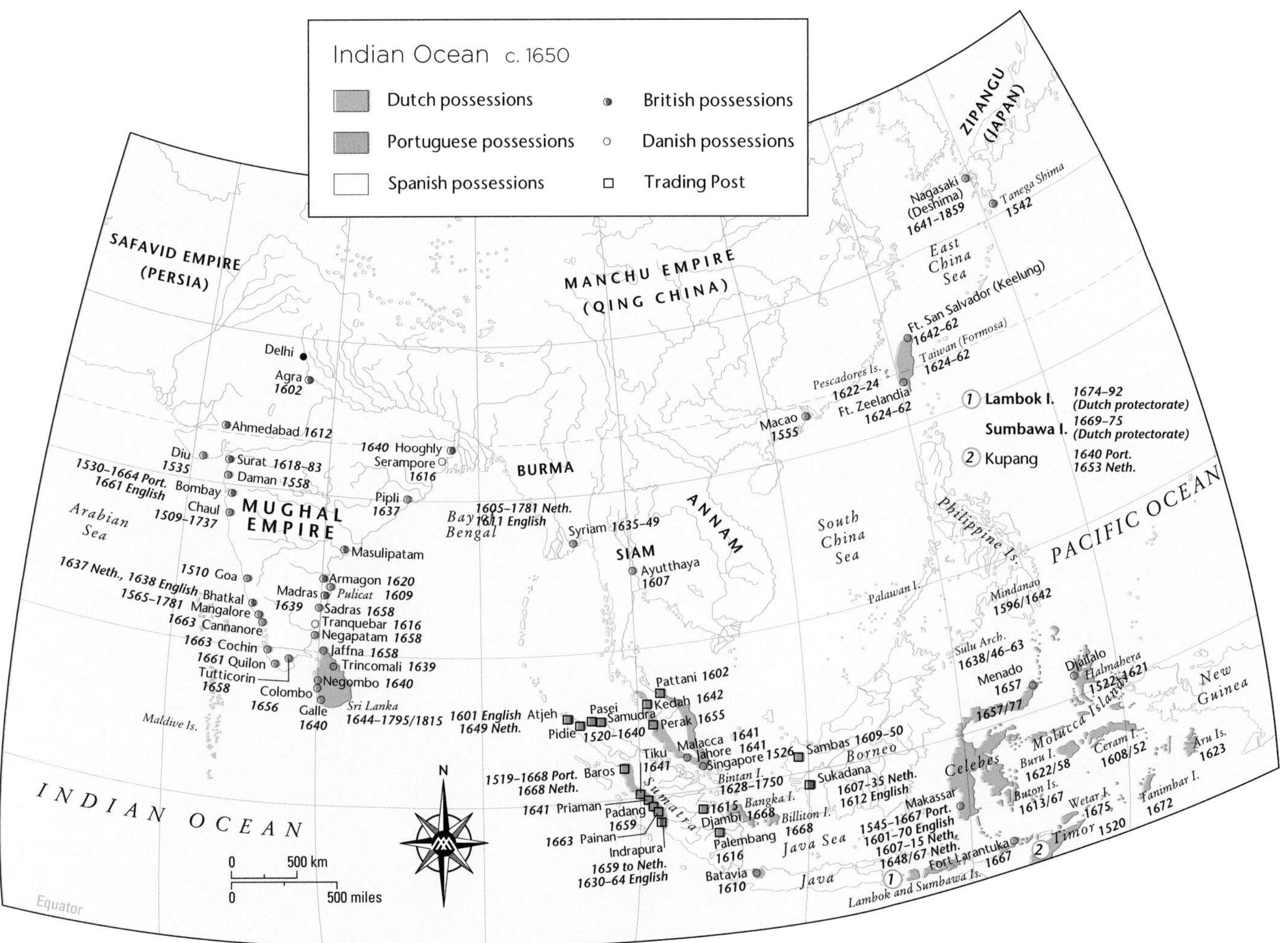

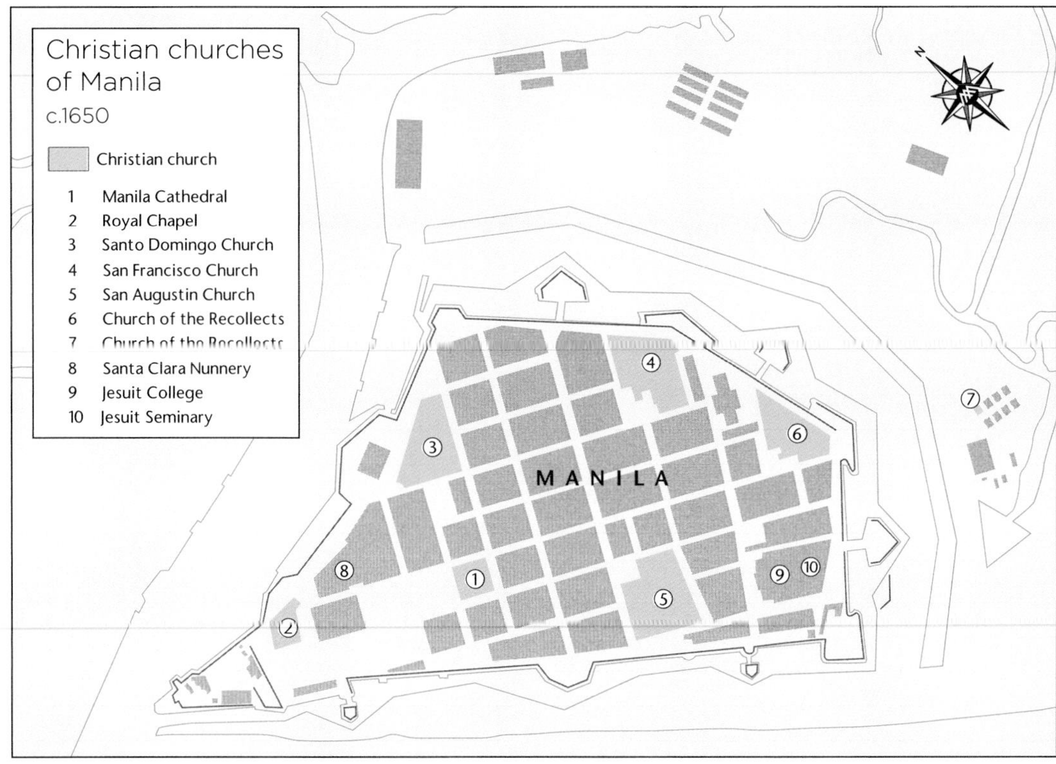

astronomy, and geography. However, when the Dominicans and Franciscans arrived in China in the early 17th century they launched bitter attacks on their Jesuit rivals, disagreeing with their acceptance of the Chinese way of life. The Jesuits remained a highly respected presence in the Chinese court. Finally, in 1704, the papacy condemned the accommodations the Jesuits had made to their Chinese converts, and after this "Chinese rites" controversy the Jesuits were expelled from China. Chinese Catholicism would be marginalized for more than a century.

A similar but much bloodier story of thwarted hoped unfolded in Japan. Francis Xavier and his fellow Jesuits arrived in Japan in 1549, and converted some 300,000 Japanese to Christianity by the end of the century. However, the Jesuit mission became inextricably caught up with Portuguese trade initiatives, and ultimately that proved their downfall – the Tokugawa shogunate began to see Christianity, and the concomitant trade it introduced, as a threat. When Franciscan friars arrived in 1593, a number of them were executed. In the early 17th century all Europeans were expelled from Japan, with the exception of one trading post, and Christian converts within Japan were savagely persecuted, especially after a failed uprising in the Christian stronghold of Nagasaki in 1637. Following tens of thousands of deaths, Japan was completely closed to foreign contacts for more than two centuries, and the small surviving Christian population driven underground.

The one significant Spanish territory in Asia was the Philippines, first claimed for Spain by Ferdinand Magellan in 1521 and named for a Spanish king. The first Catholic mass was conducted on the island of Limasawa on Easter Sunday, 1521. Within a month the king and queen of Cebu had converted. Spanish missionaries began to arrive and within 25 years about 250,000 Filipinos – half the population – had converted to Christianity. The monastic presses produced books on the catechism in Spanish and Tagalog, which helped in the rapid propagation of the new faith. Religious orders, including the Franciscans, Dominicans and Augustinians, held large tracts of land granted by the Spanish government, and acted as landlords, responsible for the material and spiritual wellbeing of their tenants. Native priests were blocked from holding authority in local parishes by the church and government; the Filipino priesthood became radicalized, and influential, nationalists.

The Protestant Reformation

The revolution that took place in the Western church in the 16th century, spearheaded by Martin Luther, would have political, social, and economic effects and would lead to the foundation of Protestantism.

The Reformation emerged against a background of growing criticism of the temporal power and wealth of the Roman Catholic church, which many felt was matched by its growing spiritual bankruptcy. This perceived corruption was epitomized by practices such as the selling of indulgences by the clergy, which absolved penitents and promised remission of their sins, while also turning the pious hopes of the laity into cash for the church. The church's political power, moreover, had never properly recovered from the crisis of the Western Schism, and kings and princes were increasingly ready to defy the papacy. However, the near-universal commitment of western Christians to the norms of the Catholic faith prevented these problems from turning into a crisis – for now.

What was new about the critique advanced by Martin Luther (1483–1546), a professor of theology at the University of Wittenberg in Saxony, in his Ninety-Five Theses on indulgences in 1517 was that he mixed widespread moral revulsion at corruption with a radically new theological critique. As his critics confronted him during the late 1510s and his case became a *cause celebre*, he argued that the church's corruption was only a symptom of a much deeper problem. The church had been trying to sell something – salvation – which Christ's gospel offered for free. With this insight, he came to argue that the church's entire authority collapsed like a house of cards: everything, from the papacy through the religious orders and the doctrine of purgatory to the miracle of the Mass itself, was a confidence trick played on Christians by a hierarchy who were using invented complexities to fleece the faithful. All that was needed was the "pure gospel," the Bible itself, which the newly invented printing press and, soon enough, Luther's own German translation was putting directly into the hands of the common people. Repudiating the pope as Antichrist, Luther taught that faith in Christ alone was all that Christians needed to be saved.

Luther was condemned as a heretic in 1521, but it was too late: he was already building a mass movement, built in part on his unparalleled mastery of the new technology of print, which allowed him to appeal directly to the people. When the movement was condemned by the Diet of the Holy Roman Empire at Speyer in 1529, a small group of German cities and princes lodged a formal "Protestation" and thereafter were known as "Protestants."

The Holy Roman Emperor, Charles V, was committed to suppressing Luther's movement, but, locked in quarrels with France and the Ottoman Empire, he was not able to launch a campaign against the Protestants until 1546, the year of Luther's death. After a crushing victory at the Battle of Mühlberg in 1547 it looked as if Luther's Reformation might be over – but Protestant hardliners, holed up in the city of Magdeburg and elsewhere, regrouped and in 1555 secured the legal right to practice the new "Lutheran" form of Christianity in the Empire.

Meanwhile, Luther's Reformation had spread well beyond the Empire's borders. The kingdoms of Sweden and Denmark had embraced Lutheranism in 1527 and 1536 respectively, there were substantial Lutheran minorities in Poland and the Netherlands, and sympathies as far afield as Italy. In 1534 King Henry VIII of England took advantage of the confusion to reject the pope's authority in his own kingdom too, although he did little more than flirt with Luther's theology and was more concerned to establish himself as Supreme Head of the English Church.

Luther's teachings rapidly permeated all levels of German society. For all his spiritual radicalism, he was socially and politically very much a traditionalist. His famous claim, in his 1520 tract *The Liberty of a Christian*, that "a Christian is a free lord over all things and subject to none" was a statement of inner, spiritual freedom. He neither expected nor intended that so many would hear it as a call to revolution. >>

The Lutheran Reformation in Central Europe c. 1560

Lutherans
Calvinists and Zwinglians
Moravians
Anabaptists, Socinians, Antitrinitarians etc.
Roman Catholics
Battle

Abbreviations

A. Archbishopric
B. Bishopric
C. County
D. Duchy
M. Margravate
P. Principality

In early 16th-century Germany the peasants' lot was unenviable. They paid taxes and levies to support clergy and nobility, and were frequently required to provide compulsory labor for their landlords. As population levels rose and land was in ever shorter supply, land that had previously been held in common – for grazing, fishing, forestry and so on – was increasingly being appropriated by overlords, eroding traditional rights held by the peasants.

The repeated unrest of the Late Middle Ages did not further the peasants' cause. But Martin Luther's new doctrine appeared to give them some hope; the doctrine of individual Christian freedom seemed to repudiate the practices of bondage and serfdom. Fired up by radical preachers who were ready to draw out the implications of Luther's message, they began to formulate demands. They called for the abolition of serfdom, a lowering of taxes, an end to the enclosure of common land, and the freedom to elect their own parish priests. They were met with implacable opposition from their landlords, and rebellions broke out village by village, starting in Sühlingen. Eventually risings extended from the Tyrol and Switzerland in the south to Alsace, Upper Swabia, and Thuringia. Pragmatic demands for concrete improvements in rights and living conditions were mixed with apocalyptic hopes for a dawning kingdom of the saints. The result was the "Peasants' War," the largest mass uprising in European history until the French Revolution.

The peasant armies were ill-equipped and untrained and, despite some inspirational leadership, they were repeatedly confronting the armies of feudal lords who were able to levy troops from their own lands and to pay for mercenaries to swell their forces. The first important battle took place at Leipheim in April 1525, where the peasants were confronted by the forces of the Swabian League, and defeated. The same pattern was repeated at Frankenhausen, Böblingen, Königshofen, and Würzburg, leaving tens of thousands of peasant casualties.

The radical reformer Thomas Müntzer was a parish priest from Mühlhausen in Thuringia, who supported the peasant cause and tried to unite the peasant troops of Thuringia, where he organized a group called the Eternal Covenant of God. Müntzer believed that if the common people sacrificed individual interests for the group, they would be demonstrating that the will of God could transform society, eradicating both social and legal distinctions. He aligned the liberation of the peasantry with the liberation of all Christendom. But in May 1525 he was captured at the Battle of Frankenhausen and was tortured and put to death.

Martin Luther's attitude was initially sympathetic and, in his "Admonition for Peace" he condemned the arrogant attitude of the sovereigns, while also urging the peasants to restrict themselves to peaceful petitioning. But he became increasingly alarmed by the violence and chaos that had been unleashed and began to distance himself from the rebels. Indeed, in his pamphlet "Against the Murderous, Thieving Hordes of Peasants" (1525) he urged the ruling class to strike down the peasants as if they were mad dogs.

The peasant cause was doomed; they were ranged against the entire ruling class, together with their knights, mercenaries, swords, and cannons, and were poorly armed, ill-trained, with no command structure. The carnage that followed was unimaginable, leaving over 70,000 peasants dead. A brutal reign of terror followed, when captured leaders were beheaded, or hanged, drawn, and quartered.

The Peasants' War (1524–25) left a bitter aftermath. Luther, having sided firmly with the authorities, had demonstrated his respectability and became the acceptable face of reform. The surviving radicals were driven into starker alternatives. Many of them became "Anabaptists," rejecting the idea of a universal church in favor of a select community of the faithful. One such group seized the German city of Munster in 1534–35, setting up a short-lived, and apocalyptic "kingdom," which was eradicated, with bloody reprisals, by the authorities. But most Anabaptists withdrew into pacifism and separatism, building localized communities in east-central Europe, the Netherlands and elsewhere in the face of persecution from Catholic and Protestant states alike. Many eventually emigrated to the relative safety of North America.

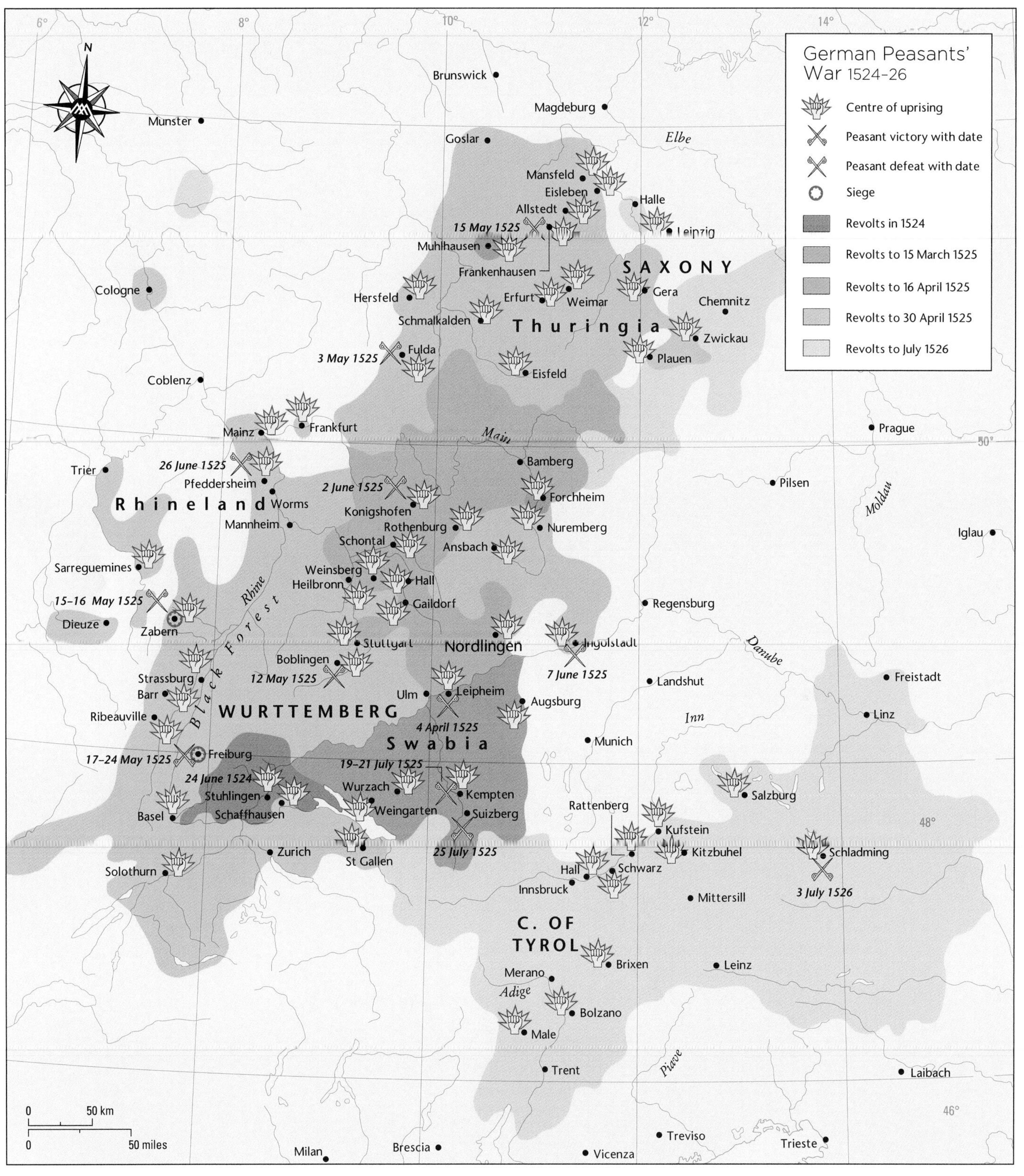
German Peasants' War 1524–26
Centre of uprising
Peasant victory with date
Peasant defeat with date
Siege
Revolts in 1524
Revolts to 15 March 1525
Revolts to 16 April 1525
Revolts to 30 April 1525
Revolts to July 1526
SAXONY
Thuringia
Rhineland
WURTTEMBERG
Swabia
Nordlingen
C. OF TYROL
Black Forest
Elbe
Main
Rhine
Danube
Inn
Moldau
Adige
Piave
Brunswick
Magdeburg
Munster
Goslar
Mansfeld
Eisleben
Halle
Allstedt
15 May 1525
Leipzig
Muhlhausen
Frankenhausen
Cologne
Hersfeld
Erfurt
Weimar
Gera
Chemnitz
Schmalkalden
Zwickau
3 May 1525
Fulda
Plauen
Eisfeld
Coblenz
Frankfurt
Mainz
Prague
Bamberg
Trier
26 June 1525
Pfeddersheim
2 June 1525
Pilsen
Forchheim
Worms
Konigshofen
Mannheim
Rothenburg
Nuremberg
Iglau
Schontal
Ansbach
Sarreguemines
Weinsberg
Heilbronn
Hall
15–16 May 1525
Gaildorf
Regensburg
Dieuze
Zabern
Stuttgart
Ingolstadt
Boblingen
Strassburg
12 May 1525
7 June 1525
Landshut
Freistadt
Barr
Ulm
Leipheim
Augsburg
Ribeauville
Linz
4 April 1525
Munich
17–24 May 1525
Freiburg
19–21 July 1525
24 June 1524
Wurzach
Stuhlingen
Kempten
Salzburg
Basel
Schaffhausen
Weingarten
Rattenberg
Suizberg
Kufstein
Zurich
25 July 1525
Kitzbuhel
Schladming
St Gallen
Solothurn
Hall
Schwarz
Innsbruck
3 July 1526
Mittersill
Brixen
Leinz
Merano
Bolzano
Male
Trent
Laibach
Treviso
Trieste
Milan
Brescia
Vicenza
0
50 km
0
50 miles
6°
8°
10°
12°
14°
50°
48°
46°
N

The Second Reformation: Calvinism

The Reformed tradition began in 1519 in Zurich under Huldrych Zwingli, soon followed by Martin Bucer, Wolfgang Capito, John Oecolampadius and Guillaume Farel. These theologians joined Luther in teaching salvation by faith and the exclusive authority of Scripture, but in contrast to Luther's spiritually focused, socially conservative reforms, they advocated a thoroughgoing purification of the church and of Christian life, and their rejection of Christ's bodily presence in the Eucharist led by 1529 to an irreparable breach with Luther.

The French reformer John Calvin (1509–64) belonged to a second generation of Reformed thinkers, which included Heinrich Bullinger, Wolfgans Musculus, and Andreas Hyperius. Forced into exile in 1534, Calvin settled in the city of Geneva, where – after nearly two decades of turmoil – he and other French Reformed refugees succeeded in forging a model Reformed Protestant republic. Before arriving in Geneva, Calvin also published the first edition of his *Institutes of the Christian Religion*, a systematic theological treatise around which he hoped the riven Protestant world could unite. The quarrel with the Lutherans turned out to be beyond healing, but Calvin, in the Zurich Consensus of 1549, did manage to unite the various Reformed cities and territories around the position that became known as Calvinism.

The model church he developed in Geneva abandoned the traditional hierarchy of bishops for a collective form of church government, with strict moral discipline applied without regard to social status. This rigorous, flexible structure, which unlike Lutheranism did not need support from rulers and could even flourish in the face of persecution, began to spread rapidly across Europe from the 1550s, in a so-called "Second Reformation." A series of German territories, and the island kingdoms of England and Scotland, adopted variants of Calvinism, and substantial Calvinist minorities sprang up in Poland, Hungary, the Netherlands, and France – in the latter two cases, helping to trigger devastating religious civil wars from the 1560s onward.

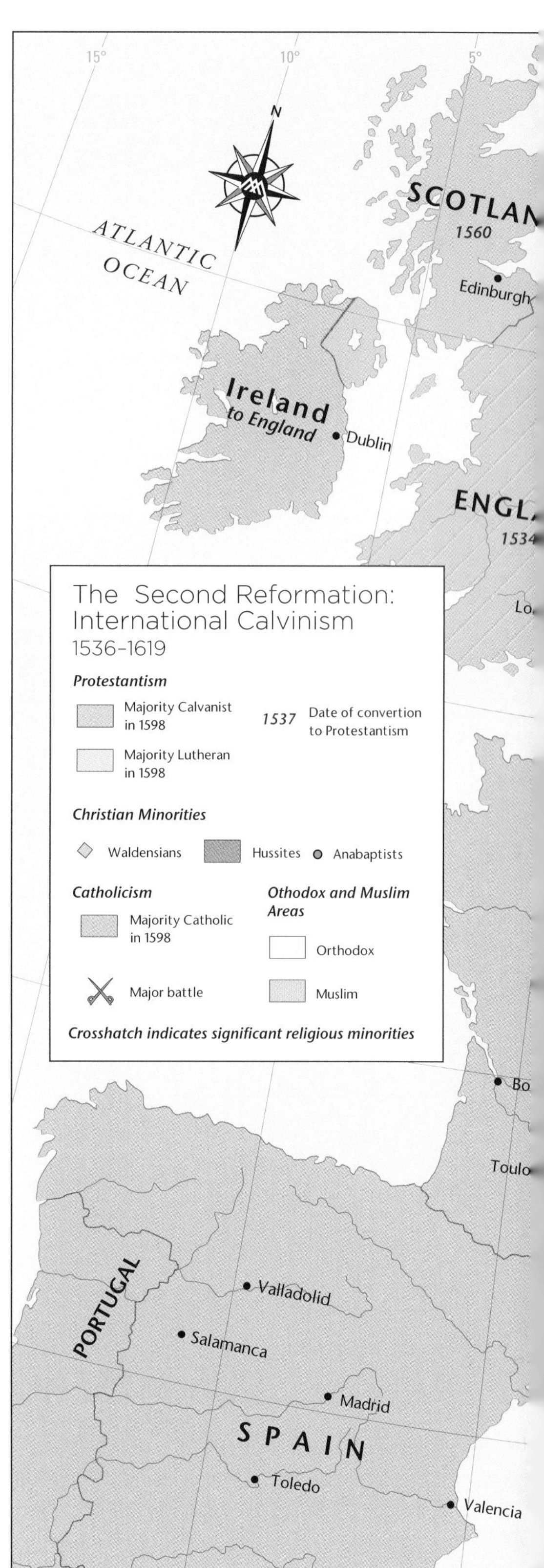

SWEDEN
DENMARK AND NORWAY
Stockholm
Estonia
Livonia
Riga
Courland
Lithuania
RUSSIA
North Sea
Baltic Sea
Copenhagen
Prussia
Danzig
Holstein
Lubeck
Mecklenburg
Hamburg
Stettin
POLAND
United Provinces
Amsterdam
Antwerp
Brandenburg
Berlin
Warsaw
Ukraine
Volhynia
Munster
Silesia
Muhlberg 1547
Brussels
Spanish Netherlands
Liege
Leipzig
Saxony
1542
Glatz
Fulda
Crakow
Podolia
Douai
Mons
Frankfurt
Mainz
Bamberg
Prague
Kuttenberg
Galicia
Bohemia
Moravia
Trier
Wurzburg
Rheims
Verdun
Brunn
Jedisan
Ingolstadt
Tyrnava
Strasbourg
Bavaria
Austria
Vienna
Moldavia
Dillingen
Austria-Hungary
Transylvania
Buda
Pest
Basel
Graz
Zurich
1523
Salzburg
Styria
Bourges
Neuhaus
Bern
1529
Tyrol
SWISS CONFED.
Hungary
Geneva
Wallis
1536
Trent
Carinthia
Wallachia
Milan
Venice
Savoy
Belgrade
Parma
Serbia
Genoa
Modena
Bulgaria
Black Sea
Avignon
Lucca
Bosnia
OTTOMAN EMPIRE
Tuscany
PAPAL STATES
Adriatic Sea
Constantinople
Rome
NAPLES
Naples
Sassari
Corsica
Sardinia
Greece
Aegean Sea
Cagliari
Athens
Mediterranean Sea
1537
1527
1536
0 200 km
0 200 miles

Wars of Religion in the Holy Roman Empire

The Wars of Religion in the 16th and 17th centuries may have been impelled by religious belief, division, and conflict, but they were also inextricably entangled with more temporal concerns, relating to territory, power, and hegemony. Germany was the heartland of the Reformation, which began in 1517, and many princes of the Holy Roman Empire, which had a quasi-federal structure, converted to the Protestant cause, leading to intermittent religious conflict. In 1531 the Lutheran territories of the Empire formed a defensive league, the Schmalkadic League, to resist any attempt to enforce the decisions of the Diet of Augsburg (1530), which had given Protestant territories a deadline by which they should return to Catholicism. The League was led by Elector John Frederick I of Saxony and Landgrave Philip I of Hesse and counted amongst its original members Brunswick, Anhalt and the cities of Mansfeld, Magdeburg, Strassburg, Bremen, and Ulm. Emperor Charles V, fearful that they would ally with his enemy France, gave the League de facto recognition until 1544, when he made peace with France.

It was clear that, in any conflict, the emperor would command greater resources. However, the members of the League believed that they were in a position to mobilize their troops faster, and therefore it would be wise to wage a preventative war. Martin Luther had been deeply opposed to a war between the League and the emperor, but his death in February 1546 removed that objection.

There were two phases to the war. In the south an initial League offensive caught Charles off-guard in Regensburg, and he escaped the League's forces by outmaneuvering them and then joining forces with papal troops, who arrived via neutral Bavaria, and heavy cavalry from the Netherlands. The second phase of the war shifted to the north, when Duke Maurice of Saxony invaded the lands of his rival and stepbrother, John Frederick I. John Frederick swiftly took ducal Saxony, but during his later occupation of Bohemia, found himself exposed and without the expected military support of the Protestants of Bohemia and he was forced to retreat. At the Battle of Mühlberg on 24 April 1547 the imperial troops destroyed the scattered Protestant formations and John Frederick was taken prisoner. It seemed likely that the Reformation would be crushed, and Charles V himself stood in triumph at Luther's grave.

Charles stripped John Frederick and Philip of Hesse of their domains, and declared a religious settlement, the Augsburg Interim, which made only minimal concessions to the Protestants. However, Magdeburg became the center of Protestant resistance, propagating the Lutheran message in effective pamphlet campaigns, which ensured the survival, and even recognition, of the Lutheran cause throughout Protestant Europe. When Maurice of Saxony changed sides to support the Protestants once again, and Henry II of France, spotting an opportunity to discomfort his old rival Charles V, invaded the Empire, Charles was forced to accept defeat.

The Peace of Augsburg (1555) was promulgated by the Diet of the Holy Roman Empire in September 1555, creating the legal conditions for Protestants and Catholics to co-exist. Princes were allowed to choose between Lutheranism and Catholicism as the religion of their domain. Their decision applied to their citizens as well (*cuius regio, eius religio*: "whoever rules, his the religion"), and any dissenters were allowed to migrate to a more sympathetic realm. No prince would make war on another prince on religious grounds. Only Lutheranism was permitted: Anabaptists and Calvinists remained outside the law. In the Catholic ecclesiastical states any bishop who wanted to convert to Lutheranism had to resign first; the refusal of the archbishop of Cologne to do so led to the war of 1583–88, when a coalition of Catholic princes forcibly removed him. The Catholics' success was a turning point. Up to this point the Catholics, faced with the energized adherents of Protestantism, had been on the defensive; Cologne proved that they could unite to fight for their cause. The Catholic princes began to enforce the principle of *cuius regio* with vigor.

The religious geography of Germany was highly complex at the beginning of the 17th century. South of the Danube was firmly Catholic, while Lutherans predominated northeast of the Elbe, and in between was a mosaic of Calvinist, Lutheran, and Catholic states. Faced with increasingly assertive Catholics, Elector Frederick IV of the Palatinate formed the Evangelical, or Protestant, Union in 1608. When the childless duke of Cleves-Jülich died both the potential successors to his duchy, where Protestants and Catholics co-existed, were Protestant and the Catholic population was therefore faced with expulsion. The Emperor refused to recognize the Protestant princes' claim, so they sought help from the Union. In response a Catholic League was formed in 1609 between Duke Maximilian of Bavaria and his neighbors. The formation of militant confessional alliances was to play an important role in the hostilities to come.

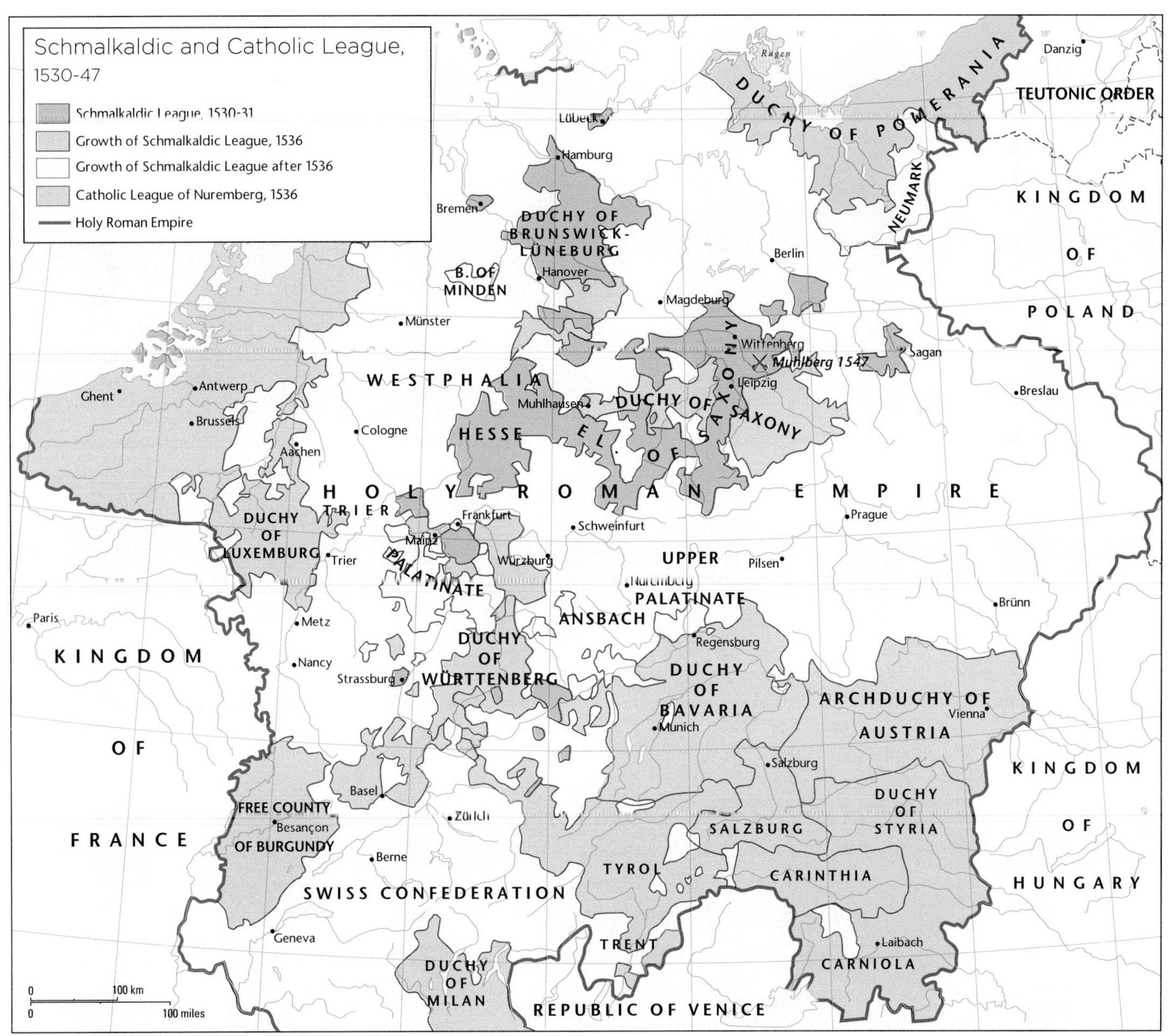

The Papal States and the Holy League

The Italian Wars, which had begun when France invaded the peninsula in 1494, were a conflict between France and Spain for control of Italy, and its mosaic of kingdoms, duchies, and republics – including the papal states – had formed a complex series of alliances and treaties as a means of containing the ambitions of their powerful neighbors. Pope Julius II (r. 1503–13), the "warrior pope," took up arms and led his troops in defense of the papal lands, joining the League of Cambrai to defeat Venice in 1509 and embarking on an unsuccessful attempt from 1510–11 to drive the French from Italy; they eventually left following a revolt in 1512.

The Italian Wars dragged on, however, and in 1527 mutinous troops of the Holy Roman Empir – predominantly *landsknechte*, but also some Italian and Spanish mercenaries, who were stationed in Italy and had not been paid – entered Rome. Despite a heroic defense by the massively outnumbered Swiss Guard, they laid waste to much of the city and brutalized its population. Pope Clement VII took refuge in Castel Sant' Angelo and was forced to pay a ransom for his life. The Sack of Rome forced the pope to reach an accommodation with the Spanish; he no longer had the resources to resist their territorial ambitions in Italy. Emperor Charles V, faced with Europe-wide criticism of his army's depredations, left the papal states intact and guaranteed Medici rule over Florence.

Meanwhile, the Protestant Reformation had been spreading unchecked in Germany. Turning to the problem, Charles favored reform and conciliation, while the papacy took a harder line. After an attempt at a negotiated settlement with the Protestants failed in 1541, Charles and Pope Paul III agreed to convene the Council of Trent (154–63), which staunchly reaffirmed Catholic doctrines while also pursuing far-reaching institutional and disciplinary reform. It became the launchpad for the Counter-Reformation.

The papal states were now subordinate to Habsburg Spain's Kingdom of Naples, but keen to reassert their power in Italy. In 1571, a Holy League engineered by Pope Pius V (r. 1566–72), which embraced all the major Catholic maritime nations in the Mediterranean except France, achieved a crucial victory over the Turks at the sea-battle of Lepanto; the western half of the Mediterranean was now under the control of the Habsbsurgs and their Italian allies. At a time when Europe was being torn apart by conflict over the Reformation this union of Catholic allies against the Ottoman Turks was seen as a significant turning point for the Catholic world.

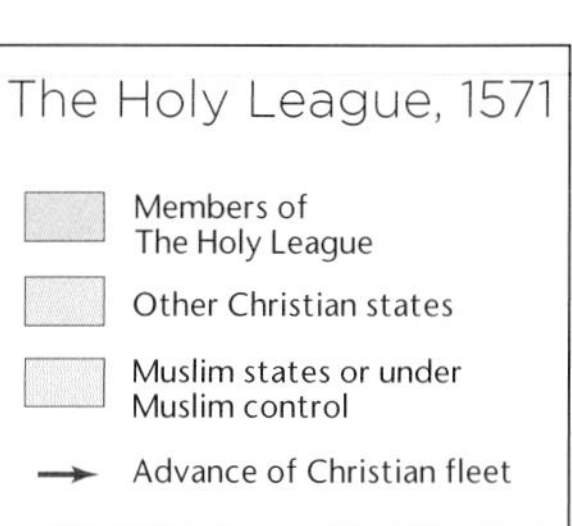

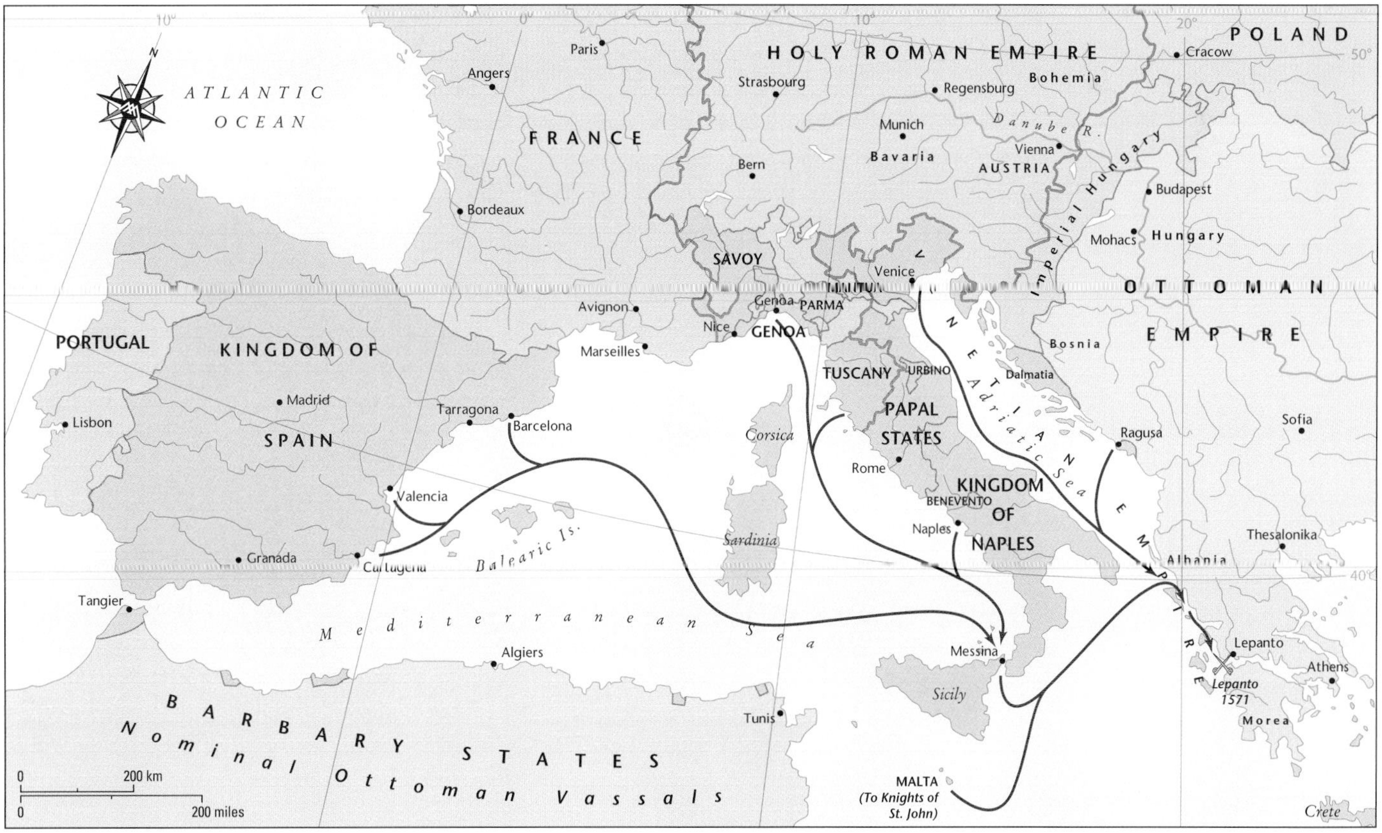

The Dutch Revolt

Sometimes called the Eighty Years' War (1566–1648), the Dutch Revolt led to the Netherlands' eventual independence from Spain and the subsequent separation of the northern and southern Netherlands, eventually leading to the formation of the United Provinces of the Netherlands, or Dutch Republic.

The revolt originated with the northern, seven provinces against the Habsburg Spanish ruler Charles V, who had inherited the throne. During the 16th century Protestantism had spread rapidly throughout the predominantly Catholic region. However, Charles V and his successor, Philip II, were determined to root out the heretical Protestant faith, which they saw as a threat to the social hierarchy and their political authority. The Dutch Protestants asserted that their humble, pious lifestyles were morally superior to the luxurious indulgence and moral turpitude of the ruling class, which was dominated by ecclesiastical nobility. Charles and Philip set out to create a highly centralized enpire, taking responsibility for taxes and legal affairs away from independent local administrators, many of whom had risen from the ranks of the wealthy merchant class rather than the nobility. This caused suspicion and resentment.

Once Philip II of Spain ascended to the throne the situation deteriorated. In 1566 an attempt by the local authorities to relax the heresy laws led to mass open-air preaching, followed by a wave of iconoclastic destruction in which churches were "cleansed" of Catholic images and relics so as to be fit for Protestant worship. With his regent in Brussels powerless to intervene, Philip dispatched the duke of Alba, in command of 10,000 troops. His violent reprisals led to a spate of executions, including the beheading of the counts of Egmont and Home, Catholic nobles who had been loyal to the king, but whom Alba considered to be unduly tolerant of Protestantism. These harsh measures only served to fuel the unrest.

Alba's leading opponent, William I of Orange, would soon convert to Calvinism himself and was the most influential noble in the States General of the Netherlands. His campaigns in 1568 to drive the duke of Alba out of Brussels were initially successful, but when he ran out of funding his army disintegrated and he became a fugitive. For four years the "revolt" was conducted by guerrilla raids and piracy, operating from bases in England and in Emden in Friesland, where the Dutch Calvinist church held its first national synod in 1571. However, Alba's repressive policies and harsh taxation pushed many previously moderate Netherlanders into sympathy both with the rebellion and with Protestantism. In 1572 the city of Brill opened its gates to the rebel fleet and the revolt spread across Holland and Zeeland with alarming speed. A turning-point came in November 1576, when unpaid Spanish troops sacked the city of Antwerp, the Netherlands' commercial capital, devastating the city and killing thousands of civilians. This led to the Pacification of Ghent, in which the Netherlandish provinces collectively agreed to expel Spanish troops and establish religious toleration. The compromise soon collapsed under pressure from Calvinist hardliners and, from 1579, a more conciliatory Spanish governor-general, the duke of Parma. The provinces split into the southern, Catholic Union of Arras, and the northern, Protestant Union of Utrecht, and the war now intensified.

William of Orange was assassinated in 1584 and succeeded by his son Maurice of Nassau, prince of Orange, who became Captain General of the Dutch army in 1587. He conducted a series of successful military campaigns in the 1590s along the borders of the southern Netherlands, but Spanish control of the south remained secure. In 1609 the United Provinces and the Spanish-controlled south entered into a ceasefire, the Twelve Years' Truce (1609–21). The Spanish demanded religious tolerance for Catholics in the United Provinces but were unable to comply when the Dutch demanded similar religious freedoms for Protestants in the southern Netherlands. Soon the conflict would resume in the context of a wider European religious struggle, the Thirty Years' War.

The Twelve Years' Truce of 1609–21 was not destined to last. The conflict was subsequently reignited by Spanish attacks on the fortress town of Bergen op Zoom and the city of Breda, and the conflict became subsumed into Europe-wide hostilities, the Thirty Years' War. Peace was finally achieved as part of the European-scale Peace of Westphalia (1648) with the Treaty of Munster between Spain and the Netherlands. This finally recognized the Dutch Republic as an independent state, which was separate from the Holy Roman Empire.

The French Wars of Religion

The eight points of the Huguenot cross symbolize the eight Beatitudes (Matthew 5: 3–12). The stylized *fleur-de-lys* around the center comprises twelve petals, symbolizing the apostles. The cross became a potent symbol for the worldwide Huguenot diaspora.

As the situation for Huguenots in France became more perilous many more Protestants chose to leave France, at great personal risk. Those that were caught were executed, imprisoned, or sent as galley slaves to the French fleet. About 200,000 Huguenots left France during the reign of Louis XIV (1638–1715), the largest migration movement in modern French history. They settled in Protestant Europe – the Netherlands, Germany, Scandinavia, Switzerland, – and even Russia, the Americas, and South Africa, They brought new, and welcome, skills to their host societies – particularly silk production and metalworking, and by the mid-18th century were largely integrated.

Protestant ideas were first introduced to France during the reign of Francis II (1415–47). Although Francis was a loyal Catholic, he was also hostile to papal claims and to the Holy Roman Emperor Charles V, and gave some encouragement to reformers.

From 1555, Calvin's Geneva began to send missionary pastors, and a flood of Calvinist books, into France, and a nationwide network of underground churches sprang up. These "Huguenots," as they were called, included at their peak about 10–15 precent of the population, and as much as half of the nobility. During 1560–62, as Huguenot numbers surged, and with the boy king Charles IX (r. 1560–74) unable to impose authority, it seemed possible that all France might soon turn Protestant.

Instead, Catholic nobles led by Francois, duc de Guise, took a stand and massacred Calvinist worshippers in the town of Wassy on 1 March 1562. The leading Huguenot nobleman, Prince Louis de Condé, took up arms to defend the Calvinists and a year-long civil war ensued. With neither party able to win a decisive victory, a compromise peace, the Edict of Amboise (1563) allowed Huguenots limited religious freedoms.

In 1567 the Huguenots took up arms again, and the Peace of Longjumeau (1568) reiterated the terms of Amboise. But the peace was fragile and religious enmities were becoming entangled in international religious confrontations. The Protestants were allied to the embattled Dutch Calvinists, and to Queen Elizabeth of England, who provided them with crucial military aid, while the Catholics were exploring an alliance with France's old enemy, Spain.

The turning point came on the night of 23 August 1572, the eve of St Bartholomew's Day, when numerous Protestant noblemen had come to Paris to celebrate the wedding of Marguerite de Valois to the Huguenot prince Henry of Navarre. After a failed assassination attempt against a Huguenot general, King Charles IX, despairing of compromise, decided instead to try to wipe out the entire Huguenot leadership, unleashing a wave of Catholic mob violence in Paris and, over the following weeks, in the provinces. Protestant minorities were all but eliminated from many parts of the country and their rights were eradicated; but in their strongholds they dug in, newly embittered.

The cycle of wars resumed, and attempts by the new King Henry III in to impose a compromise in the mid-1570s broke down. The war now took on a dynastic character. The nation's most prominent Protestant, Henry of Navarre, was now heir apparent to the throne, and the great Catholic families could not tolerate the prospect of a Huguenot king. The newly formed Catholic League took control of many of the northern cities in protest, triggering a further round of warfare. When Henry III's assassination in 1589 brought Henry of Navarre to the throne as Henry IV, the majority of the country rose against him. During this most intense phase of the wars, Henry staved off defeat, but concluded that the only route to victory and pacification was to convert to Catholicism, which he did in 1593. Paris yielded to him in 1594 and in 1598 he promulgated the Edict of Nantes, granting defined but limited rights to Huguenots within a still-Catholic nation.

During the remainder of Henry IV's reign this status quo held. However, after his assassination by a Catholic hardliner in 1610, his successor Louis XIII and his minister Cardinal Richelieu progressively squeezed Huguenot privileges. The Huguenots' military rights were broken during campaigns in the 1620s, leaving their privileges dependent solely on royal goodwill. The Huguenots' position, however, became increasingly insecure during the reign of Louis XIV, grandson of Henry IV, who came to see the existence of a Protestant minority as a threat to the absolute authority of the monarchy. Gradually the Huguenots' hard-won rights and privileges were eroded. In 1685 Louis revoked the Edict of Nantes. Huguenots had been leaving France since the first persecutions in the 1560s, fleeing to Geneva, England, or the United Provinces. The revocation now triggered a surge of hundreds of thousands into exile.

France in 1585

The Counter-Reformation 1545–1731

The reforms of the Counter-Reformation were enforced by the Roman Inquisition, established in 1542. It combated heresy and controlled doctrine and practice. Various theologians, notably the Jesuit Robert Bellarmine, attacked the doctrinal arguments of the Protestants, and the *Index Librorum Prohibitorum* (Index of Forbidden Books) was established in 1559, in an attempt to systematically keep Catholics from being lured by heresy. The punitive face of the Counter-Reformation was felt not only in the religious wars, but in the suppression of Protestant populations under Catholic rule deep into the 18th century, such as in the notorious expulsion of the Protestants of Salzburg in 1731.

THE PERIOD OF SPIRITUAL, intellectual, cultural, and moral revival within the Roman Catholic church in the 16th and 17th centuries is called the Counter-Reformation, or sometimes the Catholic Reformation, but it was not merely a reaction to the radical critique of the Protestants; its roots date back to the 15th century, when calls for reform grew out of the criticism of the worldly attitudes and corruption of popes and clergy. Martin Luther's doctrines were condemned as heresies as early as 1520, but it was always plain that a fuller response was needed. And so Pope Paul III reacted by convening the Council of Trent, which met intermittently between 1545 and 1563. Here the church defended and defined the important doctrines that were under attack: transubstantiation and the full range of the seven sacraments; the belief that both faith and good works are necessary for salvation; the doctrine that the church had the sole authority to interpret the Bible, and was also the custodian of extra-Biblical traditions handed down directly from the Apostles.

A new emphasis was placed on training and preparation for the priesthood, with every bishop being instructed to establish a seminary. Abuses that idealistic churchmen had lamented for centuries – pluralism, non-residency, nepotism, impunity – were tackled with a new seriousness and commitment. Popes and pious reformers set about the generations-long work of turning aspirations into a reality. A new catechism summarized the Council's teachings, and local variations in liturgy and music were swept away by a single, universal Tridentine Mass.

The drivers of Catholic reform on the ground were newly energized religious orders, notably the Society of Jesus (Jesuits), founded in 1534 by St Ignatius Loyola and gaining the approval of Paul III in 1540. The Jesuits quickly became a leading intellectual force in the Catholic church. They founded schools, universities and seminaries, and by 1615 had 372 colleges. They spearheaded missionary initiatives across the globe but also had some success in reconverting Protestants in Europe.

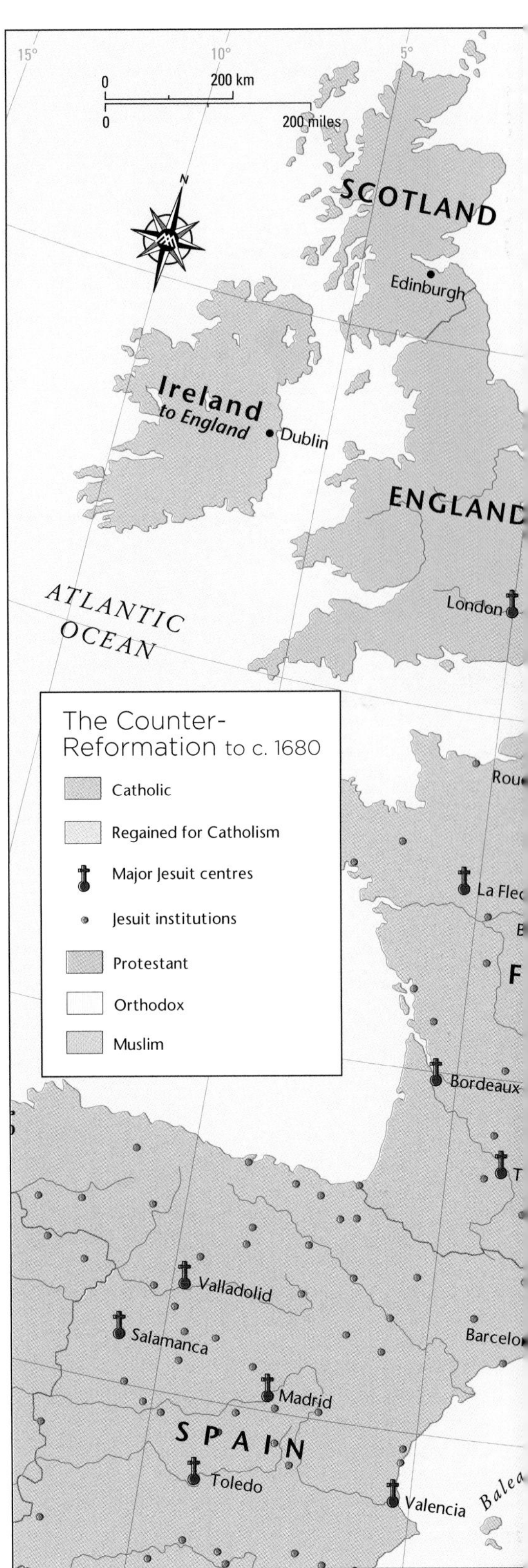

Stockholm
SWEDEN
DENMARK AND NORWAY
Estonia
Livonia
Riga
Courland
RUSSIA
Lithuania
Vilnius
Baltic Sea
North Sea
Copenhagen
Prussia
Danzig
Holstein
Lubeck
Mecklenburg
Hamburg
Stettin
POLAND
United Provinces
Amsterdam
Brandenburg
Berlin
Warsaw
Ukraine
Antwerp
Munster
Volhynia
Silesia
Saxony
Brussels
Spanish Netherlands
Liege
Fulda
Glatz
Crakow
Podolia
Mons
Frankfurt
Bamberg
Prague
Kuttenberg
Galicia
Jedisan
Mainz
Bohemia
Trier
Wurzburg
Brunn
Verdun
Ingolstadt
Trnava
Moldavia
Molsheim
Bavaria
Dillingen
Austria
Vienna
Austria-Hungary
Transylvania
Buda
Pest
Basel
Zurich
Salzburg
Graz
Styria
Neuhaus
Bern
SWISS CONFED.
Tyrol
Hungary
Wallis
Carinthia
Wallachia
Black Sea
Milan
Savoy
Venice
Belgrade
Serbia
Parma
Modena
Genoa
Bulgaria
Avignon
Lucca
Bosnia
OTTOMAN EMPIRE
Tuscany
PAPAL STATES
Adriatic Sea
Constantinople
Sardinia
Rome
Naples
NAPLES
Sassari
Corsica
Aegean Sea
Greece
Cagliari
Athens
Mediterranean Sea

The Thirty Years' War 1618–48

THE SPARK THAT IGNITED the Thirty Years' War originated in Bohemia and Hungary, where the Archduke Ferdinand (who was Holy Roman Emperor from 1619–37) was busy revoking rights and privileges that had previously been granted to the Protestant minority. At a meeting of the Estates of the Realm in Prague in May 1618 two Catholic regents were thrown out of the window (the Defenestration). When Frederick V of the Palatinate, the leader of the Protestant Union, accepted the Bohemian crown in 1619, the Catholics' worst fears were realized. A Catholic League was mobilized, and authorized to levy an army of 25,000 men.

The Battle of the White Mountain (1620), fought near Prague, marked the first victory of Emperor Ferdinand II and the Catholic League, which aligned with Habsburg Spain, over the Protestant Union, which allied with Denmark-Norway. Emperor Ferdinand now embarked on a full-scale attempt to retake Germany for Catholicism, and during the 1620s won a series of victories. But in 1630 Sweden, under the brilliant military leader King Gustavus Adolphus, joined the Protestant cause, and began to push the imperial forces back. When Gustavus Adolphus was killed in the Battle of Lützen in 1632, the Swedes lost some of their resolve, and met their nemesis in the person of the Catholic Bohemian nobleman Albrecht von Wallenstein, who brought an army of about 50,000 soldiers to the imperial side, in exchange for the right to plunder conquered territory. By 1635 the Swedes had been vanquished and the Peace of Prague protected the Protestant territories of north-eastern Germany, but not those of the south-east, Austria, and Bohemia.

The battle lines were not drawn exclusively on religious grounds. Catholic France, wary of the Empire's overweening power and anxious to secure the territories of Alsace and Lorraine, had already financed the Swedish invasion, and in 1635 joined the conflict on the Protestant side. Meanwhile Spain mounted counterattacks into French territory, even threatening Paris in 1636. The French held the Spanish back and a stalemate lasting several years ensued. In 1643 Denmark-Norway took up arms again, this time fighting on the side of the Habsburgs and the Holy Roman Emperor. The Swedes reentered the conflict, attacking Vienna in 1645. In 1647 the Swedes and French were driven back from Austrian territory, and, in the last action of the war, the Swedes captured Prague Castle in November 1648.

The Thirty Years' War was a series of protracted conflicts waged by regular armies and barely regulated mercenaries, partisans, and conscripts. Many of these new fighting forces carried out atrocities with impunity, while war profiteers exploited the conflicts for their own personal gain, plundering and exploiting, and leaving entire regions ravaged. Jews were persecuted and refugees massacred, while mass movements of people transmitted lethal outbreaks of plague and disease. The population of Germany fell by a quarter or more.

The Peace of Westphalia (1648) recognized a stalemate in which the religious divide was no longer the determining factor in international politics. The United Provinces of the Netherlands and the Swiss Confederation were formally recognized as independent republics. France and Sweden both made significant acquisitions. Brandenburg-Prussia and Bavaria emerged as the most powerful states in the Imperial Council of Electors of the Holy Roman Empire The Imperial victories of 1620–24 were allowed to stand, and Protestantism was suppressed in much of eastern and southern Germany. All parties recognized the principle of *cuius regio eius religio*, Calvinism was recognized as a permitted religion alongside Lutheranism and Catholicism, and Christians living in states where the official religion was of a different denomination were guaranteed freedom of worship. Pope Innocent X's fulminations against the Treaty ("null, void, invalid, iniquitous, unjust, damnable...") were impotent, underlining Westphalia's transference of effective power from supranational authorities, both secular and ecclesiastical – the Holy Roman Emperor and the papacy. >>

The Religious Situation in Germany at the Start of the Thirty Years War 1618

In 1630 Emperor Ferdinand II overestimated the security of his position in Germany and dismissed his most successful military leader, General von Wallenstein, from his command. Catholic France, alarmed by the Habsburgs' growing power, supported Protestant Sweden. King Gustavus Adolphus of Sweden rampaged through the Empire, winning decisive victories over the veteran commander, Tilly, at Breitenfeld (1631) and Rain (1632). But when Adolphus was slain at Lützen in 1632 (a Protestant victory) the Swedes and their German allies sued for peace. France was galvanized into action and entered the war, winning victories at Wittstock (1636) and Breisach (1638).

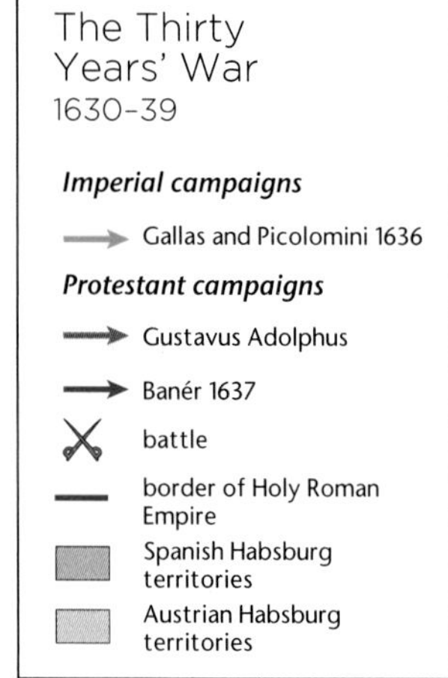

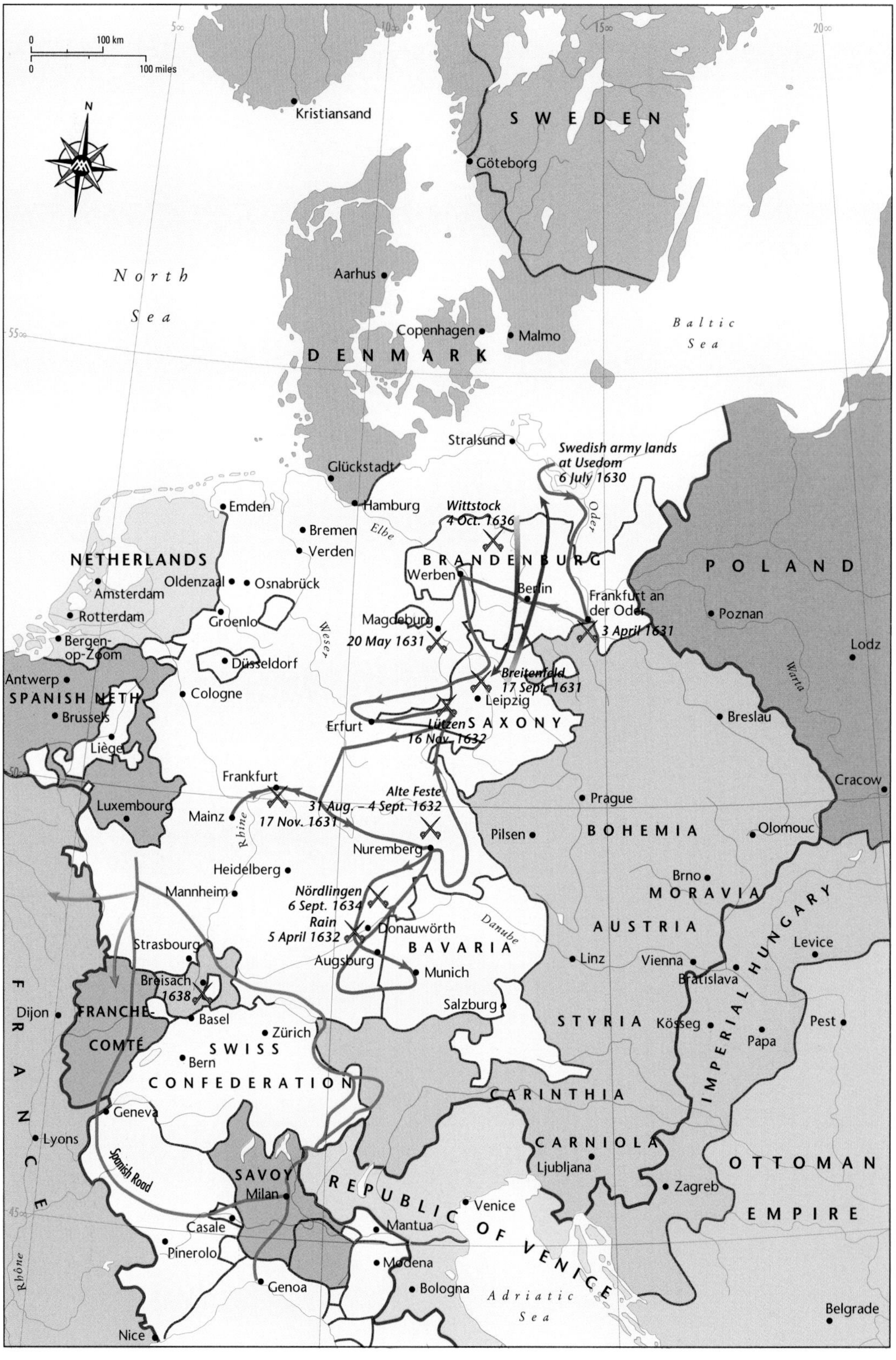

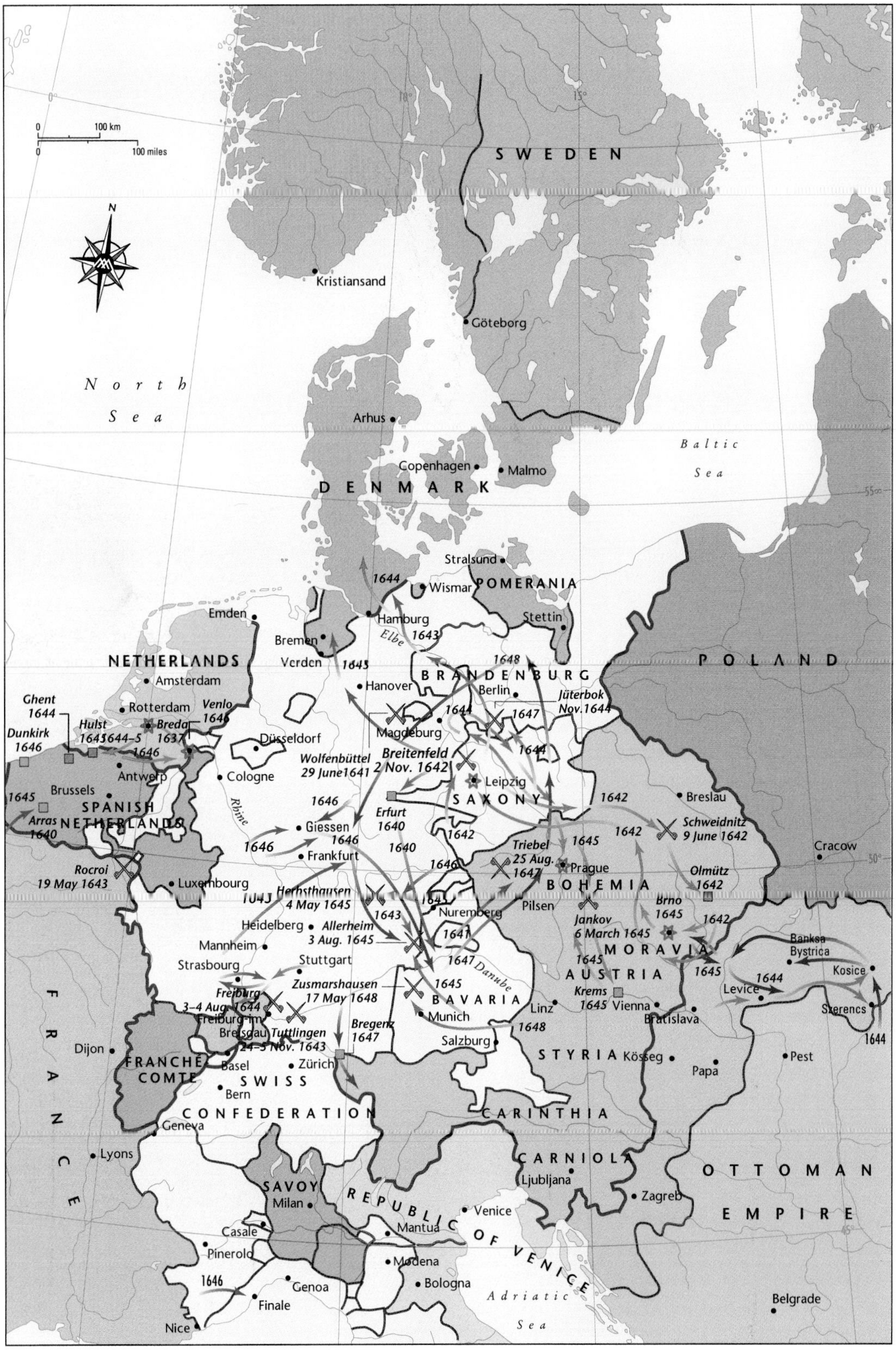

The Thirty Years' War 1640–48

Swedish campaigns, with dates

- Banér
- Torstensson
- Wrangel
- other Swedish campaigns

other campaigns, with dates

- Austrian
- French
- Dutch
- George Rákóczi, Prince of Transylvania
- Swedish victory
- Swedish defeat
- towns captured by Swedes, with date
- towns captured by French, with date
- towns captured by Dutch, with date
- siege
- border of Holy Roman Empire
- Spanish Habsburg territories
- Austrian Habsburg territories

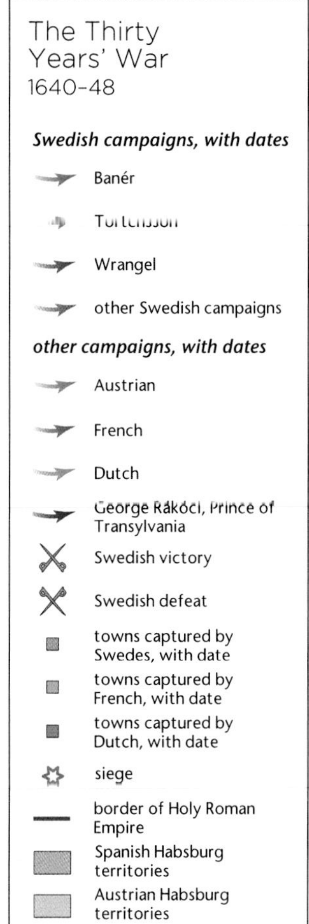

The Siege of Arras (1640) was a turning point in the long conflict. The French routed the Spanish in the Netherlands but faced defeat by the imperial forces at Tuttlingen and Herbsthausen. Their Swedish allies triumphed at the second battle of Breitenfeld (1642) and went on to besiege Vienna (1645). By now both sides were exhausted and the futility of the conflict, which was being fought over the same territory, was ever more apparent. In 1648 the war ended in a plethora of treaties, collectively known as the Peace of Westphalia.

Puritanism in England and North America

THE PURITANS were English Protestants of the late 16th and 17th centuries who aspired to rid the Protestant Church of England of remaining Roman Catholic practices. These "dissenters" sometimes formed their own Presbyterian church government, while others formed their own congregations, based on a covenant with God and amongst themselves. The movement found solid support, particularly in East Anglia and amongst the merchant classes of London, where it was linked with a desire for a new social order where traditional economic constraints were discarded.

The Puritans turned to preaching, proselytizing, and pamphlets, and the movement found influential adherents amongst the nobility and learned men at the colleges of Oxford and Cambridge. When James, king of Calvinist Scotland, came to the throne, the hopes of the Puritans were raised, but he dismissed them with the phrase "no bishop, no king." While Puritanism continued to gain popular support early in the 17th century, the government and the church hierarchy, especially under Archbishop William Laud, became increasingly repressive, causing many Puritans to flee England, some groups traveling to Protestant Holland. Those who remained formed a powerful element within the parliamentarian party that defeated Charles I in the English Civil War.

Against this background of increasing persecution in England many of the Puritans who aspired to a Holy Commonwealth, established by a covenanted community, turned to America. The Pilgrim Fathers were English Puritan settlers who first moved to Leiden in Holland in 1608, and then, in 1620, returned to England, where they raised finance for their venture. Under the leadership of William Bradford, they chartered the *Mayflower*, which took them to southeastern Massachussets, where they established the Plymouth Colony. They intended to found a "pure" church, free of royal, episcopal or even Presbyterian control. In 1629 the Massachusetts Bay Company obtained a charter from King Charles I to trade with the region that was now being called New England. Led by the lawyer John Winthrop, the Company left England in April 1630, arriving in what is now Boston in August and founded the Massachusetts Bay Colony there, which became extremely successful. Over the 1630s and 1640s over 20,000 people left England and settled in Massachusetts Bay, aiming to found the "city on a hill" – a pure Christian society and an example to the world.

These Puritan settlers were the origin of Congregationalism in the United States, a reformed Protestant tradition that emphasizes the right of each congregation to organize and order its own affairs without reference to a higher authority. Their emphasis on congregational rights and freedom of conscience arose from strong convictions about the sovereignty of God and the priesthood of all believers, which eliminates the need for priestly mediation.

While churches in New England were "sufficient," which meant that they ran themselves, independent of outside interference, they were also part of a larger network, which they could consult on matters of church governance, discipline, appointments and so on. In 1648 the ministers of the Massachusetts Bay Colony drew up the Cambridge Platform, which laid out the standards for practices such as ordaining ministers, accepting new church members, interchurch cooperation; this was a constitution of sorts, but it did not require any meetings or governing bodies. Members of the Congregational church were equal, responsible to each other under the terms of the Covenant by which they lived. Ministers were ordained members of the church, subject to the will of the congregation, giving ordinary citizens unprecedented power and the right to hold their leaders to account.

By 1740 there were 423 Congregational churches in colonial America, a third of all churches. Much of this dominance was due to the Great Awakening, a revivalist movement that galvanized religious life in the colonies. The robust self-governance and independence of this tradition would become a springboard for American independence and democracy.

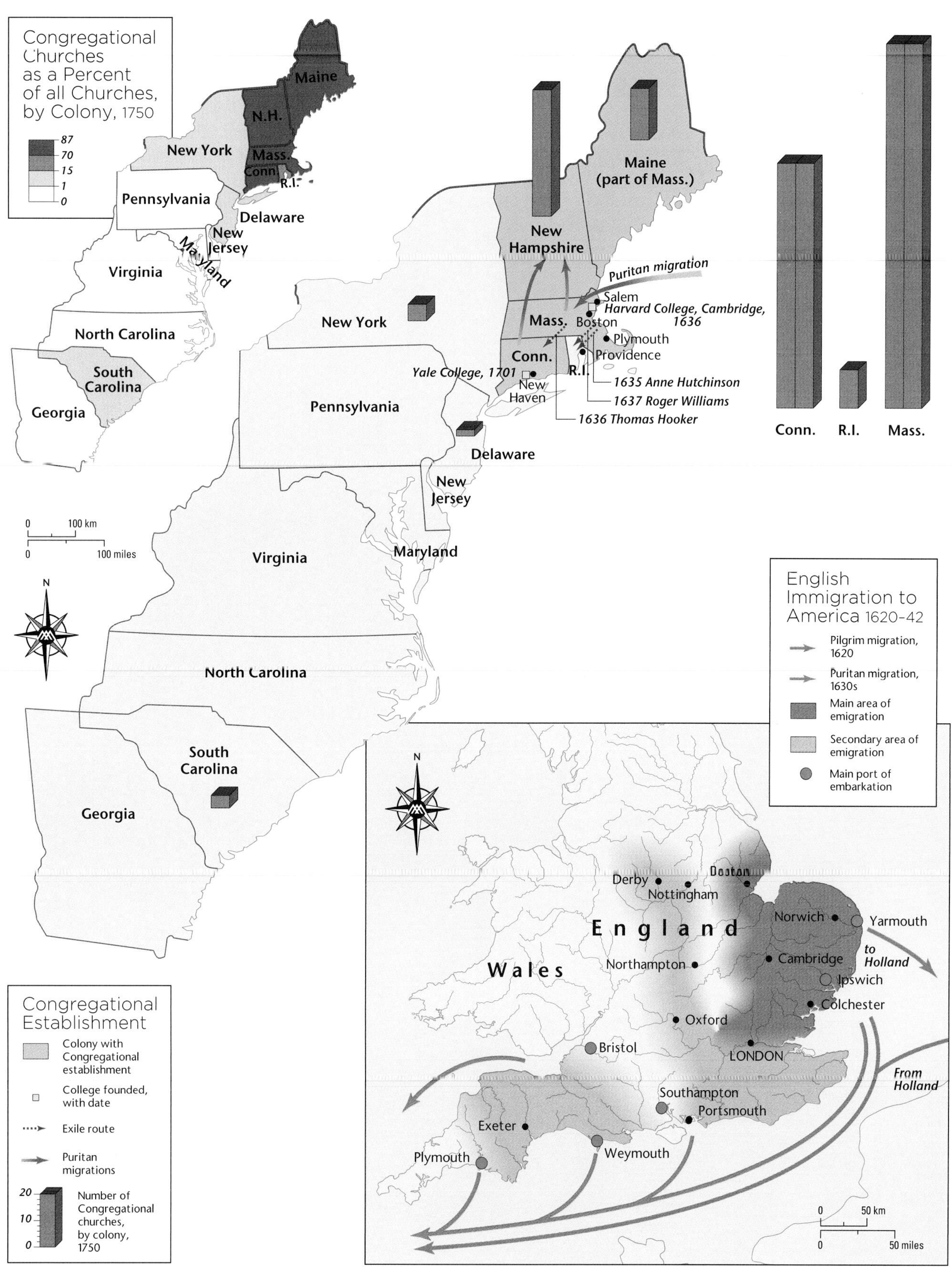
Congregational Churches as a Percent of all Churches, by Colony, 1750
87
70
15
1
0
Maine
N.H.
New York
Mass.
Conn.
R.I.
Pennsylvania
Delaware
New Jersey
Maryland
Virginia
North Carolina
South Carolina
Georgia
Maine (part of Mass.)
New Hampshire
Puritan migration
Salem
Harvard College, Cambridge, 1636
Mass.
Boston
Plymouth
Providence
Conn.
R.I.
Yale College, 1701
New Haven
1635 Anne Hutchinson
1637 Roger Williams
1636 Thomas Hooker
New York
Pennsylvania
Delaware
New Jersey
Maryland
Virginia
North Carolina
South Carolina
Georgia
Conn.
R.I.
Mass.
0
100 km
0
100 miles
N
English Immigration to America 1620–42
Pilgrim migration, 1620
Puritan migration, 1630s
Main area of emigration
Secondary area of emigration
Main port of embarkation
N
Derby
Nottingham
Boston
England
Norwich
Yarmouth
to Holland
Wales
Northampton
Cambridge
Ipswich
Colchester
Oxford
Bristol
LONDON
From Holland
Southampton
Portsmouth
Exeter
Weymouth
Plymouth
0
50 km
0
50 miles
Congregational Establishment
Colony with Congregational establishment
College founded, with date
Exile route
Puritan migrations
20
10
0
Number of Congregational churches, by colony, 1750

Missionary States in South America

Following Christopher Columbus' discovery of the New World in 1492 Pope Alexander VI awarded colonial rights over newly discovered lands to Spain and Portugal. The silver mines of Mexico and the Andes of Peru with its Inca gold were the first areas to be explored by the Spanish. Colonization was a destructive process – the indigenous population of the Americas fell by around 90 percent between 1500–1600, mostly because of disease but also because of violence. Everywhere the attitude to pre-Christian religious rituals was harshly suppressive. The Franciscans set up a zealous local inquisition and indigenous people were treated

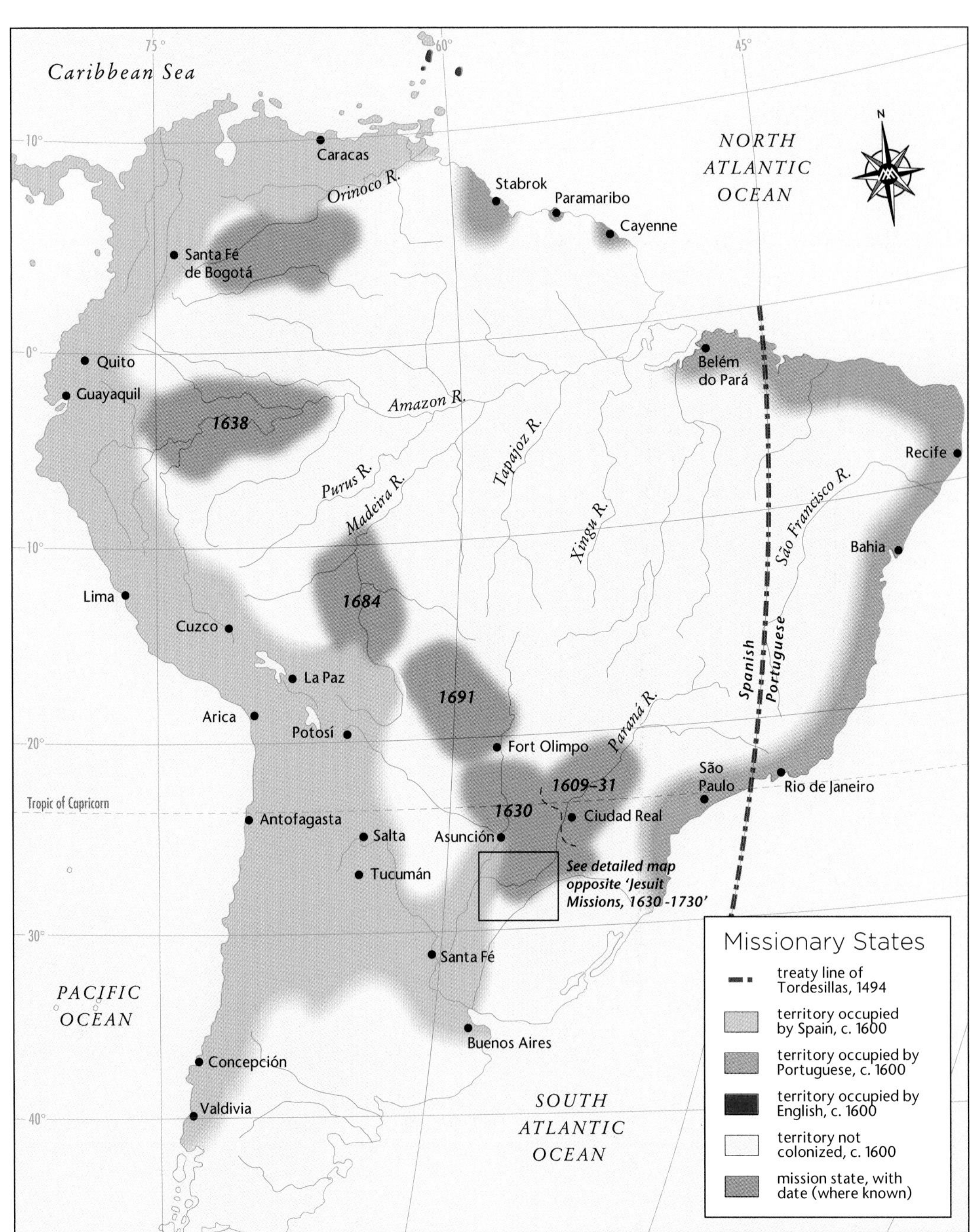

with mistrust. Pre-Christian sacred sites were neutralized by church-building. New villages and towns were laid out on a grid plan, each focusing on a church.

The interior of the continent – Brazil, Argentina, Uruguay, and Paraguay – was largely unexplored, some regions being populated by tribes that had not had any contact with outsiders. The Jesuits arrived in Brazil in 1540 just six years after the foundation of their Order, reaching the highlands of Paraguay in 1587. Armed with a self-government grant from the king, they set out to found Christian societies in the impenetrable jungles of the continent. By the 18th century the Jesuits were a preeminent power in the region, successfully holding off Spanish and Portuguese imperial claims and deriving huge wealth from the large plantations in central Chile, the ranches of the River Plate region, and vast rural estates in Chile and Peru.

The model communities the Jesuits set up in Latin America were known as "reductions." Here the indigenous peoples could be governed, taxed, and evangelized. The Jesuit reductions in Paraguay, Argentina, and the Rio Grande do Sul area of Brazil, the area occupied by the Guaraní people, were established in the early 17th century and there were 30 Guaraní missions in what came to be known as the Guaraní Republic. The reductions were vulnerable to raids by Portuguese "Bandeirante" slavers, mainly from the São Paolo region, who captured and enslaved Indians. The Jesuits began to arm their residents, and secured the permission of the Spanish crown to raise militias to act in self-defense. The militias would eventually number some 4,000 troops.

These religious communities reflected the Jesuits' own sense of organization and self-discipline, and became increasingly elaborate, with banks, postal centers, roads and river transport, schools, hospitals, and workshops. Reductions were laid out according to a standardized plan, with a main plaza, a church, college, hospital, warehouses, and housing. The reductions traded surpluses – their main products were cattle hides and yerba mate (leaves that were drunk like tea). Most structures were wood or adobe, but the main buildings, especially the churches, were elaborate Baroque structures, built in stone by local craftsmen. Jesuit presses even printed books in the Guaraní language.

But the Jesuits increasingly came into conflict with Spanish landowners, the new economic elite. In the 1750s, a joint Spanish-Portuguese army broke the independence of the reductions, after a seven-year guerrilla war in which the Jesuits fought alongside the Guaraní, who refused to leave the mission settlements; and in 1773 the entire Jesuit order was suppressed, albeit temporarily, by Pope Clement XIV, provoked by the Jesuits' stubborn independence and disregard for tradition. Many of the Guaraní rose in revolt to protect their Jesuit priests from arrest. The brutal new colonial regimes, established once the Jesuits were expelled, fed ethnic conflicts that festered for centuries to come.

Christianity and Islam in Africa

The arrival of Islam in around 640 CE, which expanded by conquest and conversion, changed the religious situation in Africa. There were no large-scale forced conversions, and the Christian communities of northern Africa endured under Islamic rule, especially in Egypt, but further expansion was impossible and their restricted rights meant that Islam gradually became the majority religion in the north, and succeeded in expanding southward into the Sahel. Islam, with its acceptance of polygamy, sat more comfortably with the traditional religions of Africa, many of which were polygamous, than did the Christian insistence on monogamy.

Various Muslim dynasties steadily consolidated their control over North Africa over the following millennium. The Arab slave trade, across the Sahara Desert and across the Indian Ocean, began after Muslim Arab and Swahili traders won control of the Swahili coast and sea routes during the 9th century. These traders captured Bantu peoples (Zanj) from the interior in present-day Kenya, Mozambique and Tanzania and brought them to the coast.

In the 1540s a Portuguese expeditionary force came to the aid of Ethiopian Miaphysite Christians who were fighting a holy war against the Muslim emir, Ahmed Granj. But this spirit of Christian cooperation was dissipated by the arrival in Ethiopia of intolerant Jesuit missionaries, who were shocked by Ethiopian Christian practices, such as immersion baptisms where both the priest and the baptized were naked, and thought the Ethiopian church was permeated with Judaic practices, such as the celebration of the Sabbath and the avoidance of pork.

Portuguese Jesuit missionaries had landed along Africa's east coastline in 1548. The missionary Gonçalo de Siveira had managed to baptize the Mwenemutapa, king of the Mutapa empire located in modern Zimbabwe, but in 1561 he was murdered following court intrigues. By this stage at least a dozen Catholic churches had been established but they disappeared by the mid-17th century, when Portugal's power on the continent was waning.

The story on Africa's Atlantic coast was very different. In 1490, in the wake of early exploratory voyages along the west African coast by Portuguese navigators, the first Portuguese missionaries arrived in sub-Saharan Africa at the request of King Nzinga of Kongo, who adopted the Portuguese title of Afonso I. The missionaries helped in the rebuilding of Nzinga's capital at Mbanza Kongo (modern northern Angola) and baptized the king. His son, Afonso, was sent to Portugal to study, where he impressed his teachers with his intelligence and piety. Afonso's son Henrique subsequently became the first African bishop in the Catholic church. Schools were opened to teach the Portuguese language and a cathedral city, named São Salvador, was built in the interior. The successors of King Afonso I maintained the Catholic faith into the 18th century, evolving an indigenous form of the faith. The Portuguese authorities tried to impose their Padroado rights by appointing bishops, which was a severe impediment to the ordination of native clergy. The Portuguese role in the burgeoning African slave trade created further problems: Franciscan missionaries who had arrived in the Kongo during the 17th century protested and in 1686 the Roman Inquisition, at their behest, issued a general condemnation of the slave trade.

Yet most slavers who engaged in the Atlantic slave trade were practicing Christians. Spanish and Portuguese traders in the 16th century were joined and soon eclipsed in the 17th by Protestant slave traders from England and the Netherlands. The European forts established along the coast of the Gulf of Guinea were dominated by the slave trade, and although a handful of Africans were converted and even ordained, the slave trade was simply incompatible with any serious missionary effort. Some Europeans even argued that the transatlantic slave trade would enable Africans to come into contact with Christianity and "civilization" in the Americas. Only with the abolition of the Atlantic slave trade from 1807 onwards could this picture change.

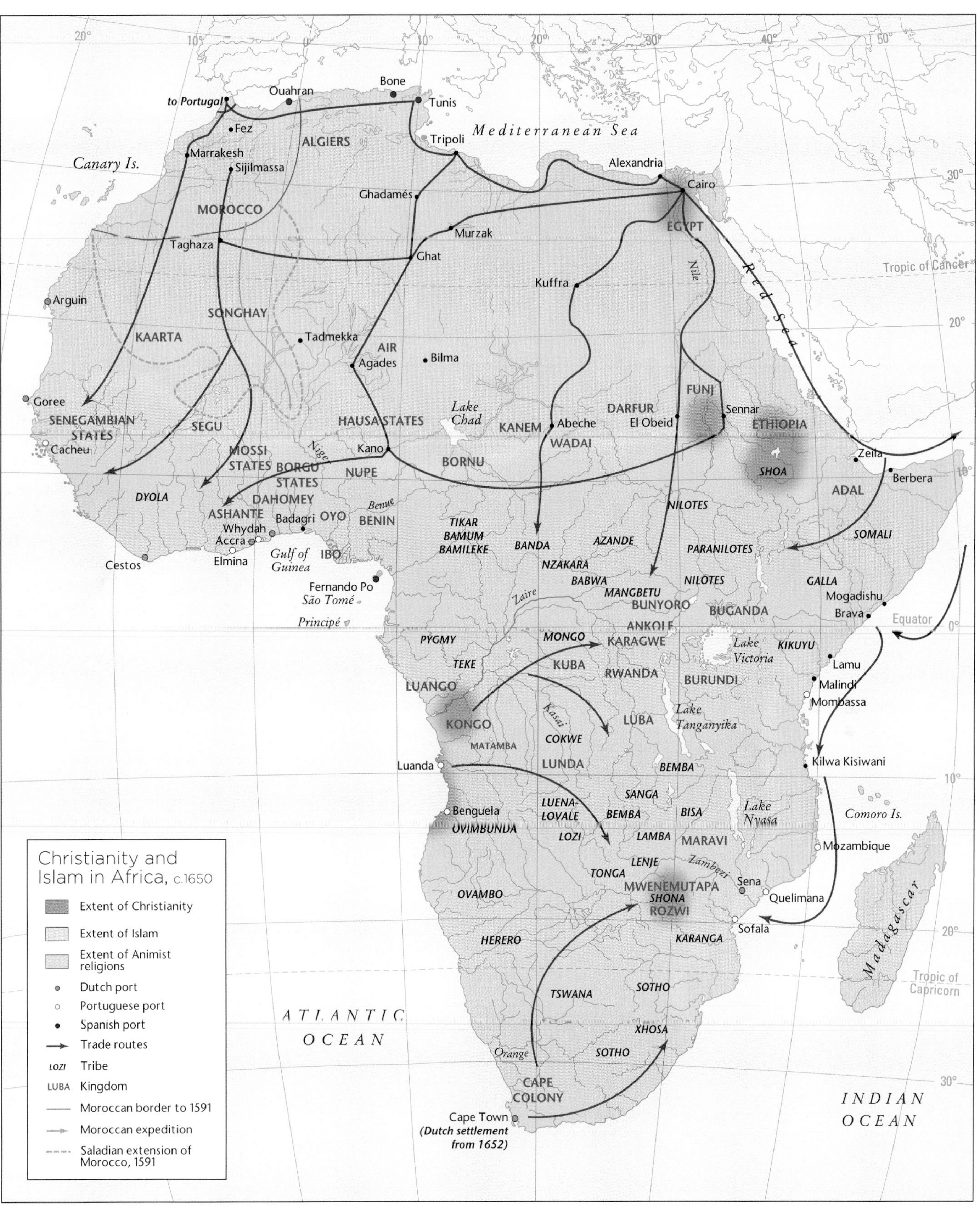
Christianity and Islam in Africa, c.1650
Extent of Christianity
Extent of Islam
Extent of Animist religions
Dutch port
Portuguese port
Spanish port
Trade routes
LOZI Tribe
LUBA Kingdom
Moroccan border to 1591
Moroccan expedition
Saladian extension of Morocco, 1591
Mediterranean Sea
Red Sea
ATLANTIC OCEAN
INDIAN OCEAN
Gulf of Guinea
Tropic of Cancer
Equator
Tropic of Capricorn
Canary Is.
Comoro Is.
Madagascar
to Portugal
Ouahran
Bone
Tunis
Fez
Marrakesh
Sijilmassa
ALGIERS
Tripoli
Alexandria
Cairo
Ghadamés
MOROCCO
Murzak
Taghaza
Ghat
EGYPT
Nile
Kuffra
Arguin
SONGHAY
KAARTA
Tadmekka
AIR
Agades
Bilma
Goree
SENEGAMBIAN STATES
SEGU
Cacheu
HAUSA STATES
Lake Chad
KANEM
Abeche
WADAI
DARFUR
El Obeid
FUNJ
Sennar
ETHIOPIA
SHOA
Zeila
Berbera
MOSSI STATES
BORGU STATES
Kano
NUPE
BORNU
Niger
DYOLA
DAHOMEY
ASHANTE
Whydah
Accra
Badagri
OYO
BENIN
Benue
Elmina
Cestos
IBO
TIKAR
BAMUM
BAMILEKE
BANDA
AZANDE
NILOTES
PARANILOTES
ADAL
SOMALI
NZAKARA
BABWA
MANGBETU
BUNYORO
BUGANDA
GALLA
Mogadishu
Brava
Fernando Po
São Tomé
Principé
Zaire
ANKOLE
KARAGWE
MONGO
PYGMY
TEKE
KUBA
RWANDA
BURUNDI
Lake Victoria
KIKUYU
Lamu
Malindi
Mombassa
LUANGO
KONGO
MATAMBA
Kasai
COKWE
LUBA
Lake Tanganyika
Luanda
LUNDA
BEMBA
Kilwa Kisiwani
SANGA
LUENA-LOVALE
BISA
Lake Nyasa
Benguela
OVIMBUNDA
LOZI
LAMBA
MARAVI
Mozambique
LENJE
Zambezi
TONGA
Sena
MWENEMUTAPA
SHONA
ROZWI
Quelimana
OVAMBO
Sofala
HERERO
KARANGA
TSWANA
SOTHO
XHOSA
Orange
CAPE COLONY
Cape Town
(Dutch settlement from 1652)

Radical Settlers in North America

In sparsely populated colonial America it was hard to adhere to conventional practices of worship; a parish could stretch for over 100 miles, and with churches and ministers often distant, anticlerical, self-reliant and sometimes idiosyncratic forms of Protestantism flourished.

From the beginning of English, Dutch, and Swedish colonization of North America in the 17th century, the settler population was religiously diverse: Anglicans in Virginia, Congregationalists in New England, Catholics in Maryland, Quakers in Pennsylvania. During the 18th century successive waves of migration brought ever more diversity, predominantly but certainly not exclusively Protestant: including Jews, French Huguenots, Dutch Calvinists, Scottish Presbyterians. A plethora of new movements emerged, sometimes collectively referred to as "dissenters," such as Baptists, Methodists, Unitarians and Quakers. In the colonies of Rhode Island and Pennsylvania religious toleration was enshrined in the constitution.

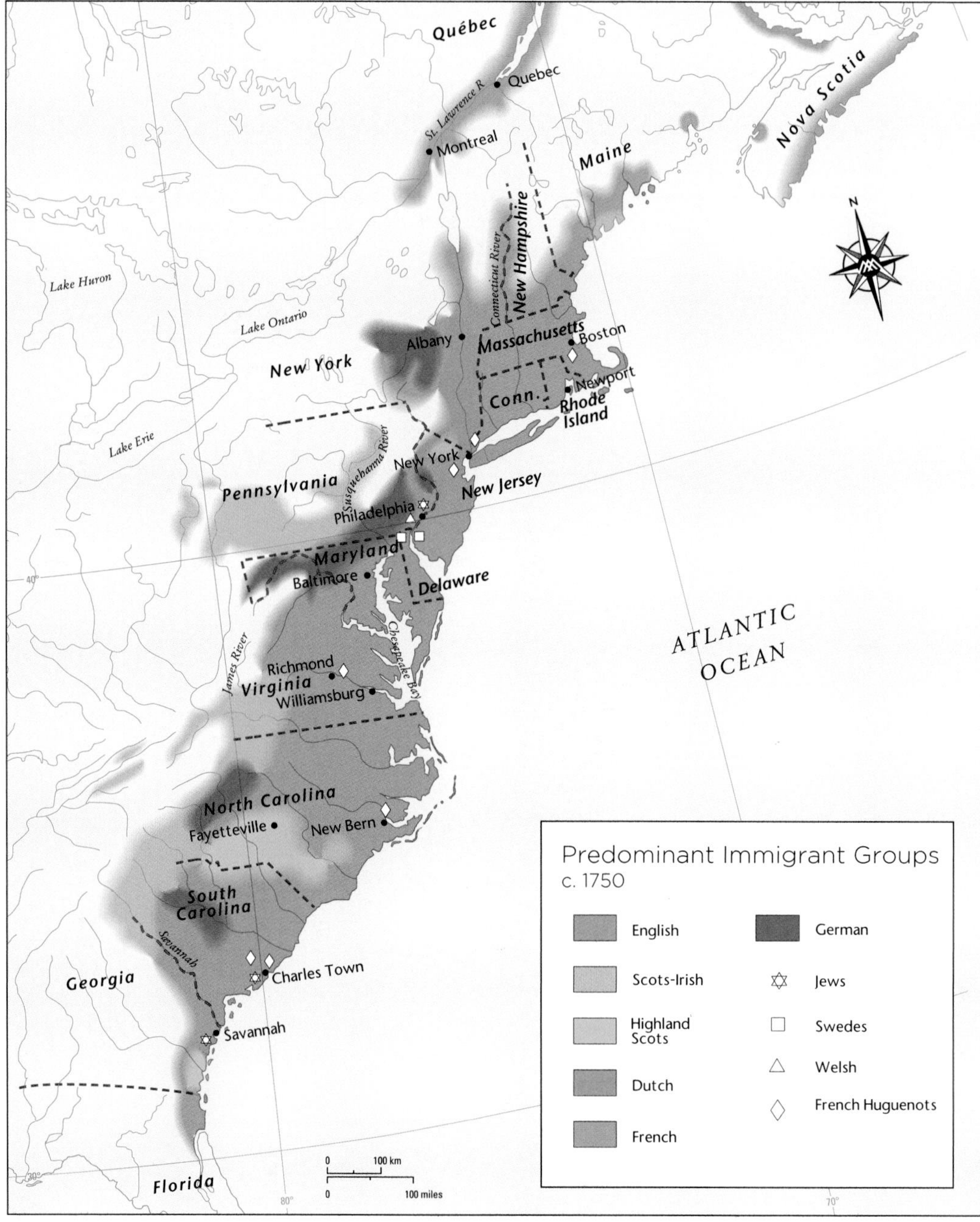

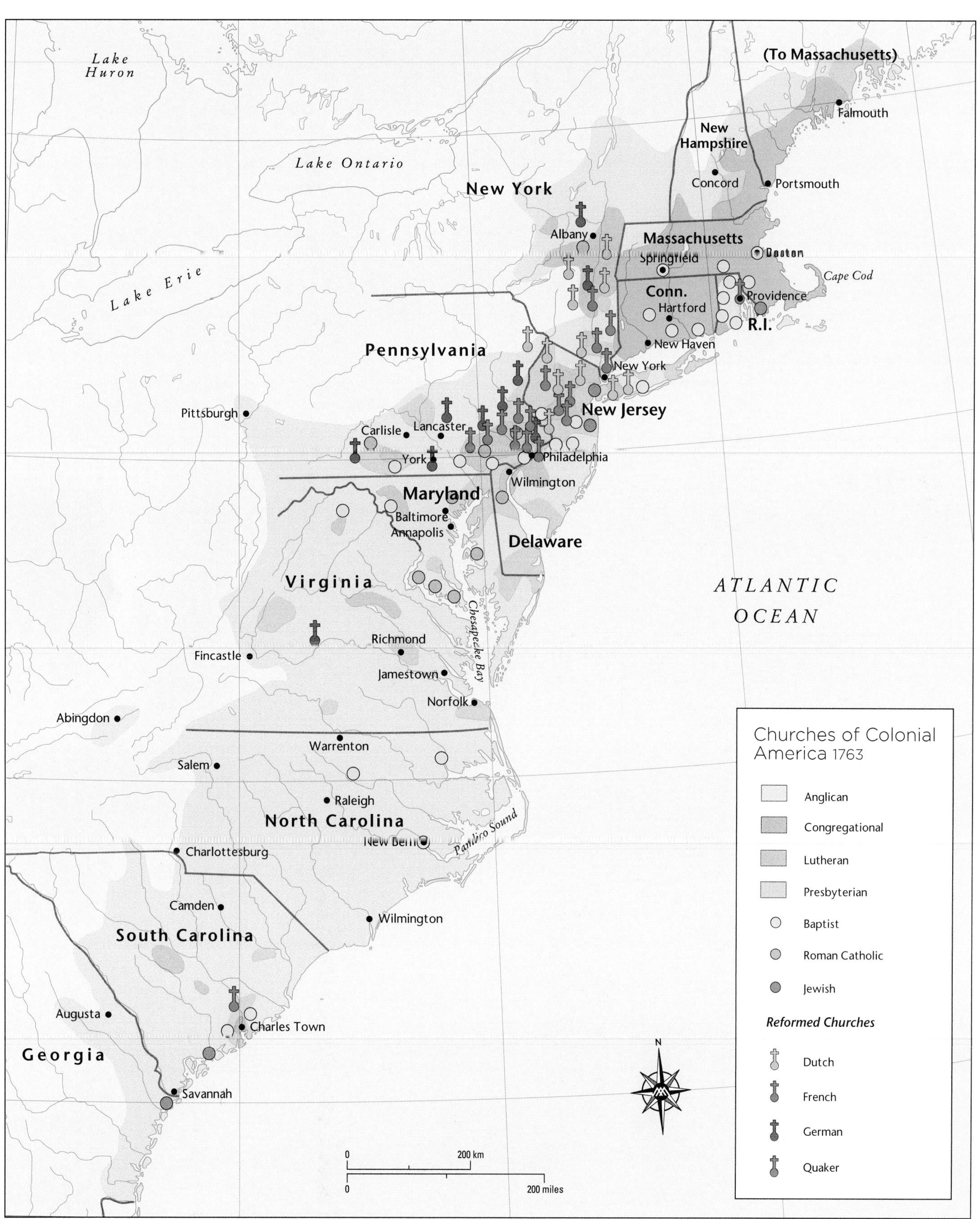
Lake Huron
Lake Ontario
Lake Erie
New York
(To Massachusetts)
Falmouth
New Hampshire
Concord
Portsmouth
Albany
Massachusetts
Boston
Springfield
Cape Cod
Conn.
Hartford
Providence
R.I.
New Haven
Pennsylvania
New York
Pittsburgh
New Jersey
Carlisle
Lancaster
York
Philadelphia
Wilmington
Maryland
Baltimore
Annapolis
Delaware
Virginia
ATLANTIC OCEAN
Chesapeake Bay
Richmond
Fincastle
Jamestown
Norfolk
Abingdon
Warrenton
Salem
Raleigh
North Carolina
New Bern
Pamlico Sound
Charlottesburg
Camden
Wilmington
South Carolina
Augusta
Charles Town
Georgia
Savannah
N
0
200 km
200 miles
Churches of Colonial America 1763
Anglican
Congregational
Lutheran
Presbyterian
Baptist
Roman Catholic
Jewish
Reformed Churches
Dutch
French
German
Quaker

Pietism, Methodism & the Evangelical Revival

George Whitefield, a charismatic English evangelist, traveled to America in 1739 and spoke to crowds of thousands. The Awakening became a movement spanning all of Britain's North American colonies and crossing denominational lines, and with particular appeal to women, socially marginalized groups and even to African slaves and freedpeople.

THE LUTHERAN DOCTRINE of pietism, with its emphasis on the study of the Bible, individual piety, and the obligation to live a good Christian life, was transported to America by radical groups from Germany, the Low Countries, Switzerland and lands further east who sought refuge in the 18th and 19th centuries.

The pietist movement had spread amongst Protestant communities on the continent in the 17th century; they initially came together in Frankfurt am Main under the tutelage of Phillipp Jakob Spener, who organized the first *collegia pietas* (pious assemblies). He purchased land in Penn's Woods, Pennsylvania, and commissioned the German-born Lutheran Dr Francis Daniel Pastorius to go to America to prepare for colonization. Pastorius played a key role in the development of Germantown, established in 1683, and now part of Philadelphia, and was a leading intellectual in colonial Pennsylvania.

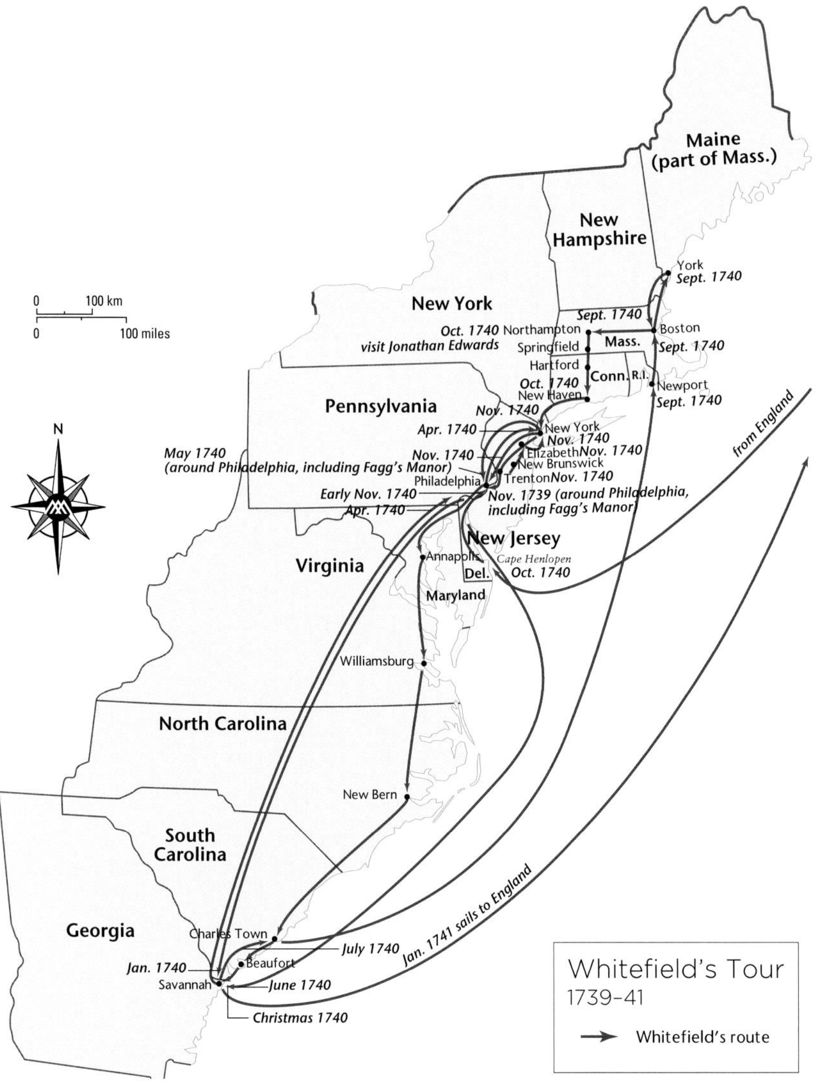

Leadership of the movement passed to August Hermann Francke (1663–1727) at the University of Halle, which became the institutional center of pietism. Count von Zinzendorf (1700–60), another Halle alumnus, gave members of the Moravian Brethren sanctuary on his estate in Saxony; the Moravian church traced its roots to the martyrdom of Jan Hus (1415). It was Zinzendorf's initiative that provided pietism with its greatest influence outside Germany, as Moravian missionaries fanned out to territories as varied as India, South Africa, the Caribbean, North America and Greenland.

The founder of the Methodist Church, Englishman John Wesley (1703–91), was influenced by the Moravians and emphasized Bible study, acts of private devotion, and good works. He and his brother traveled to Georgia to minister to the colonists and to attempt to teach the gospel to the Native Americans. Wesley sent Methodist preacher Thomas Coke to America, where he and Francis Ashbury founded the Methodist Episcopal Church, later to become the largest denomination in 19th-century America.

The Mennonites were followers of Menno Simons, the Dutchman who in 1536 had become an Anabaptist and founded one of the most enduring radical Protestant sects. The Mennonites taught "believer's baptism" only for adults who made a positive profession of faith, and were pacifists, teaching a strict withdrawal from worldly politics. They were soon joined by the Amish, followers of Jakob Amman in Switzerland. They had split from mainstream Anabaptism, favoring stricter church discipline and separation from "worldly practices."

In the 1700s the English colonies experienced "revivalism," which eventually gave rise to a larger evangelical movement known as the

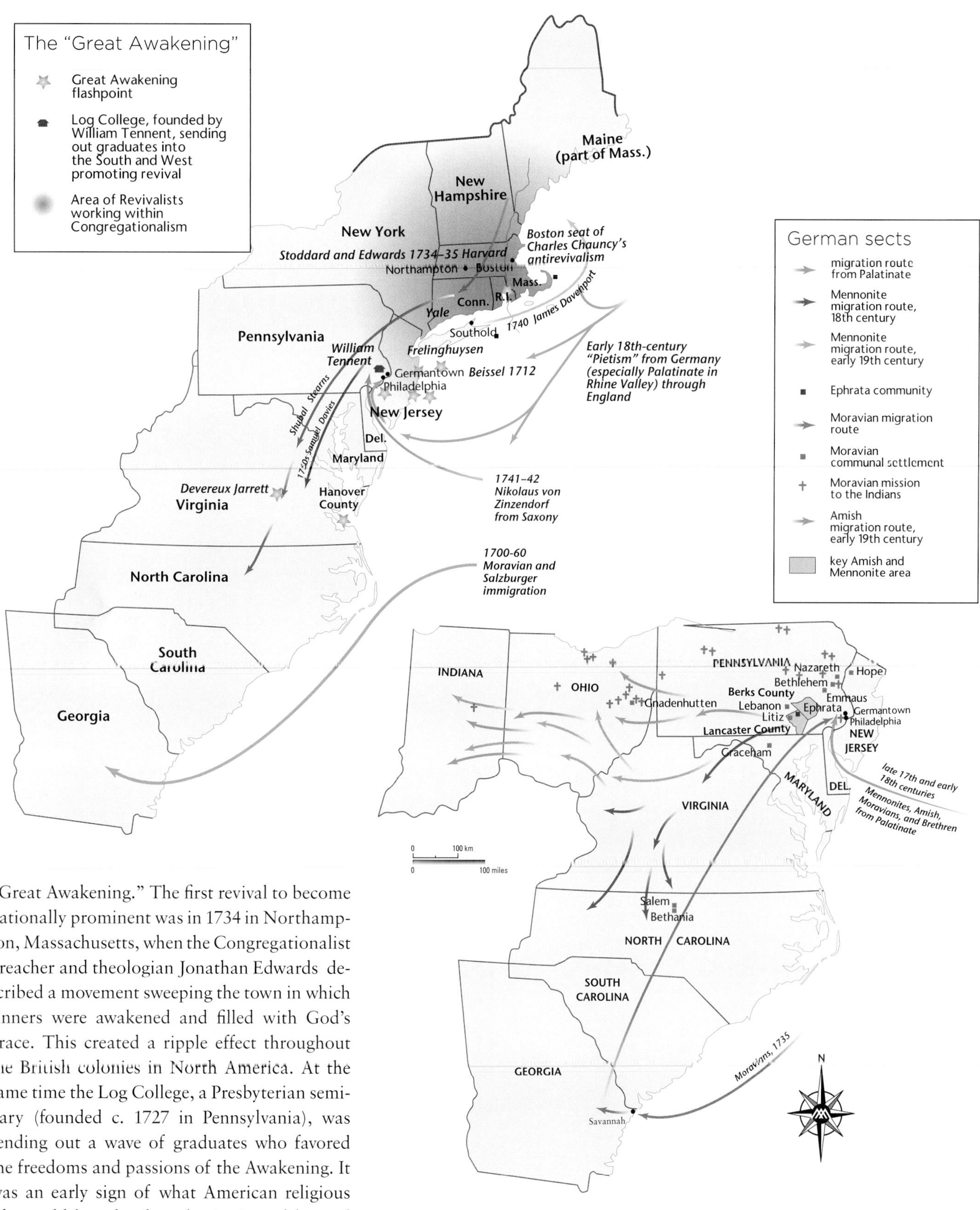

"Great Awakening." The first revival to become nationally prominent was in 1734 in Northampton, Massachusetts, when the Congregationalist preacher and theologian Jonathan Edwards described a movement sweeping the town in which sinners were awakened and filled with God's grace. This created a ripple effect throughout the British colonies in North America. At the same time the Log College, a Presbyterian seminary (founded c. 1727 in Pennsylvania), was sending out a wave of graduates who favored the freedoms and passions of the Awakening. It was an early sign of what American religious life would be: plural, enthusiastic and beyond any institutional church's control.

Protestant Missions in the Age of Slavery

The Portuguese engaged in the Atlantic slave trade as early as the 16th century, and other Europeans soon followed, setting up outposts on the African coast, where they purchased slaves from traders. Slaves were treated as cargo, transported as cheaply as possible across the Atlantic to work on plantations, in mines, and in construction. From the 15th to the 19th centuries, around 12 million Africans were forcibly shipped across the Atlantic.

The Dutch, in Brazil, the Caribbean, and South Africa, were the first Protestants to engage in slave-trading – and many of their slaves, coming from Angola and Kongo, were already Catholic. The English Atlantic slave trade gained momentum throughout the 17th century.

In America the Protestant Anglican church was the religion of the ruling class of slave-owners and many colonists rejected the idea that slaves could convert to Christianity. Despite instructions from the English government to proceed with the conversion of slaves, slave-owners argued that converted slaves were more "perverse and intractable," while slaves that were heathen were not entitled to rights or privileges.

Protestant missionaries began to arrive in the plantations from the late 17th century. They encountered slave-owners who saw the evangelizing missionaries as perpetrators of sedition. They responded by arguing that converted slaves would be more docile and manageable than "heathens." Quakers, Anglicans, and Moravians – the chief missionaries to enslaved societies – all fought to accommodate slavery within their worldview, asserting the compatibility of bondage and Christianity.

As early as 1657 the founder of the Society of Friends (Quakers), George Fox, asserted the equality of all men and argued for the better treatment of enslaved people, and it was

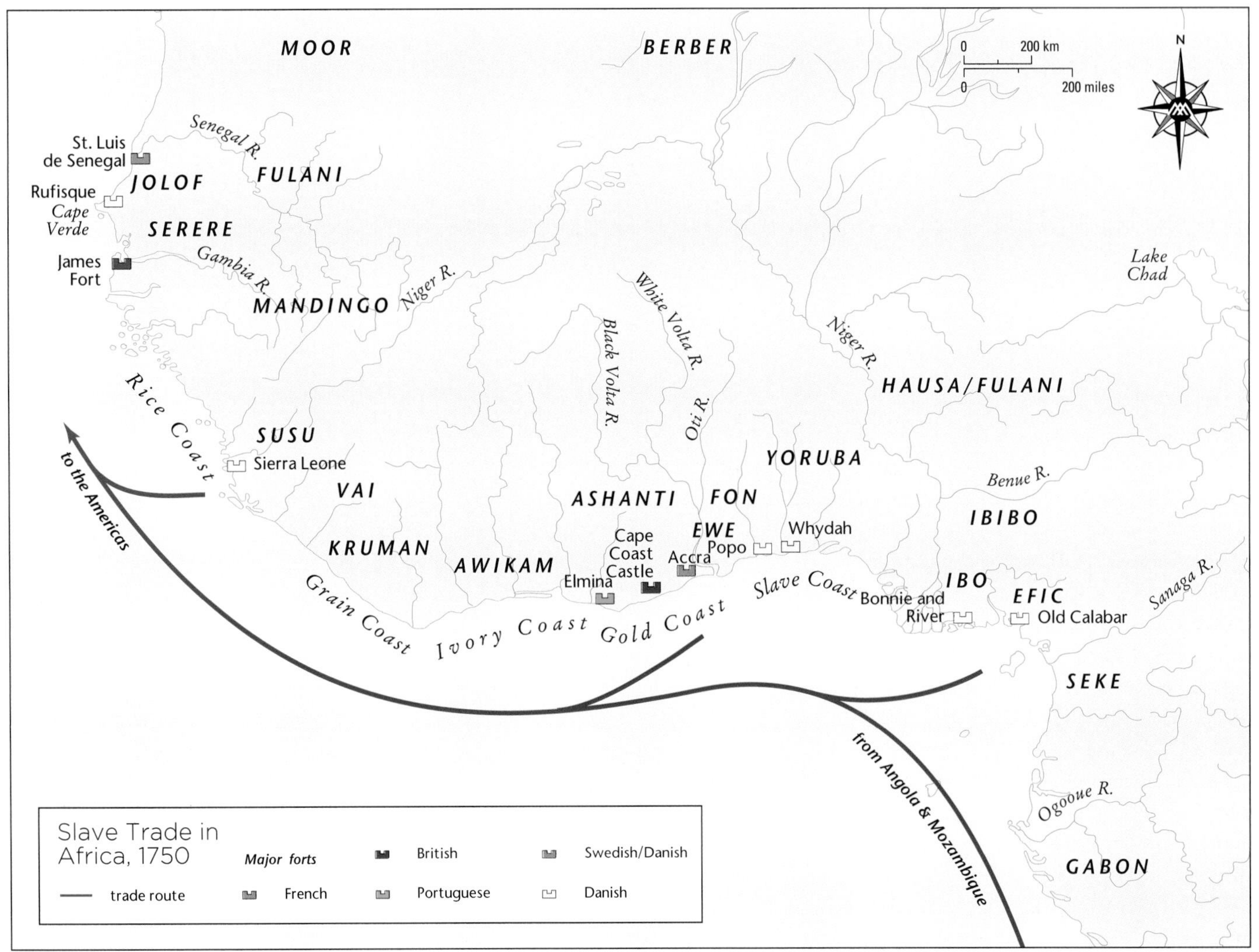

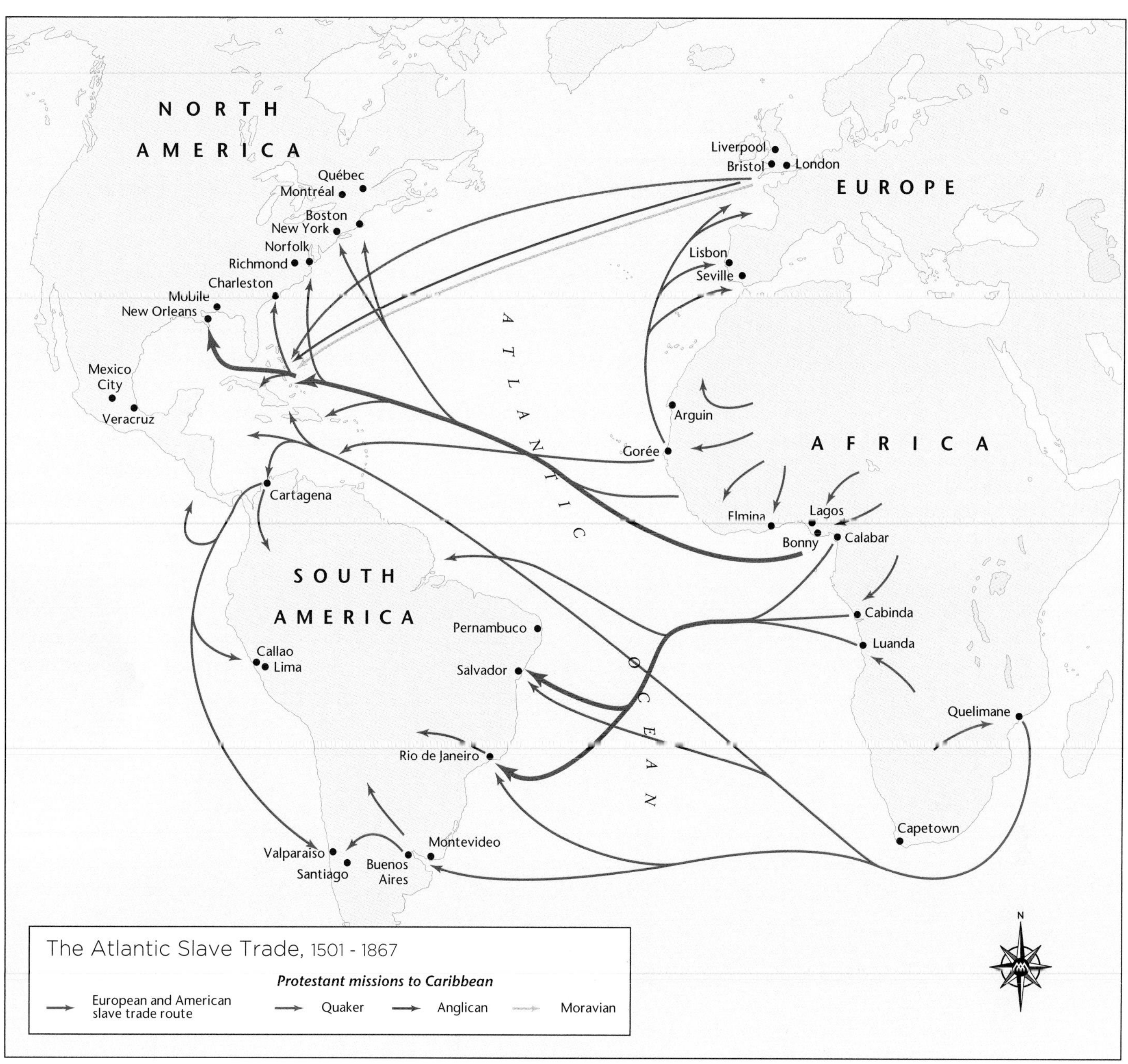

The triangular trade consisted of the export of goods to slave traders in Africa. The slaves were then exported across the Atlantic to colonies in the Americas. The final part of the triangle was the export from the Americas of goods that were the product of slave labor: cotton, sugar, tobacco, and rum.

Quakers from Germantown, Pennsylvania, who penned the Atlantic world's first principled denunciation of all forms of slavery in 1688. But it was not until 1761 that Quakers were barred from holding slaves, formally petitioning Parliament against slavery in 1783.

The Anglicans eventually committed to the policy of evangelization. Thomas Bray, the founder of the SPCK (Society for Promoting Christian Knowledge) and SPG (Society for the Propagation of the Gospel) evangelized through the circulation of catechisms, as well as the foundation of libraries and schools. The Moravians joined this effort in the 1730s, traveling extensively between slave colonies in the Caribbean and North America.

While converting African slaves can be seen as a means of controlling the slave population, the African converts appropriated Christianity, creating a hybrid or creole system of beliefs. The evangelization of the "Great Awakening" in the 1740s spread rapidly amongst the black population partly because it did not rely on education or literacy but emphasized egalitarianism.

Catholic Missions in California

From 1769 onwards the Spanish built a line of 21 Catholic missions in Alta California (New Spain), stretching from San Diego to Sonoma. This was an effective way of gaining a foothold on the new frontier and colonizing the Pacific coast for Spain. The missions lie about 30 miles apart, a day's journey on horseback.

The Jesuits had already established a chain of 15 missions, starting in 1684, in the Baja California peninsula but they were forcibly expelled from the New World in 1767. The Alta California missionary effort was in the hands of the Franciscans, and the first nine missions were established by Padre Junípero Serra. Spain already had a considerable presence in Mexico, and it was from here that the mission effort was launched, with the founding of the Mission San Diego de Alcalá in 1769.

The Californian missions were founded with the purpose of assimilating the natives into the Catholic religion. A total of 146 Franciscan friars served in California between 1769 and 1845 and 67 missionaries died there. Over the entire mission period, between 1769 and 1834, about 53,600 California Indians were baptized.

Each mission was supervised by two friars, with the assistance of five or six soldiers. Indians were initially attracted to the missions by offers of food, gifts, and trinkets. Once they were baptized they were labelled "neophytes," meaning new believer. Baptized Indians were no longer free to roam around the country, but were required – under close supervision – to labor and worship in the mission. If the friars believed the neophytes had run away, they would be rounded up by large scale military expeditions. Neophytes were kept in well-guarded mission compounds, and the friars aimed to keep them continuously occupied and ensured that they adhered to a strict daily routine of work and prayers, which was signalled by the ringing of the mission bells. Male neophytes were taught to sow, irrigate, cultivate, reap, and thresh. They were also taught to build adobe houses, tan hides and weave. Female neophytes were set to dressmaking, weaving, knitting, laundering, and cooking. The Indians were not considered free, and were not paid wages.

Five fortified bases, called *presidios,* were also built along the coast to defend the settlers against rival colonisits as well as Native Americans. Some neophytes were sent to work as the servants of the Spanish soldiers stationed there.

Farming underpinned the mission economy and, apart from the cultivation of cereal staples such as barley, maize, and wheat, the missions were also responsible for introducing seeds from Europe – oranges, grapes, apples, peaches, pears, and figs – which transformed the agricultural base of the new colony. The first wine produced in California emerged from a mission winery in 1783. The missions also generated large quantities of manufactured goods: carpentry, tools, building materials such as bricks and tiles that were baked in the mission's kilns, and ceramic pots. The missionaries brought the Iron Age to the Native Americans: traded iron was forged in the missions to make a range of items, including nails, hinges, cannons. Mission water systems introduced stone aqueducts (*zanjas*), piped water, cisterns, and fountains.

Yet the Californian missions never attained complete self-sufficiency, and all were subsidized by Spain. The development of the missions was financed by the "Pious Fund of the Californias," which dated to 1697 and comprised donations from wealthy individuals, religious bodies, and members of the Society of Jesus.

Alta California became part of Mexico following Mexican independence in 1821, and calls for "secularization" of the missions multiplied. After the Secularization Act of 1833 Indians in southern California were freed from missionary rule, and the Franciscans effectively abandoned most of the missions, which were subsequently plundered by the locals. Former mission lands were divided into land grants called *ranchos*. By 1846 some missions were used as military bases in the war between the US and Mexico. California became a state in 1850 after the discovery of gold there in 1849 attracted a flood of Anglophone prospecters and settlers.

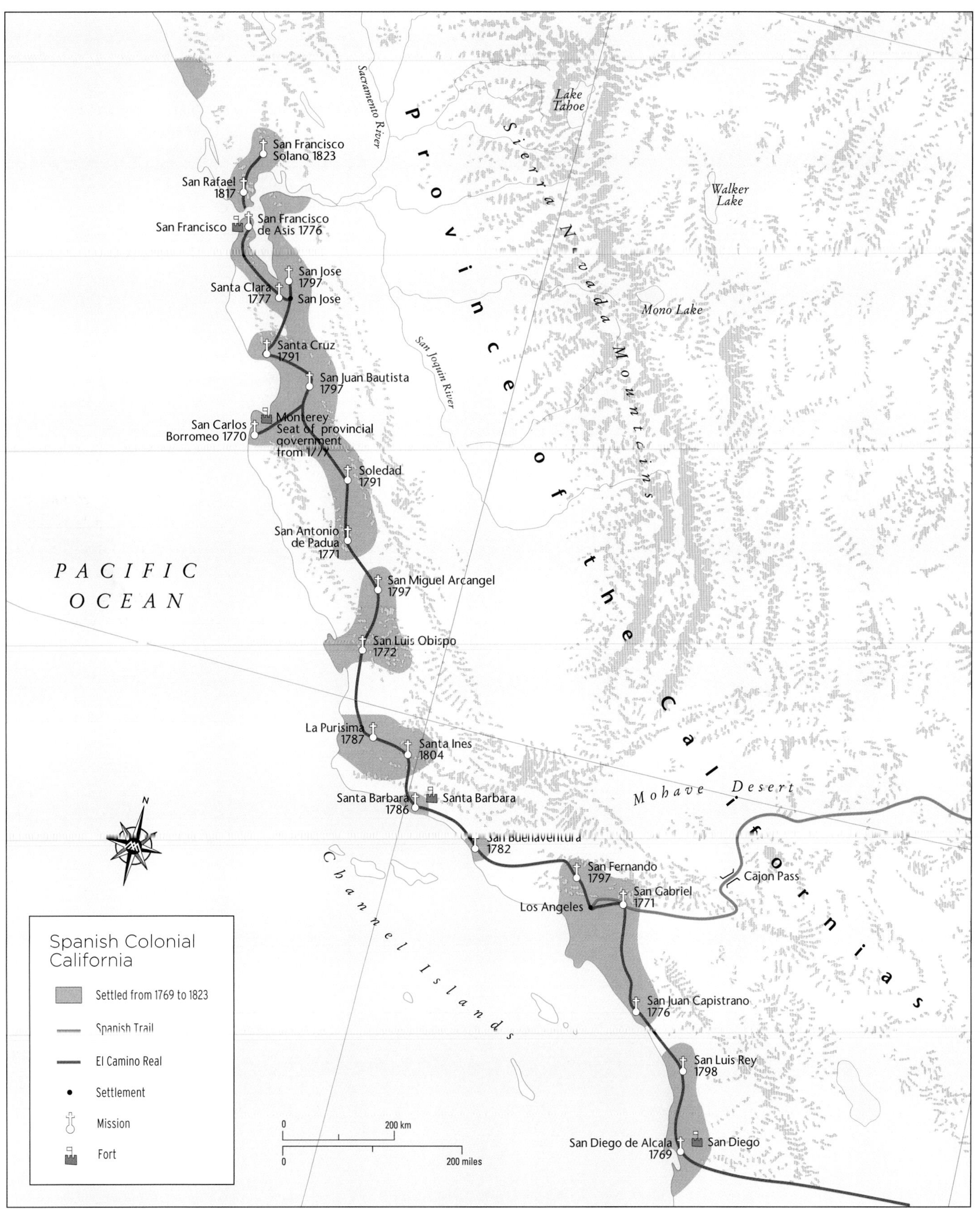
Spanish Colonial California
Settled from 1769 to 1823
Spanish Trail
El Camino Real
Settlement
Mission
Fort
PACIFIC OCEAN
Province of the Californias
Sierra Nevada Mountains
Sacramento River
San Joquin River
Lake Tahoe
Walker Lake
Mono Lake
Mohave Desert
Channel Islands
Cajon Pass
San Francisco Solano 1823
San Rafael 1817
San Francisco
San Francisco de Asis 1776
San Jose 1797
Santa Clara 1777
San Jose
Santa Cruz 1791
San Juan Bautista 1797
Monterey Seat of provincial government from 1777
San Carlos Borromeo 1770
Soledad 1791
San Antonio de Padua 1771
San Miguel Arcangel 1797
San Luis Obispo 1772
La Purisima 1787
Santa Ines 1804
Santa Barbara 1786
Santa Barbara
San Buenaventura 1782
San Fernando 1797
San Gabriel 1771
Los Angeles
San Juan Capistrano 1776
San Luis Rey 1798
San Diego de Alcala 1769
San Diego
N
0
200 km
0
200 miles

Christianity
IN THE MODERN AGE 1800–2020

Statue of Christ the Redeemer in Rio de Janeiro, Brazil, unveiled on 12 October 1931.

Christianity in the Age of Revolution

Revolutionary Europe, 1803

Revolutionary republic Allied to France

Holy Roman Empire

Catholicism was the official religion of the French state and in 1789 – at the outbreak of the French revolution – the church was the largest landowner in the country, and its institutions dominated French life from the cradle to the grave. The wealth and privileges enjoyed by the Catholic clergy and the aristocracy were prime causes of the resentment that finally erupted amongst the French people, who were also suffering from bad harvests and oppressive taxes. Enlightenment ideas, which increasingly questioned religious orthodoxy, were contributing factors in the revolutionary fervor that gripped France, culminating in the storming of the Bastille in July 1789. In the following month feudalism was abolished and with it the rights and privileges of the *Ancien Régime*.

In November 1789 France's new National Assembly passed a decree that effectively nationalized all church property; just three months later France's monasteries were closed. Dioceses were redrawn to match administrative divisions; priests and bishops were to be elected by the people; the clergy's salary scale was reformed. All clergy were required to take an oath of loyalty to the Constitution; about 50 percent of parish clergy refused, and were labelled "refractory." The pope condemned the oath on 13 April 1791, creating a schism with Rome. Following the fall of the monarchy on 10 August 1792 remaining religious orders and institutions were suppressed and "refractories" were ordered to leave the country or face arrest. Foreign religious orders, such as the longstanding English Catholic exile communities, were expelled.

With the onset of the Reign of Terror, overseen by the new Republican government, the church was openly targeted and religious practice was increasingly driven underground. In October 1793 public worship was forbidden and all visible signs of religion were eradicated, leading to an outbreak of iconoclasm. In November, churches were closed, and converted for secular use. The Gregorian calendar was banned, and the Sabbath and saints' days were eradicated, to be replaced a new Revolutionary calendar. The Revolution began to evolve its own cults and symbols: the Cult of Reason worshiped the goddess of reason in former churches. The radical lawyer and ideologue Maximilien Robespierre, head of the Committee of Public Safety, went on to inaugurate a new religion, the Cult of the Supreme Being, which renounced the "superstitions" of Catholicism, although the new religion was short-lived and Robespierre himself was executed on 28 July 1794. On 21 February 1795 church and state were formally separated; refractory priests were allowed to practice as long as they respected the laws of the Republic.

When Napoleon came to power in 1799 he accommodated religious belief and practice as a means of consolidating his control. A Concordat, signed with Rome in July 1801, recognized that Catholicism was the religion of "the vast majority of French citizens" and the church was once again brought under the control of the

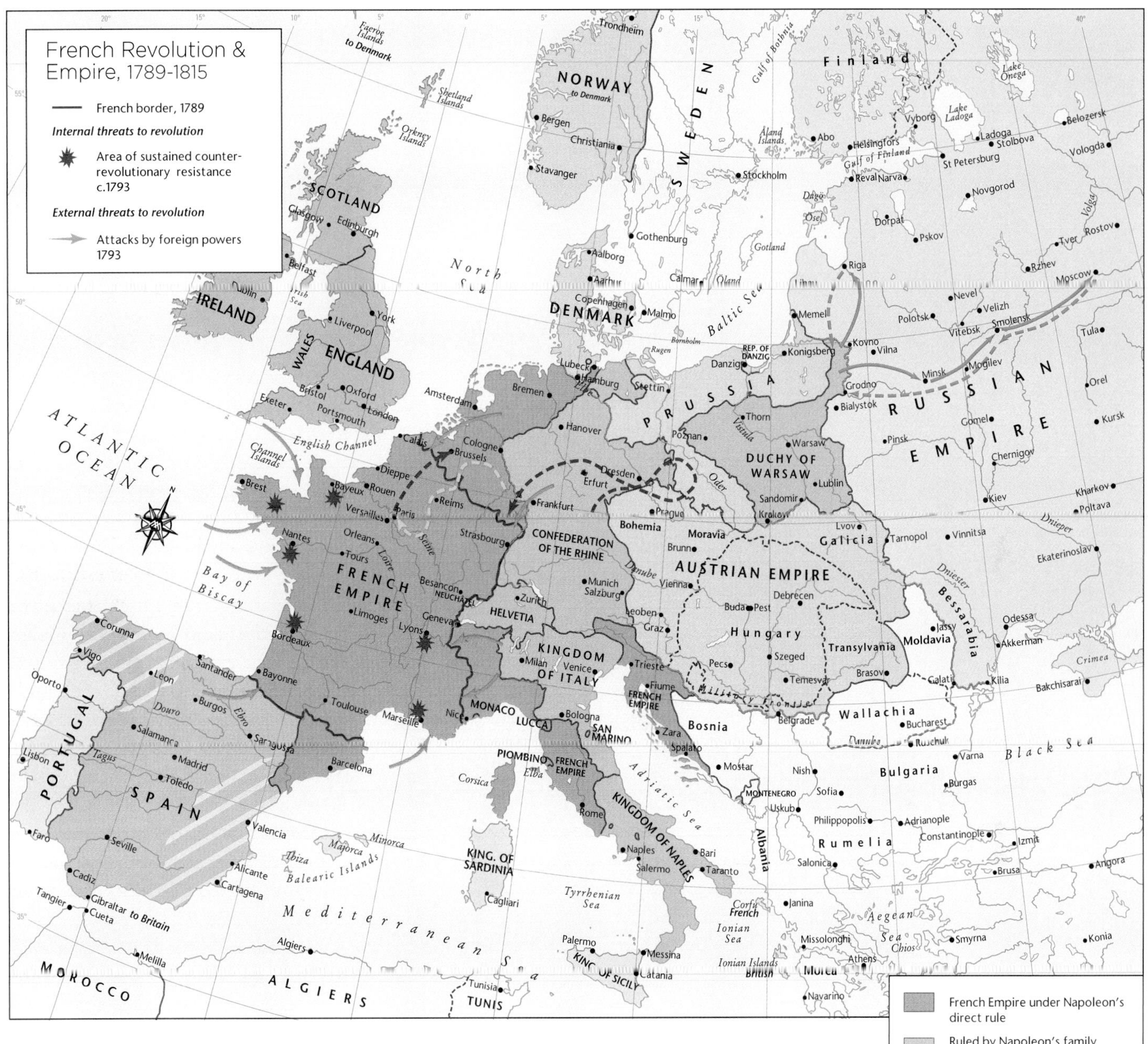

state. In 1805 the pope was angered by the incursion of French troops on papal territory and demanded their withdrawal. Napoleon proclaimed "you are sovereign in Rome, but I am its Emperor," insisting the Papal States join his continental system, which blockaded and expelled British goods from the whole of the European continent. The pope refused. Following the occupation of papal lands by French troops in 1808, the pope excommunicated Napoleon, and in 1809 the Emperor had the pope arrested and imprisoned – he remained a captive in the chateau of Fontainebleau until 1814.

Napoleon's single-minded pursuit of power and supremacy and his treatment of the pope alienated many Catholics in his empire and had long-term consequences. When the monarchy was restored in France in 1814–15, the old "Gallican" tradition in France, which asserted French distinctiveness within the Catholic world and played down papal authority, was dead. To be a French Catholic was, increasingly, to be "ultramontane," to look to the pope (beyond the mountains). Ironically, the Revolution and its aftermath helped to precipitate the assertion of papal infallibility in 1870–71.

Europe in the 19th Century

THE FRENCH REVOLUTION and Napoleonic Wars had swept away the old aristocratic-clerical dominance of the hierarchy, and Catholics all over Europe looked once again to the ultimate authority of the pope. Secular rulers negotiated a series of concordats with the papacy but it was an uneasy relationship, as monarchs sought to contain increasing liberalism.

The papacy regarded the upsurge of liberal and nationalist movements in the 19th century with great suspicion. 1848 was a year of revolutionary fervor, when a series of republican revolts against constitutional monarchies started in Sicily and spread to France, Germany, Italy, and the Austrian Empire. The revolts all ended in failure and repression, leading to a strong anti-liberal backlash. In the 1864 *Syllabus of Errors* Pope Pius IX condemned liberalism, speaking out against movements to allow freedom of worship for non-Catholics in Catholic states.

As the movement for Italian unification gained momentum, starting in Sicily in 1848, the Catholic church, and its control of territories in central Italy, was seen as a major obstacle. Liberal revolutionaries defeated the papal army in 1860 and Victor Emmanuel II, the king of Sardinia, took most papal territories, only excluding Rome itself and its hinterland, and became king of of a united Italy. Pope Pius IX retreated to the Vatican and in 1870, Victor Emmanuel marched on Rome, seized the city and made it the Italian capital.

Against this background, surrounded by the Italian army, in 1869 Pius convened the First Vatican Council, where 700 bishops from all over the world arrived in Rome. At his moment of greatest political vulnerability, the Council backed a decree, *Pastor Aeternas*, which asserted the doctrine of papal infallibility. Eventually, in 1929 the Vatican City was recognized as a sovereign microstate within the city of Rome.

When the Prussian leader Otto von Bismarck became chancellor in 1862 the process of German unification was accelerated by "blood and iron." Northern Protestants had approached the new liberalism differently, seeking to explicitly embrace the Enlightenment, through Protestant theologians such as Friedrich Schleiermacher (1768–1834) and Søren Kierkegaard (1813–55). Following German unification in 1871 Chancellor Bismarck launched the *kulturkampf* ("cultural struggle"), the conflict between liberalism and Protestant Germany against conservative Roman Catholicism. In this he was able to harness German disdain for the Catholicism of Poland, much of which now lay within the new German Empire. The Chancellor was attempting to use religion to shift the balance of power in the new empire. But Germany's Catholics, a third of the population, withstood this assault.

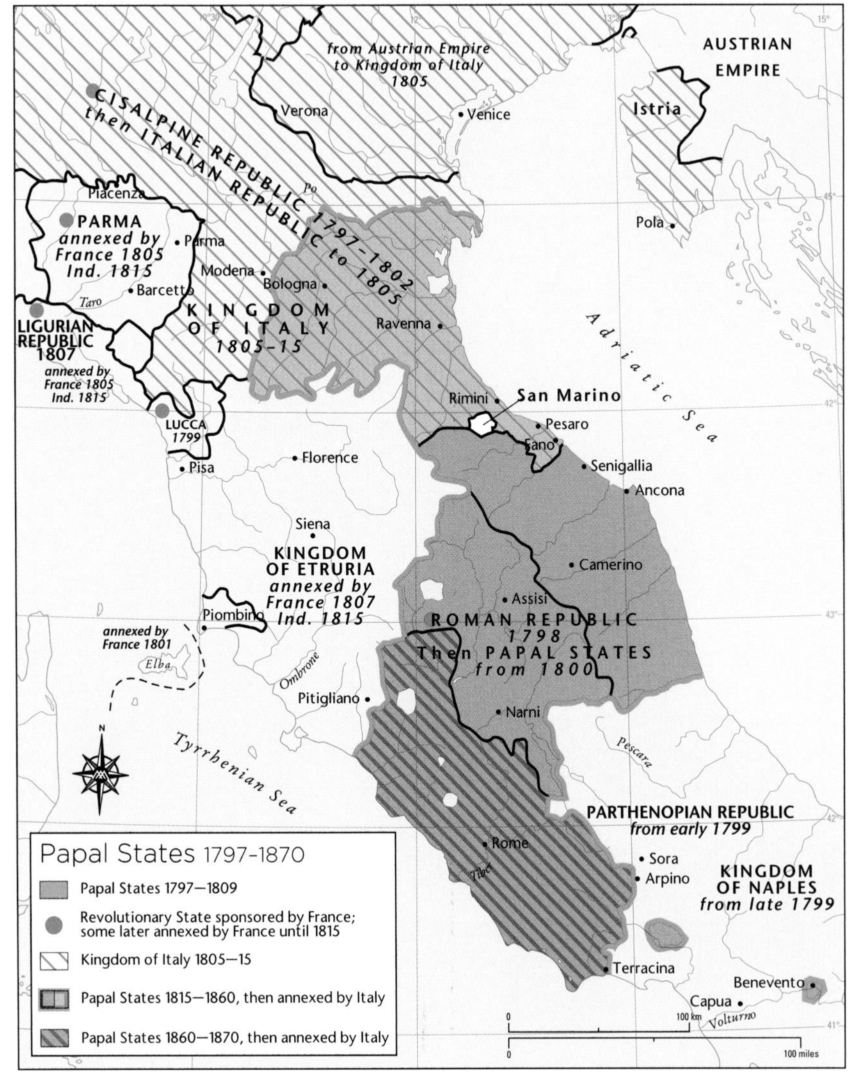

Indeed, in Protestant and industrialized northern Germany, many people were turning away from religion altogether and embracing secularism and socialism.

In 1829 the Tory government of Great Britain passed the Roman Catholic Relief Act, which ended legal discrimination against Roman Catholics, even allowing them to stand for Parliament. One motivation was to quell Catholic discontent in Ireland, which would ultimately lead to the 1916 Easter Rising, when Catholic Republicans rose against British rule.

Christian precepts were increasingly challenged by thinkers and philosophers, such as Friedrich Nietzsche (1844–1900) and Karl Marx (1818–83), whose disenchantment with Christianity was matched by excitement at the age of science. Charles Darwin's theory of evolution, first proposed in *On the Origin of Species* (1859), altered understanding of the natural world. For many it was a decisive moment, which made literal interpretation of the Bible no longer tenable. But the 19th century was also a time of visionaries and impassioned believers and reformers, who set out to spread the Christian message to the farthest corners of the earth.

Against a background of nationalist uprisings and constiututional reform traditional Catholic beliefs were passionately asserted. The 19th century was a time of Marian visions throughout Europe. In 1884 Pope Pius IX had declared in the bull *Ineffabilis Deus* that the dogma of the Immaculate Conception was revealed by God, and therefore to be believed by all Catholics.

Religion in the American Revolution 1757–87

THE AMERICAN REVOLUTION of 1775–87 saw a strange alliance between two apparently opposed religious forces. Many of the leading thinkers and politicians of the revolution were deists and freethinkers influenced by French Enlightenment philosophy and sceptical towards Christianity. Much of their grassroots support, in the generation after the first Great Awakening of the 1740s, came from revivalist and evangelical Protestants. What these strange bedfellows shared, aside from their secular grievances with British misrule, was a hostility to clerical power and hierarchical church establishments. The philosophers committed several of the newly independent American states, and then in 1791 the United States as a whole, to a policy of open religious toleration while denying special privileges or official establishment to any denomination. The revivalists eagerly seized the opportunities that this new world offered.

As the new republic's rapidly expanding population moved westward, it outran the structures of the old hierarchical churches. The Baptists and Methodists flourished in this new climate.

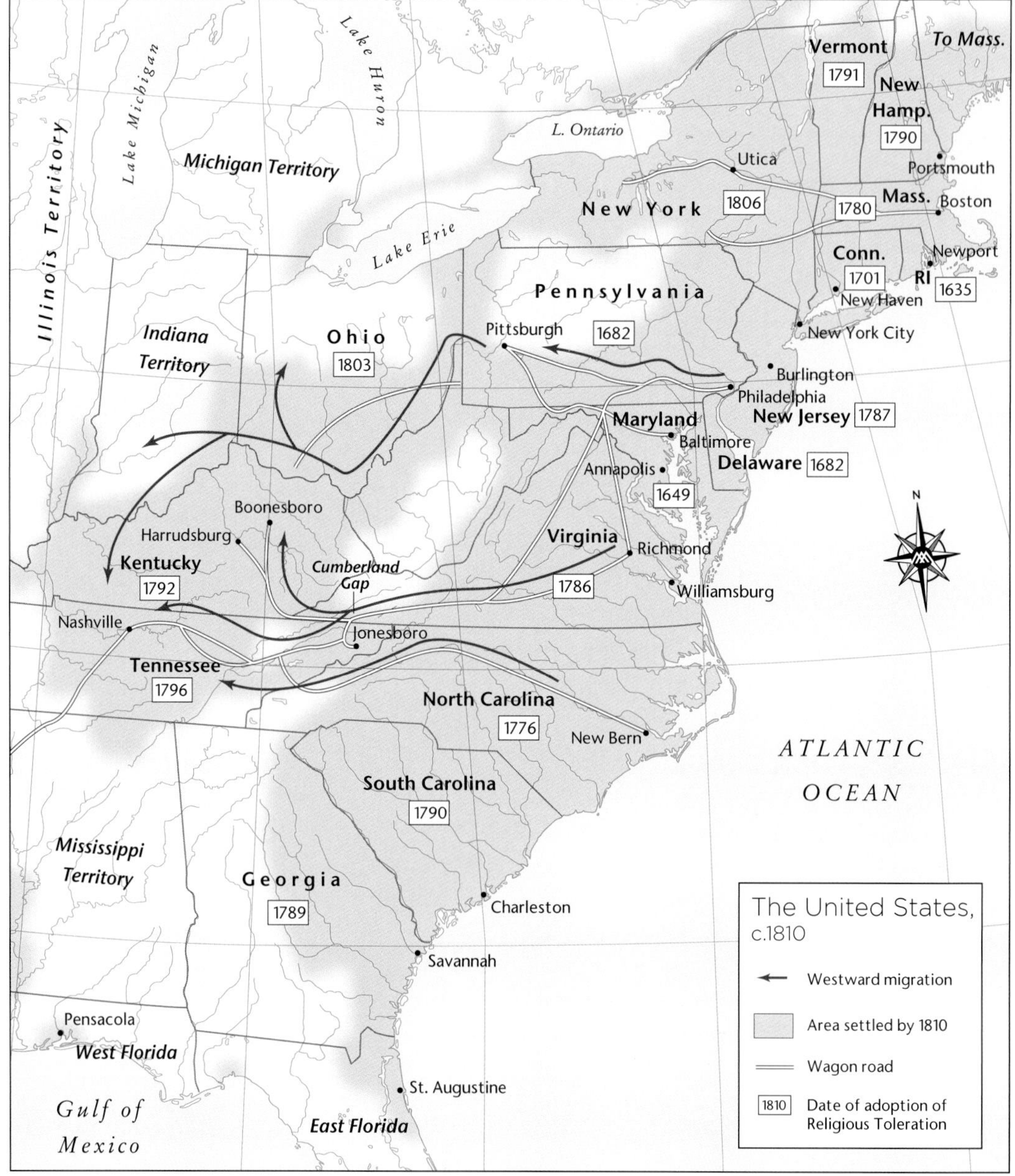

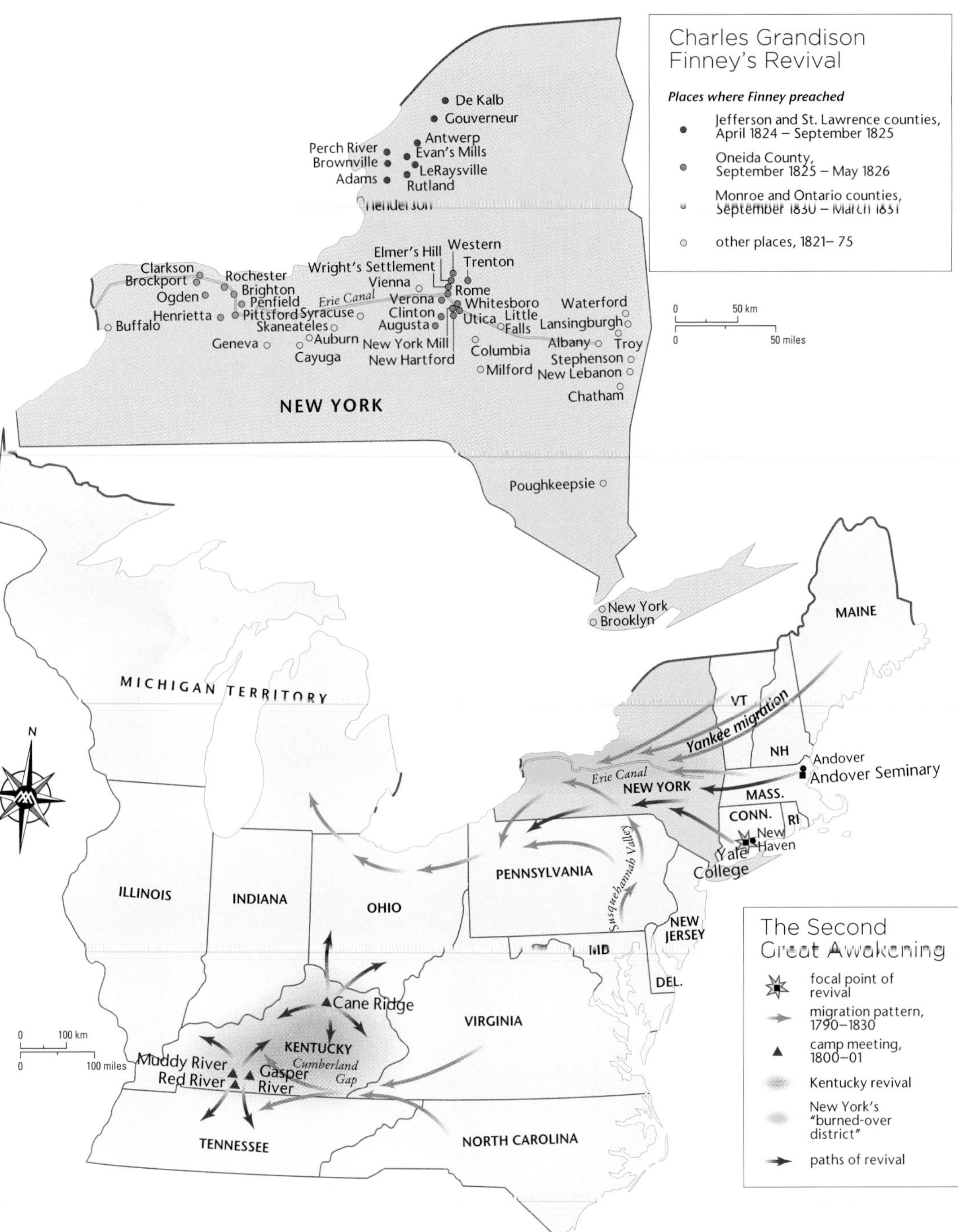

The evangelist Charles Grandison Finney (1792–1875) was a former lawyer, who underwent religious conversion and conducted emotional revivals throughout the state of New York, especially in cities such as New York. He eventually moved to Ohio where he founded a new religious school. "Second Awakening" missions often focused on "camp meetings," a kind of outdoor religious fair, which attracted large crowds, and lasted several days. These gatherings involved singing, dancing, and emotional testifying.

The result was a new wave of revivals known as the second Great Awakening, traditionally traced to the Cane Ridge revival in Kentucky in 1801. Long-established denominations such as the Congregationalists were left behind; the Church of England was almost destroyed by the Revolution, before reinventing itself as the Protestant Episcopal church. The winners of the cut-throat religious competition were the flexible denominational families such as the Baptists and, above all, the Methodists, who by 1850 comprised over a third of the US population.

Christianity and the Enslaved Peoples

Africans brought to the Americas as slaves came predominantly from West and Central West Africa and brought with them the linguistic, cultural, and religious traditions of that region. For most, those religious traditions focused on maintaining harmonious relationships with nature and supernatural forces, which included gods, spirits, and ancestors. Some enslaved Africans from the Senegambia region were Muslim, while others – mainly those from the kingdom of Kongo, which had come into contact with the Portuguese – were Catholic.

More than 12 million Africans were transported to the Americas between the 16th and 19th centuries, in conditions of the utmost degradation, and sold into slavery. Only around 5 percent of these – 600,000 people – were brought to the North American mainland, the majority being destined for the Caribbean or Brazil. While it was extremely hard for slaves to preserve their religious beliefs intact once in the New World, their religion proved adaptable and resilient. Although families and tribal groups were separated and white owners rejected the "heathen" beliefs of their slaves, some relic of their original beliefs – songs, movements, belief in the world of spirits and ancestors – did survive into the 19th century. In Latin America slaves mixed African beliefs and practices with Catholicism, which in some instances (for example "voodoo" in Haiti, Santeria in Cuba) led to the formation of an entirely new religion. In the Southern states of the United States, where the slave population was high, African religious influences were strong, and a kind of syncretic religion evolved. Symbols and objects, such as crosses, were conflated with charms carried by Africans to ward off evil spirits. Christ was seen as a healer, much like the priests of Africa.

By 1800 most of the slave population in the US had not converted to Christianity. However, in North America slaves were coming increasingly into contact with Protestant evangelists, who sought to convert them. The slave trade to America legally ended in 1808, but unlike in the Caribbean, the mortality rate for slaves was low enough that the enslaved population could continue to grow. In the North some states were beginning to abolish slavery, so that the experiences of African-Americans began to diverge dramatically according to geography.

The "awakenings" that swept the country in the wake of the Revolution led to conversion of many African-Americans, both slave and free, to evangelical religions such as Methodism and Baptism. Clergymen within these denominations promoted the notion that Christians were equal in the sight of God, and that both inner transformation and social change were possible. They encouraged methods of worship, incorporating singing, dancing, hand-clapping, and even spirit possession, which drew on African traditions. This was in contrast to white-controlled churches, which promoted formality, ritual, and obedience to one's master. Many slave-owners forced their slaves to attend their own churches, anxious that evangelical worship would lead to sedition, and keen to use Christian teaching to justify notions of divinely-ordained hierarchies and obedience. Some planters saw Christianity as a means of controlling their slave populations, and justified enslavement as a means of Christianizing African "heathens." They wel-

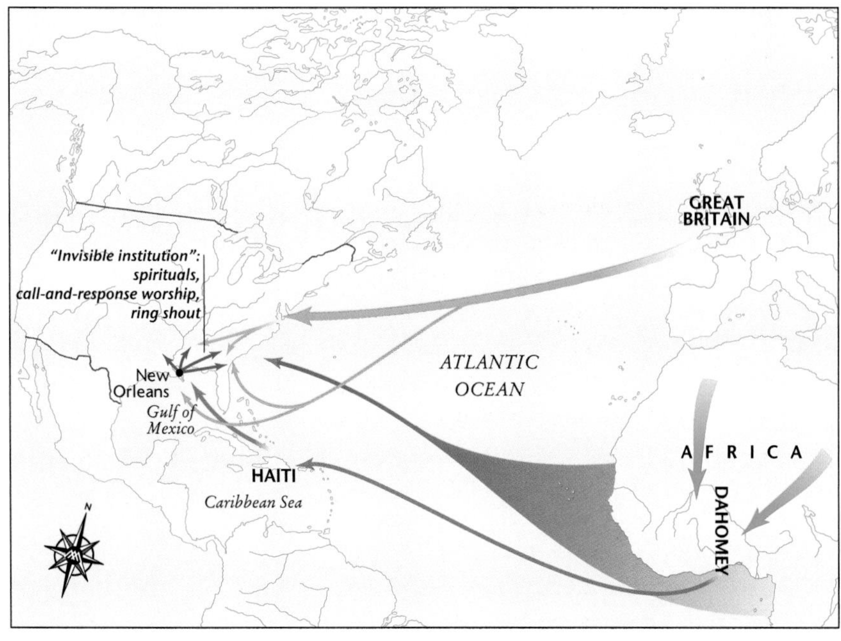

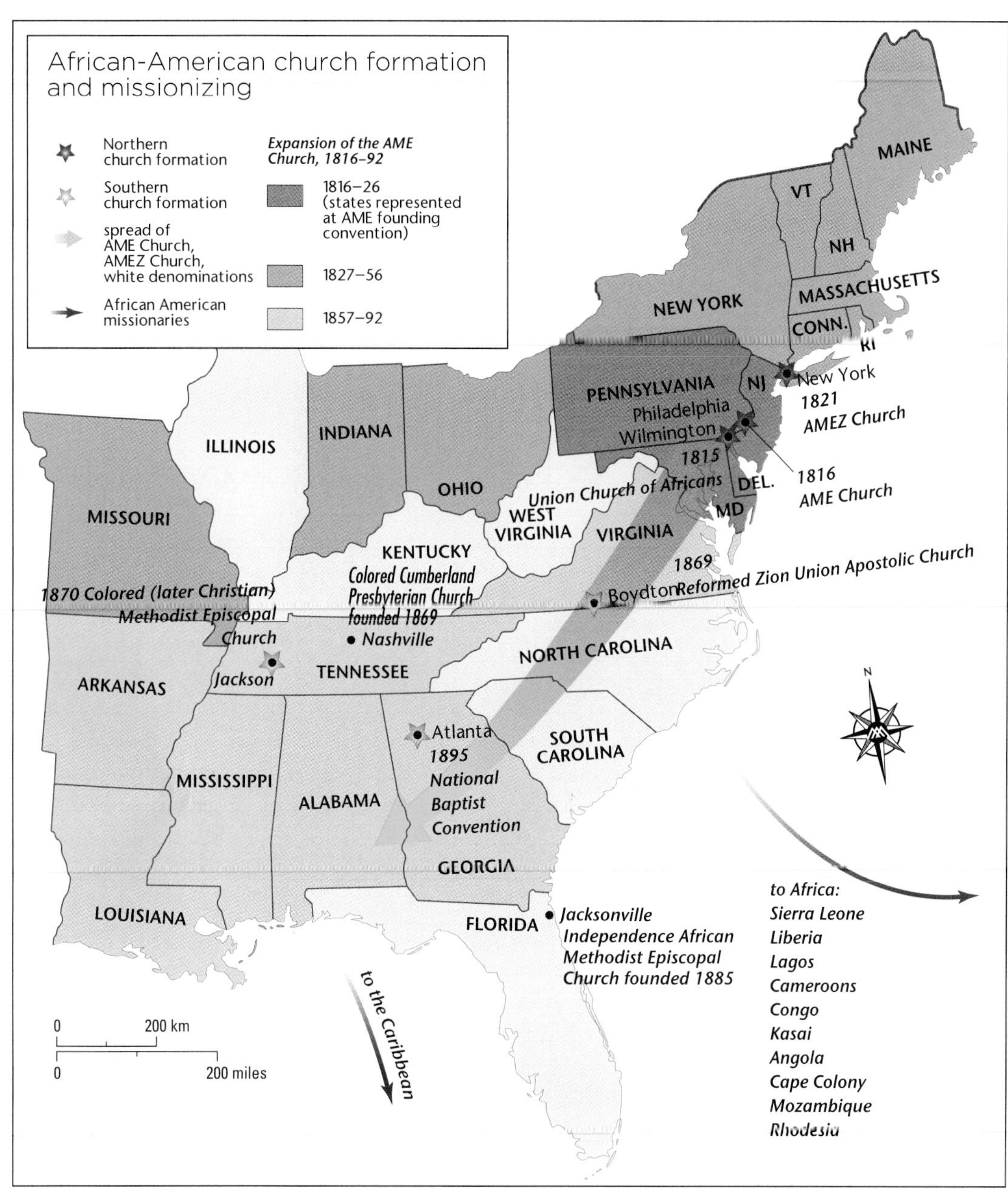

comed ministers to their plantations, and built chapels for their slaves. Fear of sedition and insurrection was never far away and in the South black churches were regarded with suspicion.

In the North freed slaves were also drawn to Protestant evangelicalism, but despite ostensible equality, discriminatory practices, such as segregated seating in church, persisted. By the late 18th century literate, educated black leaders were seeking to establish their own independent black churches, especially in cities with large freed black populations, such as New York, Boston, and Philadelphia. The first independent black denomination was the African Methodist Episcopalian Church (founded 1816), and it was soon followed by the African Methodist Episcopal Zion Church, and the National Baptist Convention. Because of the limitations placed on African Americans in the northern states theses churches also became centers of education, social welfare, and neighborhood organization, uniting the population into a community. Some of the earliest civil rights activists were African-American Protestant clergy and some of these African-American churches made common cause with white abolitionists. >>

In public slaves adhered to formalities and rituals, but in private worship could sometimes be more spontaneous. On occasion slaves in the southern United States gathered together in hidden places, such as woods, ravines or gullies, known as "hush harbors," secret meeting places where they could evolve their own form of evangelical Christianity, overseen by peripatetic slave preachers, with an emphasis on song, chanting, and preaching. Black preachers drew on biblical narratives such as the Exodus, with its inspiring example of deliverance from slavery. Most slaves could not read, so an oral tradition arose with a distinct musical expression, the so-called "spirituals," a fusion of Evangelical hymns and the celebratory rhythms and chants of African origin. These refuges from oppressive overlordship became places that helped individuals endure the brutality of slavery. They were sometimes also places where rebellion could be planned.

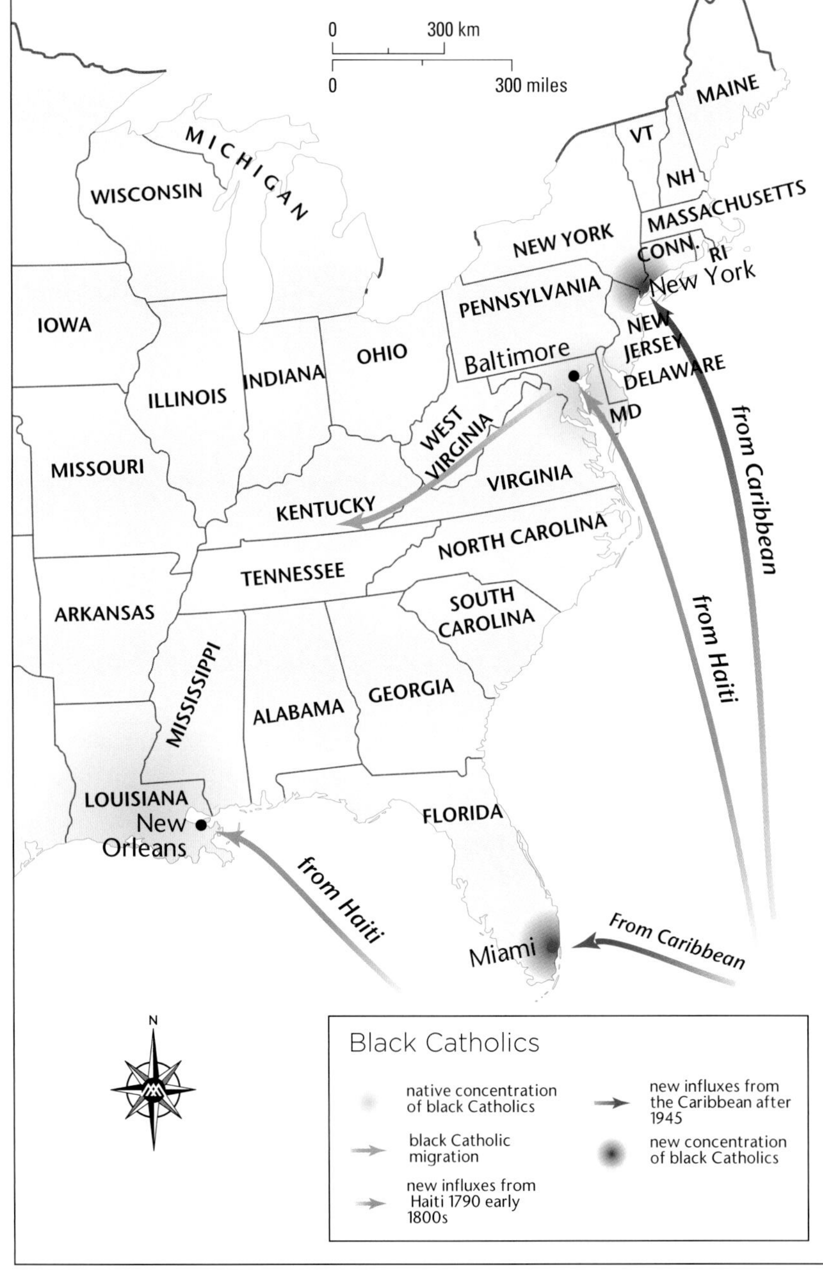

Nat Turner, who led an armed slave insurrection in Virginia in 1831, was literate, charismatic, and highly devout, holding Baptist services for his fellow slaves who dubbed him the "Prophet." His rebellion, which began on 22 August 1831, was crushed by an armed militia, and many of the participants were summarily hanged, incuding Turner. Several southern states responded by banning the teaching of reading and writing to African-Americans.

The Demerara rebellion of December 1823 was an uprising involving more than 10,000 slaves that took place in the colony of Demerara-Essequibo (Guyana). John Smith, an English pastor at the "Success" plantation, was implicated in the revolt and was eventually arraigned for "promoting discontent and dissatisfaction in the minds of the Negro Slaves towards their Lawful Masters, Overseers and Managers, inciting rebellion." He was condemned to death, but died of consumption, and was hastily interred. His unmarked grave became a rallying point for future revolts, and galvanized abolitionists back in Britain.

Jamaica, the home of extensive British sugar plantations, was the scene of many slave revolts. In 1831 the Baptist deacon Samuel Sharpe led a Christmas Day general strike for wages and better working conditions, which turned to open rebellion by tens of thousands of slaves, who looted and burned plantations into January 1832 before being defeated by British troops. This Baptist War was one of the largest slave rebellions in the British West Indies and contributed to Britain's abolition of slavery in 1833.

The slave preacher was an important figure in slave society. He (and sometimes she) presided over major rituals, such as funerals and baptisms – one of the most significant events in the slaves' lives, which involved total immer-

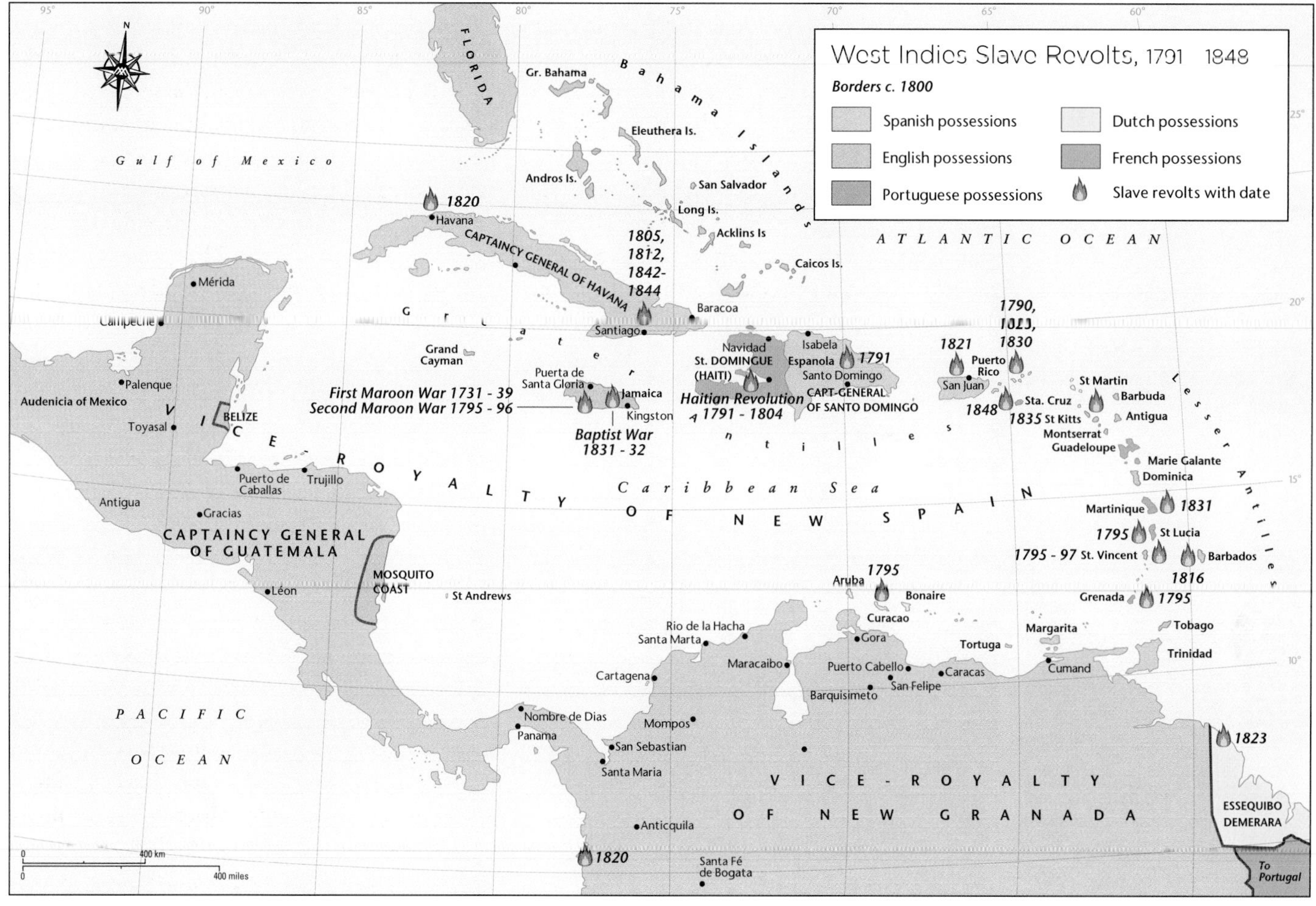

sion in a local creek or river, symbolizing the River Jordan, where the enslaved Israelites had entered the promised land. Preachers even officiated at weddings, although slaves' marriages had no legal status and families were routinely broken up for sale and simply for discipline by slave-holders. Preachers had to tread a delicate path between administering to their brethren and adhering to the commands of their masters. Some preachers experienced something close to freedom, moving from place to place to conduct prayer meetings, sanctioned by slave owners. Although somes slave preachers were accused of being their masters' mouthpieces, preaching adherence to the status quo, most slaves recognized the limitations they were operating under, respecting them as messengers of God, who preached the gospel with power and authority.

African-Americans in the southern United States also developed churches that provided independent interpretation of Christian teaching and practice. Amongst these first black Baptist churches were Silver Bluff Church in Georgia (1770s) and the First African Baptist Church of Savannah (1788). These independent churches became important means of promoting African-American interpretations of Christianity.

There was also a well-established community of black Catholics in the United States, many of whom emigrated north from the Catholic countries of Central America and the Caribbean, which had been colonized by Spain, France, and Portugal – in 1693, for example, Florida, which was still under Spanish rule, offered freedom to all the enslaved blacks who converted to Catholicism. The oldest black Catholic parish in America is said to be in Saint Augustine, Florida (1841). One of the most influential black Catholic communities was founded by refugees from the island of San Domingo (now known as Haiti and the Dominican Republic) who founded the first St Xavier Church in Baltimore (1863).

Slave revolts in Central America and the Caribbean were frequent. Jamaica, with its sugar plantations, experienced many revolts, some of them by the "Maroons," escaped slaves who lived in independent communities in the mountains of Jamaica. In Haiti a major revolt in 1791 continued until the French banned slavery in 1794. Its leader, former slave Toussaint Louverture, became the leader of the new country of Haiti, the first state to arise from a slave rebellion.

Religious Innovation in 19th-Century America

Communitarian groups carved out small communities on the fringes of mainstream society. Their challenges to the economic injustice, gender roles, and established religion that characterized American societies were heartfelt, but ultimately had little general impact.

Following the American Revolution there was a great outpouring of religious diversity, and many sects were founded that emerged from the dissenting Protestant denominations that had been founded in America by refugees from persecution in Europe, and incorporated notions of utopianism into their core beliefs. An essential tenet of many of these sects was the idea of communal living, or communitarianism. America was ideally suited for this experiment, as the frontier was continually moving westward, and land was cheap and available. The First Amendment of the US Constitution, which guaranteed religious freedom, had attracted many persecuted European groups, who hoped to found self-contained, agrarian societies in the New World.

The Protestant sect of the Shakers was founded in England in 1747. The American Shakers were founded by the daughter of a Manchester blacksmith, Ann Lee, in 1774, and she sailed to America to fulfil her mission. The Shakers believed in communal living and all property was shared. They practiced strict celibacy, perpetuating themselves exclusively by adoption – a stance which ultimately hastened their disappearance. They were pacifists with advanced notions of gender and racial equality, and favored simplicity in dress and behavior, encouraging their adherents to live in agricultural communities away from the corruption of cities.

The Rappites immigrated from Württemburg in Germany to the United States in 1803, and established a colony called Harmony in Butler County, Pennsylvania. Similar in many ways to the Shakers, the group was founded by Johann Georg Rapp. Under the leadership of his son, Frederick Rapp, the essentially agrarian community gradually evolved into mixed manufacturing and became prosperous. Eventually they

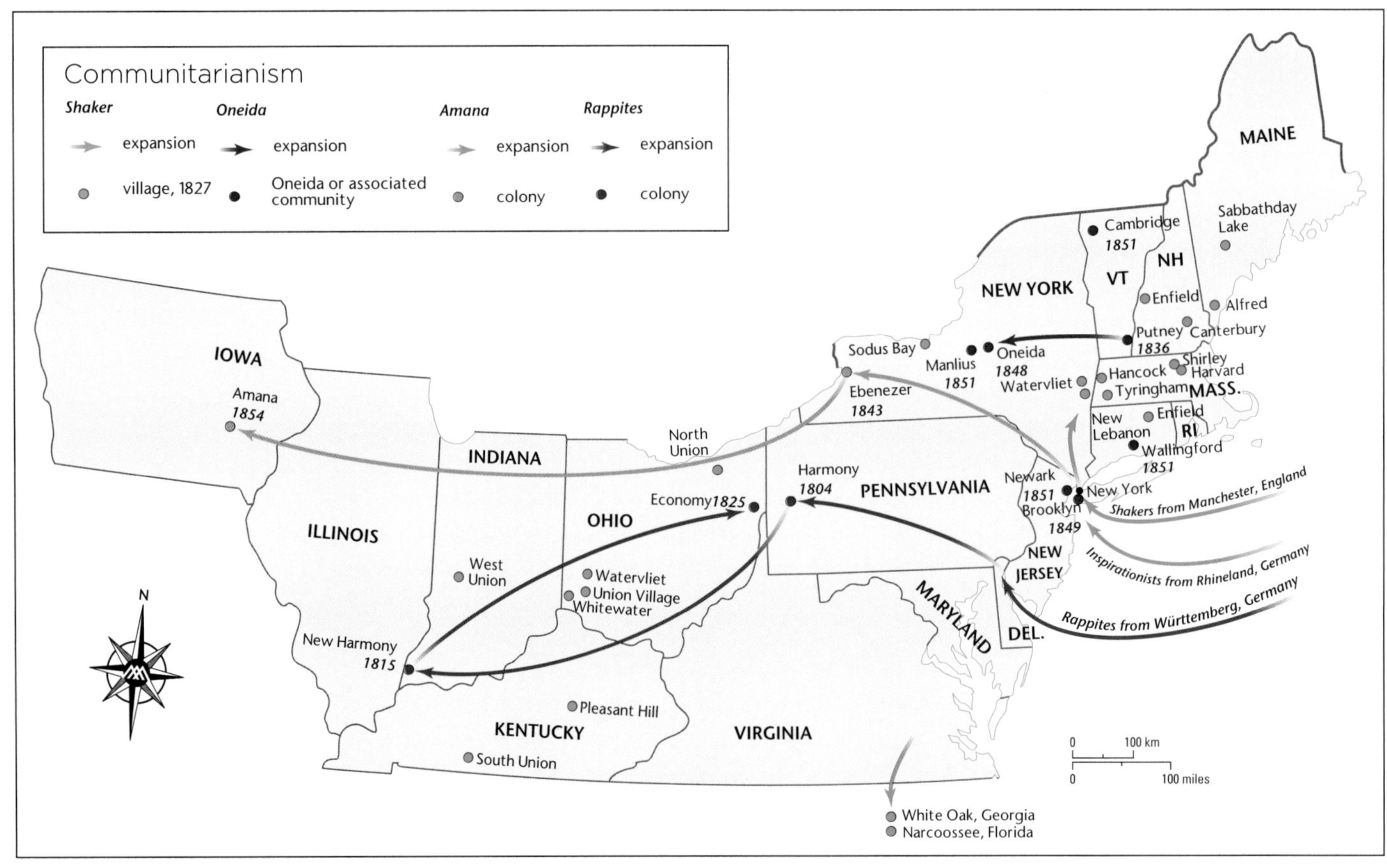

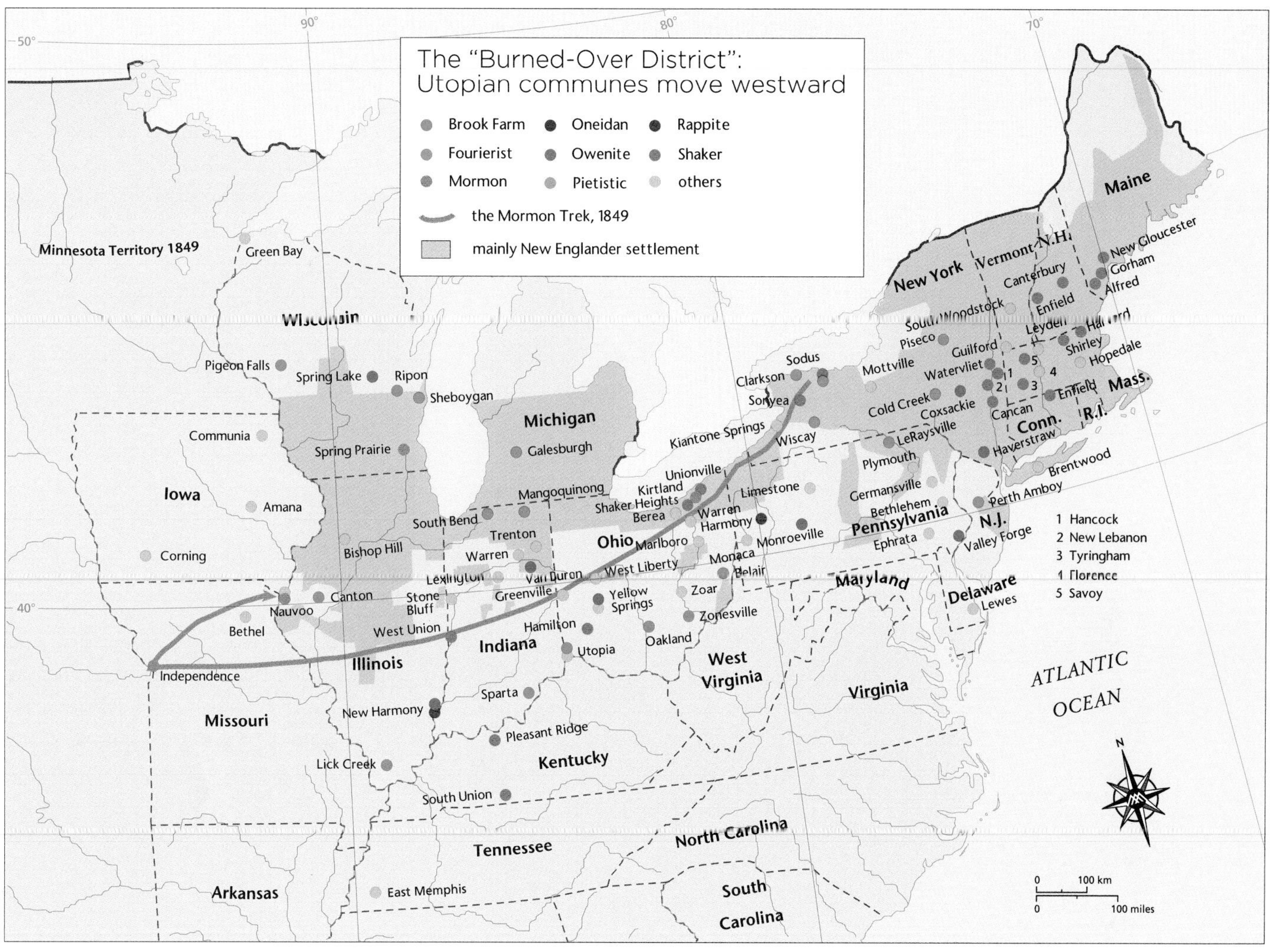

built a new community, Economy, on the Ohio River, but their practice of celibacy and several internal divisions eventually led to the dissolution of the Rappite movement in 1906.

The Oneida community was founded by John Humphreys Noyes of Brattleboro, Vermont, who was a well-known abolitionist. His followers, who became known as "Perfectionists," practiced "complex marriage;" in contrast to Shaker or Rappite celibacy, the Oneidans considered themselves all married to one another, rejecting exclusive marriage and raising the community's many children collectively. They were based at the town of Oneida in New York, where they built an economy based on manufacturing, lumber milling, and flour processing. Property was held communally. Noyes, who himself fathered about a sixth of all the community's children, fled to Canada in 1879 to avoid a statutory rape charge and the community was dissolved in 1881.

The Amana Community of True Inspiration was founded in Hesse, Germany, in 1714 by the pietistic mystics Johann Friedrich Roch and Eberhard Ludwig Gruber. In 1842 the community emigrated to the United States and established the Ebenezer Society near Buffalo, New York. In 1855 a number of members moved westwards to Iowa, where they purchased land, establishing a new home, Amana (the name relates to the Song of Solomon, and means "to remain true"). Property was held communally and members of the community opposed military service. The community survived until the 1930s, when it was reorganized, communal property was dissolved, and it became a joint-stock company, the Amana Society, with the workers as stockholders. Four Amana churches survive in the 21st century. >>

The central and western region of upstate New York appeared to be particularly susceptible to the religious revivals of the early nineteenth century. It was a region characterized by economic and social upheavals; immigrants flooded in to work on the Erie Canal, while New England migrants were searching for new farmland, and formed a transient population. The term "burnt-over" comes from a quote by Charles Finney, the father of American revivalism, indicating that the region had been so heavily evangelized that there was no longer any "fuel" (the unconverted population) left to burn. The region provided thousands of converts to mainline Protestant sects, such as the Methodists and Baptists. But it was also the home to a number of new religions and utopian experiments in the early 19th century. The pioneers that moved through the Hudson Valley combined an extraordinary range of beliefs and superstitions: from Zionism and Apocalypticism to spiritualism.

William Miller rejected his Baptist upbringing in rural Vermont, became a deist, and then a revivalist, scouring the King James Bible for evidence of the Last Days and announcing that the Advent of Christ was due in 1843, then 1844. Tens of thousands of his converts gathered in expectation of the end on the appointed day, but following the "Great Disappointment" most of them returned to the mainline churches.

However, one of Miller's followers, the teenage visionary Ellen G. Harmon, experienced a series of visions explaining that the process of Christ's return had indeed begun. With the help of a preacher named James White, whom she married, she gathered a community committed to purifying themselves in anticipation of the end. Their distinctive insistence on a Saturday sabbath gave them their name: Seventh-day Adventists. In 1855, when the Whites moved to Battle Creek, Michigan, it became the center of Adventist activity. Her views on purity extended to health and nutrition: her rejection of coffee, tea, tobacco, alchohol and some meat was adopted as Adventist practice. She was a prominent temperance activist and abolitionist.

The International Bible Studies Association, later the Jehovah's Witnesses, also grew out of the Adventist movement, and was founded by Charles Taze Russell (1852–1916), who came from a Presbyterian family in Pittsburgh. In 1875 he devoted his life to Bible study groups, and founded a group called the International Bible Students Association. He became an Adventist teacher who rejected the notion of Hell and adopted a non-Trinitarian theology that denied the divinity of Jesus. He taught that a final conflict between God and the devil, Armageddon, was predicted to take place in 1914. Although this did not come to pass many volunteers circulated books and pamphlets and a periodical, *The Watchtower*. His work is carried on worldwide by over 8 million Witnesses. The name "Jehovah's Witnesses" was adopted in 1931.

The most radical of all the new departures was the work of Joseph Smith, who founded Mormonism. Born in rural poverty in Vermont, and raised in upstate New York, Smith was uneducated and spent his childhood treasure-hunting amongst the remains of American Indian earthworks and reading the Bible. Amidst the febrile atmosphere of the burned-over district, ablaze with evangelism, he had a vision of an angel, Moroni, leading him to a secret store of inscribed gold plates that told a hidden story of how God's people had lived in the Americas since the time of Christ. Smith transcribed these revelations into the Book of Mormon (1829) and founded the Church of Jesus Christ of Latter-day Saints, which he saw as the restoration of an authentic – and hitherto lost – Christianity. The Book of Mormon was soon joined by a series of new prophetic revelations from Smith, moving further and further away from conventional Christianity.

Following the precedent of many other utopian communities, Smith moved his Church to the frontier to establish an ideal community. The first stop, in Ohio, was short-lived; wherever Smith and his followers found themselves they became involved in local politics, and were targets of sustained hostility that ultimately led to their displacement westward.

In Missouri they so alienated the locals that a "Mormon War" erupted, leading the state governor to order their "extermination." Moving quickly to found a new settlement – Nauvoo –

in Illinois, Smith once again enraged his non-Mormon neighbors and was killed by a mob (1844). The movement bifurcated: a small splinter group led by Sam Brannan sailed to California to found "New Hope," while the majority followed Smith's lieutenant, Brigham Young, to found Salt Lake City in Utah, which in 1847 was beyond the boundaries of the United States.

Utah was made a US territory in 1850 and in 1852 Brigham Young publicized one of Smith's later revelations, that polygamy should be authorized, earning widespread condemnation. The US authorities saw Utah as a personal theocracy, in rebellion against them, although after a massacre of settlers in 1857 threatened substantial retaliation, the Mormons accepted US rule. Polygamy, however, remained a gravely divisive issue, preventing Utah's admission to the Union as a state until after the Mormons renounced the practice in 1890. Down to the present, some two-thirds of the population of Utah are Mormons.

Southern Africa

In 1648 the Dutch East Indiaman *Haarlem* was stranded on the northeast shore of Table Bay, and the colony of the Cape of Good Hope was subsequently founded there. The Dutch did very little about mission in this region, quickly deciding that the local Khoisan people were depraved, bestial, and resistant to civilization. By the 18th century the Khoisan had become impoverished at the hands of the colonists, and eventually their numbers were decimated by a smallpox epidemic in 1713. The only serious missionary project in the 18th-century Cape was undertaken by Georg Schmidt, a Moravian missionary who founded a small community of converts in 1737 but was expelled by the Dutch authorities shortly thereafter: the community survived in isolation until Moravian missionaries were able to return in the 1790s.

By the early 19th century, when the Cape Colony came under British rule, South Africa was a major hub for maritime trade between Asia and Europe, and in the wake of traders came successive waves of Christian missionaries, originating in the Netherlands, the British Isles, France, and the United States. Many missionaries were intrepid explorers, traveling far into the interior. They translated the Bible and hymn books into local languages, and the coastal regions of South Africa were increasingly seen as a "gateway," through which the Christian religion would penetrate the unconverted interior of sub-Saharan Africa. Missionaries were amongst the earliest explorers of southern Africa; indeed the famous explorer David Livingstone was sent by the London Missionary Society in 1840. He converted the chief of the Bakwena tribe, Sechele, who was baptized in 1848, but lost contact with his convert. When British missionaries arrived to work with the Zulu Ndebele tribe in what is now Zimbabwe in 1859 they were

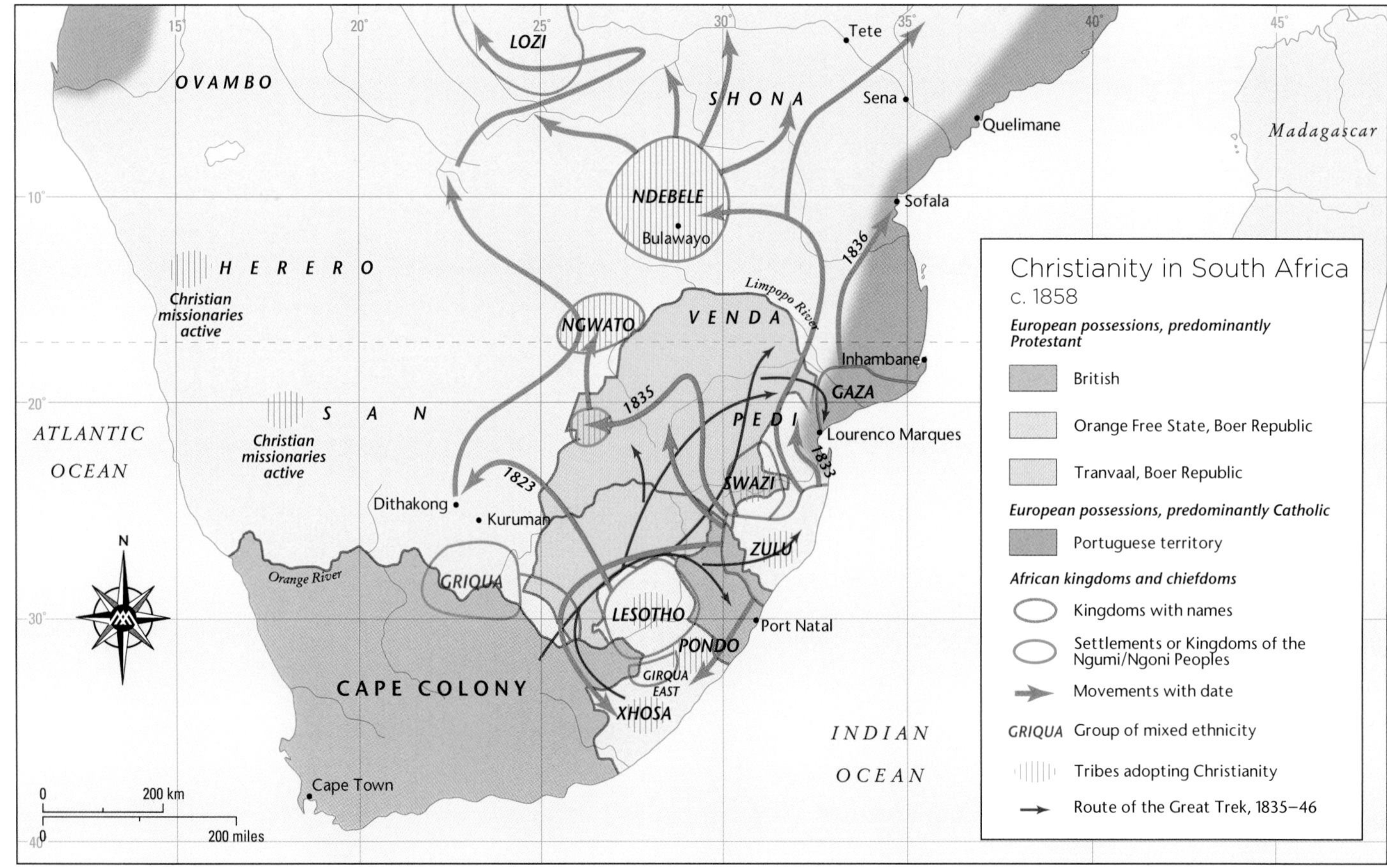

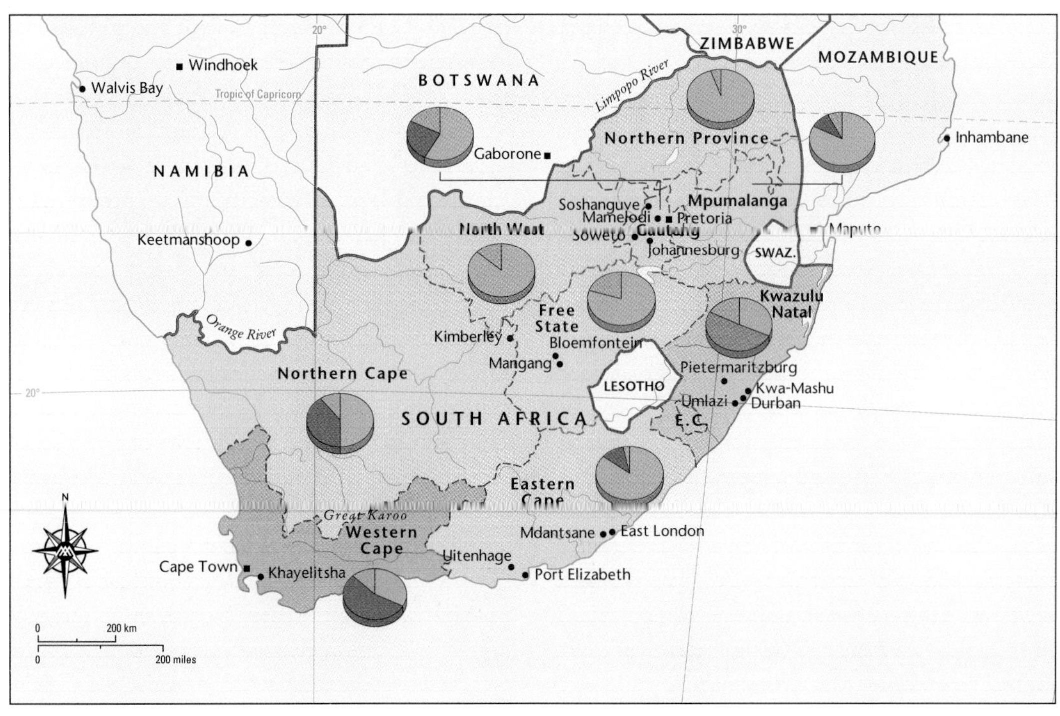

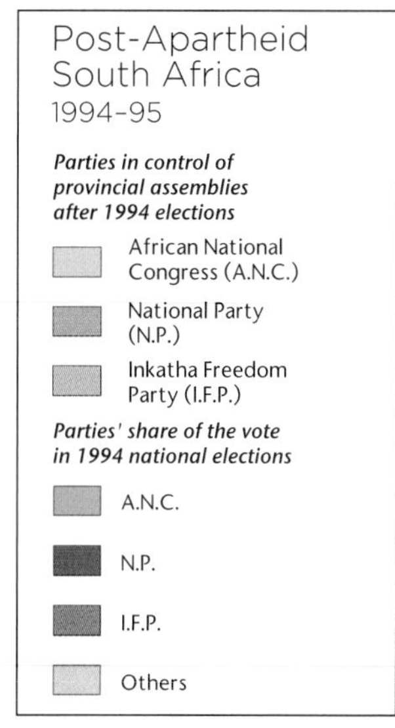

staggered to find that they already had regular Christian prayers. Sechele had turned missionary, traveling hundreds of miles to convert neighoring tribes.

Many African societies retained traditions of polygamy, and were resistant to Christian strictures on dress and traditional dances, and worship that incorporated African traditions. Many missionaries were quick to condemn customs and practices that they did not fully understand. In fact, practical and economic help, providing viable agricultural land for indigenous settlement, frequently did more than sermonizing. Many converts stayed on mission stations for safety and economic reasons rather than because of religious beliefs. The missionaries' assault on "immoral" habits such as polygamy, witchcraft, initiation rituals, and heavy drinking, made little headway and in 1884 the United Missionary Conference reported that, despite their efforts, these customs were still prevalent throughout southern Africa.

Africans wanted to worship in their own style, without missionaries acting as intermediaries. In 1881 the Dutch Reformed Church established a separate "colored" church. Independent African churches – for example, the Tembu National Church (1892), the Zion Christian Church (1910), and the Nazareth Baptist Church (1910) – developed in a society that was becoming increasingly segregated.

The white-controlled government established with the Union of South Africa in 1910 solidified, with the election victory of the Afrikaner National Party in 1948, into a policy of "apartheid," or strict separation. The Afrikaner Dutch Reformed Church taught that national and racial differences were God-given and must be preserved; in practice, this "separation" meant the systematic dispossession, subordination and oppression of the non-white majority. Other churches, both white- and black-led, opposed apartheid from the 1960s onwards, and were decisive both in eventually bringing the apartheid regime down and in persuading the Dutch Reformed Church to abandon its racial theologies. By the time of the first free elections in 1994, a quiet revolution had taken place: over 80 percent of South Africans were now members of one or other of the Christian churches.

China and the Missionaries to 1945

China's Qing dynasty (1633–1911) was weak and precarious. The arrival of missionaries in the 19th century, and colonial attempts to exploit Asia's vast wealth, took advantage of that weakness to overcome China's longstanding resistance to foreign missionaries. This had the effect of associating Christianity with colonial exploitation for over a century.

Roman Catholics had already reached China in the 17th century, but the 19th century was the beginning of the Protestant missionary effort, and it came in the wake of Britain's imperial exploitation of China, which involved trade in Indian opium to gain a commercial toehold in Asia. In the First Opium War (1839-42), Britain compelled China both to open its ports to the opium trade and to allow missions to enter. A series of Anglo-French military interventions during the rest of the century secured ever greater legal privileges for missionaries, although rates of conversion were initially low.

The Taiping rebellion broke out in 1850. Its instigator and leader, Hong Xiuquan, blended his own visions with Christian teachings to produce an apocalyptic movement, which proclaimed that he was Christ's younger brother and had been commissioned by God to slaughter demons – chief amongst them the Qing emperor. This quasi-Christian movement took the ancient capital of Nanjing and a swathe of central China. It was not defeated until 1864, in a war that cost as many as 20 million lives. The war further weakened the Qing regime, convincing many Chinese that Christianity was dangerous, but also exposed large parts of China to a form of Christianity for the first time.

Missionaries found the Chinese language extremely hard to master, and perhaps externalized their failure in a generalized and widespread contempt for traditional Chinese beliefs. There were some successes. At the treaty port of Amoy (Xiamen), the American missionary John Talmage built the first Protestant church in China. Soon his congregation was electing Chinese elders, following the Presbyterian model. Christian missionaries built a network of churches, schools, seminaries, hospitals, and publishing houses, while Chinese evangelicals began to attract large followings.

After the end of the Qing dynasty and the creation of the Chinese republic in 1912, Christianity could spread more freely: many churches

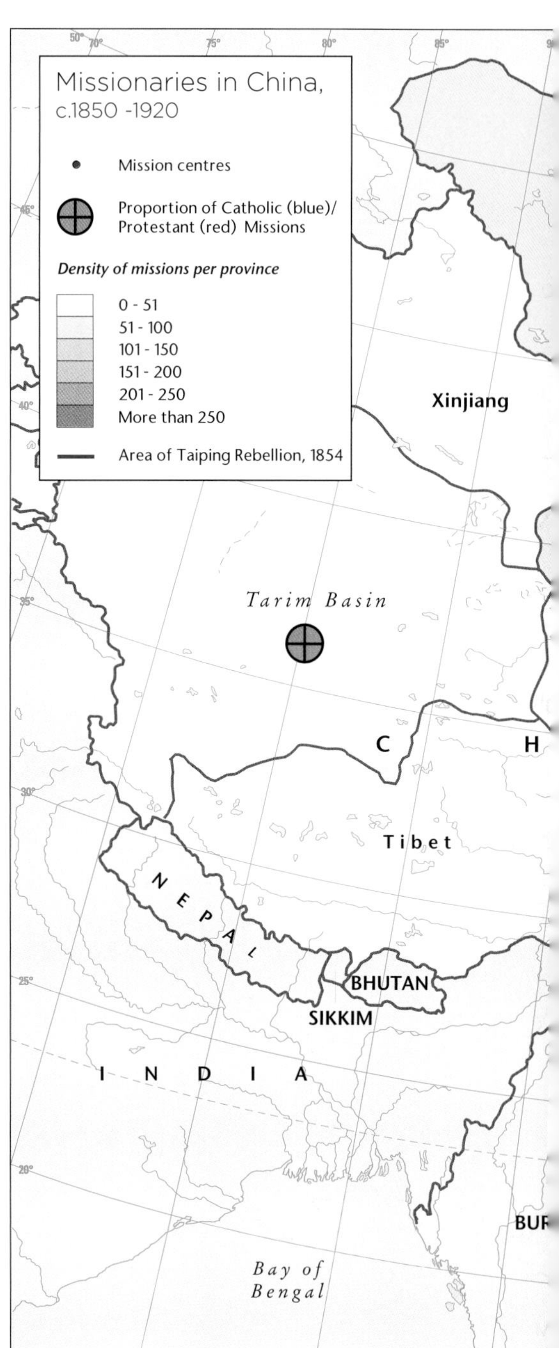

were built in some cities, and Chinese-led groups such as the Jesus Family and the Little Flock sprang up. However, most Christian churches remained dependent on missionary support. With the Nationalist governments of the 1930s keen to use Christianity as a political tool, the rising Communist insurgency either being actively hostile or wanting to fold Christianity into a Communist-led "united front," and – from 1937 – Japanese invaders regarding missionaries as enemy agents, China's still-growing Christian minority was under pressure from all sides.

India and the Missionaries to 1947

Portuguese traders brought Catholic missionaries to Goa from the 16th century onward and there were Danish/German/British missions to Tranquebar from 1706. After US independence India was the centerpiece of Britain's colonial empire and by the early 19th century the London Missionary Society had focused its attention on South Asia. Some leading Protestants, however, argued that attempts to evangelize a region that already had long-established and deep-rooted religious beliefs was doomed to failure. India was to prove an intractable challenge to the missionary endeavor.

The British East India Company, which governed India until 1858, had always been extremely wary of the risks of disturbing Muslim and Hindu sensibilities. The Company went out of its way to accept indigenous beliefs, except when they appeared completely transgressive, for example the practice of *suttee* (widow-burning). However, increasing pressure from evangelicals in Britain, and from evangelicals working for the Company, led to a shift in policy. In 1813 Parliament opened India to missionary activity. A range of missionaries fanned out over India, including the London Missionary Society (Protestant), the Baptists, German Lutherans, and the Church Missionary Society (Anglican.)

The 1813 Act also provided India with an established church, which formed part of the Church of England, and was largely financed by Indian taxation. An Anglican bishopric was set up in Calcutta and an English-style cathedral was built there. In 1835 the fifth Bishop of Calcutta, Daniel Wilson, issued a circular letter to all the Anglican missionaries in India, calling for the immediate abandonment of caste and caste distinctions in Anglican churches. The campaigns against caste and for women's rights would become major themes of 19th-century Protestant missions, fostering wider egalitarian principles. As the 19th century progressed the structures of the Church – bishoprics, churches, schools, colleges, missionaries, clergy – steadily grew but they primarily administered to British colonial administrators, merchants, the Indian Army, and Anglo-Indians. There was only limited success in gaining Christian converts.

The Company saw education as a way of creating a westernized ruling class amongst the Indian elite, and the Protestant missions were prepared to finance this policy. Alexander Duff, who arrived in Calcutta in 1830, was a pioneer of English language education, and schools and colleges spread throughout the subcontinent; English became colonial India's lingua franca. The German Leipzig society, on the other hand, which took over the former congregations of the Danish-Halle mission with its headquarters in Tranquebar, aimed to school its Tamil congregations in the Lutheran catechism, while retaining Tamil cultural identities. Consequently, the language used in the Lutheran schools was Tamil, not English.

In 1857 the Great Indian Rebellion (Indian Mutiny) sent shockwaves throughout the Empire. It was the most serious uprising against any western colonial power in the 19th century and one of its main trigger points was the increasing policy of Christianization in India, which united Hindus and Muslims in protest – the use of pig or cow fat to grease the bullets used by the Indian army offended both religions. Britain's colonial status looked vulnerable, dependent on the neutrality of some Muslim and Hindu leaders, and the active promotion of Christianity no longer seemed to be a sensible way of proceeding. In 1858 the East India Company's rule was terminated and India was brought formally under British sovereignty. Queen Victoria's proclamation of that year stated that the new government must "abstain from any interference with the religious belief or worship of any of our subjects."

Left without official support, the missionaries that remained in India were forced to concede that their enterprise was fraught with difficulty. Christianity's proclamation that it was the only true religion ran counter to many Indians' unwillingness to adapt their own beliefs and tendency to assimilate other belief systems; it became seen, therefore, as a manifestation of colonialism. The caste system ran directly counter to Protestant convictions that all men were equal in the eyes of God and that social barriers must therefore be eradicated. It is scarcely surprising that the most conversions to Christianity took place amongst tribal groups, who were predominantly animists, and the "untouchable" Dalits, who were outside the Hindu social structure. British-run schools proved popular and successful, but they did not act as centers for Christian conversion. Hindus increasingly showed their pride in their heritage and were self-confident enough to reap the benefits of British education without submitting to its belief systems. The Christian population of South Asia, concentrated in certain castes and regions, has remained constant since the 19th century, at about 2–3 percent of the population.

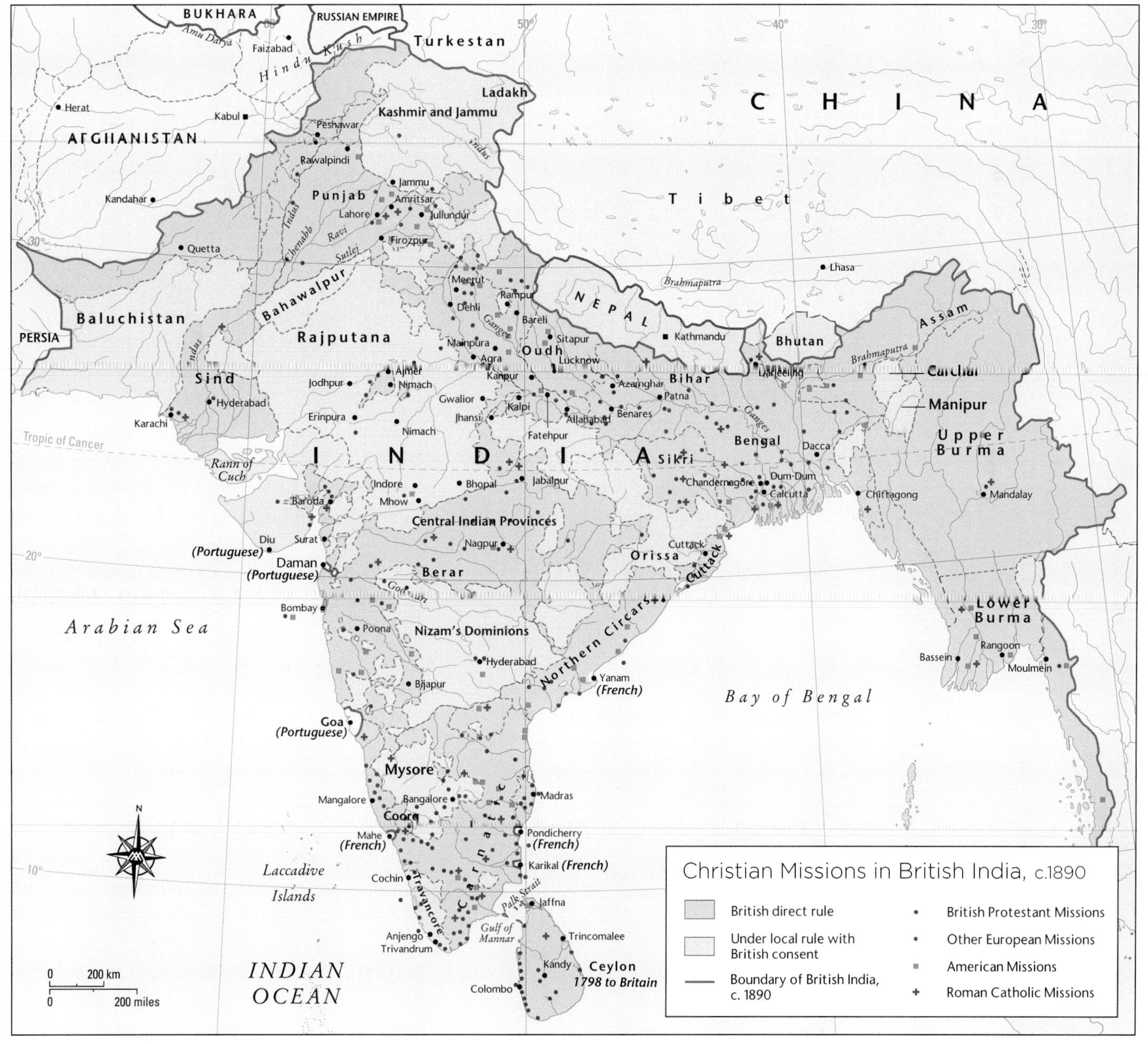

Christianity in Modern Africa

Towards the end of the 1880s the devastating trade in slaves had finally come to an end. However, the European powers still looked to exploit Africa's raw materials, and these ambitions came to a head at the Berlin Conference of 1884–5, which divided most of the African continent between the various colonial powers. The colonial regimes followed on the heels of early Christian missionary penetration of the continent's interior, and brought with them new waves of missionaries, setting in motion an ever-increasing Christianization of the population. The majority of new Christians were converts from their local religions, though there were some Islamic converts, especially in West Africa and in French-controlled North Africa.

The spread of the Christian faith in Africa represents perhaps the most dramatic advance in all of Christian history, yet the names and stories of the individuals responsible are largely unknown. In most cases the primary agents of conversion were not missionaries but African evangelists such as Bernard Mizeki from Mozambique, killed in Rhodesia in 1896. Often Christianity was attractive to African political leaders, both as a means of accessing and negotiating the power and knowledge structures of their new colonial reality, and also as a source of spiritual power when existing African traditions were seen to have failed. African leaders who found space for themselves in the new world, such as the kings of the Sotho and of the Baganda, who secured British protectorates, often did so by presenting themselves as Christian rulers.

The struggle against what might be described as cultural imperialism was, to some degree, ameliorated by such Christian champions as Thomas Fowel Buxton and Henry Venn who both encouraged local African commercial and agricultural initiatives and established the principle of the "indigenous church," whereby the nascent African church became more confident in its own interpretations and expressions of Christianity. An example of the growing confidence of the local African church community was the Yoruba linguist Samuel Ajayi Crowther, who was the first African to be appointed bishop by the Anglican Church in Nigeria in 1864. Many Africans searched for aspects of the new religion that might resemble their own religious practices and beliefs and adapted Christianity to fit existing social norms, such as the Kimbanquist Church, founded by Simon Kimbanqu, who questioned the order of religious deliverance: "Would God send a white man to preach?"

The nationalist movements that led most of colonial Africa to independence in the years 1958–66 were typically secular, and newly independent nations often nationalized missionary institutions. Yet the growth of Christianity accelerated in the postcolonial period. In some cases, it fed into the continent's conflicts. In the Rwandan genocide of 1994, longstanding ethnic differences were reinforced by Christian missionaries who perpetuated ethnic divisions. In Sudan a civil war was waged by the militant Islamist government of the Muslim north on the south (1983–2005), which is mainly Christian, a legacy of missionaries associated with British colonialism.

Islamic State and other jihadist groups have shifted their operations to sub-Saharan Africa, where radical Islam collides with weak government, corruption, poverty, organized crime, and instability. Christians are scapegoated and Christian aid workers have been held hostage in Mali, Burkina Faso, and other countries. In the middle of Nigeria, Christian families have been murdered in their homes, giving rise to accusations of ethno-religious cleansing

In 1900 there were around 9 million Christians in Africa; by 2000 the number had reached an estimated 380 million of which 147 million were "Renewalists," such as Pentecostals and Charismatics. As the gospel spread through the remoter villages and hamlets of the now independent African states, local Christianity began to define itself in its own cultural terms, producing both reform and the birth of thousands of "African Initiated Churches." These fast-growing new denominations now comprise a third or more of the continent's entire population.

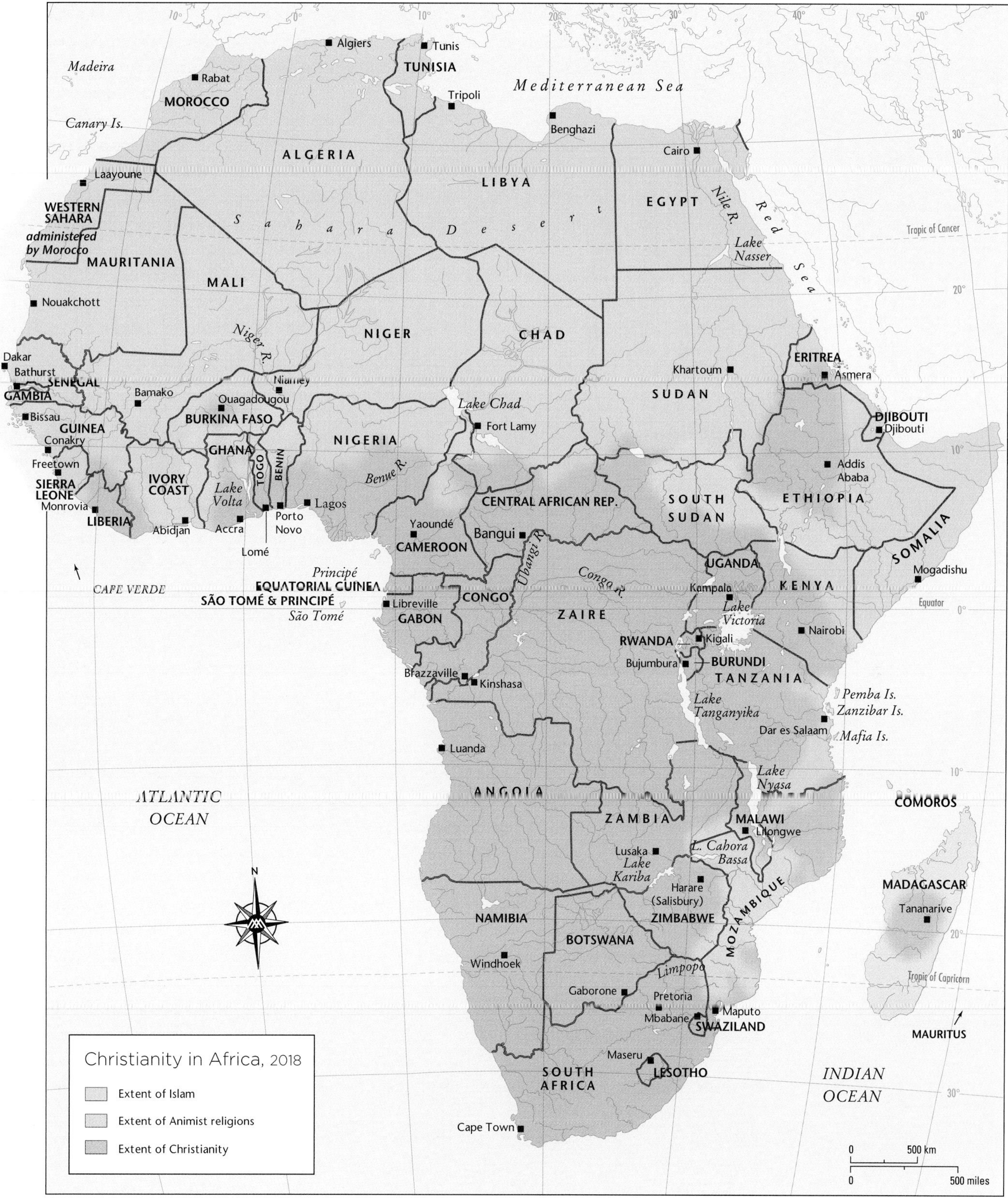

Christianity in Africa, 2018
Extent of Islam
Extent of Animist religions
Extent of Christianity
Mediterranean Sea
ATLANTIC OCEAN
INDIAN OCEAN
Sahara Desert
MOROCCO
ALGERIA
TUNISIA
LIBYA
EGYPT
WESTERN SAHARA administered by Morocco
MAURITANIA
MALI
NIGER
CHAD
SUDAN
SOUTH SUDAN
ERITREA
DJIBOUTI
ETHIOPIA
SOMALIA
SENEGAL
GAMBIA
GUINEA
SIERRA LEONE
LIBERIA
IVORY COAST
GHANA
TOGO
BENIN
BURKINA FASO
NIGERIA
CAMEROON
CENTRAL AFRICAN REP.
EQUATORIAL GUINEA
SÃO TOMÉ & PRINCIPÉ
GABON
CONGO
ZAIRE
UGANDA
KENYA
RWANDA
BURUNDI
TANZANIA
ANGOLA
ZAMBIA
MALAWI
MOZAMBIQUE
ZIMBABWE
NAMIBIA
BOTSWANA
SOUTH AFRICA
SWAZILAND
LESOTHO
MADAGASCAR
COMOROS
MAURITUS
CAPE VERDE
Madeira
Canary Is.
Algiers
Tunis
Rabat
Tripoli
Benghazi
Cairo
Laayoune
Nouakchott
Dakar
Bathurst
Bissau
Conakry
Freetown
Monrovia
Bamako
Niamey
Ouagadougou
Abidjan
Accra
Lomé
Porto Novo
Lagos
Fort Lamy
Khartoum
Asmera
Djibouti
Addis Ababa
Mogadishu
Yaoundé
Bangui
Libreville
Principé
São Tomé
Brazzaville
Kinshasa
Kampala
Nairobi
Kigali
Bujumbura
Dar es Salaam
Luanda
Lusaka
Lilongwe
Harare (Salisbury)
Windhoek
Gaborone
Pretoria
Mbabane
Maputo
Maseru
Cape Town
Tananarive
Nile R.
Niger R.
Benue R.
Congo R.
Ubangi R.
Limpopo
Red Sea
Lake Nasser
Lake Chad
Lake Volta
Lake Victoria
Lake Tanganyika
Lake Nyasa
L. Cahora Bassa
Lake Kariba
Pemba Is.
Zanzibar Is.
Mafia Is.
Tropic of Cancer
Tropic of Capricorn
Equator
N
0 500 km
0 500 miles

Pentecostalism: A Global Faith

In April 1906 a revival movement began amongst a near-destitute congregation meeting in a derelict building in Azusa Street, Los Angeles, led by an African-American preacher named William J. Seymour. This revival, traditionally seen as the starting gun for global Pentecostalism, was in fact the point where longstanding interests in holiness, "baptism of the Spirit" and spiritual gifts in certain strains of Methodism and evangelicalism, especially in England and the United States, came together. Similar revivals were taking place around the world at the same time: in Australia (1901), Estonia (1902), Wales (1904–5), India (1905–06), Korea (1906–07), Chile (1909) and elsewhere. Yet it was the fire at Azusa Street that caught and spread. Receiving the gift of "tongues" – glossolalia, or ecstatic speech – Seymour's congregation not only found the experience emotionally transformative, but also believed that they had miraculously been empowered to speak languages from across the globe. Although they generally discovered that their "languages" were not in fact comprehensible to anyone, this could not shake their experience of God transforming them from within.

The unstructured worship at the makeshift church in Azusa Street lasted for hours on end, drawing together a scandalously interracial congregation which soon numbered in the thousands. Miracles were reported; lives were upended; church establishments were horrified by the "tongue-talkers" who now insisted that only those who shared their gift had truly been baptized by the Holy Spirit. Rejoicing in the hostility they faced, these untutored missionaries fanned out across the world. Many believed that their revival was the sign of the imminent end of times, a call to bring salvation to the world before Christ's Second Coming.

Early visitors to Azusa Street took the Pentecostal message back to their home countries: the Norwegian Methodist pastor T.B. Barratt, who met Seymour in person, is credited with bringing the Pentecostal movement to Scandinavia, Germany, France, and England. The Anglican vicar of All Saints in Sunderland, Alexander Boddy, was converted by Barratt, and founded British Pentecostalism. The Italian immigrant to the US Luigi Francesco first experienced Pentecostalism in 1907 and was responsible for establishing Italian Pentecostal congregations in the US, Argentina, and Italy. In 1910 two Swedish Pentecostal missionaries brought their beliefs to Brazil, while in 1908 John G. Lake traveled to South Africa, where he founded the Apostolic Faith Mission of South Africa and the Zion Christian Church.

Nearly all Pentecostal denominations trace their origins to Azusa Street, but there is no central authority governing Pentecostalism or a clear definition of the movement. Even tongue-speaking, seen in the Azusa Street tradition as essential, was neglected by Pentecostals in Korea, southern Africa, and other parts of the world. The movement is defined, instead, by its emotional intensity, and often its apocalyptic expectancy. In 1914 several small Pentecostal groups in Hot Springs, Arkansas, formed the intensely mission-conscious Assemblies of God, which combined foreign missions with domestic outreach amongst urban populations, on Indian reservations, and in prisons. They developed Spanish-language branches, and autonomous denominations appeared in Mexico and Puerto Rico. It is believed that they are the largest Pentecostal denomination worldwide, with more than 25 million members and missions in over 150 countries.

During the 1960s, a "charismatic renewal" brought phenomena like Pentecostalism to many of the old mainline Protestant churches. From 1967, the Roman Catholic hierarchy warily accepted a charismatic movement within the church, which has made particular progress in Latin America. Many independent and non-denominational churches springing up in Africa, East Asia, and elsewhere in the 1980s adopted certain renewalist characteristics. By the early 21st century over a quarter of all Christians worldwide belonged to some part of this tradition, especially in Africa and Latin America.

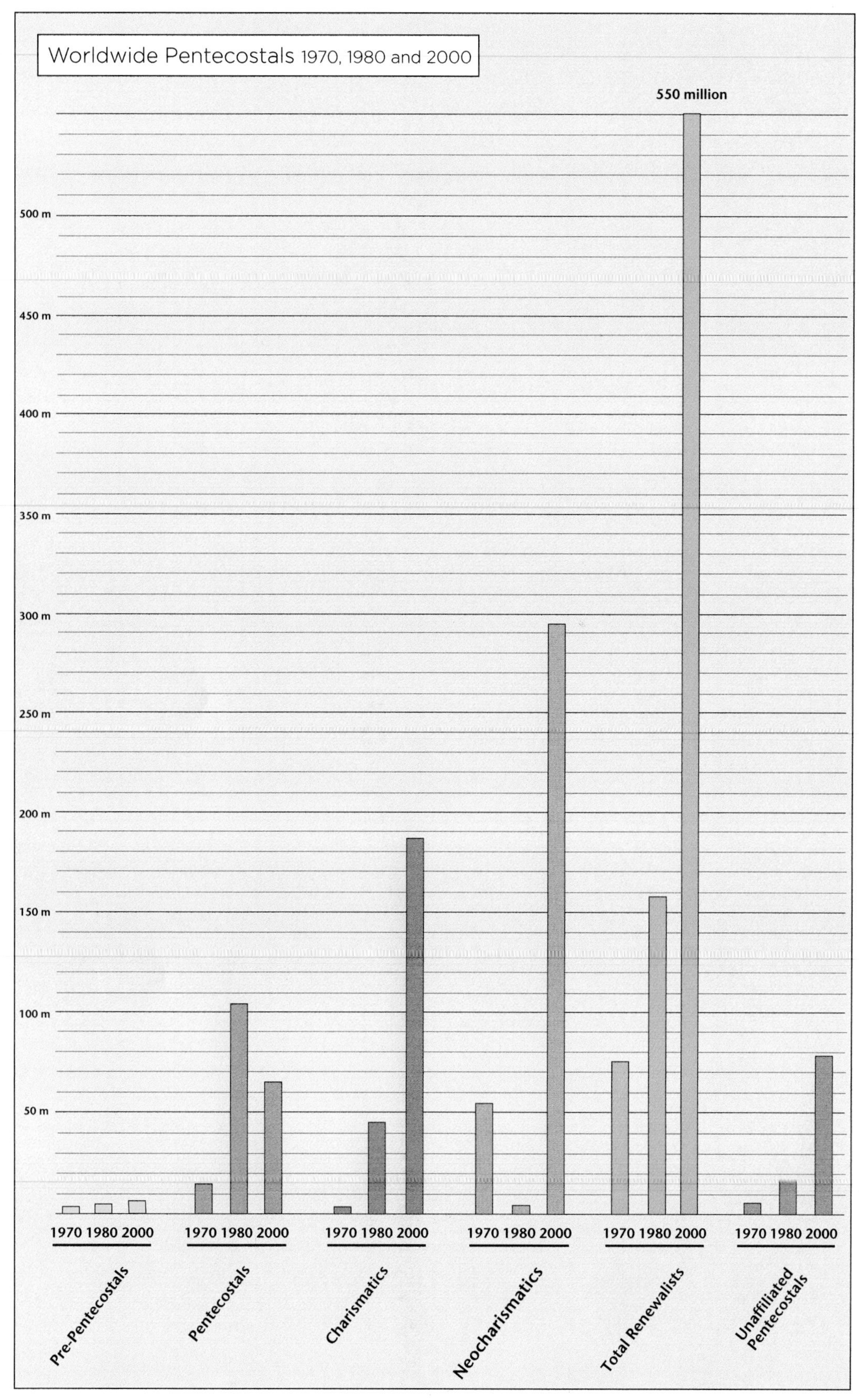
Worldwide Pentecostals 1970, 1980 and 2000
550 million
500 m
450 m
400 m
350 m
300 m
250 m
200 m
150 m
100 m
50 m
1970 1980 2000
1970 1980 2000
1970 1980 2000
1970 1980 2000
1970 1980 2000
1970 1980 2000
Pre-Pentecostals
Pentecostals
Charismatics
Neocharismatics
Total Renewalists
Unaffiliated Pentecostals

Evangelicalism & Fundamentalism in America

EVANGELICALISM EMERGED during the revivals of the Methodist movement in England between 1730 and 1840, and the contemporaneous Great Awakenings in the United States. The many streams of evangelicalism had some persistent features in common: an emphasis on individual conversion and faith in the literal inspiration of the Bible, and a scepticism towards institutional churches and political power.

The English cleric and evangelist George Whitefield was one of the founders of the evengelical movement who promoted revivalism on both sides of the Atlantic. Charles G. Finney, a Presbyterian and leader in the Second Great Awakening, has been called the Father of Modern Revivalism, who bought a commitment to Bible distribution, education, moral reform, and global mission to the evangelical movement.

In the mid-19th century a new strain appeared within Anglophone evangelicalism: Dispensationalism, which stemmed from the Anglo-Irish Bible teacher John Nelson Darby's divisions of all of time into seven different stages, known as "Dispensations." Darby argued that the world had almost reached the last dispensation, the Great Tribulation, in which a final battle would be fought out at Armageddon, followed by Christ's return and the final

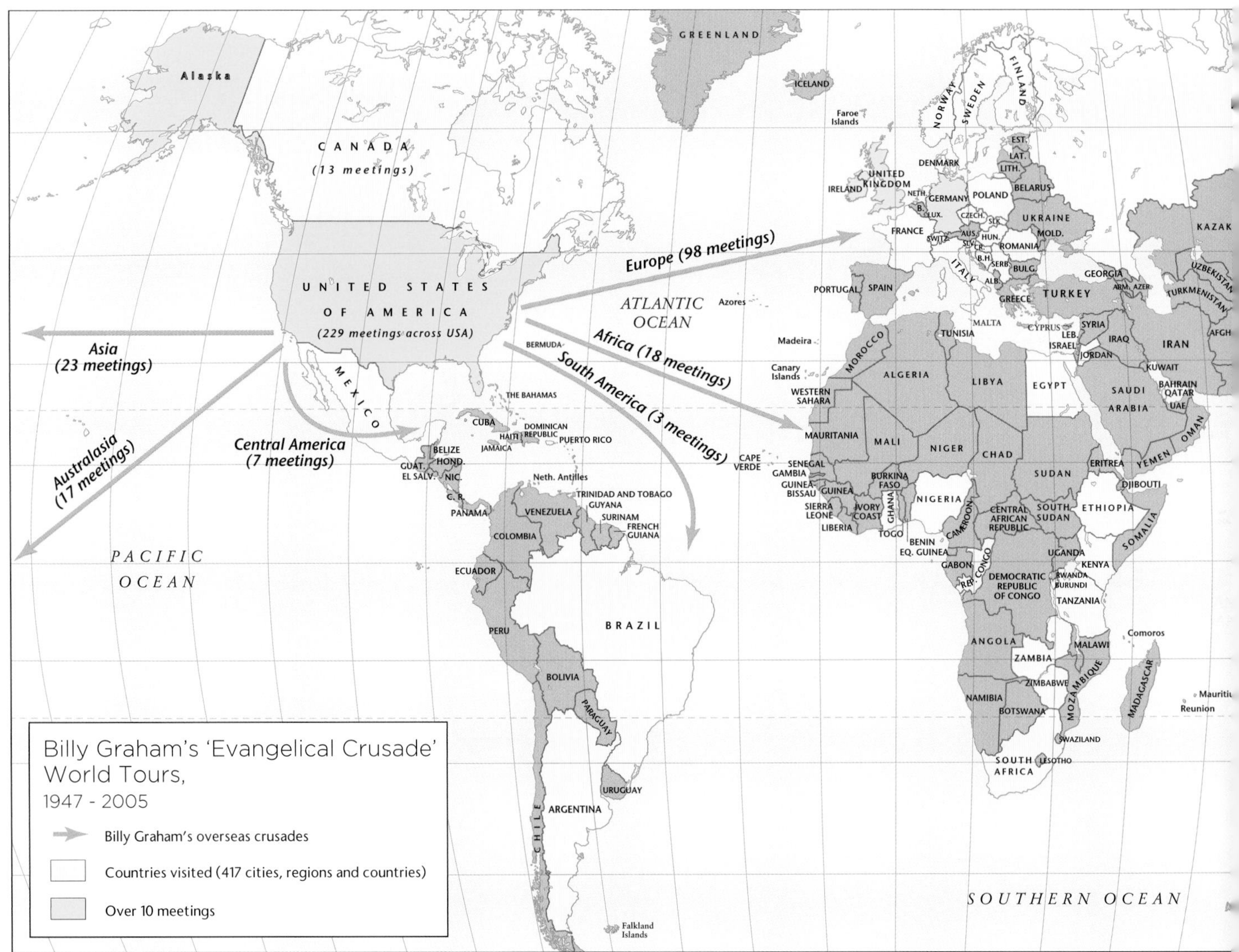

judgment. This belief system was set against a perceived background of increasing liberalism, secularism and immorality. To this may be added the theory of biblical inerrancy, refined to its modern form in the 1840s, which claims that the Bible is written without error or fault in all of its teachings and that the scripture, in the original manuscript, does not affirm anything that is contrary to fact. For growing numbers of evangelicals Dispensationalism and inerrancy were seen as indispensable bulwarks against the advance of liberal, sceptical and sometimes openly atheist principles in science, theology and biblical criticism. *The Fundamentals* were evangelical manifestoes, published in the US from 1910–15, whose advocates and defenders proudly styled themselves "fundamentalists."

In May 1919 the first World Conference on Christian Fundamentalism took place in Philadelphia. The northern Baptist churches based in Minneapolis spearheaded the campaign against modernism. The network of fundamentalist-affiliated churches in many denominations grew steadily, especially the Independent Churches of America, the IFCA, which became the leading association of fundamentalist churches across the United States. A particular focus for fundamentalist concern was Darwinian evolution: not only did it apparently contradict the Biblical creation narratives, it suggested a blurring of the line between human and animal and was felt to undermine notions both of white superiority and of shared humanity. Laws against the teaching of evolution were passed in many states, culminating in the "Monkey Trial" in Tennessee in 1925, when a schoolteacher named John T. Scopes was prosecuted for teaching evolution. The trial was a fiasco and was the beginning of a series of public reverses for fundamentalism, culminating in the repeal in 1933 of the fundamentalists' signature legal achievement, the prohibition of alcohol.

However, the cultural crisis of the 1960s, during which many of the "mainline" Protestant churches embraced left-wing political causes and lost millions of members as a result, saw a resurgence of evangelicalism and fundamentalism. In 1976 the United States elected its first avowedly evangelical president, the Democrat Jimmy Carter, but evangelicalism would soon find its home on the political right, animated in part by opposition to abortion. The Moral Majority was a pressure group, founded in 1979 by the Baptist minister Jerry Falwell, which mobilized conservative Christians as a political force. By the time of the presidencies of George W. Bush and Donald Trump, white evangelicals were overwhelmingly identified with the Republican Party. Non-white evangelicals, however, were strongly aligned with the political left.

Some conservative evangelicals, especially Baptists and Presbyterians, repudiated the separatist fundamentalist movement, electing to be called Neo-Evangelicals, shortened to Evangelicals. In 1942 Evangelical leaders formed the National Association of Evangelicals. They prospered and attracted persuasive spokesmen, the most famous being the Baptist evangelist Billy Graham, whose oratorical skills and commitment to his preaching mission attracted worldwide interest

Worldwide Evangelicalism

Evangelicalism is a fluid and diverse phenomenon that is hard to define. In a much-cited definition from 1989 historian David Bebbington identified four signature characteristics: an experience of personal conversion; a commitment to active missionary evangelism or preaching of the gospel; belief in the Bible as the word of God; and "crucicentrism," a belief in the saving power of Christ's sacrificial death on the cross. Within this broad frame, evangelicalism is highly diverse, embracing Pentecostalism, Fundamentalism, liberal evangelicalism and all points between. It has never valued institutional, doctrinal or liturgical uniformity. It is therefore difficult to quantify the number of evangelicals worldwide but there are believed to be over 550 million, concentrated in the Americas, Africa and Asia.

The global spread of evangelicalism can be traced to the missionary movements of the 19th century, when European and American evangelicals – inspired by the teachings of global mission – traveled to Africa and Asia to spread the word. In 1951 evangelicals formed the World Evangelical Fellowship (WEF), and more than 110 regional and national organizations are now affiliated with WEF, which is headquartered in Singapore.

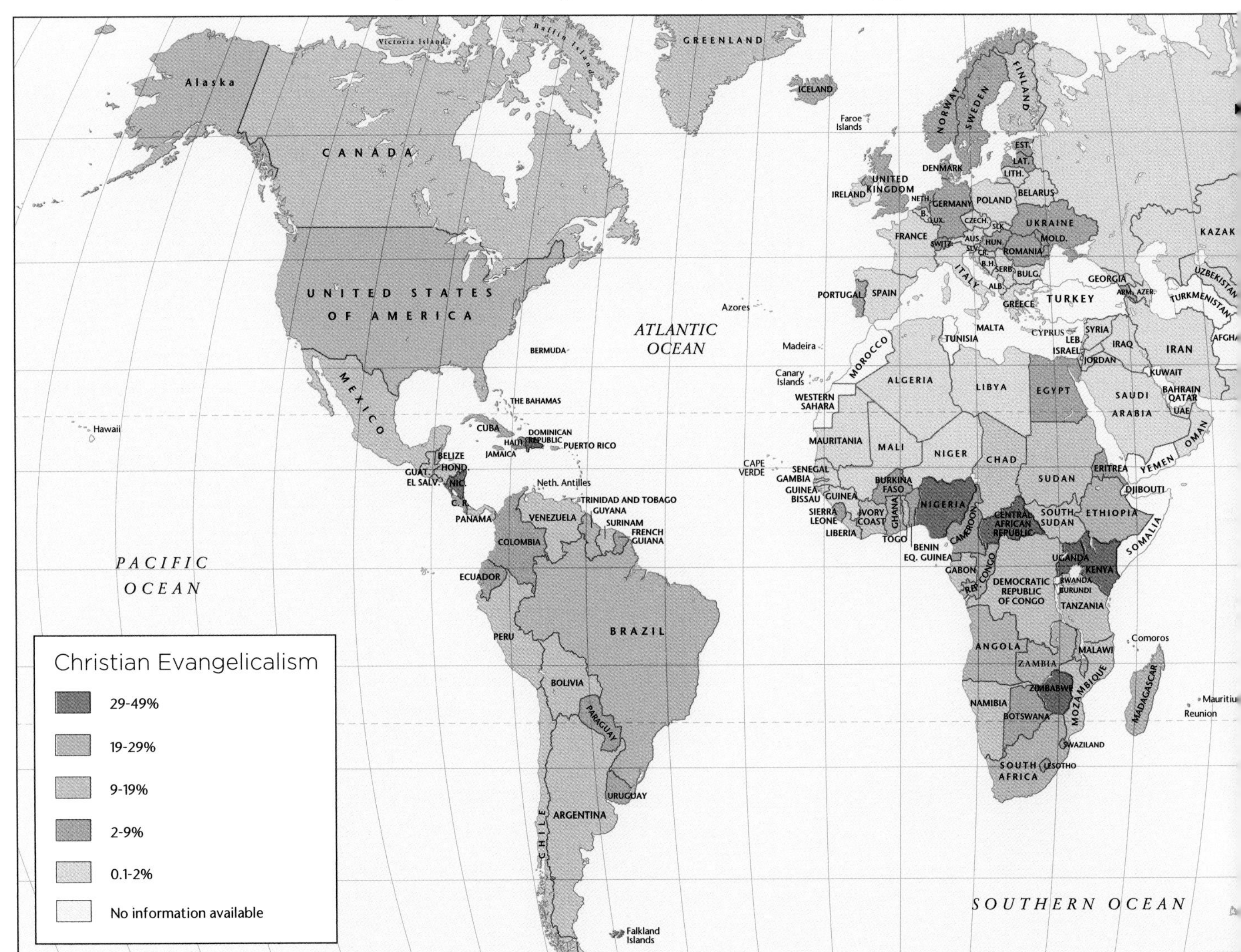

In 1974 the American Baptist preacher Billy Graham spearheaded a campaign to turn evangelicalism from a missionary-led to a genuinely globally owned movement. In that year evangelical leaders gathered together in Lausanne, Switzerland. Nearly 2,500 Protestant evangelical leaders from over 150 countries and 135 denominations came together to agree on their strategies to spread their message. Many representatives of the global South were present, bringing with them their own stories of poverty, inequality, and injustice. Many of them offered a severe critique of American missionary assumptions, arguing that evangelicals should reject the American way of life and embrace a gospel for the poor, in which social action and evangelism are seen as equally important in the Christian mission. Such arguments had long been put forward by liberal Protestants, but these were voices which Graham and many of his allies found newly compelling. From the 1970 onwards evangelicals forged a kind of evangelical humanitarianism, which came to terms with the loss of direct missionary influence in the postcolonial world, and instead pursued a new kind of internationalism.

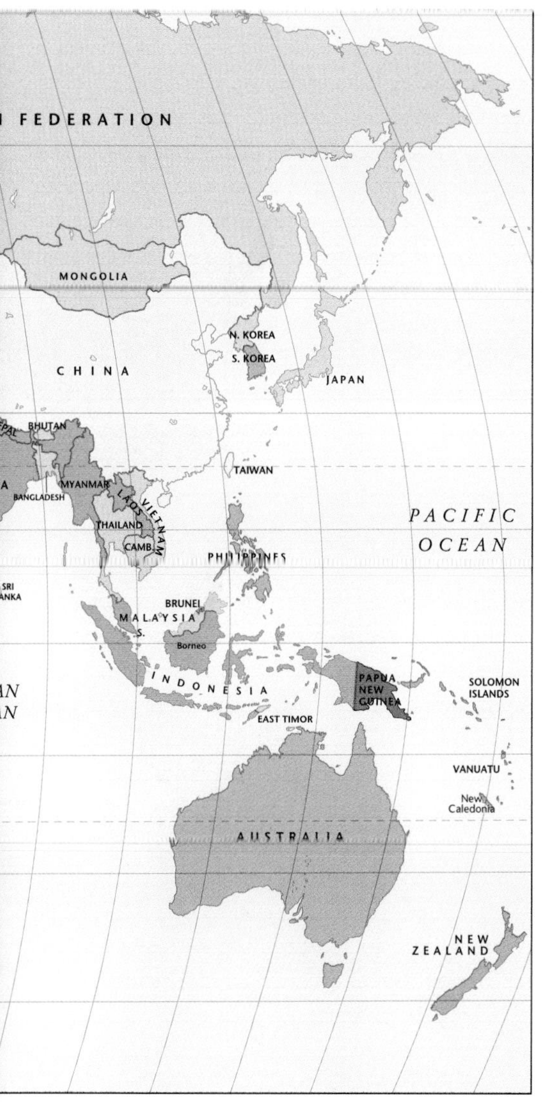

Evangelicals established the Far East Broadcasting Company (1945) and Trans World Radio (1952), which became the most significant private broadcasters in the world. By 1970, evangelicals had set up a global gospel radio network that included 45 proprietary stations and 80 transmitters, producing over 600 hours of programming per day. By 1960 the first Christian television network, the Christian Broadcasting Network, was chartered in the USA. The era of of "televangelism" had begun.

In much of the developing world evangelicalism has been associated with Western modernity. Preachers in Asian megachurches and in the evangelical churches of Latin America often embody the 19th-century German sociologist Max Weber's belief in the "Protestant work ethic," which urges people to work hard, live frugally, and abjure alcohol and drugs. Families benefit and women are empowered by the message that everyone is equal in the eyes of God. The emphasis on the Bible boosts literacy programs. In some cases, this has led to a "prosperity gospel" in which believers are taught to see and to expect worldly wealth as a sign of God's blessing, a belief which has often been accompanied by embezzlement and corruption by church leaders.

Billy Graham recognized that the future of his religion did not lie with only white Americans and embraced "the black world, the white world, the yellow world, the rich world, the poor world." The future of the evangelical movement continues to lie in the global South, shifting the world's religious axis.

Christianity in Communist Europe

In line with the Marxist principle that religion is "the opium of the people," a form of false consciousness used to perpetuate the oppression of the working class, Soviet Russia regarded Christianity with hostility and advocated the ultimate elimination of religion, destroying churches and synagogues and harassing and incarcerating, and even executing, religious leaders. However, Soviet law never officially outlawed the holding of religious views. The tactic was to confiscate church property, harass believers, and in some cases persecute them by sending them to labor camps, prisons, and mental hospitals, in the hope that this doomed phenomenon would die its inevitable death.

Many members of the clergy had cooperated with the White armies during the Russian civil war of 1918–22, although there was no nationally organized anti-Soviet stance. It has been estimated that during the first five years after the Bolshevik revolution 28 bishops and 6,775 priests were executed. However, in July 1927 Metropolitan Sergius issued his *Declaration*, which secured the survival of the church by expressing his "loyalty" to the Soviet government; many Russian churches in America and Europe severed their relations with Moscow.

Further persecutions ensued in the 1930s and many members of the Orthodox church were sent to labor camps and shot during the purges of 1937 and 1938. Nevertheless, Soviet figures record that in 1937 two-thirds of the rural population and one-third of the urban population still held religious beliefs. With the outbreak of World War II there was a rapprochement, as Stalin needed to rally the entire population against the German threat. The postwar era saw a return to the suspicious attitude of the authorities, and a new anti-ecclesiastical campaign, initiated by Nikita Khrushchev in 1959, forced the closure of about 12,000 churches. Schools were saturated with antireligious propaganda, and atheistic materials were included in the curriculum. The Khrushchev campaign led to the closure of monasteries and seminaries, and even a ban on church bells at certain times of the year.

After Khrushchev's removal from office in 1964, propaganda decreased. But it was not until the *glasnost* period in the late 1980s that many church buildings were returned to the church, seminaries began to reopen their doors, and religious societies were given control over their own finances. After the fall of the Soviet Union the Russian government openly embraced the Russian Orthodox church and there was a renaissance in religious belief. The close ties between the Orthodox church and the state that had been normal in the tsarist period continued uncomfortably through the Communist period and have resurfaced again in the close alliance with Russia's postcommunist government.

In the wake of World War II the Soviet Union extended its persecution of religion to the newly Communist Eastern Bloc. Many churches were closed, lost their prominent role in public life, and children were taught atheism. In the German Democratic Republic the head of the East German Stasi, Erich Mielke, described the church as "the legal organization of the enemy" and the government promoted state atheism. The compromises Protestant churches had made with the Nazis were still fresh in many memories; now they became opponents of the Communist government, asserting their right to take a stance on public issues. Eventually they became the champions of mass political dissent against the regime and promoted the changes in the GDR that led to the downfall of the regime.

In Poland the nation rallied to the Catholic church, which unequivocally condemned the Communist regime. Attempts were made to persecute the church and promote atheism but from the 1960s onwards the Poles developed a vocal Catholic intelligentsia and an active movement of young Catholics. Pope John Paul II (1920–2005), the first non-Italian pope since the 1520s, played a vital role in rallying Catholic opposition to the communist regimes in the 1980s. The church adopted an increasingly critical stance towards the authorities in some countries, playing a crucial role in the transition to democracy in 1989.

NORWAY
SWEDEN
North Sea
DENMARK
Baltic Sea
Riga
Klaypeda (Memel)
Kaliningrad
Gdansk
U. S. S. R.
Rostock
Szczecin
Berlin
POLAND
Warsaw
Posnan
Lodz
NETHERLANDS
EAST GERMANY
Lublin
Kiev
Halle
Dresden
Wroclaw
BELGIUM
WEST GERMANY
Przemysl
Lvov
Cracow
Prague
L.
CZECHOSLOVAKIA
Brno
Kosice
Bratislava
Debrecen
Jassy
FRANCE
Gyor
Budapest
Cluj
AUSTRIA
HUNGARY
SWITZERLAND
Arad
ROMANIA
Pecs
Zagreb
Rijeka
Belgrade
Bucharest
Black Sea
Danube
Constanza
YUGOSLAVIA
Varna
BULGARIA
Burgas
Split
Sofia
Adriatic Sea
Kotor
ALBANIA
TURKEY
ITALY
Durres
Tirana
Vione
Aegean Sea
GREECE
N
Fault Line of Faith
The Soviet Union and Eastern Europe
Soviet Union from 1945
Principal areas of anti-Soviet protest and revolt 1953–68, crushed by Soviet intervention
Only European Communist state entirely free from Soviet intervention since 1949
Only European Communist state within Soviet bloc pursuing independent policy since 1968
Only European Communist state aligned with China refusing contact with Soviet Union
Only European Communist state to accept Soviet guidance with equanimity
The 'Iron Curtain'
Members of NATO
Neutral countries

The Rise of Protestantism in Latin America

The remarkable wave of Protestant conversions in Latin America, one of the most dramatic large-scale religious shifts in modern history, reflects the emotional, social and material appeal of diverse, flexible Protestant churches, some of them bringing genuine spiritual empowerment and liberation to their people, some of them unscrupulously opportunistic. Their worship is theatrical, populist, vernacular and often offers spiritual gifts such as healing that have an immediate and practical appeal, as well as ethics and networks of self-improvement.

In 1910 Latin America was 90 percent Catholic, the result of 400 years of colonization and conversion by the Portuguese and Spanish. But in 2014 that figure had dropped to 69 percent, the result of large numbers of people leaving the Catholic Church and many moving to Protestant denominations, including the Pentecostal churches. Across the entire region, 18 countries and Puerto Rico, 65 percent of Protestants identify as Pentecostal Christians. Catholicism's long history of entanglement with political power structures and with colonial government, and its hierarchical structure in which poor and indigenous people were often voiceless, had left it dangerously alienated from large parts of the population. During the 1970s and 1980s, the 'liberation theology' movement in Catholicism drew on left-wing politics to try to rebuild its connection with the poor, but with mixed success. Protestants, meanwhile, were decentralised, less political and more unashamed in pursuing a direct and emotional connection with their congregations. Protestant Christianity has flourished in Latin America because of its exploitation of mass media. Many large evangelical churches own their own television stations and broadcast religious programmes to the most remote regions of the increasingly receptive region.

After the independence movements of the 19th century, most new national governments in Latin America decriminalized Protestantism, allowing a small number of missionaries from the USA and Great Britain to enter the region. Although the missionary effort became more organized and substantial by the end of the century, success rates were still low. Protestantism began to gain a foothold in Latin America from the 1900s when the first Pentecostal missionaries began to arrive in large numbers. With their emphasis on the spiritual gifts of speaking in tongues, healing, and forming an individual relationship with God, they invited a more passionate adherence.

The growth of Protestantism began to pick up from the middle of the 20th century because of a number of factors: missionaries began to target the more marginal populations, especially those who did not use Portuguese or Spanish as their first language; Pentecostalism, which had previously been seen as a peripheral faith, began to gain traction globally; local converts began to form independent churches and denominations, giving them freedom from missionary supervision. Protestantism was increasingly being seen as a home-grown religion, removing the foreign influences manifested by the missionaries.

Latin America's most Protestant country is Guatemala, where over 40 percent of the population is Protestant. Recent polls show that Uruguay (the most secular country in Latin America) no longer has a majority of people that identify as Roman Catholics. While Brazil is home to the largest Catholic population on earth, it accounts for just 64 percent of the population, and its Pentecostal population is the largest in the world. Denominations like the Assembleia de Deus (Assemblies of God) are attracting every larger congregations. In regions that were originally settled by German speakers, churches belonging to the Lutheran World Federation have prospered, amongst them the Evangelical Church of the River Plate in Argentina and the Evangelical Lutheran Church of Brazil.

Latin American Catholicism was imposed on the region by conquest and has never entirely rid itself of its violent colonial roots. Its close association with the political Right in modern times has made it controversial, whereas Protestants have generally attempted to remain apolitical – although this stance, too, has been accused of implicitly favoring the Right. Moreover, the Catholic church's celibate clergy and traditionalist views of women have alienated it both from conservative Latin American masculinity and also, increasingly, from the women who have long been its mainstay. The difficulty of recruiting priests is in stark contrast to the informal structures in the Pentecostal world, where women's leadership has been much more prominent despite strongly conservative views on gender and sexuality.

Los Angeles
New York
Philadelphia
Washington
UNITED STATES OF AMERICA
NORTH ATLANTIC OCEAN
Tropic of Cancer
Miami
MEXICO 81%
Havana
THE BAHAMAS
CUBA
Mexico City
DOMINICAN REP. 57%
JAMAICA
Virgin Is.
BELIZE
HONDURAS 46%
HAITI 57%
Puerto Rico 56%
ANTIGUA
GUATEMALA 50%
DOMINICA
ST. LUCIA
EL SALVADOR 50%
ST. VINCENT
BARBADOS
GRENADA
NICARAGUA 50%
TRINIDAD AND TOBAGO
COSTA RICA 62%
Caracas
GUYANA
SURINAME
French Guiana 80%
VENEZUELA 73%
PANAMA 70%
Bogotá
COLOMBIA 79%
Belém
ECUADOR 79%
Quito
PACIFIC OCEAN
Manaus
BRAZIL 64%
PERU 76%
Lima
Brasília
BOLIVIA 77%
La Paz
Río de Janeiro
PARAGUAY 89%
Tropic of Capricorn
São Paulo
Asunción
CHILE 64%
ARGENTINA 71%
Santiago
URUGUAY 42%
Buenos Aires
Montevideo
SOUTH ATLANTIC OCEAN
Falkland Is.
Christianity in Central and South America, Present Day
Percentage who Identify as Catholic
Over 80%
50% - 70%
50% or less
Protestantism on rise
Protestantism in majority

Christian Persecution in the Middle East

On the eve of World War I, there were two million Armenians in the declining Ottoman Empire. By 1922, there were fewer than 400,000. The Ottoman Empire had been beset by revolts among Christian subjects to the north; large amounts of territory were lost in the Balkan Wars of 1912–13. The Young Turk movement of discontented junior army officers seized power in 1908, determined to modernize and nationalize the Empire. In 1914 they entered World War I on the side of Germany.

Religious minorities had been allowed to maintain religious, social, and legal structures within the Empire, but were often subject to extra taxes or other measures. During the war Armenians were stereotyped as not real Turks but as western collaborators. In April 1915 several hundred Armenian intellectuals were rounded up, arrested, and later executed as the start of the Armenian genocide, which extended to 1917. The massacres resumed from 1920–23. There were executions, mass graves, and forced death marches of men, women and children to concentration camps, marking the beginning of a century of Christian persecution.

A century ago Christians accounted for 30 percent of the population in the Middle East and North Africa. Since then the proportion has fallen to less than 4 percent, the result of emigration, conversions, differential rates of population growth and some direct violence. Persecution can range from routine discrimination in education, employment, and social life to genocidal attacks – millions of Christians have been driven from their homes, killed, kidnapped, or imprisoned.

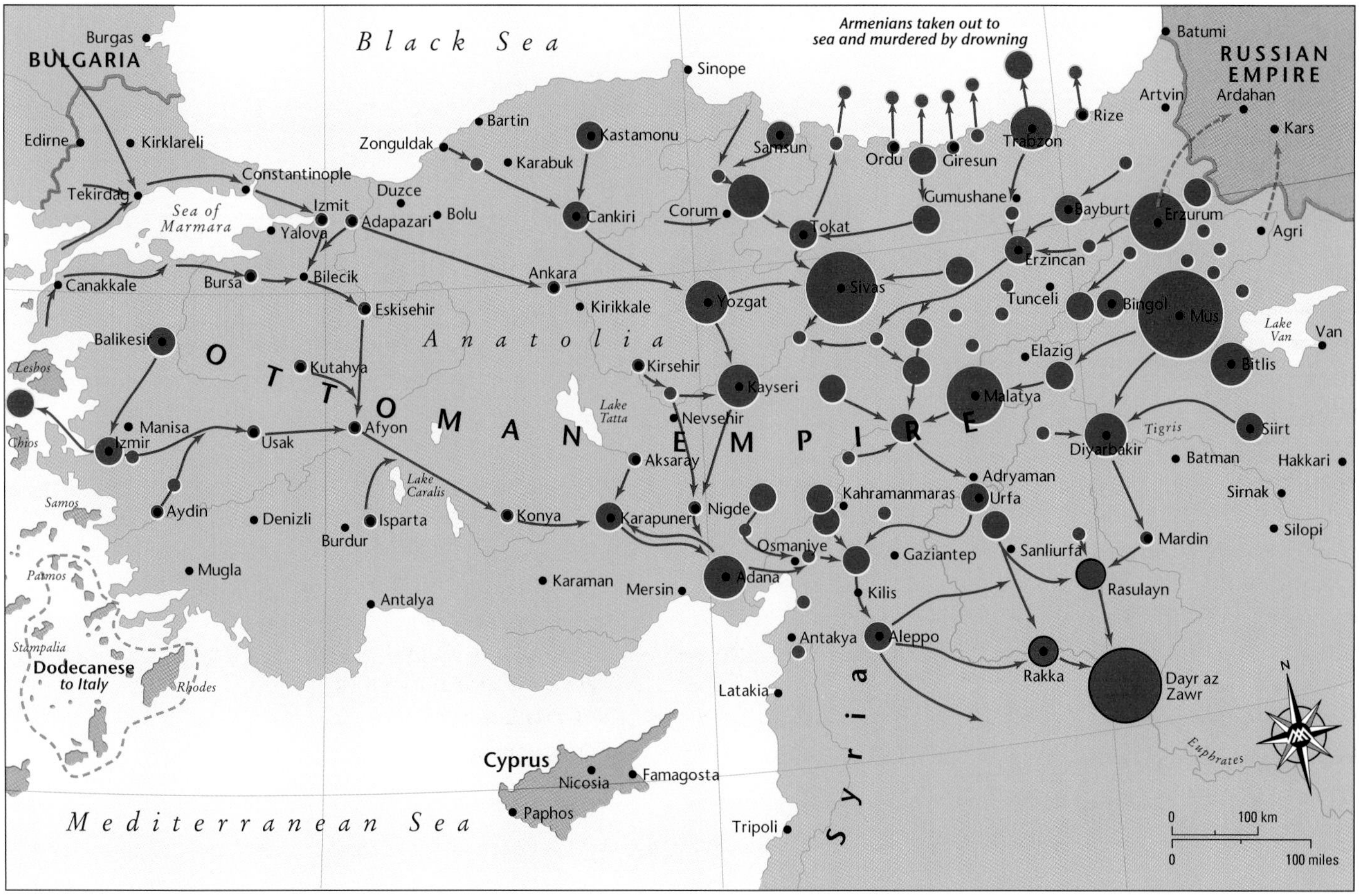

Persecutions become much more marked in countries where political failure sets the stage

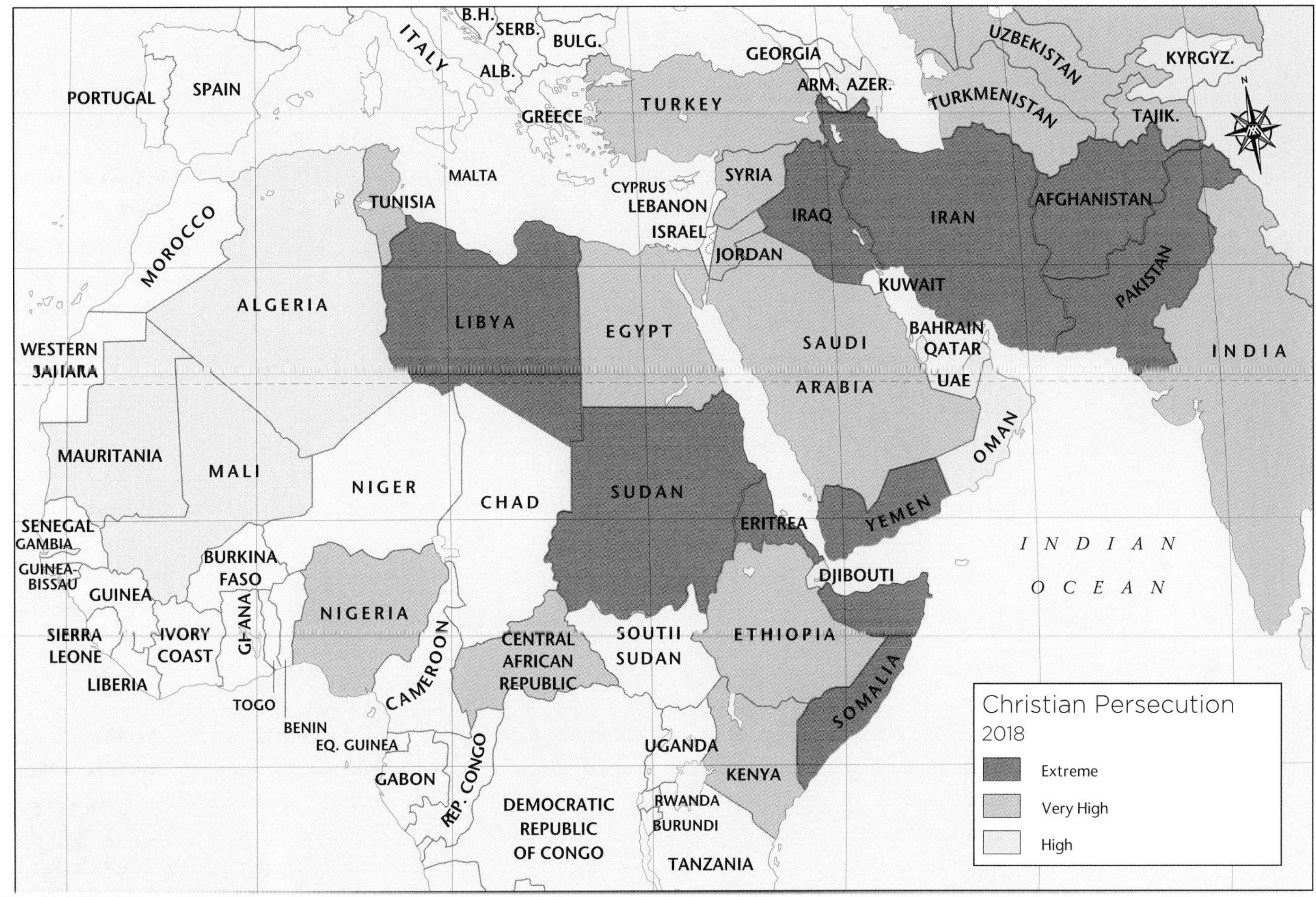

for religious extremism. Christians are also at risk in countries that have espoused religious conservatism, such as Turkey and Algeria. Finally, many of the most dangerous countries have experienced failures in their systems of law, justice, and policing, which creates situations in which extremists thrive and persecuted minorities are exposed. These factors have been particularly critical in the 21st century: the "Arab Spring" (uprisings in 2010/11) and the fall of established dictatorships in Egypt, Libya, Syria, and Iraq led to power vacuums that were partly filled by religious extremism. During the civil war from 2011, Syria's substantial Christian minorities were often targeted as suspected supporters of the Assad dictatorship.

In countries such as Algeria, Egypt, Iran, Iraq, Syria and Saudi Arabia the situation of Christians and other minorities is alarming. In Saudi Arabia there are strict limitations on all forms of expression of Christianity, and even private acts of worship. Other forms of persecution include violent threats, general harassment, detention, legal discrimination, and incitement to hatred from Islamic pulpits. In Egypt Christian Copts account for about one fifth of the population, and Islamic State has threatened to "wipe out" this community, targeting respected local leaders, bombing churches, and killing busloads of pilgrims. Christian pleas for government protection have fallen on deaf ears.

States, and state-sponsored social media, sometimes incite hatred and publish propaganda against Christians, especially in Iran, Iraq, and Turkey – the governing AK party in Turkey depicts Christians as a "threat to the stability of the nation." Confiscation of church properties and attacks on properties owned by Christians are increasing in Israel, Egypt, and Turkey.

Inevitably persecution leads to exodus: in the Palestinian territories, Christian numbers have been reduced by 87 percent, and are now below 1.5 percent of the population. There are parts of the Middle East, where Christian roots go back the longest, where Christianity now faces the possibility of being wiped out entirely.

China and Korea since 1949

China's Communist revolution in 1949 appeared to herald disaster for Chinese Christianity, but recent Chinese Christian growth is such that some some sources project that the number of Christian believers will outstrip the USA by 2030. The communist regime, always officially committed to atheism, expelled foreign missionaries in 1950 and compelled all Christians to join officially recognized church bodies whose leadership included Communist Party agents. A steadily tightening squeeze on these churches culminated in the Cultural Revolution of 1966–76, when religious practice of any kind was outlawed. But the wave of destruction during this period seems to have damaged other religious communities more severely, while Protestant Christianity, well equipped to face persecution and able to flourish without buildings or public ritual, spread in clandestine groups. Since the re-legalisation of public worship under Deng Xiaoping in 1979, Christian congregations have skyrocketed. China has also become the world's largest printer of bibles: the Amity Printing Company, a joint venture be-

tween a Chinese non-government organization called the Amity Foundation and the United Bible Societies, printed 50 million bibles between 2013 and 2016. In an era of unprecedented economic and educational growth, many Chinese are seeking to find new spiritual moorings. Chinese believers are drawn to Christianity's moral authority, its alignment with modernity, the community it offers during a period of dislocating social change, and the spiritual benefits many of them encounter in it.

There are also between 10 to 12 million Roman Catholics in contemporary China. Formal ties between China and the Vatican were cut in 1951, and partly restored only in 2018 when a provisional agreement on the appointment of bishops was reached. The Chinese regime remains strongly opposed to religious bodies which accept leadership from entities outside China, seeing them as potentially subversive.

The Communist Party appears to be uncertain how to deal with the spread of Christianity. Some officials accept that Christian communities provide social welfare that is lacking from the government, and are also appreciative that Christianity embodies moral values, which are much valued at a time when a galloping economic boom is associated with increased crime. But longstanding Chinese fears of religious subversion, and a particular concern that Christianity may be a front for American and other foreign influences, mean that a close watch is kept on churchgoers and preachers, and sermons are scrutinized to ensure that they adhere to a communist message and do not encourage subversion. Meanwhile, most Chinese Christians strive to be apolitical and to keep as low a profile as possible. This fragile equilibrium came under pressure from the mid-2010s, as Xi Jinping's government cracked down on unregistered churches and some Christians became more outspoken in asserting their rights.

The first Protestant Christian missionaries arrived on the Korean peninsula in 1884, and some prominent early nationalist leaders during the period of Japanese influence and occupation converted to Christianity, but conversions did not really take off until after World War II. Rapid growth amongst Presbyterians and Methodists then made South Korea into by far the most Protestant country in Asia: the Protestant population rose from 2.5 percent in 1960 to 27 percent in 1990, and while Protestant growth has since stalled, the Catholic community has been expanding rapidly and now stands at some 10 percent of the population. A well-known feature of Korean Protestantism is its "mega-churches" with congregations of 5,000, many of them renewalist or Pentecostal in flavor and some offering a "prosperity gospel." South Koreans saw the growth of Christianity and their country's contemporaneous economic miracle as aligned: diligent and disciplined Christians had a good work ethic and made highly productive employees. However, since the end of the dictatorship in 1987 Christian growth has been challenged by resurgent Buddhism, by growing secularism and by difficulties in reaching the rising generation. There have also been scandals about church corruption, including charges of rape and embezzlement against prominent pastors.

North Korea's attempts to eradicate Christianity have been perhaps the most thorough in world history. The North had been the initial center for early Christianity in Korea, and there was a significant "revival" in Pyongyang in 1907, but in the immediate postwar period Christians were imprisoned, tortured, and killed and many thousands fled south. Today practicing Christians are treated as foreign agents and are likely to be deported to labor camps as political criminals, or even executed on the spot. Meetings amongst Christians are almost impossible and have to be undertaken in conditions of the utmost secrecy. It is impossible to estimate how many – if any – self-conscious Christians remain in the North, although many refugees who have escaped have joined Christian churches. North Korea has built four churches in Pyongyang, but these are usually taken to be "show churches," built to disguise North Korea's brutal treatment of its Christian population.

In 1949 there were just one million Protesants in China. Today estimates vary widely; there are anywhere between 60 and 115 million Protestants in China. The majority of China's Protestants worship in unregistered or underground "house churches," where they can escape Communist Party surveillance. It is estimated that fewer than 30 million attend officially registered Protestant churches (*left*).

South Asia from 1947

Bangladesh, Pakistan, India and Sri Lanka share a common history of British colonial rule, and have experienced missionary activities from Christians that date back many centuries. Muslim majorities are found in Pakistan (95 percent), and Bangladesh (89.5 percent), while Hinduism is the dominant religion in India (80.5 percent) and Buddhism in Sri Lanka (69.1 percent). All of these countries have developed in different ways following the retreat of colonialism and have treated religious and ethnic minorities in different ways. Amongst the Christians of South Asia Roman Catholics are a distinct majority, followed by Protestants – Charismatic, Pentecostal and New Apostolic Churches are all gaining in importance. The historic Syriac and Mar-Thoma churches which predate European colonialism also retain a presence.

In modern India Christians make up 2.3 percent of the population; Pakistan 1.6 percent; Bangladesh 0.6 percent; Myanmar 4 percent; Sri Lanka 6 percent. In principle Christians and other religious minorities enjoy legal freedoms and protections in all of these countries, but what this means in practice can vary widely. Prestigious Christian schools, frequently founded as part of the missionary endeavours in the 19th century, are respected throughout the region, and their alumni are found throughout the ruling political class. Attempts to conduct missionary activities amongst the wider population are treated very differently.

Christians tend to occupy a background role in Pakistan, and inter-religious relations continue to be tense. In 2011 Shahbaz Bhatti, the Minister for Minorities, was murdered. He was a Catholic, and an advocate for the Christian minority, who was also a vocal critic of the blasphemy law, which can carry a death sentence for those deemed to have insulted the Prophet Muhammad. This law has proved itself to be dangerously open to abuse, often being used simply to pursue personal vendettas against Christians. Notoriously, a Pakistani Christian named Asia Bibi spent eight years on death row, charged with blasphemy, before the charges were dismissed as baseless by the country's Supreme Court in 2019: the ruling provoked days of protest and disruption across Pakistan. Bibi was compelled to flee to Canada and continues to receive death threats from jihadists. In neighboring Afghanistan Christian converts can face the death penalty, while jihadist groups, such as Tehrik-i-Taliban, that operate along the Afghan-Pakistani border, suppress Christian minorities and intimidate politicians and judges into following suit.

India's 28 million Christians play a more prominent role in public life. The bulk of the Christian population is in South India, especially in the states of Kerala and Tamil Nadu, but there are significant pockets elsewhere, and Christians form a majority in three sparsely populated states in India's isolated northeast. About 75 percent of Indian Christians are Dalits, or so-called "untouchables," and as Christians they are actively discriminated against; for this reason many Dalits identify as Hindus, and some argue that India's Christian population is underestimated as a consequence.

Even in India some nationalistic Hindu groups are directly opposed to Christianity and have particularly opposed attempts to convert Hindus. In 1999 the Australian missionary Graham Staines was burned to death with his two sons in their car by the nationalist Dara Singh, who accused Staines of converting poor tribal people to Christianity. In 2011 the Supreme Court sentenced the perpetrator to life imprisonment and reaffirmed religious freedom, but the Hindu nationalist government of Narendra Modi has since 2014 been putting increased pressure on Indian Christians. In 2017 a major Christian charity, Compassion International, was shut down amidst accusations that it was masterminding Christian conversions.

Approximately 6 percent of Sri Lanka's population of 21 million are Christian; the majority of them are Roman Catholic and Catholicism retains a strong cultural presence there. As in India, Christians in Sri Lanka have historically not been directly implicated in their country's bitter internal religious conflicts, but on Easter Sunday 2019 they were the target of a series of bombings from jihadist Muslims (also a small minority in Sri Lanka), killing 259 people. It remains to be seen how this will affect the long-term future of Christianity on the island.

Finally, in Myanmar the substantial Christian population of 4.3 million, like the country's rather larger Muslim community, is regarded with suspicion in a country that sees itself as a Buddhist state. The politically dominant army has increased its activities against ethnic minorities (including Christians), and in the predominantly Christian states, for example Kachim, Karen and Northern Shan, 60 churches were reportedly destroyed within an 18-month period.

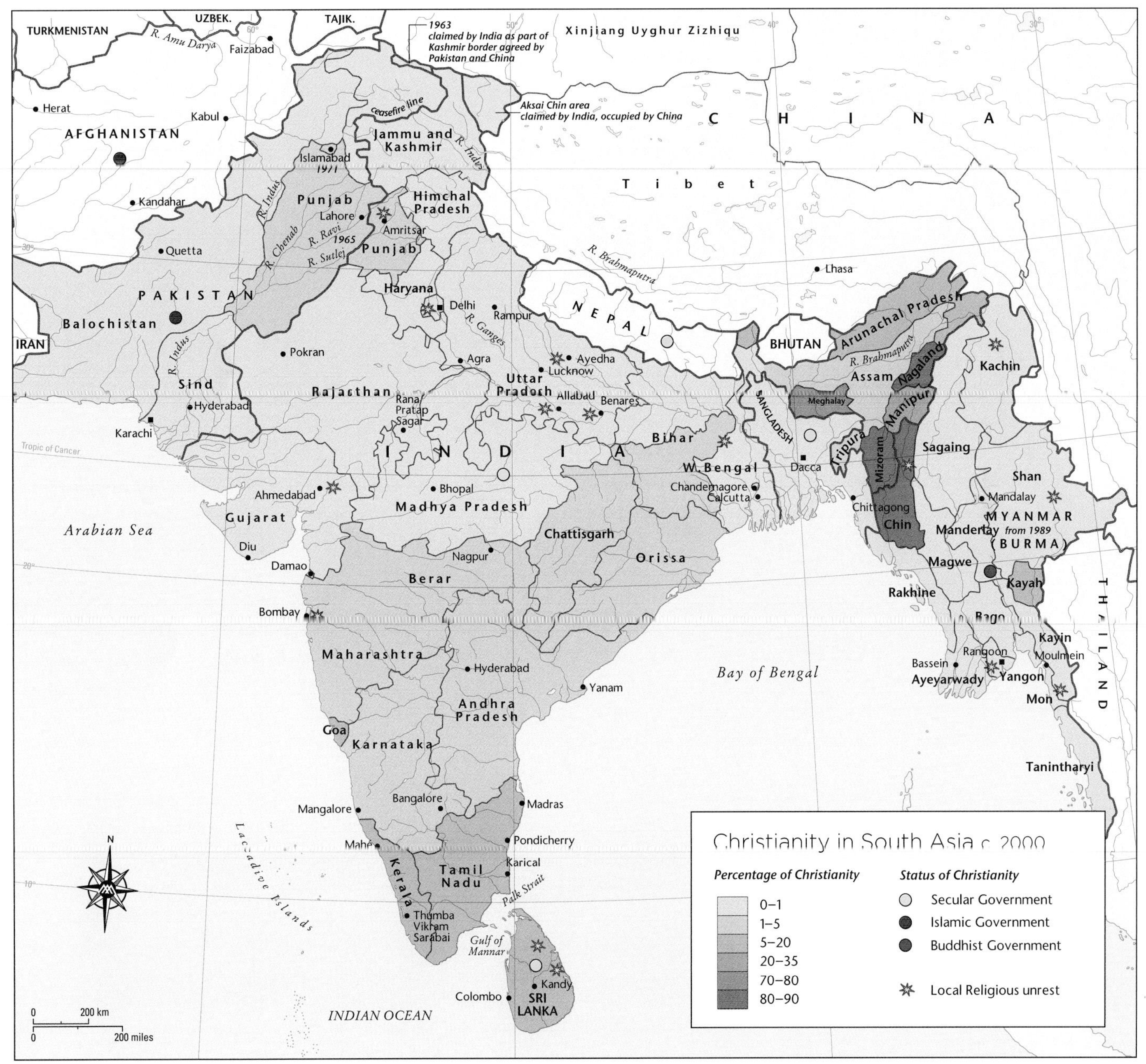

Christian Growth and Decline

Christianity is the largest religion in the world, with 2.5 billion adherents, or 31.2 percent of the total world population in 2015. The explosive growth of Christianity outside the West has made it the fastest growing global religion, and it is predicted that by 2050 there will be 3 billion Christians worldwide, of whom only 20 percent will be non-Hispanic whites. Numbers of Christians in Africa are expected to reach 633 million in 2025, with 640 million in Latin America and 460 million in Asia. About half the world's Christian population belongs to the Catholic church, with 1.3 billion adherents.

For centuries Christianity has been shaped by a largely European culture. But today the religion has become geographically diverse and is being revivified by new expressions of traditional Christian belief in Africa, Latin America, and Asia. Sub-Saharan Africa is predicted to become the region with the largest number of Christians in 2050, with 38 percent of the world's Christian population. The size of the Christian population in Nigeria alone, which is already the largest on the continent, is projected to double by 2060. In addition Tanzania, Uganda, and Kenya are projected to join the list of the top ten countries with the largest Christian populations.

The Christians of the southern hemisphere are far more conservative, theologically and morally, than their northern counterparts, generally insisting on traditionalist views on biblical authority, gender roles and sexual morality. Many of them also value the traditionalist structures and sacraments of the Catholic, Anglican, and other hierarchical churches, but many do not. One in four Christians globally identify as Pentecostal or Charismatic. In Latin America the growth of Pentecostalism is estimated to be at three times the rate of Catholic growth, and the "charismatic Catholic" movement is also still on the rise. Christianity, especially informal and unstructured forms, is also growing at a rapid pace in China, but because large numbers of worshipers have formed underground churches, it is difficult to arrive at concrete figures.

This shifting demography from north to south will inevitably cause tensions. Christians who belong to a worldwide communion will have to recognize that their churches' centers of gravity are now in Africa and Latin America – in population terms at least. In 2013 the Roman Catholic Church elected its first non-European pope of the modern age, the Argentinian Jorge Mario Bergoglio (Francis). African and Asian popes cannot be far behind.

As Christianity continues to expand apace in the southern hemisphere the traditional heartlands of this world faith, in particular Europe, are seeing a decline. Secularization, which is a specific and local phenomenon, not a generic and global one, has been gathering pace. Europe is no longer predominantly Christian as societies becoming increasingly globalized, multicultural, and multi-faith. There is also evidence of decline in the United States. The West offers powerful values, but they are largely "post-religious:" tolerance, democracy, autonomy and human rights.

A survey conducted in 2018 amongst young people in 12 European countries showed very large proportions who denied having any faith at all: the Czech Republic was the least religious country with 91 percent of 16–29-year-olds claiming no religious affiliation. Only in Poland, Portugal, and Ireland did more than 10 percent of young people affirm that they attended a religious service at least once a week. In countries like Estonia, Sweden, and the Netherlands between 70 and 80 percent of young people say they have no religious affiliation.

In surveys about a quarter of Europeans of all ages say they have no religious affiliation, indicating they are atheistic or agnostic. This is about the same proportion as Americans, but in the USA "nones" are more likely nevertheless to believe in God. In the United States Christians still represent 73.3 percent of the total population (2016). Nevertheless this number has been declining since the 1960s with each successive generation becoming avowedly less religious than the preceding one.

1900
Russian Empire 136,000,000
United States of America 76,000,000
Germany 56,000,000
Austro-Hungarian Empire 47,000,000
Great Britain & Ireland 40,000,000
France 39,000,000
Italy 32,500,000
Spain 19,000,000
Brazil 18,000,000
Mexico 14 ,000,000
2000
United States of America 282,000,000
Brazil 170,000,000
Russian Federation 147,000,000
Mexico 97,000,000
Germany 82,000,000
Ethiopia 77,000,000
Philippines 70,000,000
France 58,000,000
Great Britain & Ireland 58,000,000
Italy 57,000,000
2050
Nigeria 411,000,000
United States of America 395,000,000
Brazil 233,000,000
Democratic Republic of Congo 197,000,000
Ethiopia 191,000,000
Mexico 164,000,000
Philippines 151,000,000
Tanzania 138,000,000
Russian Federation 133,000,000
Uganda 76,000,000

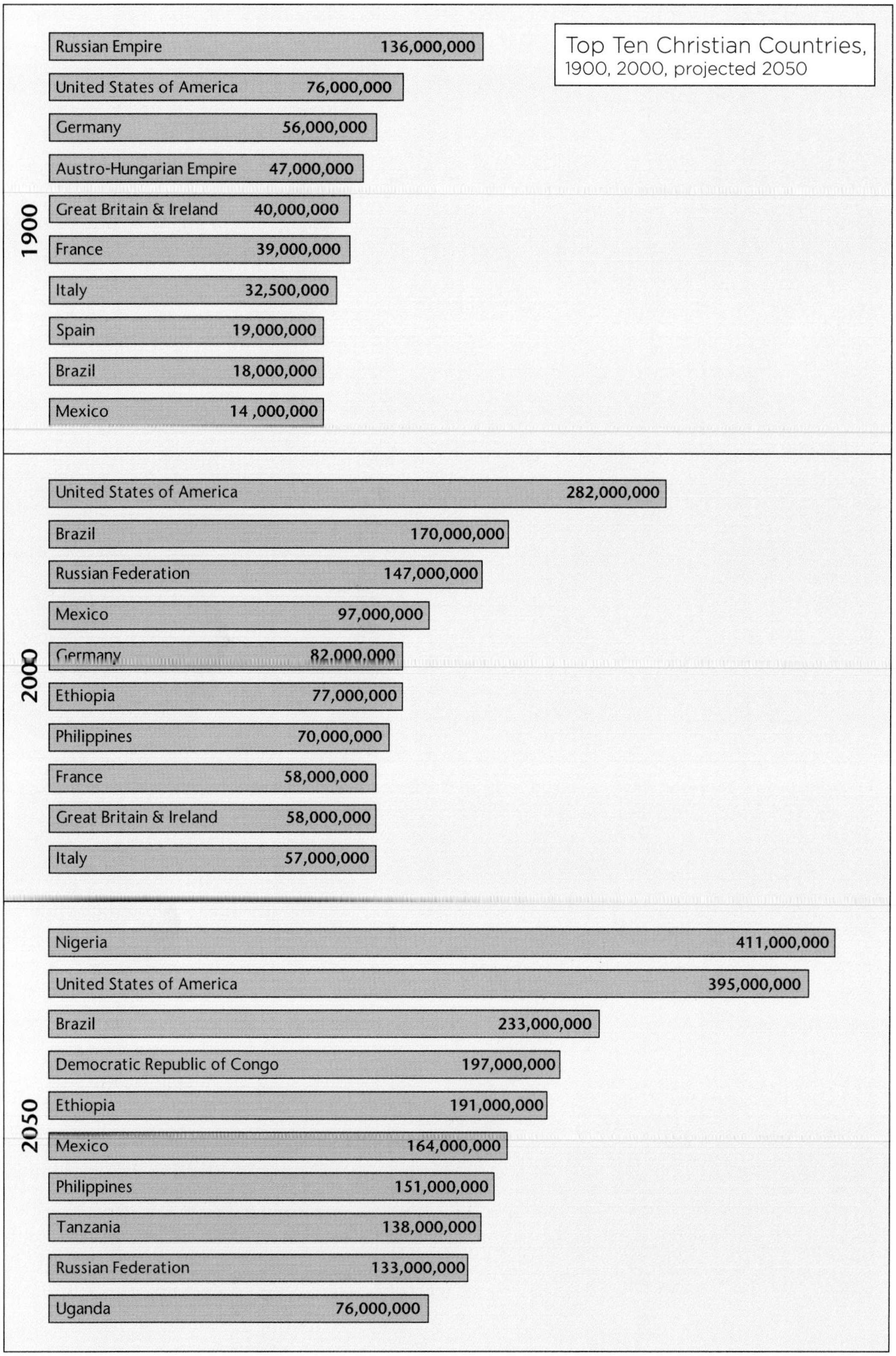

Top Ten Christian Countries,
1900, 2000, projected 2050

1910
Americas 27.1 %
Europe 66.3 %
Sub-Saharan Africa 1.4 %
Asia-Pacific 4.5 %
Middle East-North Africa 0.7 %
2010
Europe 25.9 %
Americas 36.8 %
Sub-Saharan Africa 23.6 %
Asia-Pacific 13.1 %
Middle East-North Africa 0.6 %

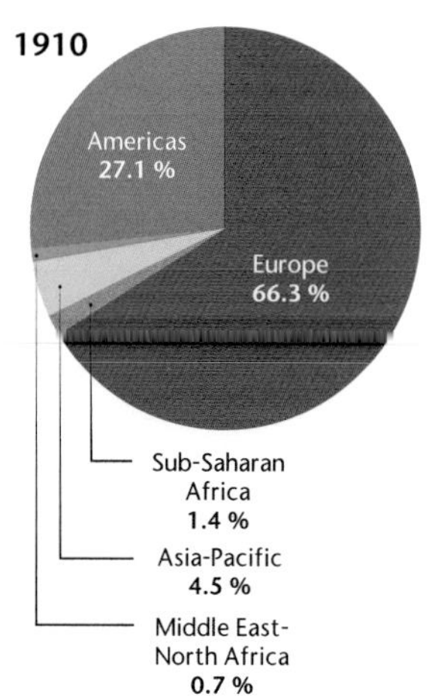

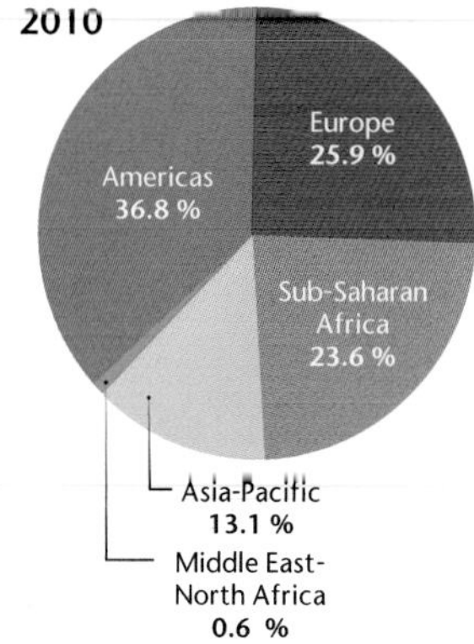

Distribution of
Christians by Region
1910 & 2010

Christianity in the Contemporary World

On 20 July 1969, the Americans Neil Armstrong and Buzz Aldrin landed on the Moon. Before either of them ventured outside, Aldrin – a Presbyterian elder – took the time to celebrate a Christian Eucharist. The sacramental bread and wine were the first food and drink ever consumed on the Moon.

It was a symbol of an ancient truth: that Christianity is a universal religion which recognizes no geographical boundaries. In the modern age, this spirit of interconnection has been technologically accelerated to draw the world's diverse Christian histories closer together than has ever been possible before.

It continues to be meaningful to depict the varieties of Christianity across the world on a map, but those regional differences are being put under pressure. Within global communions such as the Roman Catholic or Anglican churches, it is becoming progressively harder to avoid the tensions between the robustly conservative doctrines and morals of the global South and the secularized and liberalized Christianities more prevalent in the Euro-American world. But the global era is also producing new global networks, first enabled by mass media and now turbocharged by the internet, which allow minority Christian groups to gather and encour-

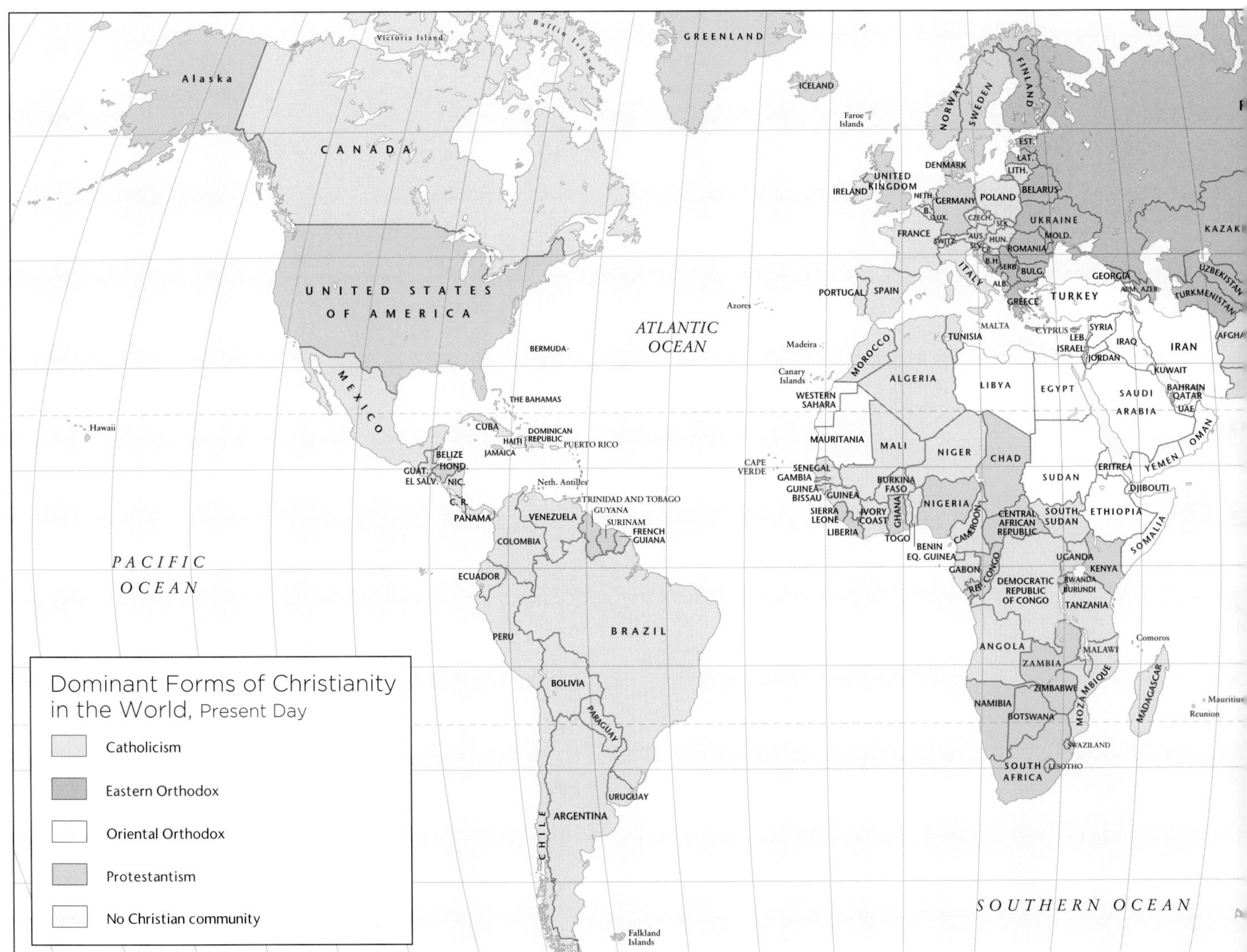

age one another virtually, and for tiny communities to discover that they are in fact millions strong.

As populations in the rich North age and decline, the global South is coming to them and bringing its churches with it. The much-heralded phenomenon of "reverse mission" – in which the newly Christianized South sends missionaries to revive secular Europe's faith – may not produce many results, but the influx of migrants will. The largest Christian church in Europe, the Embassy of the Blessed Kingdom of God for all Nations, in Kiev, was started in 1993 by the Nigerian pastor Sunday Adelaja. Established churches, too, will draw on their global networks. In the US the Catholic Church has been recruiting African priests for many years.

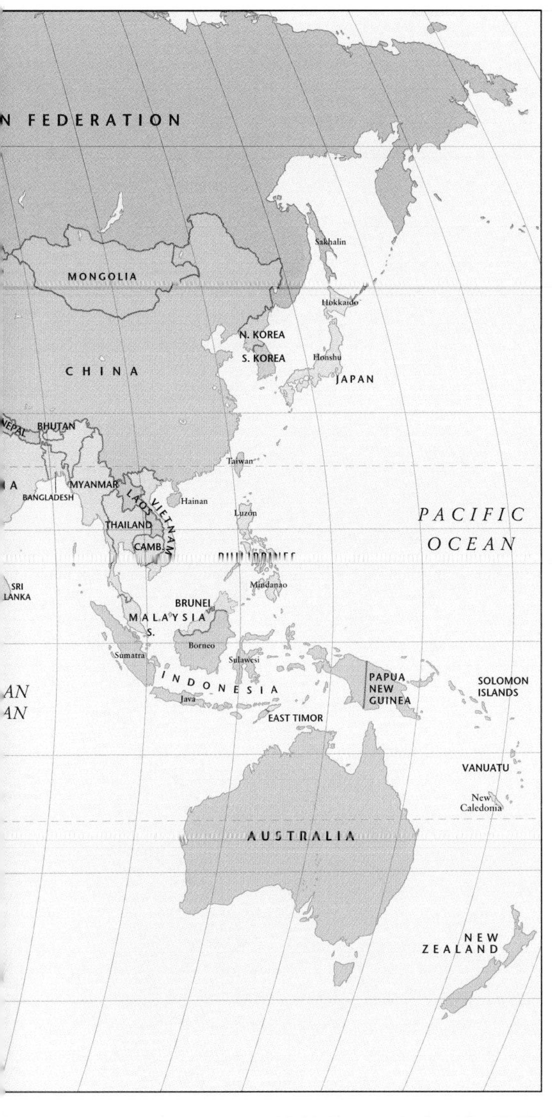

As Christianity continues to expand in the southern hemisphere, the traditional heartlands of this world faith, in particular Europe, have been seeing a decline since the 1960s. Rapidly rising incomes and an unprecedented period of peace have certainly posed a challenge to a religion that has always thrived in adversity. The rapid spread of secular education has disrupted the generational transmission of the faith and normalized scientific or philosophical perspectives in tension with traditional Christianity. The dramatic changes in the place of women in Western societies, and the wave of sexual liberation triggered by widespread contraception, seriously disrupted social norms on which Christianity had long depended. Above all, the new, secular ethical norms centered on human rights, which became established in the wake of World War II, made Christian ethics seem redundant or even erroneous. Yet traditionalist Christianity is generally not being replaced with self-conscious atheism, but with withdrawal and the spread of alternative spiritualities. The internet offers an unrivalled range of perspectives, answers, and interpretations, the "democratization of information." People may feel that they no longer need an authoritative figure who is a representative of a hierarchical organization to explain, enlighten or offer guidance, and many spiritual seekers are choosing to go their own way.

There is every reason to believe that global Christianity will flourish in the 21st century – and also face some severe challenges, although neither the successes nor the failures will necessarily come where we expect. If the Christian age is not coming to an end, however, it may be that the age in which the history of Christianity can usefully be mapped is. In a globally networked, mobile and migratory world, geography and regional difference may become less and less determinative of religious experience. Our successors in the 22nd century may struggle to produce a historical atlas of Christianity.

GLOSSARY

Acolyte
(Greek, "follower"). A lay person who assists ministers in worship services.
Alexandrian School
School of thought associated with Alexandria, Egypt. It was influenced by Platonic philosophy and tended to emphasize the divinity of Christ over his humanity.
Anabaptist
A radical Protestant movement that emerged in the 16th century, which baptizes persons when they convert or declare their faith in God, even if they have already been baptized as infants.
Anglicanism
The faiths, doctrines, and practices of the Anglican church, or Church of England, which declared its independence from the Holy See in the 16th century. Adherents in some countries are called "Episcopalians."
Antiochene school
The school of thought associated with the city of Antioch in Syria, as contrasted with the Alexandrian School. Antiochene theology was influenced by Aristotelian philosophy, and emphasized the humanity of Christ.
Apostles
The twelve disciples of Jesus, according to accounts in the New Testament.
Apostolic fathers
Group of Christian leaders and writers from the late 1st and early 2nd centuries CE, who were not apostles themselves, but had close proximity to the apostles, either by personal relationship or close connection with apostolic teaching.
Apostolic succession
Doctrine that the authority of ordained clergy derives from an unbroken succession of valid ordinations beginning with the apostles.
Archbishops
In Catholicism and Anglicanism, a bishop who oversees the other bishops in the province.
Arianism
Belief, taught by Arius in the 4th century, that Christ was created by God the Father, and although greater than man he is inferior to the Father. It was declared a heresy at the Council of Nicea in 325.
Baptists
Christian denominational family characterized by rejection of infant baptism. Baptism, usually by full immersion, is for professing believers only.
Benedictines (Order of St Benedict)
A monastic Catholic order of monks and nuns, founded in Italy in 529 CE, which follow the strict rule of Saint Benedict.
Bishop
The priest and spiritual leader of a diocese.
Calvinism
Christian doctrines taught by John Calvin (1509–64), which emphasize the sovereignty of the word of God and the doctrine of predestination – salvation is predetermined for a selected few.
Canon law
In Catholicism, the body of law related to the organization, discipline, and belief of the church and enforced by church authority.
Catechism
(from Greek *katecheo*, "instruct"). A class or manual on the basics of Christian doctrine and practice, usually studied as a precursor to confirmation or baptism.
Cathars
Heretical sect especially influential in southern France and northern Italy in the 13th and 14th centuries, and characterized by a dualistic world view and strict asceticism.
Catholic
A term meaning "universal," used by the early Christians to designate the universal Christian faith. When the Eastern church split from the Western in 1054, the West retained this term and became known as Roman Catholic. Churches in the East are known as Greek, Eastern or Russian Orthodox.
Chalcedonian Christianity
Christian denominations adhering to the resolutions and definitions of the Council of Chalcedon (451), which propounded the belief that humanity and divinity are exemplified as two distinct natures in Jesus Christ.
Christology
Area of theology dealing with the person of Christ. The vast majority of Christological doctrine was developed in the period leading up to the Council of Nicaea in 325.
Church
The worldwide body of Christian believers, a particular denomination or congregation, or the building in which they meet. The study of the nature of the church is called "ecclesiology."
Church of the East
A Christian church of the East Syriac rite established c. 410, which followed the teachings of Nestorius (428–431), emphasizing the dual divine and human natures of Christ.
Consubstantiation
A doctrine of the Eucharist associated especially with Martin Luther, according to which the bread and wine and the body and blood of Christ coexist in the elements. Consubstantiation was formulated in opposition to the medieval Catholic doctrine of transubstantiation.
Coptic Orthodox Church
The main Christian church in Egypt, which dates back to c. 50 and, according to Coptic tradition, was founded by Saint Mark. It separated from other Christian denominations after the Council of Chalcedon (451)
Council of Nicaea
Council of Christian bishops convened by Emperor Constantine in 325, which condemned Arianism as a heresy and produced the Nicene Creed.
Council of Trent
The 19th ecumenical council of the Catholic church, which took place over the period 1545–63. It reformed numerous aspects of church practice and clarified Catholic doctrine.
Counter-Reformation
The period of Catholic revival, in response to the Potestant Reformation, which was initiated at the Council of Trent.
Crusades
Wars fought against enemies of the Christian faith, primarily the Muslim Turks in the period 1095 to 1291, but later against other infidels and heretics.
Diocese
A geographical region headed by a bishop, which usually includes several congregations. In Eastern Orthodoxy, a diocese is called an eparchy.
Dispensationalism
A theological system that considers biblical history as divided by God into "dispensations," or ages, each of which is part of God's plan.
Dominican
A member of the mendicant religious order founded by Saint Dominic in 1216.
Donatism
A 4th-century North African Christian faction, named for Bishop Donatus, which emphasized the rigor of faith and taught that Christian clergy must be faultless for their ministry to be effective.
Ebionites
An ascetic sect of Jewish Christians that taught Jesus was only a human prophet who had received the Holy Spirit at his baptism.
Ecumenical council
A council of the Christian church at which

representatives from several regions are present.

Edict of Nantes
Edict signed by Henry IV at Nantes on April 13, 1598, after the end of the French wars of religion. It granted extensive rights to the Huguenots (French Calvinists), but was revoked by Louis XIV in 1685.

Eucharist
A sacrament recognized by all branches of Christianity. It commemorates the Last Supper of Christ with the sharing of bread and wine.

Evangelicalism
A tradition within Protestant Christianity that emphasizes active evangelism, personal conversion and faith experiences, and scripture.

Ex cathedra
Statements made by the pope in Roman Catholicism, which are believed to be infallible.

Franciscans
Mendicant monastic order founded by Francis of Assisi in 1210.

Gospel
"Good news." The stories of Jesus' life circulated in the early churches. Eventually four gospels came to be accepted as scriptural: Matthew, Mark, Luke, and John.

Immaculate Conception
Roman Catholic doctrine that the Virgin Mary was born without original sin.

Heresy
Dissent or deviation from a dominant theory, opinion, or practice.

Jesuits (Society of Jesus)
A religious order of the Catholic church founded by Ignatius of Loyola in 1540, dedicated to evangelization and apostolic ministry.

Justification
The state of being released by God from the guilt of sin.

Lutheranism
One of the largest Protestant Christian denominations, based on the teachings of Martin Luther in the 1500s.

Mendicants
Itinerant Christian orders that have adopted a lifestyle of poverty, preaching, and evangelization.

Mennonite
A group of denominations in the Anabaptist movement of the Christian church.

Methodism
A group of Protestant denominations that derive their practices and beliefs from the teachings of John Wesley (1703–91), and focus on the "methodical" pursuit of sanctity.

Miaphystism
Also called monophysitism, this is the belief that divinity and humanity are united in one nature in the person of Jesus Christ.

Monarchianism
General term for early Christian heretical beliefs that focused on safeguarding the oneness of God by denying the Trinity.

Mormonism
The predominant religious tradition of the Latter-day Saints movement, which was founded by Joseph Smith in New York state in the 1820s.

Nestorianism
The doctrine, named for Nestorius (d. c. 451), patriarch of Constantinople, that there were two separate persons in the incarnate Christ, one divine and the other human.

Nicene Creed
A statement of belief widely used in Christian liturgy, originally adopted at the First Council of Nicaea in 325.

Orthodoxy
The beliefs and practices of the Eastern Orthodox church, Greek Orthodox church, Russian Orthodox church ad Serbian Orthodox church.

Patriarch
Generally, an early biblical figure such as Abraham or one of the "church fathers" of the early Christian church. Specifically, the spiritual leader of a major city in Eastern Orthodoxy. The patriarch of Constantinople is the eastern counterpart of the Catholic pope.

Pelagianism
Belief system that rejects original sin and asserts the ability of humans to choose good over evil with only external assistance from God. Pelagianism was declared a heresy in the early church.

Pentecostalism
A branch of Christianity that emphasizes the work of the Holy Spirit and the direct experience of the presence of God by the believer.

Pope
The bishop of Rome, who became the recognized leader of the entire Western church by medieval times.

Protestantism
A branch of Christianity dating from the 16th-century Protestant Reformation, characterized by an emphasis on scripture, and the necessity of faith for salvation.

Quakers
A Protestant denomination started by George Fox (1624–91), who believed that a person should guided by the holy spirit in silent meditation.

Real Presence
In Catholic and some Protestant churches, the physical and spiritual presence of the body and blood of Christ in the bread and wine of the Eucharist.

Reformation
The 16th-century division of the church into Catholic and Protestant denominations.

Sacrament
A solemn Christian ritual believed to be a means of grace, a sign of faith, or obedience to Christ's commands. In the Catholic and Orthodox churches, there are seven sacraments: baptism, confirmation, the eucharist (communion), penance, extreme unction, ordination and marriage. In Protestant churches, only baptism and the eucharist are regarded as sacraments.

Schism (Great Schism, or East-West Schism)
The break between the Roman Catholic church and what are now the Eastern Orthodox churches in 1054, which was the culmination of theological and political differences between the Christian East and West

See
City in which a bishop's cathedral is located.

Theotokos
(Greek, "God-bearer"). Title of the Virgin Mary in the Eastern Orthodox tradition, used from the time of Origen (early 3rd century) onwards as an affirmation of Christ's divinity.

Transubstantiation
The doctrine that the bread and wine of the Eucharist actually becomes the body and blood of Christ.

Trinity
The Christian conception of the one God as three persons: the God the Father, the Son, Jesus Christ, and the Holy Spirit.

Universalism
Doctrine that every creature, including the devil, will be reconciled with God in the end.

Vicar of Christ
Title for the pope since the 8th century, which replaced the older title "Vicar of St. Peter."

Virgin Birth
The belief that Jesus Christ had no human father, but was miraculously conceived by the power of the Holy Spirit coming upon the Blessed Virgin Mary

INDEX

LIST OF MAPS

ACKNOWLEDGEMENTS

Red Lion Media would like to thank the following:

Cartography: Jeanne Radford, Alexander Swanston, Malcolm Swanston
Design: Karen Wilks
Editorial: Elizabeth Wyse

Images pages 8, 9, 10, 11, 14, 50, 126, Wikimedia Commons

Every effort has been made to trace copyright holders and to obtain their permission for the use of copyright material. Red Lion Media apologizes for any errors or omissions in the above list and would be grateful if notified of any corrections that should be incorporated in future reprints or editions of this book.